Crooked River Country

Crooked River Country

Wranglers, Rogues, and Barons

David Braly

Washington State University Press
Pullman, Washington

Washington State University Press
PO Box 645910
Pullman, Washington 99164-5910
Phone: 800-354-7360
Fax: 509-335-8568
E-mail: wsupress@wsu.edu
Web site: wsupress.wsu.edu

Printed and bound in the United States of America on pH neutral, acid-free paper.
Reproduction or transmission of material contained in this publication in excess of
that permitted by copyright law is prohibited without permission in writing from
the publisher.

Library of Congress Cataloging-in-Publication Data

Braly, David.
  Crooked River country : wranglers, rogues, and barons / by David Braly.
     p. cm.
   Includes bibliographical references and index.
     ISBN 978-0-87422-293-7 (alk. paper)
   1. Oregon—History—19th century. 2. Oregon—History—20th century.
3. Oregon—History, Local. 4. Crooked River Region (Or.)—History, Local.
5. Frontier and pioneer life—Oregon. 6. Frontier and pioneer life—Oregon—Crooked
River Region. 7. Pioneers—Oregon—Biography. 8. Pioneers—Oregon—Crooked
River Region—Biography. 9. Oregon—Biography. 10. Crooked River Region (Or.)—
Biography. I. Title.
  F881.B73 2007
  979.5'804—dc22

Fine Quality Books from the Pacific Northwest

ACKNOWLEDGMENTS

SOME OF THE INFORMATION in *Crooked River Country* was acquired specifically for the book, while other facts came to me over the years when conducting interviews and research for newspaper and magazine articles published earlier. The problem is how to acknowledge those who have contributed to the book when the assistance came over a period of decades. Many who provided information are now gone. Many more never suspected that I would write a book on this subject. The majority of sources I have used are newspaper and secondary, not original. But considerable information did come from interviews, reminiscences, letters, and documents.

Unless I present something as speculative (for example, the belief of water-witchers that an underground river flows beneath Crook County), I have checked out facts as best as the available sources will allow. A number of errors have been published about Crook County history and some outright lies. The errors often have been repeated unknowingly in newspaper and magazine articles. For example, much of the misinformation that Herbert Lundy presented in 1939 to accompany his James Blakely article in the *Oregonian* has been repeated over and over again, including by me, until research for this book and an article for *Wild West* on Blakely uncovered the errors.

I have been surprised at the number of falsehoods that have been told about Crook County history. A few examples that it was necessary to refute—that Prineville had an ordinance on its books forbidding residence by blacks; that Deschutes area citizens entered Prineville as a mob early in the 20th century and destroyed the Crook County courthouse; and that the FBI confiscated all local newspapers in Central Oregon shortly after Pearl Harbor. These are incorrect.

I wish to thank Rick Chrisinger, Valerie Schnoor, and others at the Crook County Library, who in 1992 and 1993 offered advice about materials available through interlibrary loan and tracked down obscure materials. Cheryl Hancock assumed this task later and did so superbly.

Irene Helms, Gordon Gillespie, Steve Lent, Garry Boyd, and others at the Bowman Museum in Prineville answered many questions, located vital information, and allowed the use of their microfilm machine.

Dorsey Griffin provided much valuable advice and information about Chief Paulina and other aspects of the region's early history.

Beulah N. Calica of the Middle Oregon Indian Historical Society gave me information about her ancestor, Billy Chinook, for an article that was never written. Keith Clark provided a copy of Chinook's letter about land encroachments. Others who helped put together the Billy Chinook story included Dr. David H. French, emeritus professor of anthropology at Reed College, and Monica Felt of the Original Courthouse Preservation Corporation.

Jerry and Doris Breese shared their recollections of James Blakely. Others helping to put together the Blakely story included Grace Bartlett of the Wallowa County Museum and Pearl Jones of the Baker County Historical Society. The *Oregonian* article about Blakely was first brought to my attention in 1967 by a high school history teacher, James Mulvahill.

People who provided information specifically for this book included Frances Juris, Dr. Ward Tonsfeldt, Dr. Denison Thomas, Robert W. Chandler, Les Schwab, Dr. John Eliot Allen, and Mary Fraser. Juris, I must mention, presented critical information about several aspects of the region's history and forcefully brought to my attention the career of Kate Helfrich.

People who provided information for a book about Central Oregon that I planned years ago included Phil Brogan and George W. Friede.

Others giving information presented in *Crooked River Country*, which may have been originally intended for an article or some other purpose, include Joanne Rife, Stuart Shelk Sr., Ham Jackson, Joe Stahancyk Jr., Norbert Volney Jr., Allan Coxey, Debbie Bowen, LaSelle Coles, Lloyd E. Lewis, Paul G. Claeyssens, Dr. Orde S. Pinckney, Judge Dick Hoppes, and Dwight Newton. Additionally, there are some who would prefer to remain anonymous.

Steve Lent read an earlier version of the manuscript and drew attention to some misspellings and pointed out areas that needed clarification. He also hunted up and made copies of several dozen historical photographs at the Bowman Museum.

Organizations that assisted in one way or another include the Crook County Library, Crook County Historical Society (Bowman Museum), Central Oregon Community College, Oregon State Library, Oregon Historical Society, National Archives and Records Service, San Jose State University, John F. Kennedy Library, Middle Oregon Indian Historical Society, and Deschutes County Historical Society.

Much of the information was researched many years ago in the offices of the *Central Oregonian*, *Madras Pioneer*, *Redmond Spokesman*, and *Bend Bulletin*.

The great bulk of information concerning areas outside the present boundaries of Crook County came from published sources listed in the bibliography. Without this previous research by other writers, this book would not have been possible.

My apologies to anyone I have failed to mention. I am sure there were many. Although many supplied me with information, the responsibility for this book's final form and interpretation is my own.

TABLE OF CONTENTS

ILLUSTRATIONS

Steins Pillar stands northeast of Prineville in the Ochoco Mountains.
Bowman Museum, Crook County Historical Society

1
WHERE LIES THE SUBJECT

NOT MANY PEOPLE have ventured into the desolate northeast corner of Jefferson County, Oregon. Roads are few, and reasons for traveling on them fewer. There, just west of the John Day River, where county lines separate Jefferson County from Wasco to the north and Wheeler to the east, nothing much of monetary or ascetic value is to be found. What anyone who goes there may find instead are mysteries.

One such mystery is a road. Or rather what was once a road, long ago, beyond the memory of those who live in the vicinity and unrecorded in any official source thus far identified. What remains of the road are mere impressions, here and there, faint and yet unmistakable. Obviously an old road. Junipers with trunks a foot and a half thick now stand between its shoulders. Yes, a very old road. And a very strange road. Most roads can be seen to go from one place to another, normally in as straight a line as the terrain allows. No such pattern can be deciphered from the remnants of this road, which appears to have wandered hither and thither around Fir Tree Canyon, Arrastra Canyon, Currant Creek, Dry Creek, and Muddy Creek. Nobody knows who blazed the road, or why. During the 1980s, three researchers seeking answers to questions about it were told by old-timers that the road used to end at Rock Fort.

Which only leads to the mysteries surrounding Rock Fort. Who built it? Why did they build it? What happened to the builders or to those who lived within it? Where did they go?

Rock Fort today consists of a chimney and some stone walls. An examination of the site, however, reveals that these are the mere remnants of what was once a very large stone building with several other structures nearby. Nobody knows anything about its origins or fate or what purpose it served. Some people believe that it used to be an army post, but no official records of such a post have been found. Indeed, no records of any sort have been discovered that relate to the structure except as a ruin. Whether the mysterious ruin is related to the mysterious road, or whether their proximity is a coincidence, is anyone's guess.

In the same area, in Fir Tree Canyon, is a gruesome place called Skull Hollow. There, in pioneer days, someone discovered human skulls and skeletons. Again, a mystery: nobody knows who the dead people were or how they came to die together at that particular place. A popular theory has been that they were men escorting a pack train who were killed by Indians. Possibly they were taking supplies east to the gold camps around Canyon City or farther to the nearly legendary mining mecca of Auburn when they were ambushed by Paiute warriors under

Chief Paulina. But nobody really knows. It is known that at another time Indians attacked a pack train at Currant Creek, but the men escorting it fled to safety. On the same creek whites massacred a party of Indians and afterwards heaped their bodies into a pile and burned them. Or so it is said.

In the same area there is mystery about missing money. The money had been robbed from a bank. The outlaw was caught near Currant Creek and lynched. But if he were really the robber, the money should have been with him. It has never been found. Or at least not by anyone who has reported it.

Finally, there is the mystery of Arrastra Canyon. It births the name of the canyon itself. An arrastra was a horse- or mule-powered very heavy grinding stone employed to extract gold from rock. It was not a device someone normally carried around with them while traveling across the country. Spaniards built them at mining sites. However, the canyon earned its moniker when 19th century prospectors crossing it came upon an old arrastra. They could not guess who built it, or why anyone would construct it in an area devoid of gold. Neither has anybody since then figured out the mystery. The popular theory is that long ago Spaniards exploring Central Oregon built it. It is as good a theory as any other, but, again, nobody really knows. It, like the road and the fort and the skeletons and the missing bank money, remains a mystery.

And all of that is in one tiny corner of the region.

Mysteries abound in Central Oregon, and anyone attempting to relate the history of the region is forced to acknowledge that some part of the story might someday be altered substantially by the solving of one or another such enigma. Mysteries creating holes in the history of any large region is not uncommon. What is strange is that there are so many in the story of this region, which was one of the last to be settled within the United States. Because settlement came so late, logically Central Oregon's history should be definitive, clear, and relatively complete. However, this is not the case.

Of course, the greatest mystery about any region, or about any country or continent for that matter, concerns the time of arrival of its first native inhabitants. That is a mystery that may never be fully solved. Nor the manner in which they arrived, though they could have drifted into Central Oregon individually or in small groups rather than as a large tribe. Scientists claim that the region was better watered, and had more and larger lakes, during a waning ice age around 10,000 years ago. It is unlikely that any tribe would have ventured into such an isolated region without having first received detailed reports from scouts or hunters or trappers, and, in the case of Central Oregon, if they had received such reports they might have decided not to enter. In later millennia, at least, compared with localities to the west, east, north, and south, the country between the Cascades and the Blue Mountains was not attractive. It was also difficult to enter.

Natural features form barriers between Central Oregon and the rest of the world. Today, with many multilane paved highways as well as air transport, it is hard to imagine how difficult it was to enter in olden times. Doubtless if they had sought the kinds of abundant natural resources that later attracted westerning white Americans, many would have undertaken the journey. But a stone-age people without horses saw no value in bunchgrass pastures, or in lumber and gold. While Central Oregon also had fish, wildlife, and plant foods, the areas around it had them in greater abundance. Penetrating the natural boundaries to tap desert resources perhaps struck most prehistoric people as not worth the effort.

Central Oregon was surrounded by barriers on every side. Anyone seeking to journey south from the Columbia River encountered obstacles in the form of deep river canyons. The Deschutes canyon in particular straightjacketed travel to its east side, and fords were few. The John Day canyon to the east, with the Ochoco and the Blue mountains hugging it, discouraged travel in that direction. Only by traveling between the rivers and their great gorges could anyone other than the most venturesome enter from the north. The Cascades were an insurmountable barrier on the west during winter and scarcely less so during other seasons. To the east were smaller ranges—the Ochocos, the Blues, the Strawberrys, and the Mauries—but still very discouraging to travel. The south offered as a barrier the vast sageland known variously as the High, Artemesia, and Great Sandy desert.

Before relating the history of Central Oregon, it is first necessary to do a quick overview of the region's geography:

"Central Oregon" during the 19th century was understood to mean everything between the Cascades and the Blues, from the Columbia to California. This included Wasco and Sherman counties in the north as well as Klamath, Lake, and Harney counties in the south. Today, however, the designation is usually understood to mean only four counties: Deschutes, Jefferson, Wheeler, and Crook. For the purposes of this book, the label of "Central Oregon" will be kept loose, applying to most of the area first mentioned when discussing the 19th century, and then with the focus narrowing as time advances. This has less to do with the structures of governmental forms than with the degree of interconnection between localities in past times and present. Harney County in the 19th century, for example, was more tied to Crook County economically and socially than it is today. However, the emphasis of this history will be on the four counties today identified as Central Oregon for as long as they were the southern part of Wasco County, and then Crook County itself, from the time of its creation until the middle of the 20th century with the death of its last pioneer leader.

After one travels a couple dozen miles south of the Columbia, the terrain is mostly gently rolling hills studded with junipers, sagebrush, and rabbit brush. This area is southern Wasco and northern Jefferson counties, including the whole of the Warm Springs Indian Reservation, down to the great canyon of the Metolius. When the pioneers arrived, bunchgrass grew abundantly here, as it did throughout the region, and wildlife was relatively plentiful.

South of the reservation is the Metolius, a whitewater river that has its origin in a spring erupting from the 3,000-foot level on the north side of Black Butte. Other springs junction with it, until the river is formed and shoots down the deep canyon that ends at man-made Lake Billy Chinook. Before the lake was created, the Metolius flowed into the Deschutes from the west, while Crooked River entered the same waterway from the east. Cove Island—an 800-foot-high volcanic plug formed in prehistoric times by lava flowing into the Crooked River and filling its gorge—overlooked this scene and was called "the Plains of Abraham" by pioneers. South of the Metolius are the Three Rivers community and the bleak sageland known as the Lower Desert. Westward are the Cascades, and farther south are Black Butte and resort communities.

Within Jefferson County stand the towns of Madras, Metolius, and Culver. All are situated on the railway, and as will be observed later probably would not exist today were it not for the railroad. East of these towns are yet more gently rolling hills, more flat sageland, and many isolated farm and ranch buildings. Geological features include, among many others, Whetstone Creek, Muddy Creek, Trout Creek, Hay Creek, Crater Butte, Devil's Canyon, Slaughter House Gulch, Poison Hollow, Axehandle Ridge, Suicide Well, Gooseberry Mountain, Iron Mountain, and, covering many square miles across southeastern Jefferson County, the Petrified Forest.

Deschutes County, south of Jefferson, is dominated by three major geological features. On its west are the forested foothills and mountain crags of the Cascade Range. Directly east are juniper and sagebrush-laden flatlands. These two areas are now heavily populated, especially along the highway between Redmond and Bend. South lies the desert variously known as the Artemesia, the High, and the Great Sandy. It appears on most maps as the Great Sandy. Also, there are the great lava lands where the first astronauts trained for moon walks. The Paulina Mountains, with Paulina and East lakes, lie just north of LaPine at the southern boundary of the county.

Mount Jefferson, the largest mountain in Central Oregon with an elevation of 10,495 feet, is located in the southwest corner of the Warm Springs Indian Reservation. Moving south down the Cascades within Jefferson County are Goat Peak, the Cathedral Rocks, North and South Cinder peaks, Rockpile Mountain, Minto Pass, Porcupine Peak, Three-Fingered Jack (7,792 feet), and Santiam Pass.

Traveling further south down the range one encounters Mount Washington, Belknap Crater, the Three Sisters, Koosah Mountain, Horse Lake, Elk Lake, McKenzie Pass, Cultus Lake, Crane Prairie reservoir, Wickiup reservoir, Davis Lake, Willamette Pass, and Waldo Lake. The above-mentioned Three Sisters area includes Broken Top and a number of other mountains that were named in the 1840s by members of the Jason Lee mission in Salem and by later pioneers: the North Sister (Faith), the Middle Sister (Hope), the South Sister (Charity), Mount Bachelor (originally called Brother Jonathan, then The Bachelor, then Bachelor Butte), The Wife, The Husband, and the Little Brother.

South of Jefferson County and east of Deschutes County is modern Crook County. Its western region, like much of its two neighboring counties, is covered by a vast scrub-cedar woodland that is the largest juniper forest in the world. Two distinct geographical areas are separated by Mill Creek, nine miles east of Prineville. West of Mill Creek is the county's more fertile terrain. Most of the population is here, including the town of Prineville and the hamlets of McAllister, Wilton, O'Neil, Lone Pine, and Powell Butte. The rich Ochoco and Lone Pine valleys are located here, as well as the irrigated farmland of Powell Butte and Grimes Flat and the Prineville, Ochoco, Barnes Butte, and Stearns dams. Farms tend to be green and small, the ranches heavily-grazed.

East of Mill Creek is the dry and rugged "Upper Country." Except for irrigated farmland near Paulina, this section is forest, range, and mountains. Ranches tend to be large and sparsely grazed. Geographic names here include such Western gems as Painted Desert, Horse Prairie, Lame Dog Creek, Shotgun Creek, Antler Prairie, and The Badlands.

Crooked River is the only major waterway in Crook County. Flowing from the Ochoco Mountains and the nearby desert, the Crooked moves westward through Prineville and Lone Pine to junction with the Deschutes in Jefferson County. It is an ancient river, and its gorge is such a deep, steep, narrow slash in the earth that it attracts tourists, suicides, and murderers. The river itself is shallow and meandering. Before a dam regulated its flow, Crooked River became a mere dribble most summers and sometimes dried up entirely.

Other significant waterways in the western portion of the county include Ochoco Creek, McKay Creek, and Bear Creek. Ochoco Creek was originally labeled on maps as Achona, Chawa, and Chawy. Whatever the name, it always sounded like a sneeze. Ochoco itself is pronounced "Oh-cha-coh," unlike how it is spelled. McKay Creek was originally called Cottonwood, but changed apparently after a man named McKay lived near it for many years. It is pronounced in the original Scottish "Ma-kie," rhyming with "sky." There are numerous other creeks in the county. Some waterwitchers claim that there also is an underground river. They believe it comes south from the Dalles area and flows almost directly beneath the Prineville Airport.

Prineville lies upon both Crooked River and Ochoco Creek. The Crooked River skirts the town at the south and has often flooded the neighborhoods there. The river frequently changed course; old photographs show different channels. Ochoco Creek flows through the north part of town. Prineville sits upon an ancient lake bed and the water table is high. Some people who dig holes to a depth of only three or five feet strike water.

According to Dr. John Eliot Allen, emeritus professor of geology at Portland State University, the closest fault is the Brothers fault that goes through Bend. Crook is at very low risk for earthquakes, although not for volcanoes. Apparently no strong earthquake has been focused in Central Oregon for thousands of years.

One mountain range is partly in Crook County and two others are wholly within it. The Ochoco Mountains border it on the north. The Maury Mountains, or "the Mauries," are in the middle of the county south of the Crooked River. Often the name is locally mispronounced "the Mallories." Between Crooked River and Ochoco Creek, and including both Stearns Butte and Juniper Butte, are the Pup Mountains.

Some geologists claim that millions of years ago eastern Crook and western Grant counties were the location of a three-mile-high range they call the "Mesozoic Alps." Everything between the "Mesozoic Alps" and the Cascades, they believe, was covered by a vast inland sea.

The best known individual mountains in Crook County are Lookout, Powell, and Grizzly. Lookout Mountain, with an elevation of 6,926 feet, stands more than 20 miles east of Prineville and about seven miles east of Howard. It is the county's premier winter recreation area, with trails for cross-country skiers, snowshoers, and snowmobilers. Powell Butte, elevation 5,215, is actually two buttes and is well known because it gave its name to a nearby hamlet, the second most populated community in Crook County. Grizzly Mountain, elevation 6,025, is located northwest of Prineville, near the Jefferson County line. Originally named Blue Mountain, it became known as Grizzly sometime in the 1870s after a man killed a bear there. When, in 1956, the Ochoco Telecasters needed a place to put equipment for relaying Portland television signals throughout Central Oregon, they chose Grizzly because of its elevation, easy access, and proximity to Prineville, Madras, Redmond, and Bend. One unusual geological feature is Steins Pillar. This 350-foot-tall basalt chimney from the volcanic age is located ten miles north of the Ochoco Highway near the Mill Creek Road.

East of Prineville and stretching into other counties are 845,855 acres of federal forestland. As late as the 1940s, its conifers were primarily old growth.

Most of the marsh at Prineville has been filled in. The process continues even today. The town's industrial park off Gardner Road was built atop fill dumped into a marsh.

Prineville is the only incorporated town in Crook County. Wilton, McAllister, and O'Neil—towns no more—lie along the Crooked River Road, which leads to Terrebonne just over the Deschutes County line. Lone Pine lies north of the road in a rich verdure valley. Powell Butte is about halfway between Prineville and Redmond. Howard lies in the northeast part of the county. Roberts is situated a few miles south of Prineville Lake, which itself has a large population of users during the summer months. Paulina and Suplee are at the extreme eastern edge of the county. Post is located between Prineville and Paulina. The community of Marks Creek is east of Prineville beneath the Ochoco Mountains. Fife, near the G.I. Ranch, is in the southeastern part of Crook County. Many other communities that once existed in Crook County, such as Grindstone, Scissorsville, and Ochoco, have disappeared.

Crook County covers 2,982 square miles. At the widest points, it is 72 miles east to west, and 58 miles north to south. According to the 2000 census, the county had more 19,000 people, of whom 17,679 were white, 1,082 Hispanic, 275 multiracial, 274 Native American, 110 Asian, and 16 black.

East beyond Crook County is the southern portion of Wheeler County. The big town there, with a few hundred people, is Mitchell. Prone to floods, and high in the Ochocos, Mitchell stands on the eastern limits of Central Oregon. This is also—barring those few hardy adventurers who chose for one reason or another to reside in cabins in the Cascades or shacks on the Great Sandy—perhaps the most difficult place to live in the region: isolated, rugged, and subjected to violent extremes of weather.

Into this vast region, minus the modern improvements, but still blessed with the vegetation and other natural features that had existed during prehistoric times, came the first people to enter Central Oregon, many thousands of years ago. Shoes woven of sagebrush bark rope found at a cave in northwest Lake County have been radiocarbon dated to 9,000 years ago. Archaeological investigations in the area where the Deschutes and Metolius meet unearthed traces of human habitation dating back almost 8,000 years. Of similar age, the discovery of Kennewick Man on the Mid-Columbia has raised some questions about whether these early inhabitants were genetically related to modern Indians, who probably arrived around 7,500 years ago. Kennewick and similar human remains appear to be from an older extinct population, probably closer related to western Pacific islanders, especially the Ainu of northern Japan.

People living in Central Oregon about 5,700 B.C. became unwilling witnesses to one of the most devastating volcanic explosions ever. Oregon's highest mountain was Mazama, with an estimated elevation of 12,000 feet, or several hundred feet higher than Mount Hood. Located in the Cascades in what is now western Klamath County, Mazama suddenly and very violently erupted, doubtlessly accompanied by earthquakes that shook the Pacific Northwest. Thirty-five cubic miles of pumice and ash shot into the sky; winds first blew it east, then northeast, over Central Oregon. Altogether, ash covered 5,000 square miles. The number of people killed by the explosion or suffocated by ash or starved by the destruction of flora and fauna is unknown. It certainly created havoc throughout the region. Mazama itself collapsed, leaving only its rims to form a bowl, eventually filled by rainwater to become a very deep lake with an island toward its west side. Crater Lake is the sole remnant of the volcano, except for the deep frosting of ash that covers a layer of subterranean earth throughout Central Oregon.

Whoever may have lived in Central Oregon when Mazama erupted, Sahaptin-speaking Indians occupied the region later. They also lived in parts of western Oregon, south-central Oregon, and northern California. The great Lalaca Nation, which in 1776 split into the Klamath and Modoc tribes, was Sahaptin, and carried on a brisk trade in slaves and other wares with the Columbia River Indians.

Probably, the Sahaptins once occupied the entire Oregon outback. The northern edge of Central Oregon was still theirs when the first whites arrived.

About a thousand years ago another people began migrating north from their homeland in Arizona. These people spoke the Numic—or Plateau Shoshonean—language. They formed several nations, including the Bannock, Shoshoni, and Ute, but those who entered southeastern Oregon were the Northern Paiute. They called themselves the "Nomo" (the People). Some historians have claimed that the Cayuse and Nez Perce of northeastern Oregon drove the Paiutes south, but physical evidence and Paiute oral tradition indicate that the Paiutes were pushing these Sahaptins north. Their northern neighbors certainly viewed them as eternal enemies, calling them "Teewalka" (Enemy to be Fought). Paiutes apparently had expelled Sahaptins from southeastern Oregon, forced the Klamaths to retreat from their eastern-most encampments, and were expanding across Central Oregon when the whites arrived.

The Paiutes were not an organized political and military tribe. Bands numbering about three to ten households each, usually (but not always) related by blood or marriage, comprised their nation. They had no hereditary chiefs, no ownership of land, no fixed territories. Nomadic wanderers, each band had habitual campsites they used and abandoned year after year. They lived in tule mat houses in winter, in sagebrush breaks during summer, and in other quick-to-assemble and quick-to-take-down dwellings. They chose leaders based upon individual skill and personality, not upon hereditary right, social custom, or law. Anyone dissatisfied with a chief, or with life in a certain band, could simply leave and join a different group. A successful leader could attract many to his band. Perhaps the epitome of this came in 1878 when most Paiutes followed Chief Egan in the last great war against the whites. Marriage among blood kin was taboo, so usually Paiutes married members of other bands. They also sometimes married Cayuse, Nez Perce, Klamath, and other non-Paiutes. They practiced polygyny and polyandry, but seldom. The husband usually lived with his wife's family.

They believed that spirits could visit them in their dreams. When thus visited, they obtained supernatural powers to heal, cast spells, and predict future events. Some became shamans. Paiutes held shamans (who could be either men or women) in awe, but occupational hazards existed. Because they claimed supernatural power, they were expected to produce supernatural cures. A band might kill a shaman who failed. The shamans' influence declined in 1847 after a smallpox epidemic killed many Indian elders throughout the Pacific Northwest and northern California. The government outlawed shamanism in 1870, but it enjoyed a brief resurgence during the next decade as the Ghost Religion.

One aspect of Paiute belief held that a dead person's ghost would be awakened if a living person spoke his name or even thought about him. Because of this belief, Paiutes unfortunately preserved little history. Speaking of the past would arouse the dead.

Town of Paulina in the upper country, ca. 1910. *Bowman Museum, Crook County Historical Society*

The bands wandered peripatetically season after season, in pursuit of food. Sometimes they could not find sustenance and the weak ones starved. What they could find was the flora and fauna of the desert, everything from elk to insect larvae. The Paiutes utilized elk, deer, antelope, sagehens, groundhogs, rabbits, mountain sheep, mud hens, geese, ducks, other birds, salmon, trout, suckers, minnows, bulbs, camas, wild onion, cattail root, bitterroot, tule root, arrowroot, serviceberries, gooseberries, huckleberries, raspberries, currants, wild cherries, chokecherries, sagebrush seeds, cattails, rushes, saltbrush, fescue, wheatgrass, Indian rice grass, and bluegrass, as well as ants, crickets, caterpillars, and larvae. Centuries in the Great Basin had taught them how to survive in times of near starvation diets.

Two archaeologists mapped the Paiute bands and their territories. Unfortunately, the maps disagree. Beatrice Blyth wrote in 1938 that the Juniper-Deer Eaters (Wa'dihichi'tika) occupied the area between the Cascades and the Ochoco Valley. She believed that the locality between the sites of Prineville and Dayville was unoccupied, while the area east of Dayville belonged to the Root Eaters (Hu'nipwi'tika). But her contemporary, Omer C. Stewart, believed that all the area between the Cascades and the upper John Day River was occupied by the Hunipuitoka, or Walpapi band.

What can be said with certainty is that the Walpapi chief Paulina had his main camp in the Paulina and Beaver Creek valleys of eastern Crook County. He fought wars against the Klamaths, Modocs, and Warm Springs Indians that may have been hereditary.

When Peter Skene Ogden first explored the Crooked River in 1825, he found Paiutes there. The region may have been a war zone between the Paiutes and the Sahaptin and Chinook tribes further north and west. Chief Ochoco, who camped often on the site of Prineville, was a Paiute. Little is known about him except that he was peaceful toward white settlers and was a close friend of the famous Paiute chief, Winnemucca II. It is not even known if the Ochoco Valley was named after him or if he was named after the valley. Mrs. Ada B. Millican wrote in 1921 that the Paiute word "ochoco" meant a willow-fringed stream.

In 1853–1855, Joel Palmer, the Oregon Superintendent of Indian Affairs, negotiated treaties with the Sahaptin and Chinook tribes of Central and East Oregon. The Indians ceded to the U.S. government all the territory east of the Deschutes River. That this was actually Paiute territory mattered little to Palmer and less to the Indians attending the treaty councils.

On the opposite side of the Cascades, shortly before Palmer began the treaty talks in 1853, a baby was born to the Blakely family in the town of Brownsville. The baby was named James, but he was usually called Jim. He would later cut a wide swath in Central Oregon history.

2

FUR MEN
1820s–1830s

FUR TRAPPERS WERE THE FIRST WHITE MEN to enter Central Oregon. Some of them, French Canadians probably in the employ of the Hudson's Bay Company, renamed the river the Indians called "Tawah-na-hi-ooks" as the "Des Chutes," or river "of the falls." Probably such traders were the source of information about the "Crooked River" that appeared in a map produced in 1824. Not only is the map reasonably accurate, it already carried the name Crooked River.

The first person who left a detailed record of the region was fur-brigade leader Peter Skene Ogden, a son of Chief Justice Isaac Ogden, a Tory who had fled to Canada to escape the American Revolution. Peter was hired by Canada's North West Company, traveled to Oregon in 1818, and became a partner before the North West Company's merger with the Hudson's Bay Company in 1821. He earned a good reputation among both whites and Indians, and married the daughter of a Flathead chief.

At Fort Vancouver in 1825, Chief Factor John McLoughlin instructed Ogden to cross Central Oregon on a journey to the Snake River. The Hudson's Bay Company wanted to trap out the fur-bearing animals in the Snake watershed, so that American trappers entering the region from the east would find nothing to encourage them to remain. McLoughlin also directed Finan McDonald—who in 1807 had entered the

Hudson's Bay Company brigade leader Peter Skene Ogden found few beaver, but left the first written record of the Crooked River Country. *Bowman Museum, Crook County Historical Society*

Northwest with the first British party coming over the Rockies in what is now British Columbia—to cross the central Cascades and rendezvous with Ogden. Accompanied by French Canadians, Indians, and probably some women and children, Ogden went south from the Columbia along the Deschutes. In December, he found McDonald's party waiting for him at the junction of the Deschutes and Crooked rivers. Together they turned east up the Crooked River.

Ogden's notes reveal that the region neither thrilled nor disappointed him. Crooked River "looks well running through a fine Plain and well lin'd with Willows." Its valley had grass seven feet high, but desert sands lay only 200 yards distant. When the party reached Ochoco Creek, they turned to follow it. Ogden's men tramped 20 miles in search of beaver, but found few. They returned to the Crooked River and followed it eastward. Although Ogden believed that the river offered good potential for beaver, he discovered that the Nez Perce had recently trapped the area out. He also found little to eat. Before they reached the John Day, members of his party were reduced to consuming horse meat.

Ogden returned to the Crooked River twice in 1826. During the last journey he learned to distrust the Paiutes. He had earlier expressed sorrow at their apparent poverty and had treated them well. Because they had returned traps lost the previous year by McDonald, he also had judged them honest. But one October night they set fire to dry grass near his camp, which could have been disastrous were it not for the alertness of the watch. The trappers seldom saw the Paiutes. Ogden became the first of many visitors who remarked upon seeing Indian sign without seeing Indians. Ogden again returned in 1829, going through Central Oregon into California and all the way to the Colorado River.

Most of the Hudson's Bay Company expeditions coming into the region, instead of descending down the Deschutes from the Columbia, used Santiam Pass over the Cascades. This was the route Finan McDonald took in 1825 to rendezvous with Ogden. They were following a trail into Central Oregon that Indians had been using for generations. Joseph Gervais, an independent trapper who sold his pelts to the Hudson's Bay Company, also used the Santiam when he crossed over from his farm at French Prairie to spend autumns trapping in Central Oregon.

How many Hudson's Bay or independent trappers entered the region cannot be guessed. Probably few, and most likely the area proportionally better profited an independent trapping in the eastern Cascades foothills than major expeditions such as Ogden's that ventured all the way to the Ochocos and Pups. When John Work—an HBC chief trader—led a trapping expedition returning north from Utah in July 1831, the party skirted Central Oregon on the east, never going farther west than the John Day. Indians are alleged to have later massacred a party of Hudson's Bay packers at Powell Butte.

The first prominent American to enter the region did so as part of a daring plan to wrest a fortune from the Oregon Country. Speculator, entrepreneur, adventurer—call him whatever one would—Nathaniel J. Wyeth already had learned to think big and act bold. However, like many such fellows, by his thirties the Massachusetts native had experienced a reverse in his fortunes and was looking for a way to recover. Indeed, he wanted to become bigger, richer, more influential than ever. Having heard a great deal about Oregon, Wyeth became convinced that a magnificent future could be established there if a man had enough money, enough courage, and a good plan. And he formed a plan. He believed that the United States would become the sole proprietor of Oregon after the joint governing agreement with Great Britain expired in 1838. Wyeth would go to Oregon with others and develop a fur business that would rival the Hudson's Bay Company. When the British departed, his firm would fill the vacuum.

To this end, he organized the Pacific Trading Company and in 1832 recruited a couple dozen investors willing to join him in a cross-continent venture. Less than half that number continued all the way to Fort Vancouver, however, and the company was dissolved because its resources became exhausted. But Wyeth did not abandon his dream so easily. After examining Oregon first hand and satisfying himself that it offered all the opportunities he had believed in, he returned to the East to organize a new company, recruit new employees, and secure new capital.

He returned to Oregon in 1834, and this time he did not remain on the west side of the mountains. Leaving a fort he had built on Sauvie Island at the Willamette-Columbia junction, Wyeth led a party of trappers on an expedition east along the Columbia that turned down the Deschutes. They spent the stormy winter of 1834–1835 in the western districts of Central Oregon, going a dozen miles or more south of present-day Bend. They traveled by canoes south on the Deschutes until they were stopped by Benhall Falls. Enduring harsh winter conditions, where in some areas the snow stood four feet on the ground, and subsisting at times only on the meat of deer and swans, Wyeth continued to explore the Deschutes country until early February.

After returning to the lower Columbia, Wyeth continued his efforts to establish a trading empire for another year. He did build Fort Hall on the Oregon Trail in Idaho, but eventually sold it to the Hudson's Bay Company and abandoned his plans. He really did not know enough about the fur business to make a go of it, and the desertion of the Hawaiians he had brought over for labor, coupled with the killing of 14 other employees by Indians, helped persuade him that Oregon was not the oyster he believed it would be.

Mountain man Stephen Meek guided the ill-fated Lost Wagon Train in 1845. *Bowman Museum, Crook County Historical Society*

3

PILGRIMS
1838–1853

MISSIONARY ACTIVITY across the Northwest began after four Nez Perce had journeyed to St. Louis in 1831 to ask Gen. William Clark for information about the "White Man's Book of Heaven." In 1838 at The Dalles of the Columbia, early missionaries Daniel and Jason Lee, H.K.W. Perkins, and Ben Wright arrived from Western Oregon to establish the Wascopam Mission near the site of an ancient Indian village. Indians from far distances visited it, about 2,000 from various tribes wintering nearby in 1839–1840. It became one of the largest missions in the Pacific Northwest. Although far from Crooked River, from here began the settlement of the vast interior, and to here the people of the outback would look for government and supplies for many years.

An orphan Indian boy later earning a place in Central Oregon history was raised at this Methodist Mission Society station. As a child when living with his uncle, he became an expert fisher and hunter. When he was 12, the missionaries took him in and gave him white boy's clothes. They also gave him a white name: William McKendue. Later, he would be known as William Parker and other names, but history remembers him as Billy Chinook.

Chinook adapted readily to life at the mission, and tended the garden and cattle. In 1843, he met a military officer from the East leading an expedition of 25 men. Lt. John C. Fremont of the U.S. Army Topographical Engineers had secured an assignment to explore parts of Oregon and California through the influence of his powerful father-in-law, Sen. Thomas Hart Benton of Missouri. This was Fremont's second excursion into the Far West. The United States and Britain still disputed ownership of the Northwest, and California belonged to Mexico, so Fremont's expedition was supposed to be peaceful. However, he dragged along a cannon in case of trouble. Kit Carson was his guide. At the Wascopam Mission, on November 24, 1843, Fremont heard a strange proposal and recorded it in his memoirs:

"At the request of Mr. Perkins, a Chinook Indian, a lad of nineteen, who was extremely desirous to 'see the whites,' and make some acquaintance with our institutions, was received into the party, under my especial charge, with the understanding that I would again return him to his friends. He had lived for some time in the household of Mr. Perkins, and spoke a few words of the English language."

They gave the boy—Billy Chinook—a mount to ride, plus another horse to carry his bedding and clothes. The expedition then traveled south from The Dalles, crossing the Tygh Valley into the Warm Springs country.

Fremont followed the Metolius, until he suddenly found himself in the river bottom below a steep wall of the river gorge. They would have to cross the swift, very deep, river. After probing here and there, discovering that the water was too deep to ford at most places, Fremont at last crossed the Metolius at a spot where it was only three or four feet in depth and about 100 feet wide. This locality was later called Pitt Ford. He camped there a couple of nights. The ford was anything but ideal. One of the expedition's mules went too low into the water and a load of sugar became molasses. Climbing up the gorge's south wall was even more difficult than the descent of the north side had been. Before making the ascent and camping on top in a marshy area surrounded by pines, Fremont discovered the fish for which the "salmon river" later became famous. He reported seeing one salmon that was 12 inches in diameter.

After camping several days at Fly Lake, where the party left several cannon balls, Fremont continued southwest to Squaw Creek, then Bull Creek Springs, across Tumalo Creek, and finally to the Deschutes. He followed the river south, and was greatly impressed by its many falls and by the nearby grasslands. He got a chance to use the brass cannon he had been dragging along when he encountered Klamaths, then turned east and left Oregon.

"Our Chinook Indian had his wish to see the whites full gratified," Fremont later recorded. "He accompanied me to Washington, and, after remaining several months at Columbia College, was sent by the Indian Department to Philadelphia, where, among other things, he learned to read and write well, and speak the English language with some fluency."

Chinook wintered with a Quaker family in Philadelphia, and then "was glad to go back to his people" when Fremont arrived to return him to the West. Fremont wondered about his future.

"The Quaker family had been interested in him and careful to give him such rudiments of practical knowledge as he might be able to put to good use. But he was twenty years old when he left the Columbia with me; intelligent, with set character formed among the habits of Indian life, as ineradicable from Indian manhood as his love of free range from a wild horse. How far his brief education was likely to influence his life was made strikingly clear to us when on the evening he reached Washington he exhibited the parting gifts which he had received from his friends. Among these was a large Bible which had been made attractive in his eyes by its ornamentation. 'Chinook been a Quaker all winter,' he said; and opening this at the blank leaves for 'Family Record'—'Here,' he added, with the short Indian laugh of pleasure, 'Chinook put the name of all wife, and all horse.'

"The knowledge which his eyes had taken in would be useful among his people. He was the son of a chief and the stories he could tell of his life among the whites would add to his importance; and the kind treatment he had received would dispose himself and them to be friendly to the Americans."

Chinook accompanied Fremont to California, and reached The Dalles in 1851. With him were a California Indian wife and a herd of Mexican cattle. Those who remembered the boy welcomed him home. He acquired a farm, and his white neighbors looked upon him as a good, honest man, and a decent Christian.

However, Billy Chinook found Oregon different than how he had left it. More white people had entered, arriving year after year in their long wagon trains. Several of these immigrant trains crossed Central Oregon, and their doing so became stories of tragedy.

What became famous as the Lost Wagon Train was organized on April 28, 1845, at Oregon Encampment on the Missouri River. The numbers given in the various sources differ wildly, but roughly 1,000 men, women, and children, with 100 to 300 wagons and 2,000 head of cattle, formed the caravan. All went well until they reached Fort Boise. There they met Stephen Meek, brother of "mountain man" Joe Meek and cousin of President James Polk. Stephen Meek, himself a long-time mountain man, said that he knew a shortcut that would save them 200 miles. Because they had been forced to move slowly, with wagon wheels and oxen raising dust, with children cramped inside the little wagons, with the cattle wandering from the train, the weary pilgrims listened. Meek's assurances of the route's safety were especially welcome because they had heard rumors of Indian trouble along the Oregon Trail. Everyone voted for which route they would prefer. The majority elected to pay Meek's price of five dollars a wagon in exchange for his guiding them over the shortcut.

The caravan left the Oregon Trail on August 24, following the Malheur River. The impressions these heavy wagons left upon the Oregon desert are still visible in places, two deep ruts infamously known as the Meek Cutoff Trail. Their route led west across the Malheur country to Harney Lake and then the Wagontire Mountain vicinity, before turning north toward the upper Crooked River watershed.

Disaster followed disaster. For days, the immigrants had trailed Meek across rugged desert terrain that gradually tore wagons to pieces. Sometimes their horses and oxen—hooves leaving a trail of blood across the desert—refused to move. People drank alkali water, which induced fever and death. As one body after another was lowered into the parched ground, Meek followed advice that he should stay a short distance from the wagons so that the bereaved immigrants would not attack him. His departure created the legend that Meek "led astray and deserted" the immigrants. He did lead them astray, but he never deserted them. After they found good water, Meek almost returned, but a man who had lost several family members threatened to kill him on sight. After facing down this adversary, Meek rushed to The Dalles for help.

The immigrants had found the upper reaches of the Crooked River and headed westward. Widely spaced out, and sometimes taking different branch routes, some wagons came upon the Ochoco Valley with its willows and tall grass. There, on the site of what later became Prineville, they rested. They were there on September 22 when the rescue party arrived from The Dalles.

More than two decades later Barney Prine would use iron rims from their wagon wheels in his blacksmith shop, but it is unlikely that they left behind much else. Twentieth century Prineville children were told how members of the Lost Wagon Train hid their valuables nearby, intending to retrieve them, but never returning. Supposedly, caches of long abandoned goods lay in the basalt outcrops, awaiting discovery, somewhere near those old wagon ruts.

After leaving the Ochoco Valley, the guides from The Dalles led the wagons to Hay Creek and the Deschutes rim. After spending a night at the future site of Gateway, the pilgrims had to double the teams on each wagon to climb up to the Shaniko Plain. To ford the Deschutes they used the wagon beds as rafts, after which they tackled the big canyons south of The Dalles. All told, the Lost Wagon Train of 1845 arrived after the deaths of 23 or 24 people.

The second wagon train to enter Central Oregon was the Clark Massacre Party in 1851. Members suffered less from the natural elements than had those of the Lost Wagon Train, but before it had reached Oregon the caravan was attacked by about 30 Indians. Two members of the small party were slain, another one shot and partly scalped. In Central Oregon, the train camped for several days on the Deschutes, allegedly where Bend's Pioneer Park is now located.

A couple of years later, a resident from Western Oregon's Lane County rode to Fort Boise to join his family. Elijah Elliott knew that a wagon road through Willamette Pass should be ready before the summer ended. He believed that it would skive three weeks off the time the wagon train otherwise would have to spend reaching the west side of the Cascades if it stayed on the Oregon Trail. All they had to do was go through the Vale area, up the Malheur River, and across the Great Sandy Desert—starting on the Meek Cutoff.

The 1,027 people and 250 wagons that followed Elliott in 1853 suffered many of the same hardships endured by members of the 1845 train. Wagons had to be lightened so the weak animals could continue pulling them, and pilgrims hid furniture in desert coves—where it allegedly remains to this day. The train crossed what would later become southern Crook County, fording Bear Creek twice but staying south of the Maury and Pup mountains. It continued on into the Cascades, where the wagons became trapped in the Willamette Pass vicinity. With winter approaching, the immigrants faced the same fate as the Donner Party had in California's Sierra Nevada in 1846–1847. But the 16th man sent over the Cascades for help was found by a boy from a Lane County settlement. Men with food-laden wagons hacked their way through the mountain timber to rescue the stranded train.

A member of the Donner party, Virginia Reed, wrote to a cousin that her family alone had not eaten human flesh to stay alive, and concluded: "Remember, never take no cutoffs and hurry along as fast as you can." The immigrants who took the Meek Cutoff could have used that advice. In the following year, however, an Oregon bound train of 125 wagons came this way with considerably less difficulty.

Members of the original 1845 Lost Wagon Train allegedly found what became Oregon's most famous lost mine: the Blue Bucket. The Lost Wagon Train, in fact, is sometimes called the Blue Bucket Train.

There are numerous stories about who found the mine and how. One is that Solomon Tetherow discovered gold when the train dry camped at the head of Crooked River. According to this version, Tetherow noticed yellow stones being uncovered by his cattle while driving them across a dry gulch. He picked one up but dismissed it as a worthless rock. After gold was discovered in California, he saw nuggets that had been brought to Oregon and exclaimed: "Why I could have picked up a blue bucket full of them at the head of Crooked River." Wooden blue buckets were popular at the time and in common use. Another account says that Dan Herren found a yellow stone thrown to the surface by a mole or gopher and beat it out on a wagonwheel. Another says that boys found the nuggets in a dry creek bed and saved them in a blue bucket to use as sinkers. However discovered, after gold was found in California word spread far of the Blue Bucket Mine.

Chief Paulina led war parties against the whites and nearly every non-Paiute tribe in Oregon east of the Cascades.
Bowman Museum, Crook County Historical Society

4
EXPEDITIONS
1852–1867

fter the United States secured control of the southern half of the Pacific Northwest in a treaty with Great Britain (1846), federal, territorial, and later state officials attempted to learn more about the new possessions. The efforts included expeditions ordered by these governments into Central Oregon. Some were strictly exploratory, though most of the army expeditions focused upon establishing white control. All military and civil expeditions prior to the death of Chief Paulina in 1867 ran the risk of attack from Paiutes.

One of the first official expeditions into Central Oregon was a survey party that departed from Eugene on August 21, 1852. The Oregon territorial government had sanctioned the seven-man expedition for the purpose of designating a new route between Fort Boise and Eugene as an aid to immigration. They planned to cross the Cascades south of Diamond Peak, ford the Deschutes, and then find their way to Fort Boise through hundreds of miles of thick stands of sagebrush.

At first all went well: they crossed the mountains and the river without trouble, traveled east to Bear Creek and then Silver Creek, and discovered deep wagon ruts that they could follow over the desert: the Meek Cutoff Trail. Things got nasty in mid-September. Upon reaching Harney Lake, they were attacked by Indians. None of the expedition members were wounded or killed, and they decided to continue east. Five miles out from the lake, however, another group of Indians attacked them. Outnumbered 11 to 7, the surveyors had to fight for their lives. By the time they had fought off the Indians, 3 of the whites had been wounded. They abandoned their plans and instead turned north looking for the Oregon Trail. When they found it, they followed it all the way to The Dalles, where they arrived on October 3. From there, they hurried on to Portland.

The first post-Fremont military expedition to enter the region was sent by Secretary of War Jefferson Davis to discover a potential route for a transcontinental railroad. Led by Lt. Henry Larcom Abbot, the party included two future Union generals, George Crook and Philip Sheridan, and the geologist and botanist for whom Newberry Crater would be named, Dr. John Strong Newberry. The party entered Oregon from California in 1855, going past Klamath Marsh and hugging the foothills of the Cascades all the way to The Dalles. Abbot was not impressed with Central Oregon, judging it a vast wasteland sliced by deep canyons, with only rare spots where anything worthwhile could be grown, and forbidden to those who might wish to enter it by the daunting barriers of mountains, deserts, and steep canyons. Nature, he observed, had preserved it for the wandering Indian. Needless to say, after Davis received this report, he did not shortlist Central Oregon for the railroad.

The next important military expedition through the region came in the spring of 1859 after the army commander of the Department of the Columbia, Gen. William S. Harney, sent Capt. Henry D. Wallen to look for a route from The Dalles to Salt Lake City that would be shorter than the trails then being followed. The existing trails consumed time by swinging wide around mountain ranges and big rivers. That the army had been skirting the whole region until this time is a good indication of Central Oregon's reputation as an almost impassable place, an American Tibet. But Harney may have observed that settlers had begun to penetrate it. Already there were crude ranches south of The Dalles. Indeed, news of this may have been partly responsible for the Department of the Pacific commander, Gen. John E. Wool, issuing an order in the summer of 1856 forbidding settlement by whites on lands east of the Cascades, in order to decrease the incidence of conflicts with Indians. Harney himself revoked this order on Halloween Day 1858, after the conclusion of the 1855–1858 Yakima War on the Columbia plains.

The Dalles itself was evidence of how important the region might soon become. The first house had been built there in 1850, the first store a year later. Several houses had gone up before 1854 when it became the seat of Wasco, at that time the largest county in the United States, with 200,000 square miles within its boundaries (larger than California), later to be cut away to form 17 Oregon counties and portions of Idaho, Montana, and Wyoming. The Dalles was incorporated in 1857, and by the time Capt. Wallen reached it the following year it had three hotels, two grocery stores, two saloons, a general mercantile, drug store, bakery, newspaper, steamship line, saddlery, assay office, warehouse, and cigar store.

Wallen rode south out of Fort Dalles on June 4, 1859, with 9 officers, 184 enlisted men, 154 horses, 344 mules, 121 oxen, 30 wagons, and 60 head of cattle to be butchered along the trip for provisions. Entering the forbidding outback, he saw the usual dismal scenes through Tygh Valley and along the Deschutes until he turned to follow Crooked River. This was an area unseen by Abbot and Fremont. What Wallen found came as a delightful surprise.

Seldom, he reported, had he seen such a beautiful and fertile country as that of the Crooked and Ochoco streams. He doubted that there was a better place for raising livestock anywhere in the United States and believed that the pioneers who had settled other areas of Oregon would never have bothered to do so if they had first seen the Ochoco's more bountiful pastures and forests.

When the party reached the forks of the Crooked River, Wallen sent Lt. John Bonnycastle with a detachment back to the Columbia, seeing if a new route could be found in the process. Wallen continued down the river's South Fork, which he found less impressive than the valley behind. There was little fodder for the horses, mules, and cattle, and the water, fully exposed to the desert sun, was warm and caked with alkali. He described the Indians as "Digger Snakes," i.e. Paiutes who lived on roots and insects as well as fish. Wallen said that the Indians of the Crooked River country were not formidable because they were armed only with bows and arrows.

Wallen went over the Meek road via Buck Creek through a place he named Whirlwind Valley (later renamed Gilchrist Valley) to Silver Creek and the Harney country. He then led his party to the Malheur, where he could turn north again. Wallen arrived back at The Dalles on October 17.

The army would not abandon the idea of penetrating the region in order to reach Salt Lake City. Meanwhile, Idaho gold discoveries soon sent prospectors and all sorts of opportunists wandering across Central and Eastern Oregon. They needed protection from belligerent Paiutes, as did gold shipments bound for Portland. An Ohio transplant named Evelyn had established a ferry at Tygh Valley to carry prospectors over the Deschutes. He scuttled it in 1855 when the Yakima War erupted along the Columbia. At the same location five years later, Tygh Valley rancher John Y. Todd built a bridge. It gave immigrants and soldiers a safe way to cross the Deschutes, though getting past other natural barriers remained a problem.

The army decided that a west-east route between Eugene and Salt Lake City would be preferable to a north-south road over the rivers and canyons of Central Oregon. Accordingly, it ordered Maj. Enoch Steen to go toward Harney Lake from Fort Dalles in the spring of 1860 to lay out the trail. Leading a company of dragoons and 20 infantrymen, Steen followed Wallen's tracks down the Deschutes and Crooked rivers and set to work. He was moving toward the upper Deschutes on June 29 when he received a courier from Capt. Andrew J. Smith, who had charge of a survey crew left working at Harney Lake, reporting that Indians had attacked them. Steen hurried back over his own trail and junctioned with Smith on July 4. The road was forgotten, and instead Steen and Smith established Camp Union, 30 miles northwest of Harney Lake on the banks of Silver Creek to protect themselves and others from the Indians. The temporary cantonment stood not far from the modern-day junction of Riley. (The "Steen's Military Road" of later fame was no part of the route Maj. Steen had been ordered to build in 1860, but instead ran from The Dalles to Todd's bridge, east to Canyon City, and then south to Fort Harney, which would be built on Rattlesnake Creek in 1867 about 16 miles east of Burns.)

Military expeditions into Central Oregon were hampered in the early 1860s by the drawing off of manpower and wealth to the East because of the Civil War, but continued despite the problems this posed because settlers and gold shipments had to be protected from Paulina and other hostile Paiutes. Some of these expeditions had value beyond their role in countering Paulina.

One was the expedition of Capt. John M. Drake, which left Fort Dalles with 7 officers and 160 cavalrymen on April 20, 1864. Drake's encounters with Paulina will be discussed later. Suffice to note here that after Drake had established Camp Maury near Snow Mountain, a patrol that he sent out discovered ocean shells along the banks of Beaver Creek. Amazed, some of the soldiers took a few of the shells with them when they returned for supplies at Fort Dalles and showed them to a pastor who was knowledgeable about geology. He told the soldiers that the presence of the fossilized shells meant that at one time the desert they now patrolled had been the floor of an ocean. This was the first evidence of what is now regarded by scientists as a geological fact for Central Oregon.

Another military expedition established the first white settlement in what would later become Deschutes County. Col. George B. Currey ordered volunteer forces in Oregon to establish posts in the central and eastern regions to protect settlers and travelers. One of the posts would be near the junction of the wagon roads over Santiam and McKenzie passes. Commanding it would be Capt. Charles La Follette from Polk County. In the summer of 1865, he led 40 infantrymen accompanying wagons loaded with several tons of supplies up the Santiam. With harsh mountain weather already setting in, they came upon the construction crew building the road. The soldiers pitched in and helped complete the last seven miles of the route to Fish Lake. They stopped on Squaw Creek on September 28 and began building their post, named Camp Polk in honor of their home county. They stripped all the branches off the tallest tree to serve as a flagpole, laid out a parade ground, and built two cabins on one side and six on the other. One of the north cabins was for La Follette and the camp doctor, the other for their commissary stores, while the six south of the parade ground were barracks for the enlisted men.

Everyone then settled in for what proved to be a boring winter: few travelers passed through because of widespread fear of the Paiutes. The Indians who went past looked hostile but made no overt moves, and two months dragged by without any communication from the west side of the mountains. Food consisted mostly of meat, both from the mule deer that were abundant thereabouts and 22 head of cattle sent to them by the garrison at Camp Watson in the Ochocos. With no travelers to escort, no Paiutes to fight, and the nearest settlers in need of protection located 100 miles away in Tygh Valley, there was really little need for Camp Polk. The army reached this conclusion during the winter. Late in May, the post was abandoned and its garrison returned home to Polk County. The old post would remain a mere stopover place, a temporary shelter for those crossing the mountain passes, until Samuel Hindman homesteaded 280 acres nearby in about 1870. The town of Sisters would grow up from this beginning.

Most of the army posts in Central Oregon were small, temporary affairs such as Camp Polk, but not Fort Harney. Located on 640 acres about 18 miles north of Malheur Lake on the road to Canyon City, it had 25 buildings and 50 soldiers.

Established in 1867, it lasted for 13 years, during which time it had the only hospital in the region and the first post office in what became Harney County.

While these military projects were undertaken, and the Paulina War raged across the region, settlers continued to venture into Central Oregon, and wagon road companies continued to make money from the travelers.

Warm Springs Indians, 1885. *Bowman Museum, Crook County Historical Society*

5

EMPTY EXCEPT FOR INDIANS AND GOLD
1853–1864

B Y THE EARLY 1850s, large numbers of whites already had moved across East Oregon. Indians became alarmed. Many of the newcomers seemed intent upon securing not only every parcel of available land, but also unavailable land.

"We are tormented almost every day by the white people who desire to settle on our land and although we have built houses and opened gardens they wish in spite of us to take possession the very spots we occupy," wrote Billy Chinook to Joel Palmer, the Oregon Superintendent of Indian Affairs, in November 1853. "We resist and tell them that this is our land, they reply that Government gives them [the right] to settle in any part of Oregon Territory and they desire to take land in this very spot.

"Now we wish to know whether this is the land of the white man or the Indian. If it is our land, the white must not trouble us. If it is the land of the white man when did he buy it?...If we lose our country what shall we do? I know the whites are strong, they have ammunition and guns and power. We cannot resist them, but we ask them to leave us our homes for we are poor and have no power. Be so kind as to answer us and tell us what you think."

At the same time, Palmer received another letter from the same area, this from a white settler who complained that Indians continually trespassed upon land that was formerly theirs but now his. Because the 1850 Donation Land Law authorized citizens of the United States to file upon and settle land, this man could not understand why the government failed to protect him and others by removing the Indians from the neighborhood.

Palmer termed Chinook's letter "a picture of Indian wrongs no less true than sad and painful." He wrote the white settler that his claim would become valid only when the Indian title was extinguished, which had not yet happened in Oregon.

On June 22, 1855, Palmer signed a treaty with the tribes of Middle Oregon, by which the Chinook- and Sahaptin-speaking people ceded almost everything between the Cascades and the Blue Mountains. They retained an area north of the Metolius between the Deschutes and the Cascades, afterward known as the Warm Springs Indian Reservation. For at least a generation the Warm Springs Indians and Paiutes had been fighting for control of this area.

However, although the Teninos and Paiutes had lived in the Metolius area for a long time, and probably were among the Indians who had worn a trail through the forest toward Mount Jefferson while hunting and huckleberry-picking, the people who settled on the new reservation were mostly from the northward. The Warm Springs (or Wayampam) and Wasco tribes had occupied most of the territory from the Columbia in the north to a few miles below the Three Sisters in the south, from the Cascades in the west to the Blue Mountains in the east. There were three bands of Wascos to be moved: the Gigwaladamt from Cascade Locks; the Dog River People from Hood River; and the People of the Narrows from three villages in The Dalles bridge area. Four bands of Wayampams were to go with them: the Tenino, near neighbors to the east of the Narrows people on the Columbia; the Wyam from Celilo Falls to the mouth of the Deschutes; the Taih from Tygh Valley; and the Dock Spus from the junction of the John Day with the Columbia.

In March 1856, 17 chiefs and other leaders from these bands accompanied 5 white representatives to the new reservation to locate sites there for future villages. The Indians expressed satisfaction with these areas, but one suspects they had little enthusiasm for exchanging their abodes on the wide Columbia for locations along creeks and streams just north of the Lower Desert. The Wascos would move there only when promised improvements were completed, but the Wayampams agreed to go onto the reservation immediately.

One Wayampam who was decidedly less than enthusiastic was the Taih (Tygh) chief Que-pe-ma. After the Tyghs arrived on the reservation, he persuaded them to ignore the farm plots set aside for their use. He had no quarrel with the size of the allotment; he simply despised the very occupation of farming. Que-pe-ma became a thorn in the sides of the white agents and the pro-white chiefs. In late 1865, at a time when the reservation was still being raided by Paulina's Paiutes, he led about half the reservation's residents away to the Yakima Indian Reservation in Washington. After several months of stirring up trouble there, Que-pe-ma rode back to Warm Springs. A season of poor hunting finally persuaded the Tyghs to join the other reservation Indians in farming. But Que-pe-ma's wanderlust had not ended, nor had the concern that his independent behavior created.

The government and settlers were determined that the two tribes, as well as the still uncooperative Paiutes, must live on the Warm Springs Reservation. Among those forced to move there was Billy Chinook. He had to give up his farm and in 1857 go down with about 500 other Indians. He made the best of the situation, acquiring a ranch and a large two-story house. The remaining Wasco bands moved down in 1858.

But the Chinook- and Sahaptin-speaking tribes who ceded Central Oregon had not lived there; the Walpapi Paiutes did. And the Paiutes had ceded nothing. While U.S. officials might ignore this technicality, white immigrants who met Paiutes on the trail experienced greater difficulty in doing so. The Paiutes attacked them.

The withdrawal of the Warm Springs Indians onto the reservation strengthened the Walpapi Paiutes. They had been dominant in Central Oregon but challenged by other tribes. With those tribes now confined to the reservation, the Paiutes could treat the region as their exclusive domain. However, the new Indian agency had been established on ground where the Paiutes often hunted, fished, and gathered berries and roots, and they did not intend to stop just because white people drew a line on a piece of paper.

The Paiutes continued the old war against their neighbors. In April 1859 they attacked the reservation, killed four Warm Springs Indians and stole more than 100 horses. The enraged victims set out in pursuit. Fifty-three Warm Springs Indians led by agency physician Thomas Fitch rode across the Crooked River country and over the Ochocos. They located a Paiute camp on the John Day and attacked, killing ten warriors and capturing the women and children. They also captured two adult brothers, whom they sent as prisoners to Fort Dalles.

The agency people hoped that the Paiutes would think twice before they attacked the reservation again. But in August, perhaps at full fighting strength, the Paiutes attacked more ruthlessly than ever. The screaming Paiutes rode through the camps, cutting down warriors, old men, women, and children. Panic and chaos followed the raid. "For God's sake, send some help as soon as possible," Fitch begged in a letter directed to "any white man." "We are surrounded by Snakes [Paiutes]. They have killed a good many Indians and got all our stock. Don't delay a single minute."

Indians and white reservation employees fled in large groups to The Dalles. Most returned the following month, escorted by 15 U.S. dragoons sent south to temporarily protect the reservation from future inroads.

At this critical period a new group of people entered the outback: prospectors. In 1860, gold had been discovered in Idaho at Orofino, and some Californians passing through Portland on their way to these new mines stopped to listen to J.L. Adams when he related the story of the Lost Wagon Train and the Blue Bucket gold. The Californians questioned Adams closely concerning his personal knowledge of the mine. Adams assured them that he himself had been part of the ill-fated train and knew the exact location where the nuggets had been found. Three other men present said that they could confirm it because they too had been with the Lost Wagon Train. The Californians asked Adams to lead them to the mine and he agreed, provided they could raise a party big enough to fight off the Indians.

A large expedition left Portland in August 1861. From The Dalles, they went down the Deschutes to Crooked River, and followed the latter to its headwaters. They emerged in the same desert that the Lost Wagon Train had crossed, with equally lugubrious results. They suffered for days. The Californians began to doubt Adams' story, and the three men who had confirmed it admitted that they had not been part of the lost train. Adams insisted that he could lead them to gold if they would be patient. The Californians continued to follow him until he led them to alkali water, then they forced him to change direction. Although they would no longer allow Adams to guide them, they demanded that he find gold. He did manage, just barely, to escape with his life.

Despite such fiascos, prospectors continued to venture into the outback looking for the lost mine. Indians posed a danger everywhere except to the northeast in what is now Baker County. There the Paiutes, Cayuse, Umatillas, and Bannocks allowed one another to hunt, fish, and gather in peace in a sort of neutral zone, and white men experienced little trouble in the area. And there, on October 23, 1861, Henry Griffin, prospecting in the vast swampland of the Powder River valley, struck gold on China Creek. Almost overnight tents and mining claims covered the ground. By 1863, wild, lawless Auburn, Baker County's first seat, had 6,000 people, making it Oregon's largest city.

Men found gold on the North Fork of the John Day at the same time as others found it in Baker County. Indians killed men sent for supplies. The miners were starved out. The following spring a party of 18 prospectors on their way to Idaho crossed through the country and one of them, an ex-49er named William Aldred, decided to pan along Canyon Creek. He did not accumulate anything except mud in his pan, but after wading in the creek found $4.50 worth of gold in his longjohns. Aldred thought this impressive; his friends did not. They resumed their journey to Idaho. Upon reaching Auburn, however, they learned that the reports of gold in Idaho had been exaggerated and the mines were overrun with miners. They decided to return to Canyon Creek. They arrived to find its banks occupied by hundreds of prospectors. Soon Canyon City, on the banks of the John Day, became the second largest metropolis in Oregon, after Auburn.

Oregon now consisted of two white sections: the commercial western region along the Willamette and the Columbia, and the gold-rich eastern region along the Powder and upper John Day rivers. Between the two sections lay Central Oregon, dominated by hostile Paiutes. Merchandise fetched stupendous prices in Auburn and Canyon City. Portland merchants and eastern Oregon miners believed it vital that the routes connecting these areas—principally The Dalles-Canyon City Road along the John Day River—remain open.

However, whites who entered the Ochoco region often did not leave it alive. How many people the Paiutes killed cannot be reckoned or guessed. Even today the skeletons of victims are sometimes found. Yet many white people defied the dangers and entered, almost always on their way to someplace else. During this period, only a handful of people actually tried to settle anywhere in the vast region between the Cascades and the Blue Mountains.

6

PAULINA WAR
1859–1867

HIS WHITE CONTEMPORARIES called him Paulina, or Paunina, or Polina, or Polino, and similar names. He is best remembered as Paulina, and many Central Oregon geographical features are named for him. While Chief Ochoco enjoyed camping in the Ochoco Valley, Paulina often resided 50 miles east in the Beaver Creek and Paulina valleys.

He became the fiercest enemy the white people ever encountered in Oregon. He also hated the Warm Springs Indians and made war on Modocs and Klamaths. The source of this vitriolic enmity is unknown. Paulina was not a mere horse thief, as author Phil F. Brogan (1964) suggested. Perhaps he was whatever passed among Paiute nomads for a nationalist. In any case, he stopped white settlement in Central Oregon for almost a decade, brought economic woes to Canyon City and even Auburn, and killed uncounted numbers of people, both white and red.

It will be recalled that after the April 1859 raid at Warm Springs, Dr. Thomas Fitch led Indians from the agency over the Ochocos to the John Day Valley and attacked a band of Paiutes. They killed ten warriors and captured the women and children. Fitch also seized Paulina and his brother Wahveveh. They were taken to Fort Dalles and imprisoned there, evidently for only a short time. Because this is the first significant mention of Paulina and Wahveveh, it is not inappropriate to speculate that the slaughter of all the other males in their band and the capture of the women and children may have been the primary source of their hatred for both whites and Warm Springs Indians. But it is only speculation.

What role, if any, Paulina played in the following August 1859 attack on the agency is unknown. Because he did emerge soon afterward as the principal Paiute war chief in Oregon, it is possible that he led most of the raids. From 1859 until the mid-1860s, the Paiutes assaulted the reservation repeatedly. The Warm Springs Indians became their own best defenders, but they never knew when or where their enemy would attack. In response to the pleas of white travelers and isolated ranchers as well as agency Indians, the state had finally sent out the First Oregon Cavalry to attack hostile Paiutes and build fortified camps for the protection of travelers.

On April 20, 1864, Capt. John Drake left Fort Dalles with a company of cavalry, moving into the Oregon outback while another company left Fort Walla Walla in Washington Territory, to approach the Paiutes from the east. While Drake's men were camped at the junction of Crooked River and the North Fork of Crooked River during the night of May 17–18, the captain's reconnoitering Warm Springs Indian scouts returned to report spotting an Indian camp of nine lodges and many horses about 15 miles away. Drake told Lt. McCall to attack them at dawn. He assigned him a detachment of soldiers and a group of scouts led by their chief, Stockietly, known to whites as Stock Whitley.

Lt. McCall found the lodges on what is now Upper Watson Springs. The Paiutes were camped against a hill, protected by the rocks. Deciding upon a trifurcated attack, McCall led one party, Lt. Stephen Watson a second, and Stock Whitley the third. The men spread out and approached the lodges. McCall had chosen the most difficult position to reach and was not there yet when a lookout raised the alarm. The Paiutes ran up the hill, where they took shelter behind boulders.

Watson and Whitley charged the fleeing enemy without waiting for McCall. The Paiutes held their fire. Watson's men and the scouts all fired their pistols as they charged up the hill, using up ammunition. Watson reached the summit, and the Paiutes opened fire. They shot the lieutenant in the face, killing him, slew two of his men, and wounded five others. They also gunned down one of Whitley's scouts and wounded Whitley and a civilian who had volunteered to accompany the soldiers. The survivors retreated. They afterwards accused McCall of failing to come to their assistance. McCall took the wounded men to safety and sent two riders to Drake with a note asking for help.

Drake was about an hour from camp when the riders found him. He immediately detached 40 men and galloped to the site of the battle. There he learned that the Paiutes had escaped. The soldiers went up the hill to retrieve the bodies of the dead, which had been stripped and mutilated, as was the Indian custom. The soldiers burned the lodges; Drake found these so well-stocked with provisions and plunder that he suspected this might have formed Paulina's base camp. The soldiers also rounded up about 50 horses.

They took their dead and wounded to Camp Maury, located near modern-day Post at the base of the Maury Mountains. Stock Whitley suffered from his wounds for three weeks before he died. Watson's name was given to a later military camp on Fort Creek in the eastern Ochocos in the Mitchell locality. Drake's men remained in the interior until early winter, but they had no more encounters with the Paiutes. "The Indians are very active and enterprising," Drake wrote at Camp Maury, "constantly lurking about our camp. The signs of their movements in the night are plainly to be seen every day; but they are extremely difficult to trail, always scattering out before leaving the place of their operations, and never coming or going away by the same route twice."

J.W.P. Huntington, the new Oregon Superintendent of Indian Affairs, decided that another treaty would be necessary. He sent word to the Paiutes, Klamaths, and Modocs that a parley would be held at Fort Klamath. Perhaps he hoped that Drake's expedition would encourage attendance.

Many Indians showed up, but fewer than two dozen Paiutes. In fact, the principal Paiute chiefs—Winnemucca, Ochoco, Paulina, Wahveveh, and Howluck—all stayed away. Naturally this disappointed Huntington. After concluding treaties with the Klamaths and Modocs, he started north with Dr. William Cameron McKay and other Warm Springs scouts. McKay, the agency physician, was half-Indian, half-Scot, a step-grandson of Dr. John McLoughlin, and had been educated in the East. He served Superintendent Huntington as a scout and, like Billy Chinook, also had been employed by the government as an interpreter.

While moving north from Fort Klamath along the Deschutes, McKay and the scouts suddenly came upon a Paiute camp. They killed the three men they found and took three women and two children prisoners. Imagine Huntington's delight when he learned that the captives included Chief Paulina's wife and son.

About the same time, Billy Chinook inflicted yet another blow. Paulina's band included a shaman, Tamowins, whom the Paiutes believed possessed great powers. He had even concocted something for Paulina that he promised would make it impossible for bullets to harm him. Chinook and other scouts, however, killed Tamowins.

Paulina learned in late 1864 or early 1865 that his wife and son had been taken to Fort Klamath. He may have tried to negotiate their release, but if so, he failed. Huntington would be satisfied with nothing less than Paulina's mark on a peace treaty. Paulina and his band rode down to the fort for a parley. On August 12, 1865, Paulina agreed to Huntington's terms, which included that he and his band remain on the Klamath Reservation.

That did not end the Paiute problem. In fact, at the very time Paulina went onto the reservation, warfare in eastern Oregon became bloodier than ever. Paiutes killed people all across the region, from the Owyhee country in Idaho to the Deschutes. They attacked wagon trains, ranches, and even towns. Military camps protected only the soldiers inside. Paiutes killed four in a party of five prospectors on Murderers Creek on the South Fork of the John Day, and captured 300 head of cattle while raiding at Indian Creek near Canyon City. Capt. L.L. Williams lost a pitched battle with Paiutes at a place between Camp Wright on the Silvies River (near modern-day Burns) and Harney Lake. The army sent a detachment from Camp Watson south to assist Camp Curry in the Harney country. At Beaver Creek, on the detachment's return trip, Chief Wahveveh attacked. After Capt. L.L. Williams abandoned Camp Wright in April 1866, Wahveveh burned the buildings to the ground.

Paiutes and their Bannock cousins also waged war in Idaho and Utah, while Howluck did the same in northern California. The whole region became hazardous for whites. In addition to their alarm about the danger to the local population, government officials and businessmen alike were further infuriated because the outbreak disrupted traffic with the gold towns.

Adding to these problems, on April 22, 1866, Paulina and his band disappeared from the Klamath Reservation. It is uncertain whether he responded to a summons from other Paiutes or if he had tried to abide by the terms of the treaty until his people began to starve after promised provisions never arrived. Whatever his reason for leaving, he bought weapons from other chiefs and returned to the upper Beaver Creek and Paulina valleys. From there, he waged war against the whites and non-Paiute Indians. Travelers, prospectors, isolated ranches, stage stations, and settlers all became targets again.

A Tennessee lad who would write his name large in Eastern Oregon's history, Lt. Reuben Bernard, led the First U.S. Cavalry out of Camp Watson to search the outback for hostiles. He and his men rode across 630 miles of this rough country in 26 days, leaving destruction in their wake. Going south from the Crooked River to Silver Creek, then to Harney and Malheur lakes and, afterward, east to the Owyhee River, they destroyed Paiute camps and won two pitched battles. Bernard ended the long sweep by routing 80 warriors on Rattlesnake Creek. One Indian Bernard did not rout was Paulina, busy slaughtering peaceful Modocs in the Sprague River valley while the cavalry looked for him up north.

Barely had Bernard returned to quarters before Paiutes raided the Elk and Dixie creek areas near Canyon City and stole horses from a Baker County ranch. Paulina or Wahveveh probably led the Canyon City area attacks, where about 50 Paiutes killed settlers, burned buildings, and stole livestock. It is certain that Paulina burned ranch buildings and stole stock that September on Bridge Creek; generally his territory in the upper Beaver Creek area lay north of Snow Mountain, Wahveveh's to the south. Camp Watson in the John Day Valley was too distant to provide protection, and Camp Logan on the upper John Day had been abandoned. Camp Watson could not even protect itself: in August, Paiutes took 54 mules and 18 head of cattle from the soldiers there. The Dalles-Canyon City Road along the John Day River became a trail of death. Business in Canyon City ground to a standstill. Settlers had to close rural schools.

The Oregon legislature passed a joint resolution calling for the U.S. Army to intervene. Governor George L. Woods went further, demanding that the army wage a war of extermination against all Paiute men, women, and children. Appalled army officers in Oregon rejected this demand, but Wood appealed over their heads to Secretary of War Edwin M. Stanton. Elements of the federal government had become genocidal regarding the treatment of hostile Indians throughout the West in the wake of the Great Sioux Uprising of 1862. It had been the largest massacre of civilians within the United States up to that time. Without any warning, the Lakota, who had been living in peace with their white neighbors, rose up and devastated much of Minnesota, leaving more than 10,000 people on the run and murdering by official count 644 men, women, and children (other accounts claimed that they killed as many as 2,000 people).

After that outrage, the Lincoln Administration, as well as the later Johnson and Grant administrations, pursued a policy often taking on aspects of what today would be called ethnic cleansing, aimed at hostile western Indians until they finally surrendered and occupied reservations. In consideration of this policy, Secretary Stanton approved Wood's bloodthirsty request and sent Gen. George Crook to implement it. Wood also proposed that Warm Springs scouts be used as attacking units, and this too was ordered. The army selected Dr. McKay and John Darragh to lead the scouts. Darragh had built the first New York skyscraper and a number of other buildings, including the Waldorf-Astoria, and had been prominent in Wasco County affairs. Only 36 years old, he was an unsociable and morose man, but able. Billy Chinook enlisted as a scout in his command. Lt. William Borrowe told the scouts at the time of their enlistment to take no prisoners regardless of age or sex.

Chinook and the other Warm Springs Indians had more reasons than ever for wanting to kill Paulina. The Walpapi chief had continued to raid the agency. He arranged peace talks with Queapama, chief of the Wascos. But during the parley, Paulina had one of his braves murder Queapama.

Another Warm Springs chief, Poustaminie, a Tygh, fell victim to Paulina's brother. Wahveveh attacked the Tyghs while they were building a bridge. The Tyghs fought until told that Chief Howluck—Paulina and Wahveveh's ally in southern Oregon and northern California—was coming up with reinforcements. Poustaminie approached the Paiutes and laid down his weapons to show his peaceful intentions. They murdered him.

That summer, Billy Chinook and about 25 other scouts spotted a Paiute camp on Dry Creek, 13 miles south of Ochoco Creek. Chinook had orders not to attack if he located the enemy, but he could not pass up this opportunity. The Warm Springs Indians hid and waited through the night. At dawn, Chinook led the attack into the camp. After a close and bloody battle, they killed or captured all 32 Paiutes. Chinook's scouts, probably all Wascos, had avenged Chief Queapama.

Scouts also located Paulina above Lake Harney in snow, 2,000 feet up on Steens Mountain. Paulina retreated to a cave protected by boulders. He managed to repel the attack, but Chief Wahveveh and two other Paiute braves were killed.

James Clark's stage station on the Dalles-Canyon City Military Road was located on the John Day, about a mile below the mouth of Bridge Creek near today's border between Jefferson and Wheeler counties. Clark had built his house and corrals there in 1865 despite the Paiute danger. One September morning, Clark and his 18-year-old brother-in-law, George Masterson, were cutting drift wood on the river. They saw Paiutes galloping downhill toward them from the Ochoco country. They jumped onto their horses and raced toward the house, where they had left their guns. Clark's family was absent, visiting in the Willamette Valley, and there was no one to cover them. When Clark and Masterson realized that the Indians would outrace them they turned and rode up Bridge Creek, still pursued.

After several miles Masterson's horse became too exhausted to continue and Masterson told Clark to go on and save himself. The Paiutes pursued Clark for several more miles before they gave up and turned back to kill Masterson. He had hidden in bushes along the river. Clark rode eight miles to C.W. Myers' station where he found a group of packers. They were led by William "Bud" Thompson, a bold, proud, intolerant young man who would later play an infamous role in Crook County's history. Clark, Thompson, Perry Maupin (a son of nearby stage station operator, Howard Maupin), John Atterbury, three other white men, and a group of Warm Springs Indians rode back to the Clark ranch. The Paiutes had gone. Clark and the others hollered for Masterson. After five hours submerged in the creek, he finally risked leaving his hiding place. The Paiutes had not found him, but the creek nearly froze him. Clark's house lay in ashes, feathers covering the ground from mattresses that the Indians had slashed open. Four horses belonging to Henry Wheeler had been stolen from the corral.

Clark, Thompson, and their posse trailed the Paiutes. They caught up with them at the head of Cottonwood (now McKay) Creek. In the ensuing fight, they killed four, but Paulina and the others escaped. Clark built another house, but forever after the stage station was known as Burnt Ranch. (Today's maps locate "Burnt Ranch" several miles west of the original site.)

Pioneer stage line operator Henry Wheeler lost more horses than the four at Clark's station. Altogether he lost 89 horses and $20,000 worth of property to the Paiutes, a tremendous ruination for that time and place. The narrowest escape for Wheeler himself came in that same bloody autumn of 1866. He and H.C. Paige, a Wells Fargo messenger, were driving a stagecoach three miles north of modern-day Mitchell when Paiutes with rifles appeared and ordered them to stop. Paige opened fire. An Indian shot Wheeler through his face, blasting away the upper gum and teeth and a piece of jawbone. Wheeler hung his whip on the brake, jumped off the stage, and unhitched one of the horses while Paige got the other. They mounted and fled toward the C.W. Myers stage station on Bridge Creek, six miles away, with the Indians in hot pursuit. Halfway there Paige's horse threw him. Wheeler caught the horse while Paige held off the Paiutes with his rifle, then Wheeler helped Paige remount. The pair escaped with bullets flying around them. They later returned with a posse to find the stagecoach destroyed and the horses gone. But the Indians had left untouched $10,000 in cash, not realizing that it had value.

Gen. Crook believed that winter was the best part of the year to attack the Paiutes. Accordingly, when wintertime arrived, McKay, Darragh, and regular army troops left The Dalles for the outback. (Historian Keith Clark has published McKay's journal, an excellent account not only of the campaign, but for understanding the difficulties of early travel in Central Oregon.) McKay spent a snowy, hazy, and cold Christmas camped at the mouth of the Crooked River gorge.

He returned to Warm Springs without encountering the enemy, but resumed the hunt again during a bitterly cold January. Snow fell hard, covering the ground with up to 20 inches. They went down Cottonwood Creek to Lone Pine, and soon afterward heard a rifle being fired. McKay sent out scouts to investigate, and they found a man's footprints. The next morning, McKay and Darragh took 40 men to follow the tracks, which led them to a Paiute camp on the Crooked River at the base of canyon walls towering 1,200 to 1,500 feet above. McKay and Darragh divided their forces, some to attack on foot from the left while others would ride in from the right. They hoped to surprise the camp, but the steep terrain caused them to make too much noise when descending. Most of the Paiutes escaped; however, the scouts killed three, and captured two children. Because of the orders issued to wage a war of extermination, it is surprising that they took two children prisoners.

They then spotted 40 to 50 Paiutes further up the river, at a creek then known as Tawawa, and rode to attack them also. The Paiutes had the high ground and were entrenched in a rock fortification. The scouts climbed up close enough to exchange shots with them, killing three, but between themselves and the rock fortification lay ground so level that McKay and Darragh calculated they would lose a quarter of their men if they tried to rush over it. When darkness fell, they disengaged. With only one man and two horses wounded, they counted it a victory.

In Superintendent Huntington's annual report, quoted by Keith Clark in articles about William McKay, Huntington related an example of the extermination policy which presumably occurred at this time: "The scouts under the command of Lieutenants McKay and Darragh surprised a camp of Snakes in a narrow [canyon] on a small fork of Crooked River, killed all the men seven in number and took fourteen women and children prisoners. Their officers directed them to carry out the orders. They remonstrated, but finally reluctantly <u>killed</u> and <u>scalped</u> all the <u>women</u> and <u>children</u>, they offering no resistance."

Huntington hotly opposed the extermination policy. The exact incident he refers to above is not mentioned in the accounts presented by historian Clark. Despite the evidence of two children taken prisoner on Crooked River, the scouts generally followed the order. It is uncertain whether the scouts disliked the policy because it was inhumane or because they were being forced to kill valuable slaves while also inviting Paiute retaliation.

McKay and Darragh returned to the Crooked River less than a fortnight later, this time approaching from the south over the Pup Mountains. Scouts found a man's footprints and followed them for four miles, where they discovered many tracks. They reported back to McKay, who at midnight told Billy Chinook to take 30 men and try to locate and destroy these Paiutes. McKay followed him the next morning, a very snowy January 20, and encountered Chinook's party returning with nine scalps. They had attacked the Paiute camp at daybreak and killed everyone in it. McKay and Darragh decided to go further and see what other Paiutes they could flush out while the deep snow made tracking easy. They traveled three miles further, where they killed a man, woman, and child. Soon after that they found another camp, surprised it, and killed five women and a child. They then returned to camp. Darragh boasted: "If our horses could have stood it we should have got the last Snake in this section," but also noted that they had (against orders) taken a total of six children as prisoners.

Chief Paulina continued to wage war against all comers until April 22, 1867. That day was the anniversary of his departure from the Klamath Reservation. It was also the day some of his enemies caught up with him.

Paulina and his braves stole 25 head of cattle and two horses from the Andrew Clarno stage station on Sunday night, April 21. As James Clark, survivor of the Burnt Ranch incident, was driving a stagecoach on The Dalles-Canyon City Road, he spotted them as they rode away. He turned the stage around and hurried back to Howard Maupin's station, where he told Maupin what he had seen. Clark, Maupin, and Clark's passenger, William Ragan, tracked the Indians to a camp near Trout Creek in what is today eastern Jefferson County. They eluded the lookout, dismounted in a secluded location, and crawled as close to the camp as they dared.

Historian Dorsey Griffin (1991) has collected into a book the numerous accounts of what happened next. He clearly demonstrates how many different stories can arise from the same incident, many of them perfectly logical, some just plain silly. He has done original research suggesting that the whites waited through the night and attacked Paulina's raiders at dawn while they were still "in their blankets." Suffice it to say that at some point the white men opened fire with their rifles. The Paiutes fled into the brush and nearby hills. According to many accounts, Maupin wounded (with a shot to the thigh) a tall Indian dressed in an old blue cavalry coat. When the white men entered the camp, Clark recognized the wounded man as one of the Indians who had chased him the previous year. He asked Maupin for permission to finish him off, and, after receiving it, shot him three times. After a search of the area failed to turn up more Indians, the group returned to the camp, looted it, scalped the dead Indian, and rounded up Clarno's stock.

Only later did they learn that they had killed Paulina himself. Warm Springs Indians confirmed it from members of Paulina's band who sought refuge on the reservation. Not until July 12 could McKay, down in Harney County, record: "Snake prisoners [say] that the Indian that was killed by Mopin and Clark was Pallina and no mistake."

The question of who killed Paulina is one that has intrigued Griffin and other historians. Maupin claimed that he did it. Such diverse figures as Bud Thompson and James Blakely believed him. Others credited Clark. Even Maupin's own family, in defending Maupin's claim, admitted that Clark had shot the Indian after Maupin did, while still insisting that Maupin killed him. At the time nobody seemed to care much, satisfied to say that Clark and Maupin killed Paulina. The accounts in fact credit them with killing four out of eight Indians, without giving any explanation of where they found the other three. The implication was that they had killed all four together, yet every account of the shooting—even the contemporary newspaper account that predated the discovery of Paulina's identity—only describes in detail the killing of the one who turned out to be the infamous chief.

Paiute problems continued in Eastern Oregon, but the Walpapis ceased to be a menace. White settlement of Central Oregon began in earnest. In September 1872 the government established the 1,778,560-acre Malheur Reservation for the Paiutes. Only 12,000 acres were tillable. Here, bands under Winnemucca II, Ochoco, Natchez, Egan, and Owitze settled, until the 1878 Bannock War.

7
ROADS ENTER THE WILDERNESS
1846–1880

OTHER THAN THE PAIUTES, the greatest impediment to the white settlement of Central Oregon remained its natural barriers. Passes over the Cascades were impassable during winter. Even after wagon roads were built through the mountains and towns were established in Central Oregon, no traffic could cross the snowbound Cascades during winter. There were alternative routes between the Willamette Valley and Central Oregon, but even they were doubtful, and dangerous. The route south from the Columbia and The Dalles, which was hazardous anyway because of the canyons and the Deschutes, was impossible for heavy wagons during winter. Nor was the Yreka Trail from California to Canyon City more certain. In wintertime, Central Oregon was almost separated from the rest of the world.

Even during summer, travel was difficult and in places quite dangerous. Several passes allowed immigrants and other travelers to cross the Cascades. The two best known, the Santiam and the Willamette, had been used by countless generations of Indians and later by the mountain men and trappers who first explored Oregon. But other, lesser known routes between the regions were also used. Samuel Barlow, equipped with a franchise from the territorial legislature to locate an alternate road, had discovered an almost passable route between Wamic and Sandy in 1846. It became completely passable after he cut down and removed trees. He operated his Barlow Road, just south of Mount Hood, for tolls, and it became much used by Oregon Trail immigrants. The pass was not entirely safe, though, as illustrated in late 1861 when four Indians were hanged for committing murders there.

Minto Pass, now part of the North Santiam Highway, had been used earlier by Indians, but they tended to avoid it as a place of misfortune. Two great battles had been fought in the pass during older times, both victories for the northeastern Oregon Cayuse over the Willamette Valley Molallas. Hogg Pass was discovered by Andrew Wiley three miles north of Santiam Pass, and nearby Wiley Pass was discovered by the same hunter in 1859. Perhaps the least accessible important pass was the McKenzie, which even today is closed for many months each year. Two companies formed in 1870 to build a road across it failed. The following year, however, John Templeton Craig and others established the McKenzie Salt Springs & Deschutes Wagon Road Company to push a route along a canyon past old Camp Polk and across the lava beds to the Deschutes. Much tree-clearing and road grading was necessary, making for hard labor. But this company succeeded where others had failed, and in 1872 began to collect tolls ranging from a nickel for a single sheep, to two dollars for a wagon drawn by two horses.

The road was immediately used by Willamette Valley stockmen who desired to drive their cattle into Central Oregon's vast plains of tall bunchgrass. After the cattle became fattened there on the cheap, the ranchers could then drive them back over the pass to the west side or take them to miners at Canyon City and on the Powder and Salmon rivers, to towns in California, or army posts in Nevada.

For more than a century, there were only two bridges over the Deschutes: Todd's and later Maupin's. Andrew Jackson Tetherow, a son of Solomon Tetherow, wagon master of the Lost Wagon Train, established a ferry in the Deschutes Canyon in the mid-1870s at the mouth of Ferry Canyon.

From the south, the Yreka Trail skirted the region on its way from California to the booming gold town of Canyon City. It entered the state in present-day Klamath County and went northeast past Silver Lake, Christmas Valley, Hampton Buttes, Whirlwind Valley, and between the Benjamin Lakes before turning up the South Fork of Crooked River, then on to Long Hollow, Twelvemile Creek, Grindstone Creek, and finally to the John Day headwaters and Canyon City.

On the east lay the Ochoco, Blue, Maury, and Strawberry mountains. These were not as daunting barriers as the Cascades or the great canyons, but they were barriers nevertheless, and in any case most people wishing to enter Central Oregon took a different route. There were also, in the southeast, the old Meek and Elliott and the new Steen trails. Despite the tragedies associated with the first two in particular, people used them. For example, a Yamhill County physician led a party of about a dozen men from Eugene in August 1858 to seek Central Oregon gold. He followed the Elliott road across the mountains, then broke off to search along the Crooked River, Hampton Buttes, the Maury Mountains, then back onto the Elliott road to follow it to Bear Creek. However, he followed Bear Creek to Crooked River, and the Crooked River to the Deschutes, and crossed the Cascades over the new Barlow Trail.

Perhaps the most enterprising entrepreneur in Central Oregon in the period prior to Paulina's death was John Y. Todd, who built a toll bridge on the Deschutes, a thousand feet below the top of the canyon walls. First, he had operated a pack mule train to the Orofino mines in Idaho. The business made him a great amount of money, and like many tycoons he sought investments to produce yet more cash. This led to the construction of a toll bridge and toll road (about five miles north of today's Maupin) in partnership with Robert Mays and Ezra L. Hemingway. Mays, like Todd, was a Tygh Valley rancher and blacksmith, and was in the process of becoming a prosperous man in his own right. Hemingway stayed at the bridge to collect tolls.

Flood waters, apparently caused by spring runoff after a heavy winter snowfall in 1861–1862, carried away the bridge. Not long afterward, Todd decided to move to the Farewell Bend area farther south on the Deschutes. He sold his Tygh

Valley properties, and Mays bought the bridge. Mays rebuilt the bridge, in the process making it wider, and improved the access roads down both sides of the gorge. But the bridge would finally be known as Sherar's Bridge.

Joseph H. Sherar had gone to the California gold fields from his native Vermont in 1855. He found no gold, but earned plenty of cash as a farmer, road builder, and pack train owner. In 1862, he relocated to Oregon and began to operate a pack string between The Dalles and Canyon City. His company is credited with first crossing and naming Antelope Valley, Muddy Creek, and Cherry Creek. In his travels, he used Todd's bridge and realized its potential more than its builder or Mays did. In 1871, he bought it for $7,041.

For the next four decades, Sherar oversaw the bridge, and it was as familiar a landmark as any in the region. Hiring Indians as workmen, he improved the road from Eightmile all the way to Bakeoven. He maintained the road better than other toll operators in the region, and the Sherar's Bridge route became the most preferred for entering Central Oregon. Not taking this success for granted, Sherar continually strived to improve accommodations for weary travelers. In addition to a large stage station at the bridge, he built an enormous barn and a three-storey inn with 33 rooms. It became one of the first and most famous hostelries in the outback.

Howard Maupin and his son Perry seized an opportunity to profit from the traffic over Sherar's road. They put a ferry on the Deschutes farther down the road. This was at the site of the village that since 1909 has been known as Maupin. W.E. Hunt later acquired this little enterprise, which afterward became known as Hunt's Ferry.

The first roads through Central Oregon followed the old Indian trails, which tended to be the easiest routes to walk rather than the swiftest between two points. Usually the Indian trails were along ridges rather than over the muddy, brush-clogged lowlands. Gradually, white road builders such as Sherar and transporters like Henry Wheeler began to cut shorter routes. Speed mattered. And the traffic became heavy during the Eastern Oregon gold rush.

On average each day in April 1863, 200 pack animals and 10 to 12 freight wagons departed The Dalles toward Canyon City. The pack trains often included as many as 50 mules. In addition to being driven down from The Dalles, some of the Canyon City-bound trains came over McKenzie Pass, although not in April when snow still blocked it. The freight wagons that soon replaced the pack trains were more practical to move over the roads, but also more dangerous. Mules were sure-footed. Wagons, loaded with up to 5,000 pounds of freight, could wobble too far toward the edge of a road in a steep canyon, sending animals, driver, and freight hurtling to destruction. Nobody knows how many lives were lost on the narrow routes high on the walls of Eastern and Central Oregon gorges, but the number probably is quite high. Hauling freight on such roads, especially the harrowing one through Cow Canyon near the Deschutes, was a tightrope act.

Freighters in Central Oregon fastened bells to the harness of their lead teams. Many children of pioneer settlers would recount later how they heard bells at night as freighters drove past their ranches or homesteads. The bells had two principal purposes: to warn others on the narrow canyon roads of their approach, and to set a rhythm for the horses to step in unison.

Pioneer Roads in Central Oregon (1985) by George McCart, et al., relates the story of what happened one morning on the grade above Sherar's Bridge, when no bells were ringing and no one was sent ahead to be sure that the road was clear. Very early one morning, two freighters—one above the canyon and one at the bridge below—decided separately to proceed over the grade before anyone else drove onto it. One, with a loaded wagon, started up from the bridge at about the same time as the other with an empty wagon started down toward the bridge. They met on a stretch of the road where it was impossible to pass. Whatever the depth of their consternation, and one assumes that there was at least some consternation when they realized the problem they had created for themselves, they found a sensible solution. They took apart the empty wagon, placed its pieces off the road, and moved the loaded wagon a few yards past it up the grade. Then both drivers put the empty wagon back together so it could continue down to the bridge.

Felix Scott Jr. had profited during the California gold rush by hauling supplies. When the Salmon River strikes occurred while he was living in the Willamette Valley, he saw a chance to repeat his success by taking supplies across Oregon to the Idaho miners. In doing so, he would follow a trail across McKenzie Pass pioneered by missionary Henry Spalding and three other men when they drove cattle from the Willamette Valley to graze in Central Oregon. Most of Spalding's cattle had perished in the harsh winter of 1861–1862, but his trail remained. It was, however, little more than a path. Scott, with his brother Marion and partner John McNutt, in 1862 and 1863 gathered the resources necessary to expand this path into a wagon road adequate for heavy freight wagons. According to one source, the Scotts assembled 40 laborers, 60 yoke of oxen, 9 freight wagons, and 900 head of cattle and horses. Another source says the Scotts had only 17 yoke of oxen and 700 head of cattle. In any case, Lane County residents who saw the business advantages of a road to the Idaho mines contributed labor and about $1,000 cash.

Building the Scott Trail was hard work. After two weeks of intense labor, the crew had proceeded less than 40 miles from the terminus of the old road, near Vida. The grades were so steep that on occasion a wagon had to be hitched to almost 30 yoke of oxen on the ascent, and then to big fir logs hitched behind them in order to slow the descent. On the lava beds, men had to smash through hard rock using sledgehammers. Following Spalding's path most of the way, the Scotts went up the McKenzie River to Scott Creek and then along an Indian path. By the time they got across the mountains, winter was imminent. They decided to wait out the season in Central Oregon rather than risk trying to cross the Ochocos at such a time. On lower Hay Creek, in present-day eastern Jefferson County, they built Central Oregon's first known log cabin. After the snows melted, they continued their efforts east toward Idaho.

The Scotts returned to the cabin early in 1866. They trailed over 400 head of cattle across the Scott Trail through McKenzie Pass. They were not alone in using the route: a man named Ritchie drove 100 head at about the same time. Another man, Cunsil, herded 100 heifers shortly afterward.

Indians raided the area on March 16, 1866, when the cabin on lower Hay Creek was occupied by Marion and Presley Scott, Charles S. Hardison, John B. Evans, Thomas J. Evans, Lem Jones, and a "Mr. Mills." They rode away with seven saddle horses and a load of camp equipment.

Three major wagon road companies were formed in 1864, whose promoters declared their intention of crossing the outback. The Dalles Military Wagon Road would run from The Dalles to Fort Boise; the Oregon Central Military Wagon Road from Eugene to Silver City, Idaho; and the Willamette Valley & Cascade Mountain Wagon Road from Albany to Vale.

The first named actually had its origin in a different, financially troubled firm that had been organized by several business leaders in The Dalles in 1863—The Dalles & Boise Road Company. In the following year, the company laid out a rough "road" from Cross Hollows south of The Dalles to Canyon City, and extended it to Boise in the following year. However, the contractors, who had not received full payment because of the company's cash woes, seized part of it, and other difficulties beset the project. The contending parties eventually agreed to cooperate rather than fight. Together with several prominent stockholders they formed The Dalles Military Road Company.

Their purpose was really not to operate a road, but rather to acquire government land grants, which were available to road builders. The operators blatantly hijacked part of an existing public road, took over the property of The Dalles and Boise Road, and paid $1,500 to buy a bridge over the Deschutes. Altogether, they may have spent $6,000 "building" the road. The road in places consisted of little more than a clearing through the sagebrush. But, in the summer of 1869, the state certified that it had been completed, and the company was handed 685,440 acres of land. The company abandoned the road itself, and concentrated on selling acreage. After a plan to market it to settlers at the federal homestead "preemption" price of $1.25 an acre failed, the firm in 1876 sold the whole grant to a San Francisco liquor wholesaler for $125,000. His heirs eventually organized the Eastern Oregon Land Company to sell and lease out the grant in subdivided parcels, which it continued to do from offices in Moro and Grass Valley until 1945.

The Oregon Central Military Road was promoted by a former state surveyor-general, B.J. Pengra, and Eugene business leaders. The Eugene people believed a road to Idaho would allow them to more easily sell and ship merchandise to the booming Idaho gold towns, thereby profiting themselves and their community. Pengra secured a contract by which his company would be awarded land grants as the road was completed. The state certified the road by 1870, and the company received 2.5 million acres of land running in a band from Eugene via the Sprague River, Klamath Marsh, and Lakeview, to the Jordan Valley. As in the case of The Dalles Military Wagon Road, after the land was granted, the road itself was abandoned. Eventually the Booth-Kelly Lumber Company and affiliated interests, which would later have timberlands in the Ochocos, acquired much of the road company's real estate. The original grant itself, though, was south of what is today recognized as Central Oregon.

In contrast, the Willamette Valley & Cascade Mountain Wagon Road would play a critical role in Central Oregon for a long time. Linn County ranchers from Western Oregon, including Luther Elkins, started the road in 1864. They capitalized their company at $30,000, and built less than 10 miles in the Sweet Home area before they asked the federal government for help. This came in the summer of 1866 when the U.S. government turned over 800,000 acres of national domain to the state, to be granted to the company as the road progressed—six square miles of land for every mile of road completed—on condition that the route, for military purposes, traverse Central and Eastern Oregon. The company could collect tolls on the road, and sell the granted land. This sounded fair. Of course, such an assessment ignored the dishonesty of the company's operators and corruption in state government.

By 1868, the company claimed that the road was finished all the way from Albany to the Snake River. At the western end, a tollgate was built three miles east of Sweet Home that collected fees on a scale ranging from three cents a head for a hog or sheep, to $3.50 for a wagon drawn by a six-horse team. These tolls brought in $1,000 to $3,000 a year. A labor force was hired to maintain the road, with each worker paid a dollar for a 10-hour day.

However, as in other cases, the company was less interested in exploiting the road than cashing in on the land grant. The builders laid its route through the best available land in each area it traversed, acquiring some of the finest real estate in the outback—a total of 861,512 acres, almost half of it in Central Oregon.

It certainly did not deserve these grants. The portion of the road crossing the Cascades was only six to seven feet wide, just enough for one wagon to squeeze through between the trees. Foot-high tree stumps were left standing in the road. Although a wagon could pass over them, it required careful maneuvering and keen handling of the draft animals. The route had many fords across streams, and instead of building up earth over marshy areas, the company laid down a loose base of logs. The route was open only during the warmest summer months. Come September, it would be closed off again. But at least this Cascades portion of the road had some slim evidence of being a transportation reality.

Not so for the many miles of "road" east of the mountains. Trees were notched, sagebrush torn out, and some stakes driven into the ground so that travelers could see where the "road" was. The small construction crew built its route at rates of up to 15 miles a day! Instead of constructing new road near Burns, the company simply appropriated a significant portion of the Steens Trail. Many portions of the road almost immediately disappeared under sand and sagebrush. Although the company continued to manage the western section of the route, and, of course, collect tolls for doing so, it abandoned everything east of the Deschutes in the 1870s. Everything, that is, except the land grants.

In 1905, early historian F.A. Shaver summarized the judgment of most writers regarding this road operation: "The company never attempted to build roads and the road that was constructed was the work of immigrants passing through the country...It is considered one of the most brilliant fakes ever perpetrated on the American public." About 400,000 acres of land granted to the company was located in what became Crook County. Many later residents there were damaged badly by the swindle.

The government granted alternate sections over the route—along the Crooked River to Prineville, then along the Ochoco, back to Crooked River, and then along the latter for 40 miles to Paulina, then Grindstone, Twelvemile Creek, Long Hollow Creek, and continuing southeast past Snow Mountain to Silver Creek and the Harney Basin. The road originally had been chartered to extend to Canyon City, but the company had obtained a change in the contract in 1870 to its eventual destination at Fort Harney. By following the new route, it could claim some of the most fertile acreage in the Crooked River country, much of it already occupied and developed. No matter that others had settled there—sometimes more than a decade earlier—or that they had sweated and labored to build houses, barns, and corrals. The company now claimed it all and had the government's support. Settlers found themselves labeled as trespassers and had to either pay rent or leave.

Led by Elisha Barnes, the settlers fought back. They claimed that the company had never fulfilled its side of the contract and that Oregon's governors had fraudulently signed over the land grants. Barnes wrote a letter to the U.S. Secretary of the Interior in 1878, laying out the facts. The department investigated—a government surveyor who examined the road reported that the settlers told the truth. Years passed while farmers lobbied the Oregon legislature, Congress, and the federal executive department to declare the grants forfeit. President Grover Cleveland called the grants "unblushing frauds" and said that the promoters responsible had tried "to pervert and prostitute the beneficent designs of the government." But the original promoters had sold the lands.

The great Paris banking house of Lazard Freres bought the grant in 1879. David Cahn and Alexander Weill were later owners. Was it fair to hold later purchasers—buying land in good faith—as being liable for the misdeeds of the original promoters? This question could only be settled by the highest judicial authority in the country. In 1893, the U.S. Supreme Court upheld the grants as valid. Many settlers, including Elisha Barnes, were forced to leave the farms they had spent years developing. Others swallowed their pride and remained on the land as tenants.

Meanwhile, a promoter even more ambitious than the wagon road swindlers was planning a road of a different sort. Col. T. Egenton Hogg, an engaging conversationalist whose tall, slender form was topped by curly brown hair that framed a distinguished beard, first visited Oregon in 1871 to further his plans for a transcontinental railroad. The focus of his interest was Yaquina Bay on the central Oregon Coast, which he planned to make into one of the world's major ports. It would be the western end of his railroad, while its port would do a heavy sea traffic with San Francisco and the Orient. The railroad would go from Yaquina Bay to Corvallis, Albany, over the North Santiam, and then across the outback to Boise. Portlanders laughed at the scheme—at first.

However, in 1877, Hogg went to London to seek money from rich Britons. Many English capitalists, led by firms such as Baring Brothers, had been investing in American business enterprises the same way 20th-century Americans pumped cash into the infant industries of developing countries. Some of these men, notably Francis Kerr and Capt. Henry Mosely, responded to Hogg's pitch. Kerr and Mosely actually traveled to Oregon and accompanied Hogg to Prineville to view the outback.

Hogg promptly bought control of the notorious Willamette Valley & Cascade Mountain Wagon Road Company with its right-of-way and land grant. In 1880, he incorporated the Oregon Pacific Railroad Company and sold $15 million worth of 20-year bonds. Portland capitalists laughed no longer. If Hogg succeeded, Newport, on Yaquina Bay, would be the big city of Oregon, not the town they themselves had bet their own fortunes upon. The Portland *Oregonian* attacked the project less than a month after the railroad was incorporated, claiming that the firm had few assets and the area around Yaquina Bay no value whatever. But during the following summer Hogg had 1,400 men working on the route, making it easily the largest construction project launched in Oregon up to that time. Hope—indeed, *belief*—that Central Oregon would soon have a railroad connection to both the Pacific Coast and the East rose throughout the region. People made decisions about moving to or investing in Central Oregon based upon the promise that soon Col. Hogg's railroad would cross it. The disappointment was great, however, when Hogg's impossibly grand scheme eventually collapsed: his transcontinental railway never materialized.

Most crime in Crook County at the end of the 1880s was small stuff—a rather quiet period between earlier Vigilante action and later range wars—and usually only sheep stealing occurred. There were some shootings and robberies, but not many.

In regard to the more far-reaching crime of swindling, however, the promoters of the Willamette Valley & Cascade Mountain Wagon Road never did serve time. They were not unique. Land fraud prevailed throughout the West. The biggest federal public assistance program ever remains the Homestead Act passed in President Lincoln's time. Other giveaways, such as the Timber and Stone Act (1878), followed in Washington, D.C.'s long-term effort to transfer its vast western public domain into the citizenry's hands. Many Westerners took advantage of these acts whether they qualified for the land or not. Yet nothing in Oregon equaled the fraud perpetuated by the Willamette Valley & Cascade Mountain Wagon Road Company.

8

THE MONOPOLY
1860–1880

THE GOLD RUSHES to Idaho and East Oregon had a big impact on The Dalles. This happened because neither the Willamette Valley road companies nor Col. Hogg's railway had yet (and of course never would) create a transportation-controlling metropolis in Linn County or on the coast. The connection from Portland to the gold fields was via the Columbia, not over the Cascades, and the interlocutor between the city and the mining towns was The Dalles. This route originally was served by a myriad of barges, rafts, sailing ships, and boats, and a few steam paddle-wheelers. In 1860, the owners of these vessels united under the umbrella of one corporate entity, the Oregon Steam Navigation Company, or OSN. Led by Capt. John C. Ainsworth, Robert R. Thompson, and Simeon G. Reed, it quickly drove out the remaining competitors and created a water transportation monopoly that soon embraced almost the whole Pacific Northwest.

Steamboats operating between Portland and The Dalles were built at Portland, those plying between The Dalles and points east were constructed near The Dalles. On the rapids-strewn Columbia, in contrast to the placid Mississippi, ship owners used sternwheelers rather than the more elegant (but harder to steer) side-wheelers. By the time it dissolved in 1880, the OSN would have 26 vessels of various sizes and models.

It controlled the key portages around the rapids on the Columbia, and established inland express and stagecoach companies to supplement the steamer traffic while preventing the development of competition. Stockholders reinvested their profits to continually build up and expand the operation, and they sought to concentrate all traffic and business into Portland. They slashed rates to undercut any competitor, but other times kept the rates high enough that shippers, land promoters, and farmers throughout the Northwest complained loudly. They were so intolerant of competition that the charge has been leveled, without proof, that the OSN stirred up Paiutes in the outback to attack rival stagecoaches, freighters, and pack trains.

Through a subsidiary, the Oregon & Montana Transportation Company, they tapped the eastern mining towns all the way to Helena, Montana. In 1864, the OSN carried 36,000 passengers and 21,834 tons of freight between Portland and The Dalles. Its profit for that year was reported at $783,339. In 1862, the OSN built a 14-mile-long portage railroad bypassing impassable rapids at The Dalles and Celilo Falls to further secure its monopoly on the Columbia.

The Dalles benefited directly from the great river monopoly, and grew accordingly. By 1864, the year its flour mill opened, the town already had a daily newspaper. Its population was estimated at 2,500. Sometimes there were as many as 10,000 people, most of them transient miners, staying in the big metropolis of East Oregon, and the local government had taken over the old army fort and subdivided its real estate. Floods that damaged the town in 1862, 1866, 1876, and 1880, and fires that devastated the business district in 1871 and 1879, failed to retard its growth. However, the end of the mining boom in the 1870s cut its population by more than half. Local merchants and other businessmen would not give up on the town, and worked hard to develop its trading ties to the two supply centers southward, Prineville and Canyon City, and to the rich wheat farming country of Southeast Washington. The town remained the most important commercial and political center in mid-Oregon. The Dalles boomed again in the early 1880s when the Oregon Railway & Navigation Company, an extension of the transcontinental Northern Pacific, built its line through, with 500 workers living in the town in 1883.

For many years, The Dalles also was where the people who lived in Prineville, and indeed anywhere in Central Oregon, went to record deeds or transact other legal business. While Central Oregon remained part of Wasco County, The Dalles was the county seat.

9

EARLY SETTLEMENTS
1867–1900

HALF A YEAR after Paulina's death, the first people intent upon permanently settling in the Crooked River region arrived from Linn County. David Wayne Claypool led Raymond and Calvin (or George) Burkhart, Capt. White, William Smith, and Elisha Barnes to the mouth of Mill Creek on Ochoco Creek, where they cut logs to build houses. They erected three structures during that autumn and winter. For food, they shot mule deer that were abundant along the creeks.

Claypool, a 33-year-old Indiana native, had crossed the plains with his parents, who settled near Lebanon in the Willamette Valley. He had served in the Yakima War before marrying Louisa Elkins and fathering five children.

Barnes was a Kentuckian, who had joined the California gold rush. He prospected until 1852, then returned home to bring his family west. Barnes had married Susanna Glenn, by whom he had seven children. Her sister later married Harney Basin cattle king Pete French.

In spring 1868, as the Paiute threat continued, these earliest settlers removed themselves and their transportable property to Camp Polk, near modern-day Sisters. Leaving their teams and property with Capt. White, they returned on snowshoes to Linn County.

A fortnight after their arrival, Elisha's 19-year-old son, George W. Barnes, returned to the Ochocos with William Elkins, Ewen Johnson, and another man, joined by Capt. White from Camp Polk. Elkins and the unknown man left after only four days, leaving White, Barnes, and Johnson. Days later, Paiutes raided the unoccupied buildings, taking guns and other property before burning down the Claypool house. When the three men returned and discovered what had happened, they carved willow sticks into six-foot-long fake guns, hoping to fool any hostiles who spotted them, and hurried to the Warm Springs agency. They then climbed on foot over the Cascades toward the Willamette Valley. At Elephant Rock they encountered a steady-eyed youth mounted on a fine horse helping his father drive a herd of cattle into the outback. His father fed them dinner, and the next morning a good breakfast.

The youth who accompanied his father was only 15 years old. Straight as an arrow, with thick hair and a polite manner, the boy already had led a life filled with adventures. "I grew up in the saddle," James Blakely once said, and this superb rider had quit school in the seventh grade to become a cowboy. He had been only 12 years old when he helped his father and another man trail 500 steers to California, where his father sold them for $20,000 in gold. The father, also named James, was one of Oregon's most prominent citizens: the founder of Brownsville (where the younger James was born shortly before Joel Palmer secured Central Oregon from the Indians), a captain in the Rogue River War, a member of the legislature, a major stockraiser, and was financially involved in a sawmill, newspaper, grist mill, and woolen mill.

The younger James credited the Presbyterian principles he had learned from his father for the way he lived his life. And James the younger lived a life of restraint, seldom drinking liquor, never taking tobacco or coffee, always leaving the table hungry. Although he sometimes ate venison and beef in these early years if nothing else was available, this cowboy who would write his name large in the beef country of Central Oregon became a staunch vegetarian.

The year the Barnes party met him, Blakely and his father were driving 600 head of cattle over the Santiam to Fort McDermitt in Nevada. The younger Blakely first saw the Prineville area in 1868, again driving cattle eastward. In 1869, he drove 500 head down to the big Miller & Lux outfit in California. Instead of returning to Brownsville, he rode to the Ochocos and established a homestead on Willow Creek, 14 miles north of Barney Prine's new cabin. He signed on as a driver for a stage line established between Sacramento and Portland that year, but quickly determined that he preferred a rancher's life and returned to Willow Creek. Soon relatives followed the 17-year-old pioneer into the area, and the ranches of Kennedy and Ellen Montgomery, S.W. Wood, and Perry Read joined Blakely's along Willow Creek.

Meanwhile, Claypool and additional settlers had returned to the Mill Creek area. Putting up a schoolhouse became their priority. Built of hewn logs in the summer of 1868, the subscription school originally had 17 students and operated three months a year. They hired William Pickett to teach. In April 1869, they organized the Ochoco School District, with William S. Clark as chairman, George H. Judy as secretary, and Ewen Johnson, William Marks, and Edmund F. Veazie as directors. James A. Crawford had replaced Pickett as teacher. Needing money for repairs, wood, and books, the district put up a tax levy in 1873. Voters rejected it 11-2.

They needed a steam-powered sawmill to provide lumber for the new houses. Ike Schwartz built it sometime in the early 1870s. They ran it at Mill Creek as a community service, not for profit.

Other communities also appeared in the region, most significantly Prineville and Scissorsville. Francis B. "Barney" Prine was a tall, broad-shouldered gambler who, according to writer Fred Lockley, had muscles like steel wires. Born in Kansas City on New Year's Day 1841 into a Methodist preacher's family, he accompanied his parents across the plains when 12 years old. The Prines settled on the forks of the Santiam in a community of Southern Democrats. At 27, Barney went south from The Dalles into the Ochoco Valley.

Here flowed the Crooked River, at that time a crystal clear waterway lined by willows, wild currants, pussywillows, wild gooseberries, service berries, and choke cherries, and dotted with beaver dams. Here, in mid-1868, Prine built a thatch-roofed cabin using 10 x 14 foot willow logs, and then he attached onto it a small blacksmith shop. Iron for the shop came from wheel rims abandoned in the Ochoco Valley meadows by the 1845 Lost Wagon Train. Two years later, he converted part of his small habitation into a store, with $80 worth of merchandise, and a saloon stocked with a single case of Hostetter's Bitters. He had hauled his inventory down from The Dalles. Barney's brother Dave with wife Elizabeth arrived. William Pickett, the schoolmaster from the Mill Creek district, moved there, and other people began drifting in. A year after Barney started business, a former Forty-Niner named William Heisler opened a competing store.

Francis B. "Barney" Prine built a thatched-roof log store and saloon in the middle of the wilderness, but moved on before Prineville became the region's key community.
Bowman Museum, Crook County Historical Society

What the Crooked River region needed was a good road from the civilized areas. None existed, despite the Willamette Valley and Cascade Mountain Road's claim to have established one. In the summer of 1869, Lew Daugherty and William Clark from Mill Creek blazed one, which the merchants of The Dalles paid for. The road ran from Bakeoven (Maupin vicinity), to Cow Canyon, to Hay Creek and Willow Creek, and into the Ochoco Valley. This made The Dalles the source of supplies for the entire region between the Cascades and Dixie Pass and all the way south to the California border. Freighters carried supplies not only to Prineville, but also to Canyon City—two towns where ranchers, farmers, and prospectors came to "stock up" on food and dry goods. Settlers might buy enough provisions and supplies to last the year.

But they did not buy them from Barney Prine. Alexander Hodges had moved to the Prine community in 1870, followed in 1871 by his enterprising brother, Monroe Hodges. Monroe had been looking for grazing land and liked the tall grass in the Ochoco Valley. He met with Barney Prine in the latter's cabin. During their conversation, Prine said that he intended to leave the area and Monroe Hodges revealed that he had decided to stay. They dickered for the cabin. Prine sold Hodges the cabin and squatter's rights for $25 and a pack horse. A few days later, after paying some men to build a house for his family, Monroe Hodges rode to The Dalles and filed a homestead claim on 80 acres running from what is now

Main Street to the mesa west of town. He platted the
townsite, naming it Prineville in Barney's honor, and
began to sell lots for $10 apiece. People complained
about the high price. He made the streets especially
wide, a feature still commented upon by visitors. Barney returned a few years later and helped his brother,
Dave Prine, lay out the town's first race track.

Stagecoach service may have started from The
Dalles as early as 1869, after the Wasco County
Court had authorized Clark and Daugherty to build
the toll road between Bakeoven, off the Steens road,
to Prineville. This was a harrowing route for freighters
and travelers alike, particularly going down the narrow and very dangerous grade through Cow Canyon.
After negotiating the canyon, the route went down
Trout Creek, along Hay Creek past the Parrish place,

Monroe Hodges laid out
Prineville and helped
develop it into a prosper-
ous cowtown. *Bowman
Museum, Crook County
Historical Society*

and across Grizzly Mountain to Prineville. Everyone entering Central Oregon
from the north was obliged to go over this hazardous road, which was dusty when
not muddy, and impossible when icy.

Stage service over this road, which was being advertised in 1872, required
watering stops and inns. The latter were established at existing ranches, or ranches
were established at stations built for the purpose. Most early Central Oregon
ranches were better known as "stations," rather in the Australian manner, than
as "ranches." The stagecoaches would leave the big Umatilla House hotel in The
Dalles at 7 a.m. Mondays, and arrive in Prineville at 6 a.m. Thursdays, presumably at the Hodges Hotel. In later years, the stagecoaches took only two days to
reach Prineville, with a stopover at Bakeoven, and left The Dalles three times a
week. Various firms ran the route before Mack Cornett took it over. Lige Haight
built a toll gate about halfway up the Cow Canyon grade.

A church was not built in Prineville until 1879. That may not surprise anyone familiar with the early history of a town that grew up around a saloon and a
race track. Some tough hombres lived in the region during its early days, including Bud Thompson, Til Glaze, and the dapper gunfighter Hank Vaughan. Prine
said later that horse thieves caused bad trouble the first few years until residents
lynched a few. Compared to some other places, though, such as Missouri, Texas,
and Arizona, it was relatively peaceful and mild.

The 1870 census for the "Ochoco District" listed 160 people, including 22
farmers, 10 stockraisers, 10 farm laborers, 8 farmer-stockraisers, 2 herders, 1
millwright, 1 lumber manufacturer, and 1 blacksmith; 25 women were listed as
housekeepers. Almost half of the people in the district had been born in Oregon.
Of the 37 household heads, only 3 were over 50 years old. About 2,000 head of
cattle and several thousand sheep grazed in the Ochoco Valley.

These people are known to have settled in the Crooked River country by 1870—

At *Bridge Creek*: Christian and Meta Meyer; Frank Huat; James Clark; Al Sutton; Wick Cusick; H.C. Hall; _____ Marshall; William Saltman; J.P. Brown; William and Ann Monroe; Thomas and Mary Monroe; Jeff Moore.

At *Squaw Creek*: Jerome LaFollette; Samuel M.W. Hindman.

At *Willow Creek*: James M. Blakely; John B. Evans; Thomas J. Evans; Andrew Warren; Kennedy and Ellen Montgomery; S.G. Woods; Allan Hash; Harland Garrett.

On *Crooked River*: William H. Anderson; Abe Henkle; John Powell; Thomas J. Powell; Emily Powell; A.G. Tetherow; S.J. Newsome.

On *McKay Creek* (formerly *Cottonwood Creek*): George and Susie Millican; Joel Long; John Latta; James McKay; Albert Allen; Jake and Lizzie Gulliford; William Gulliford; Jasper Gulliford; David E. Templeton; Thomas Lister; Calvin Pell.

At *Ochoco* and *Mill* creeks: Elisha and Susanna Barnes; Capt. White; David Wayne and Louise Elkins Claypool; William Smith; George W. Barnes; George Burkhart; Raymond Burkhart; Ewen and Nancy Johnson; Albert Allen; A.C. Belieu; Anthony Belieu; I.N. Bostwick; Charles Brotherhead; William S. Clark; John Claypool; John Crabtree; A.B. Fry; Reason Hamlin; Thomas B. James; George H. Judy; George McDowell; James W. McDowell; William McDowell; John Miller; Jack Rose; James Slater; Edmund and Harriett Veazie; _____ Vining; Abraham Zell; Richard P. Miller; W.H. Marks; Haley Anderson; Lew Daugherty; Harry Smith; James Lawson; William G. Pickett; Jake Narcross; John Luckey; John M. Toms; Anthony B. Webdell; Edward G. Conant; Samuel and Eliza Slayton; Thomas L. Logan; James Marks; Bluford Marks; Att. Marks; James H. Snoderly; Hardy Holman; John Holman; John Lee; Orange Morgan; _____ Smith; John C. Davis; D.H. Hale; William Foster; Mrs. Nancy Leach; Lysander S. Logan; R. Streithoff; Henry F. Smith; John Zell.

At *Beaver Creek*: Marcus D. Powell.

At *Camp Creek*: Abe Hackleman; John Jaggi.

At *Trout* and *Hay* creeks: John Atterbury; Henry Coleman; William and Mary Gates; Z.B. Offatt; James M. Grater; William J. Coleman; R.B. Reed; Edmund F. Veazie.

In *Prineville*: William G. Pickett; Barney Prine; Dave and Elizabeth Prine; Larkin and Mary Vanderpool.

In 1871, more people arrived. Among the more significant were the Hodgeses in Prineville, Benjamin Franklin Allen on Allen Creek, and Bud and S.G. Thompson on Hay Creek.

Benjamin F. Allen was a stern-looking, big-jawed man who had been born 38 years earlier in Illinois. He married Matilda Tate, by whom he had seven children. In 1868 they came to the Willamette Valley via Panama. The Allens lived for a while in Halsey, and in 1871 homesteaded in Central Oregon on Allen Creek near Cougar Rock. Ben built a log cabin there and entered the sheep business. He became the richest man in Central Oregon.

Bud Thompson already has been mentioned as helping pursue Paulina after the burning of James Clark's station. Born about 1847 into the family of an abusive schoolmaster, Thompson came west in a wagon train as a child. His father had a 320-acre farm nine miles north of Eugene. His elder brothers fought in the Rogue River War.

At age 14, Bud Thompson joined the Eastern Oregon gold rush. He crossed into Idaho, and briefly worked for Joachim Miller's express company before returning home. Later, in the fall of 1862, he became a printer's devil at the *Eugene Herald*. He worked three years for the newspaper, which, as one of the state's few Democratic newspapers during the Civil War, was periodically suppressed by the government. In 1864, Thompson fled into East Oregon after he broke a political prisoner out of a stockade. Returning to Eugene, he worked as a compositor and foreman for the *Eugene City Guard*, and at the end of a month took it over in lieu of the wages owed to him. He sold it a year and a half later for $1,200. Thompson then went to Roseburg, where he started a newspaper in opposition to an established journal run by Henry and Thomas Gale. It led to a gunfight with the Gales in which Thompson received serious wounds.

About this time, Thompson and his brother, S.G. Thompson, bought ranches at Hay Creek; they had six. The 23-year-old gunfighter remained busy on the west side, taking charge of the Democratic organ in Salem at the request of party leaders. He later claimed as his reward the rank of colonel during the Modoc War (1872–1873).

These settlers came, slowly at first, then in ever greater numbers. Gradually the demographic patterns of later Crook County emerged. It did not happen at once. Originally, the Mill and Ochoco creek areas had a larger population than the nearby marshy Prineville locality. Population centers were small, and their locations determined by available farmland and grass. A dozen years after its founding, Prineville still only had 200 or 300 people. And for awhile, it was not even the most populous town in what became Crook County.

In 1871, four men carrying a load of grain from Mitchell to Prineville discovered gold on Scissors Creek, northwest of Big Summit Prairie near Round Mountain. After delivering their grain and obtaining supplies, they returned and began mining. Other prospectors followed and the town of Scissorsville grew up along the creek. By 1874, it had a saw mill, two saloons, a dancehall, hotel, mercantile store, and post office. At its peak in the 1870s, according to U.S. Forest Service sources, Scissorsville allegedly had 1,700 people, a population Prineville would not match for another 60 years. Even as late as 1888, historian Hubert Howe Bancroft mentioned Scissorsville (by then a hamlet after the mining boom declined), noting that Prineville was the Crook County seat and "Ochoco, Willoughby, Bridge Creek, and Scissorsville…the subordinate towns."

Other towns, villages, and hamlets came into existence, some of which survive today. Many have long disappeared, all traces of them now covered by tangles of sage or the wind blown soil of the Great Sandy. Many of these communities were satellite neighborhoods of The Dalles.

Shaniko, the most important town to develop between The Dalles and Prineville, originally stood at the south end of the Sherar road in what is now southeast Wasco County. It began in 1864 when a miner from Nevada, Thomas Ward, hired stage station operator James Clark to build a store and 16-room inn on a place where two hollows formed a cross. The hamlet was called Cross Hollows until after 1878, when the store, inn, and a blacksmith shop were bought by a German immigrant named August Scherneckau. Indians pronounced his name as "Shaniko," and that later became the community's name.

It was during the 1860s, too, that white settlement spread east from The Dalles along the south bank of the Columbia, across the northern edge of Central Oregon. What became Sherman County became host to several cattle ranchers, though few of their holdings were based on land titles. Instead, they relied upon local territorial rights established by grazing activity. A few years later, more cattlemen arrived and settled along Rock Creek. They grew hay and grain, and in 1875 began to raise sheep. The cattlemen continued pushing farther east into modern Morrow County during the 1860s. Until the 1870s, they did not establish longterm ranches because they had no plans to remain. When cattlemen and sheepmen did settle, post offices were opened at Vinson and Willow Forks. The Vinson office was later moved to the junction of Willow and Hinton creeks, where a store was established by Henry Heppner. More people moved to the area and the town that became Heppner had a population of 318 by 1880. That same year, residents in the vicinity began to grow wheat, which soon became Morrow County's major crop.

The Jefferson County area also was first entered by cattlemen. The first to come was James M. Blakely, mentioned earlier. Blakely established his headquarters on Willow Creek below Grizzly Mountain and ranged cattle over many parts of modern Jefferson, Deschutes, and Crook counties. As noted above, friends and relatives of Blakely followed him to Willow Creek, and in May 1872 the area's first post office was established, named Willoughby, with Robert Warren as postmaster. It was discontinued in 1879, replaced by a post office west of the mountain at Cleek, a hamlet that grew up around a stage station. Later it was moved to the Edmonds ranch and finally to the Grizzly Store.

Postmaster Robert Warren's place also was the site of the first Grizzly-area school, built in the 1870s to accommodate about 20 children. Margaret Morrow recalled in Alice M. Farrell's *Jefferson County Reminiscences* (1957) that some of the pupils walked six miles to attend school, resting during the day while other children played so they would be ready for the walk home. In session for two or three months a year for grades one through eight, the Grizzly School was typical of others in early Central Oregon: the teacher roomed and boarded in the houses of the parents of children; the building doubled as a church, Sunday school, and general social center. The whole community would gather there for Thanksgiving dinners, Christmas programs, and other special events.

The Grizzly locality also was the site of Central Oregon's first commercial sawmill—the foundation for the region's industrial development. The area's earliest sawmill had been started in 1860 on the Warm Springs Indian Reservation. In 1877, an English immigrant, Charles C. Maling, having settled on the upper waters of Willow Creek, built a steam sawmill. Maling prospered when selling lumber to the people moving to Prineville and surrounding areas. He later built a planing mill in Prineville. A second sawmill, installed much later by Charles Durham, an Englishman who had accompanied Maling to Central Oregon, was put in on a tributary of Trout Creek, about nine miles east of Hay Creek.

Logs hauled from Grizzly Mountain were used to establish the first homestead on The Cove, near the junction of the Metolius, Deschutes, and Crooked rivers. Clark Rogers filed the claim in 1879. He lived on The Cove for nine years, until he traded it to T.F. McCallister for a house and lot in Prineville.

After the Grizzly area, other communities began to appear in adjacent localities, such as Hay Creek. Culver had its start when Ben Beeman settled in the vicinity with his wife and daughter. An early Central Oregon community that was well known was Cross Keys. A post office originally had been established as "Trout Creek" near that stream in 1878 to serve the growing population of ranchers. Its name was changed to Cross Keys in 1879.

Though ranchers laid claim to all the grasslands from the Tygh Valley in the northwest to Wagontire Mountain at the southeast, pioneers shunned the drier areas of Central Oregon. No homestead cabins appeared on the High or Lower deserts, but ambitious immigrants looked for any land that had the promise of tall grass and clear water.

Cattlemen were also beginning to arrive in the Deschutes country. As will be discussed in more detail later, John Y. Todd sold his Tygh Valley properties and in 1877 bought a ranch at Farewell Bend on the Deschutes. He ranged his cattle there and north to Squaw Creek in the Sisters area and up to the Metolius. Opposite Todd and other settlers on the east bank of the Deschutes, notably Joel Allen, Steve Staats, and Sid Stearns, the first claim was made on the west side in the late 1870s by a rancher who arrived from Missouri, Marshall Clay Awbrey. After ranching for years without much success on what later became part of Bend,

Awbrey removed to Tumalo. His name remains known in the region because it was given to Awbrey Butte.

The entry into the Deschutes country came not only via Cow Canyon, but through the Santiam and McKenzie passes. Camp Polk, though abandoned by the army, remained a stopover for travelers. It was to Camp Polk that the Claypool and Barnes families fled after the Paiutes raided their budding settlement on Mill Creek. In the summer of 1873, near the old camp, Samuel Hindman filed a homestead claim on 280 acres of land and on 75 acres of water rights on Squaw Creek. He built a trading post on his new ranch and in 1875 established a post office with himself as postmaster. The mails went via the Hindman ranch from Eugene to Prineville, carried by contractors such as John Templeton Craig. Meanwhile, others had begun to take up claims in the neighborhood. Late in 1874, Mr. and Mrs. J.B. Claypool and two other families arrived over the Santiam and settled on Squaw Flats. A few years later, David W. Claypool settled near Indian Ford Creek. The Indians who had camped on Squaw Flats for many years—perhaps generations—got an unpleasant surprise when they next came through and discovered that white people had taken up claims there. However, soon they were good customers at the Hindman store.

Distant Black Butte was a weather indicator. Early settlers learned to look at the amount and level of snow on the mountain to decide how severe conditions were in the Cascades. A heavy snow pack meant that it was not safe to go over the passes, a light pack in spring meant it might be time to plant seeds. The dangers of the former were illustrated by the fate of John Templeton Craig.

Craig, an Ohio native who had worked on the Scotts' road building crew, and who in 1871 became president of the toll company, had secured a postal contract to carry mail up the west slope of McKenzie Pass to Camp Polk. He was in his mid-fifties in December 1877 when he strapped on snowshoes and started up the pass with a bag of mail on his back. When he failed to return on schedule, Willamette Valley friends sent a letter to Hindman to ask if Craig had ever arrived. The letter had to go via Portland and then on OSN steamers to The Dalles, then south to Prineville and west to the Hindman post office. The answer was then sent back that Craig had never arrived. Early the following year, two men climbed about halfway up the pass to a cabin, which had been built as a stopover for mail carriers. They had to dig through the snow and then remove a log in order to see inside. They saw Craig curled up inside the fireplace. Apparently he had been unable to rekindle a fire that had burned out and had crawled onto the cooling ashes in a desperate attempt to get warm. There he froze to death.

The first whites to settle in Central Oregon had done so along The Dalles-Canyon City Road. Christian W. Meyer and "Alkali Frank" Huat established a stage station and inn on Alkali Flat, five miles east of Mitchell in 1863. Meyer diverted water from Bridge Creek to irrigate an orchard, garden, and grain field. Andrew Clarno, mentioned earlier as Paulina's last stolen stock victim, arrived on the John Day from California in 1866 with 300 heifers. He built a house with lumber hauled from a sawmill on the Columbia, and with his partner William Snodgrass sold cattle to buyers from the Union Pacific Railroad and to butchers in Portland. One early day pioneer in the same vicinity was Dan Leonard, who in the early 1860s built an inn by a bridge across the John Day along the Condon-Fossil road. In 1878, he was shot to death in his bed. His estranged wife was tried for the murder, acquitted, and later became a lawyer.

Howard Maupin settled in the Antelope Valley in 1863 to operate one of Henry Wheeler's stage stations. Nathan Wallace bought Maupin's property seven years later and set himself up as a storekeeper, blacksmith, and stage station manager. The following year he became the first postmaster of Antelope. The whole town was moved in 1881 after the stage route was moved a couple of miles west.

Many small communities were established in the mountainous region of eastern Central Oregon in what today is Wheeler County. These included Waterman Flats, a stage stop with an inn, post office, and livery stable that began in 1862 when Ezekiel Waterman settled there; Caleb, named for Caleb Thornburg on Badger Creek, 12 miles southeast of Mitchell, began when E.B. Allen and S.G. Coleman established ranches in the vicinity sometime after 1865, and eventually built a hotel, post office, saloon, blacksmith shop, livery stable, and stores; Richmond, named for the Confederate capital, and serving the Shoofly region, was a town that traced its beginnings to the 1870s when R.N. "Mose" Donnelly settled there, later donating land upon which the town was built; Contention, 14 miles north of Mitchell, named thus because of arguments between its first settlers, "Pike" Helms and Jerome H. Parsons, until Parsons' daughter Frankie returned home from a finishing school and persuaded locals to rename it Twickenham; and Spray, named for the woman who platted it in 1900, Mary E. Spray. Antone was not named until the 1890s, but had its start in 1864 when George Jones settled in Spanish Gulch and began to raise stock, farm, and prospect. Miners at Spanish Gulch and Mule Gulch were prosperous and persistent, which made Antone a notable community for several decades. The name came from Antone Francisco, a Portuguese native who settled there. Later it had a post office, school, stage station, and blacksmith shop.

Mitchell originally was a stagestop on The Dalles-Canyon City Road established in 1867. It was named for the notorious John Hipple Mitchell, bigamist and swindler, who three times entered the U.S. Senate as a freshman representing Oregon. It was founded by blacksmith William "Bawdie" Johnson. The lower level, the business district along Bridge Creek including the saloons, was known as "Tiger Town," while the upper section with its houses and church was nicknamed "Piety Hill." By the time it was platted in 1885, Mitchell had two stores, a hotel, and a blacksmith shop. What no one realized before 1884, though, was that due to its location in a gorge of Bridge Creek, it was going to be subjected to repeated floods.

Fossil, which would one day become the Wheeler County seat, traces its founding to ranchers who first settled near there in the mid-1870s. Thomas Benton Hoover established a post office at his ranch in February 1876, and named it Fossil because he had discovered fossils nearby. Hoover and Thomas Watson later moved the Fossil post office to the junction of Butte and Cotton-wood creeks in 1881, where they had decided to build a store.

Closer to the regional center at Prineville, there were a multitude of communities. Some still exist, while others, including the boom town of Scissorsville, are long gone.

George Millican, when a boy, moved west with his parents from their native New York. He lived in Central Oregon during the Paulina War, and after the chief's demise moved his cattle to the Ochoco country. He eventually ranged his livestock in the Great Sandy, including along the Bend-Burns road. P.B. Johnson opened a store there, and it became known as Millican. Johnson was the first postmaster.

Twelve miles west of Prineville, on a ford of the Crooked River, Francis Forest established a cattle ranch that eventually covered 1,200 acres of land. He built a store at what was soon being called Forest Crossing, and later simply Forest. It would be here, years later, that the histories of Jefferson and Deschutes counties began with a rally led by Deschutes country residents protesting the building of a new courthouse in Prineville.

Dr. James R. Sites in 1875 filed a homestead in a beautiful area west of Prineville on the Crooked River. He later moved to Prineville, but his farm was the foundation of what became the hamlet of Lone Pine.

Earlier, in 1872, Philip G. Carmical had established a stage station on the road that ran along the south bank of Crooked River to Prineville. In pioneer times it was known as Carmical Crossing and sometimes as Carmical Station. After three brothers named Charles, George, and Walter O'Neil opened a store there very early in the 20th century, the hamlet became known as O'Neil.

On the extreme southeastern edge of the region, between Paulina and Burns, Logue Cecil settled on the site of Camp Curry on upper Silver Creek in 1871. Robert Baker filed claims along Silver Creek in 1876.

East of Prineville at the Crooked River headwaters, James Elkins in 1872 established a horse ranch on the Willamette Valley and Cascade Mountain Wagon Road and the Yreka Trail along Grindstone and Beaver creeks. Also, Billie Adams and William Noble had settled along Beaver Creek in 1871, and other settlers soon joined them. This was the beginning of the town of Paulina, which in 1880 opened a post office.

However, by this time Scissorsville and Prineville were the only communities of any significant size in the region.

10
BANNOCK WAR
1878

PRINEVILLE GREW. Monroe and Alexander Hodges owned most of the valley and promoted the town. People drifted in—mostly cattle raisers seeking grazing land who stayed at the Hodges Hotel—and ended up buying town lots.

Early cattle families often owned houses both on their ranches and in town. During the early 1880s, Bud Thompson and James Blakely lived in houses at the corner of West Fourth and Claypool, with Thompson on the southwest corner and Blakely on the northwest. Later, distant cattle barons including John Todd of Farewell Bend wintered in Prineville so their children could attend the good schools.

Although the Union Church (for use by all denominations) would not be built until 1879, the First Baptist Church organized without a building in 1873. The first Sunday school started in 1878 with Marion Powell as superintendent. In later years, Prineville would be known for having a church on every corner, but also known for its many saloons. In local politics the church crowd often contended with the saloon crowd.

The first professional man to settle here was Dr. Lark Vanderpool, an in-law of Alexander Hodges. A Missouri native born in 1831, Vanderpool developed an interest in medicine. Although he lacked the money to go back East for a formal education, he studied medicine in whatever books he could find. The Oregon State Medical Board licensed him to practice. He did so in Benton County until he moved to Prineville, where he rented a room for a drugstore on the north side of the Hodges Hotel. From there he sold a variety of mixtures, including Smith Brothers cough syrup that he made from juniper berries and sage. He appears to have been quite good at concocting remedies, and it is claimed that years later he developed a cure for skin cancer that became lost when he died without passing along the formula. He was Central Oregon's only doctor, riding horseback long distances at night to tend injuries and deliver babies.

Doc Vanderpool. *Bowman Museum, Crook County Historical Society*

Dr. James Roland Sites of Polk County, who possessed a more conventional medical education, stayed in Prineville from 1874 to 1878, hoping that the climate would improve his health. Sites went back to Polk County, but returned again for his health in 1882 and remained seven years. The 1880 census lists a 39-year-old physician at Prineville named James Richardson. Dr. H.P. Belknap arrived in 1881. The popular Doc Vanderpool moved to Dufur in 1883 after he lost his drugstore when the hotel burned down.

Other professional men arrived. John E. Jeffery became publisher of the town's first newspaper in 1880. Named the *Ochoco Pioneer,* it lasted only a few months. Elisha Barnes' son George, meanwhile, had been reading the law. After being admitted to the bar in 1880, he became Prineville's first lawyer. A later law partner of Barnes' was Benjamin Franklin Nichols, a pharmacist when he opened a drug store upon his arrival in 1877, at the corner of Third and Main where the Bowman Museum now stands. Joseph Hunsaker took over the store in 1879 and retained Nichols as manager.

The Hodges Hotel was sold sometime in the 1870s, and Dan Richards was running it by 1880 as the Occidental Hotel. Then or soon afterward, William Circles owned it. By that time, Oliver Jackson and his wife had built the Jackson House at the corner of Main and Third streets. A.B. Culver took over management or ownership in 1880. The Jackson House (aka Culver Hotel) became the first of a series of hostelries built on the "hospitality block." Both of these hotels were described in a western Oregon newspaper in 1879 as having 30 to 35 rooms each, being well furnished and managed, and serving better food than any other hotels in Oregon.

Some industry existed. Charles C. Maling built his planing mill on Prineville's main street. Two years earlier, just south of town, James A. Allen had put in a grist mill. Until Allen's Prineville Flour Mill came along, the only grist mill in Central Oregon had been a small one at the Warm Springs agency. Allen sold out to Prineville's first big mercantile business, Breyman & Summerville. To manage the mill, they found 26-year-old David F. Stewart, who arrived on Christmas Day 1879. Stewart bought an interest in the Prineville Flour Mill the following year, and Breyman & Summerville sold their remaining interest later. Stewart would be associated with various partners in the mill. A Republican born and raised in West Virginia, he became one of Prineville's most active civic leaders, and his name will reappear often in these pages.

Prineville remained unincorporated throughout the 1870s. People pretty much did whatever they pleased—Barney Prine later told writer Fred Lockley that it was a rough place in its early days. Other accounts confirm this. The arrival of businesses, the founding of log cabin schools, the establishing of churches, and the increase in population did not mask the fact that Prineville existed mostly because of cattle and sheep. Cowboys, gamblers, and others drifted through town, perhaps trailing cattle or heading for the gold towns further east. The frontier character of the community is illustrated by its reputation as a place where gunplay could become lethal and where the mail from The Dalles was sometimes brought down by a friendly Indian. A pony express system existed from The Dalles through the Warm Springs area, but letters sent by that means cost a lot of money.

On June 3, 1878, two toughs, Van Allen and Jeff Drips, rode in and coolly announced that they had decided to take over the town. Local residents balked. They had warrants issued for the pair's arrest. Wasco County Deputy Sheriff James Chamberlain attempted to serve the warrants, but Allen and Drips resisted. The townsfolk sprang to arms. They gunned down Allen, but Drips escaped on his horse. Another deputy, Jerry Luckey, caught him that night. Instead of returning Drips to Prineville, Luckey took him to the county seat at The Dalles. There, a jury acquitted Drips of all charges. Perhaps it was this incident that led to talk that year about creating a new county out of Wasco with Prineville as the seat. Local opposition killed the idea.

In June 1878, an old difficulty suddenly returned: Paiutes. News arrived that the Bannocks of Idaho had held off the army in battle, crossed the Snake, and allied themselves with Paiutes led by Chief Egan. The Paiutes and Bannocks headed west off the Malheur Reservation. Egan now led the largest force of warring Native Americans since the Plains Indians had gathered two years earlier at the Little Bighorn. And everybody remembered what that had led to.

Frightened Ochoco Valley residents built a stockade in Prineville, and makeshift forts went up at Paulina and Long Creek. Chief George of the Wascos left Warm Springs and crossed the Deschutes into the Hay Creek country to tell Bud and George Thompson and Perry Maupin that he would know if the Paiutes approached, and if that happened, he would take all their families and horses onto the reservation for protection and then help them fight the invaders.

This was no idle promise; the reservation Indians were still good fighters. (It had been Warm Springs Indians serving with the army in California in 1873 who captured Captain Jack and ended the Modoc War after dozens of soldiers, including a general, had been slain.) The previous year, 1877, Paiutes had raided the Warm Springs reservation, stealing several girls and horses. The

Warm Springs tribesman astride a horse without a saddle, 1890. *Bowman Museum, Crook County Historical Society*

reservation warriors had tracked them across Combs Flat to their night camp on Crooked River, where they had attacked the raiders, burned their camp, and recovered the girls and stock.

Bud Thompson had been in The Dalles with other Ochoco stockmen including his brother and George Barnes when he heard of the Bannock outbreak. They galloped south immediately; Thompson covered the 96 miles to his ranch at Hay Creek quickly. Thompson, the "colonel" from the Modoc War, took charge of defenses in the area. He designated Dr. David Baldwin's sheep ranch on Hay Creek as a rallying point for all the settlers if the warriors approached.

Throughout the vast outback people abandoned farms, ranches, mines, and villages for the safety of large towns, military forts, and the west side. The population of Fort Harney, usually 50 men, swelled to more than 300 with the influx of refugees from that vicinity. Travelers moving through Eastern Oregon who were as yet unaware of the outbreak were astonished to find the entire region deserted, with no signs of life at one abandoned ranch house after another. Excitement ran high in Prineville, where some of the refugees had fled.

James Blakely was not at home. His father had summoned him to Brownsville to take 450 head of yearlings and two-year-old steers to Fort McDermitt. Blakely, with a Warm Springs Indian named Clanic and five other men, trailed them east over the Cascades into south-central Oregon on their way to Nevada. They did not know that the Paiutes and Bannocks were approaching the same area from the opposite direction. Pursued by Capt. Reuben Bernard's column, the Indians already had massacred settlers in Happy Valley and chased Peter French and a big branding crew across Diamond Valley. When Blakely learned of the warriors' approach, he and his men had no choice but to scatter the cattle and flee.

Reuben Bernard, now a 45-year-old veteran of 98 Indian and Civil War battles, had never brought Paulina to bay, but was determined to get Egan. On June 22, a Saturday, his scouts found the Paiutes and Bannocks camped on Silver Creek. Altogether, Egan had about 2,000 people with him, while Bernard had 285, including volunteers, among them the very irritated Pete French.

Bernard attacked at dawn, Sunday. He led the cavalrymen in a charge down the creek while scout Orlando Robbins and Pete French led 35 men from above it. The soldiers rode wildly through the camp, shouting and firing their rifles and pistols, panicking the Indians. They rode over or gunned down men, women, and children racing from their lodges, while the chiefs threw themselves against the horse soldiers to give their warriors time to take cover in the boulders and trees. After two charges through the camp, Bernard stopped the assault and built breastworks in anticipation of a counterattack. Instead, after dark the Indians placed the wounded Egan onto his favorite red blanket, set fire to piles of sagebrush so that the soldiers would mistake them for campfires, and silently rode away.

Three days later, Gen. Oliver Otis Howard's command junctioned with Bernard on Silver Creek. He decided to follow the Paiutes, but not too closely because he did not want to send them hurrying to the Columbia before the army could fortify the river. Howard wanted to keep them inside East Oregon.

Men at Canyon City, concerned about war parties entering Grant County, decided to go out and look for them. James Clark led about 15 men west towards Dayville. On June 29, Clark and his party caught up with some Indians at Murderers Creek—and promptly wished that they had not. Seeing about 50 warriors, Clark ordered a retreat to protection in the canyon of the South Fork of the John Day. A running battle developed in which two of Clark's men were wounded and another shot dead. Three had to hoof it when their horses were shot out from under them. Clark's men killed several Indians. Another party of about the same size encountered Indians in the nearby hills, but only two men sustained wounds. Meanwhile, Indians attacked the Billy Stewart ranch on Murderers Creek, killing the men and torturing the cattle to death.

The invaders ravaged Grant County. In one location after another, the same scenes of bloodshed and devastation were repeated. When they passed close to Canyon City and John Day, people crowded into the deep mines for protection. Indians under a flag of truce approached a makeshift fort at Long Creek. They tried to induce its occupants to come out. Although the warriors promised them that they would not be harmed, the settlers remained inside. The Indians resumed their journey.

Gen. M.V. Brown rode into Prineville with the Linn County militia. Bud Thompson raised a company of 15 scouts for him and rode up Crooked River. Among Thompson's men was a young cowboy named Charley Long. Although fear gripped both Prineville and the community of Paulina, the Paiutes did not approach either. They rode through Grant County towards the Columbia. There, later, they were defeated in engagements near Pendleton by the U.S. Army and the Paiutes' traditional enemies from the Umatilla Reservation. A Cayuse sub-chief assassinated Egan during a parley and scalped him. An army surgeon later cut off Egan's head, which was preserved in a San Francisco museum.

Blakely, who returned to the Harney region that autumn to round up his father's cattle, blamed the war on white men married to Indian women rather than on the Paiutes themselves. The government was less charitable. That winter, soldiers surrounded the Malheur Reservation to prevent anyone from escaping, then rounded up 543 Paiutes and Bannocks for a march to the Yakima Reservation. About 100 soldiers and 50 wagons accompanied these Indians on the 350-mile journey in sub-zero temperatures. Shivering in blankets, they went north via Canyon City and The Dalles. Some died. Innocent Indians were caught up with the guilty, while many participants in the war escaped punishment.

In 1879, Paiute prisoners of war at Fort Vancouver were removed by the government to the Warm Springs Reservation. In 1884, other Paiutes led by Chief Owitz were taken to Warm Springs from the Yakima Reservation. The Paiutes became the reservation's third tribe, joining their ancient enemies, the Wascos and Warm Springs. Chief Paulina's descendants would share the land and resources there with descendants of the men who fought him long ago on the Great Sandy and in the shadowy Ochoco woods.

This did not mean that Indians always remained on their reservations. Some moved freely from one reservation to another, and Winnemucca II and Chief Ochoco traveled pretty

Indian camp near Prineville. *Bowman Museum, Crook County Historical Society*

much wherever they wanted. The Tygh chief Que-pe-ma, who earlier had given white authorities a hard time about farming, led his tribe off the Warm Springs reservation in 1872, going to the Umatilla, and staying there until he decided to return to Central Oregon in 1880. Individual Indians, families, and groups drifted off the Warm Springs agency and wandered about Central Oregon at will, no less then than now, but their presence was more noticeable when the white population was smaller. They often camped at the east end of Prineville, and sold huckleberries, handicrafts, and other goods throughout the region. A year after the Bannock War, an army surveyor, Lt. Thomas W. Symons, reported the "dense haze" that hung over Central Oregon from fires that Indians lit to drive game into blind canyons, arroyos, or other terrain where they could be more easily hunted.

Fear of Indians survived in the Crooked River country for many years. Once two boys became lost a short distance from Prineville when night arrived sooner than they anticipated. They were terrified that they would be discovered by Indians and killed. They began to slowly make their way back to town. Climbing down a hill, they suddenly found themselves trapped on a ledge. They remained on it all night, too frightened to move. Dawn revealed that the ledge was only a few feet off the ground.

About the time of the Bannock War, sheepherder Jim Kelsay made a shocking discovery in the Ochoco forest. At a small glade, he noticed an old log where someone appeared to have cut six notches. The notches were evenly spaced. When he approached the log he saw that each notch had a horse's skeleton facing it. A halter chain was tied at each notch, and the iron remains of saddles, bridles, and halters lay amid each of the skeletons. Six horses had been tied to the log and left. The horses chewed into the log when they began to starve, creating the notches, until at last they died of thirst. Kelsay showed Dean Huston the skeletons in 1883, and other people saw them after that.

The horse skeletons remain one of Central Oregon's oldest mysteries. Popular belief associates the strange skeletons with a half dozen outlaws who fled Grant County in 1863. According to the story, one Saturday night when the prospectors on Whiskey Gulch were cleaning their sluice boxes of the week's accumulation, six masked riders appeared, held the miners at gunpoint, took the gold, and rode away. They went to Dayville, where they robbed the bank.

They then rode west toward the Ochoco Mountains, at that time part of Chief Paulina's domain. A posse from Dayville pursued them through the Antone and Mitchell districts. It tracked them into the mountains of the northern Ochoco forest to a place known to this day as Burglars Flat. They never found the outlaws. People expected to hear of men spending freely, which would at least reveal their identities. They heard nothing. The men seemed to have disappeared into thin air with their horses and gold. Most believe that the Paiutes got them. People still dig holes near the notched log, trying to unearth stolen gold.

Other stories of lost gold accompany tales about the deaths of pioneers at Indian hands. An example is the case of two prospectors on Snow Mountain who later were said to have kept gold buried beneath their cabin. Indians attacked the cabin, killing one of the prospectors. The other escaped, but the Indians believed the silence coming from the cabin was a ruse to draw them out from the cover of trees. They waited until night, then set fire to the building. When morning came, they examined the ruins, then began to trail the prospector who had escaped. They tracked him about seven miles toward Izee and killed him.

Later, the story of the burned cabin with its hoard of gold attracted many searchers. The size of the cache tended to grow with the telling. Over the years, hundreds searched the Ochoco forest near Snow Mountain without finding it. Someone discovered the foundation of a cabin across the canyon. Men dug down there to a depth of three or four feet. But no gold.

Finally, in June 1934, H.D. Still came upon a pile of rocks on the south side of Snow Mountain. He had been hiking with a friend, I.D. Basey, and told him of discovering the pile, which he believed might once have been a fireplace. Old stumps in the area showed axe marks. The next day they dug near the rock pile. Beneath a foot of soil they found ashes. Further digging revealed that earth had washed over the ruins of a burned cabin about 20 feet square. In the ashes they found a boot containing the bones of a human foot. Amid other bones they found buttons, part of an axe scabbard, and an open jackknife, rusted. They also found a pair of shoes of different sizes, burned spoons, cooking utensils, 44-caliber shells, a knife, fork, and spoon set, rings off a pack outfit, bits of a wool blanket, burlap, and other cloth, and—significantly—arrowheads. No guns. And no gold.

The last Indian fight in the region did not occur until 1898. John Hyde had a homestead two miles northwest of Izee, on the upper South Fork of the John Day. A Columbia River Indian shot at him. Hyde and neighbors formed a posse and found the man's band camped north of Izee on Deer Creek on October 26. The posse demanded that the Indians hand over the offender. The band refused, and a gunfight erupted. The offender and posse member George Cutting were killed, another Indian wounded. The Indians fled to the head of Murderers Creek, where they scattered to prevent being followed.

However, Central Oregon residents did not view all Indians as a threat. They got along well with most of them. Indians continued to frequently camp within Prineville's town limits. Even in the early 20th century, people working in the courthouse there could look out the east windows and see Indians hunting rabbits in the open fields where Third and Elm streets now intersect.

In September 1880, politics was the talk of the day in the predominantly Democratic Ochoco district, as revealed by a letter from Prineville written at the time. Most supported Democrat W.S. Hancock for president over Republican James Garfield. People also discussed dividing Wasco to create a new county.

"Our town is growing quite rapidly," boasted the writer. "Several more or less pretentious residences have been erected this summer and fall.

"Mr. Selling, from Portland, has a large store building nearly completed. This will make three dry goods establishments in the place. We also have a variety store, a drug store, furniture store, harness and saddlery establishment, several blacksmith shops, a planing mill, two livery stables, and two first class hotels, one of them kept by Oliver Jackson and the other by Dan Richards."

Actually Ben Selling—at one time president of the Oregon senate—only had an interest in the store, owned by Henry Hahn and Leo Fried. Julius Durkheimer, Fried's brother-in-law and one time mayor of Burns, also had an interest. Hahn & Fried competed with Breyman & Summerville. Its owners later became principals of the Portland wholesale grocery firm Wadhams & Company. Hahn and Fried also formed the Prineville Land & Livestock Company, a ranching operation that ranged sheep and cattle in what is now Crook, Jefferson, Wheeler, and Wasco counties. The pair moved to Portland in 1889, selling their store to Mose Sichel.

The 1880 letter failed to mention that the town also had four saloons. Til Glaze (known for his fine fiddle playing), Dick Graham (who doubled as the coroner), Henry Burmeister, and R.R. Kelly were the proprietors. A couple of years later, John Gagen established a soda bottling plant in Prineville.

Residents incorporated Prineville on October 23, 1880. Elisha Barnes became the first mayor. The common council ordered at its first meeting that a fine of not more than $20 be levied for *all* offenses. It also enacted a speed limit: six miles an hour. That was also the year the Freemasons chartered their oldest club in Central Oregon, Prineville Lodge #76.

A traveler from England went through the town in 1881, describing it as "a very lively and bustling place" that was growing fast. He observed that stockmen from more than 50 miles around in every direction drew upon it for supplies from three large general stores; on a summer day, he wrote, a dozen heavily-loaded wagons could be seen leaving Prineville with supplies for their ranches.

The community's main economic support was cattle, sheep, and farming. Eventually, the largest stock outfit within Central Oregon was Mays & Son, running 10,000 head of cattle. The mercantile firm of Breyman & Summerville also established a livestock business. Their outfit, Breyman, Luckey & Summerville, had about half as many cattle. Drugstore owners Joe Howard and Tom Baldwin became partners with Farewell Bend rancher Sidney Stearns, establishing the firm of Howard, Baldwin & Stearns. Later Stearns bought out his partners. Dr. David Baldwin established a big sheep ranch at Hay Creek, the Baldwin Land & Sheep Company. Other big Hay Creek ranchers included brothers Bud and S.G. Thompson.

The Thompsons had the same problems as many other Central Oregon stockmen: stock thieves, as well as the arrival of more and more homesteaders who threatened the power of men such as Bud Thompson, Elisha Barnes, and John Summerville. It distressed them. They wanted to do something about it.

11

BLOOD ON THE SNOW
1882

A **LL ACROSS THE WEST**, the influx of homesteaders alarmed ranchers. In several
places, the big stockmen organized
themselves into vigilante groups, ostensi-
bly for driving out rustlers, but actually
to attack homesteaders. Some researchers charge that this is what happened
in Central Oregon.

Homesteaders feared Bud
Thompson. The murderous young
man had acquired local influence
because of his political connections
and his new wealth. The big ranchers
who disliked homesteaders looked to
him as a leader. Elisha Barnes smiled
upon Thompson, and Barnes had
become a power to be reckoned with
in Central Oregon.

One homesteader who distrusted
Thompson was Lucius Lambert
Langdon, a Massachusetts native living 18 miles northwest of Prineville
on Newbill Creek, a tributary of Wil-

Col. William "Bud" Thompson became a
Vigilante leader, but later claimed he merely
witnessed their reign of terror. Photo from
Thompson's autobiography, *Reminiscences of
a Pioneer.*

low Creek at the edge of the forest below Grizzly Mountain. Langdon was about
30 and had married Emma LaFrancis seven years earlier. They had two small
daughters. Langdon had built a house and barn, and had begun to fence his farm.
But a man arrived who claimed part of his land.

A.H. Crooks insisted that he owned land immediately behind Langdon's barn
that Langdon knew belonged to himself. Contemporary accounts of their dispute
mention a lawsuit, but no record of one has been found. Collateral descendants
of Langdon assert that the Wasco County clerk made a mistake filing Crooks'
land claim and that the dispute might have ended if the parties involved had gone
to The Dalles to investigate. It also has been claimed that Crooks was a hench-
man of Thompson's group. But it seems probable that the dispute arose honestly
between two homesteaders who each believed himself in the right.

Elisha Barnes, Prineville's first mayor and president of the livestock association that ruled by Vigilante guns. *Bowman Museum, Crook County Historical Society*

Accounts differ about what happened on Wednesday, March 15, 1882. According to the most popular account, Crooks and his son-in-law, Stephen J. Jory, went onto the disputed land to blaze property lines at the edge of the forest. At noon they left their axes leaning against a tree near Langdon's barn and went home for lunch. Langdon discovered the axes and waited with a rifle for the men to return. When they walked back, he shot and killed both of them. Garrett Maupin, a 28-year-old sheep raiser and son of Howard Maupin (and himself responsible for killing a shepherd who allegedly attacked him with a butcher knife two years earlier), happened to be riding along the road at the time, heard the gunshots, and rode over to investigate. He saw Langdon riding away and found the bloodied bodies of Crooks and Jory in the snow.

This story tallies with a front page account that appeared in the Portland *Oregonian* five days later. "The shooting was done just over a small knoll back of Langdon's house, a short distance from the road, and not discernable from it," the newspaper reported. "Mr. Garrett Maupin was passing along the road at the time, and heard the shots, and some one say, 'You have killed me.' He went immediately to where he heard the shots and found the two men dead and Langdon leaving on a horse armed with a Winchester rifle."

Another report says that Lucius Langdon heard chopping while inside his house, grabbed a shotgun, and went out to investigate. He found Crooks and Jory. When they attempted to draw their guns, he shot both. He returned to the house, where he informed Emma of what had happened and said that he would ride to The Dalles to turn himself in. After leaving the house, he decided to ride to the ranch of his brother, George, 12 miles away on Mill Creek, and borrow money for the trip.

The Langdon family's account claimed that Langdon, already threatened earlier, gunned down Crooks and Jory when they ignored his order to stop walking toward him with a pistol and an axe.

The victims' wives allegedly witnessed the shootings from a quarter mile away. They hurried over. They did not move the bodies, but placed their aprons over their husbands' faces.

Maupin carried word of the murders to Prineville. Men rode up to Langdon's that afternoon to view the bodies. Justice of the Peace Powers held an inquest; Dr. Belknap and other members of the coroner's jury found that the pair had died from gunshot wounds inflicted by Langdon. Crooks had been shot through the lungs; Jory either in the back, or the face into the brain.

Bud Thompson formed a posse with saloonkeeper Til Glaze, lawyer George Barnes, Sam Richardson, and Charley Long. Thompson led this group, which he later called "men of unquestioned courage and discretion," to Mill Creek, suspecting that Langdon might have gone to his brother's cabin. He was right. A barking dog alerted the Langdons to their approach. The murderer fled on foot across the snow and escaped. The posse recovered Langdon's horse and gun. According to two accounts, one by Thompson and one by a descendant of George Langdon, they also arrested George Langdon and took him to Prineville. Thompson claimed that 11 other men were at the cabin, who he and Long held at bay with shotguns, but his contemporaries ridiculed this tale. He allegedly concocted it to justify his later activities.

The following day another posse formed. Its members asked James Blakely to lead it, but he replied that Deputy Sheriff John Luckey should take charge. Apparently, Luckey did not accompany the posse, which consisted of Blakely, Joe Schoolin, Lucian Nichols, and Robert Smith. They left about four o'clock, taking

the road over Grizzly Mountain to Willow Creek to see if Langdon had doubled back to his ranch. They reached the house at dusk. As happened at the other house, a dog began barking. Langdon ran out and mounted a white horse, jumped a ditch, and started for the road. Blakely called out. Langdon turned and rode up to him, saying, "Jim, I knew it was you." Emma Langdon was screaming in the doorway but stopped after Blakely identified himself. Everyone went inside.

While Emma Langdon fixed dinner for the men, Blakely rode over and told the Crooks family that Langdon had been arrested and would be taken to Prineville. The *Oregonian* later reported: "Langdon requested the men

James M. Blakely eventually led the Moonshiners against the Vigilantes. *Bowman Museum, Crook County Historical Society*

Jackson House (aka the Culver Hotel; later the Prineville Hotel) where Vigilantes shot Lucius Langdon, and Gus Winckler fled James Blakely's gun. This is a later view after electricity came to town. *Bowman Museum, Crook County Historical Society*

making the arrest to guard him from mob violence, and the same request was made by his wife. This the party promised to do."

The posse returned to Prineville with Lucius Langdon and W.H. Harrison, a young hired hand of Langdon's who had asked to accompany them. Justice Powers had issued a warrant for Harrison's arrest, but Blakely and Schoolin had decided to ignore it because Harrison had been in town at the time of the murders. Blakely said later that the posse returned between one and two o'clock, (another account says about midnight, and another 2:30). They stopped at the livery stable and sent for John Luckey.

Luckey arrived a few minutes later. Apparently, deputy Luckey and W.C. Foren prepared shackles for Langdon. Foren, a 51-year-old Tennessee native with a wife and nine children, was a deputy marshall as well as a blacksmith. Luckey, 39, was also a blacksmith. Bud Thompson appeared, but no one paid any particular attention to him. Perhaps other men also arrived and stood around watching the shackles being prepared. Luckey, Foren, and Blakely took Langdon to the Jackson House, where he could be put on the morning stagecoach to The Dalles. Harrison continued to accompany the group and Blakely said he learned only later that Luckey had considered the hired man to be a prisoner. At the hotel, Luckey asked Blakely to help guard Langdon, but Blakely was tired and went home to bed.

"Things were beginning to look a little suspicious," reporter Herbert Lundy later had Blakely say in an account of what happened. Whether Blakely came to that conclusion later or at the time, he did notice that a "good many men" had gathered around the hotel. Blakely named the Barneses, 29-year-old blacksmith Eugene Luckey, merchant John Summerville, and store manager Gus Winckler. Thompson later claimed to have been inside helping to guard Langdon. John

Luckey, in a letter to the sheriff at The Dalles, mentions only Foren as a guard. The *Oregonian* said that Luckey "placed a guard of four men to protect" Langdon and Harrison. At least four men were in the lobby that Friday morning, March 17, 1882: deputy sheriff John Luckey, deputy marshall W.C. Foren, Langdon's hired hand W.H. Harrison, and, shackled and asleep on a barroom lounge, Lucius Langdon.

John Luckey later reported in his letter to the sheriff at The Dalles: "At about 5 o'clock in the morning, as I was sitting at the stove with my back to the front door, the door was suddenly opened and I was caught and thrown backward on the floor and firmly held, while my eyes were blinded and immediately a pistol was fired rapidly 5 or 6 times. I heard someone groan just about the time the firing ceased. Harrison was hurried from the room. I could tell it was him by his cries. I went to Langdon and found him dead. I looked around and a masked man stood at each door, warning by ominous signs for no one to undertake to leave the room. So soon as they were satisfied that Langdon was dead they quietly left the room. At daylight I took some men and began the search for Harrison, and found him hanging from a banister of the Crooked river iron bridge."

Under a front page headline, "MOB VENGEANCE," and a lower headline, "The Assassin of Crooks and Jory Shot, and an Innocent Man hung by a Mob at Prineville," the *Oregonian* said that at the Jackson House "the guard were overpowered by a masked mob of twelve or fifteen, who covered each member of the deputy sheriff's party with a pistol and commenced shooting at Langdon who was killed almost instantly." Thompson, in his dubious account of these events, also asserts that there were 12 to 15 masked men.

Prineville's iron bridge, the site where W.H. Harrison's body was strung up by Vigilantes. The bridge later was dynamited to release pent-up water and flotsam during one of the Crooked River's many floods. *Bowman Museum, Crook County Historical Society*

But is this what really happened? James Blakely later said that store-owner, Leo Fried, had told him a quite different story.

According to Blakely, Fried had entered the hotel after Langdon was murdered. The killers, unmasked, had remained in the lobby with Langdon's body, time had passed, and things had quieted down. Harrison was seated by the stove. The men were talking about Langdon. And then the hired man made a fatal mistake. "Well," said Harrison of the person these men had just murdered, "he was always good to me." The men grabbed and dragged him screaming from the room. "I've got a little boy," he begged. Outside the hotel, the men put a rope around his neck. One man mounted his horse, took the other end of the rope, and galloped down the street, dragging Harrison to death. They took him to the Crooked River iron bridge and strung up his lifeless body.

Til Glaze's wife often told her son how she cowered in fear that night listening in the dark to Harrison's screams and pleas as they dragged the young man to death. Blakely slept soundly until the wild clanging of the school bell awakened him the next morning. He found a crowd gathered at the bridge and learned the details of the murder. According to the descendants of George Langdon, when Emma Langdon learned of her husband's fate she found John Luckey and called him every hard name she could think of. They claim that she then bought a pistol and tried to find him, but Luckey hid in the livery barn. While possible, it is unlikely that a Prineville store sold pistols in 1882 or that the widow of a small rancher would have enough money to buy such an expensive item on impulse.

The *Oregonian* reported that a coroner's inquest was held over the dead bodies, and that "so far none of the perpetrators of this terrible outrage have been identified. Langdon leaves a wife and two small children. Nothing can be ascertained to implicate Harrison in the murder of Crooks and Jorry [sic], and his only offense was that he was employed by Langdon."

Luckey considered the matter settled. Blakely said that Luckey had a personal reason for not bringing to justice the man who dragged Harrison to death. The murderer's identity was common knowledge.

The same week that the murders occurred, some ranchers formed the Ochoco Livestock Association. Composed in part of the men who had broken into the Jackson House, it was the formal organization for those who called themselves "Vigilantes." They chose Elisha Barnes as president, Joe Hinkle, vice president, and S.J. Newsome, treasurer. They ordered that no one could ride the range without a permit from them. When James Blakely started to leave town to tend to his cattle, the Barnes brothers told him he would need a permit. "I was born in this Oregon country and I'll be damned if anyone is going to tell me when I can go out after my own stock," snapped Blakely. He then sent away for five new six-shooters to be handed out to his men as protection against the Vigilantes.

The Vigilantes began sending out skull and crossbones notes to anyone they suspected of rustling or speaking against them. March of 1882 marked the beginning of their reign of terror over Central Oregon.

The domineering by the Vigilantes was possible due to a combination of circumstances. First, the organization's bosses were already the social and financial leaders of the region. Second, some members were willing to shed blood without much hesitation. Third, they became the local government, thanks to their roles in the community, and because of Thompson's influence at Salem. But perhaps the best break for the gang was that no local opposition emerged after the murders of Langdon and Harrison. While ranchers James Blakely, Al Schwartz, and Steve Staats condemned them for murdering Harrison, no group felt compelled to bring the guilty men to justice. Nor did people overlook the fact that while Harrison was innocent, Langdon had killed two men before being shot himself. The knowledge made it easier to do nothing. Finally, no one, including the Vigilantes themselves, could have predicted how ruthless the group would become, or that some members would use the organization as cover to settle private scores.

Portraits on the wall behind Martha Mogan are of her husbands, Mike and Frank, both gunned down in Prineville saloons by Vigilantes. *May Smith and Frances Juris*

12
REIGN OF THE VIGILANTES
1882–1883

THE NEXT MURDER came two and a half months later. A private dispute may have been the cause, but some believed that Bud Thompson was behind it.

Michael W. Mogan was a 26-year-old cattle raiser living in the Antelope area with his wife, Martha, and 28-year-old brother, Frank. The census listed Frank as a farm hand. But the census is inaccurate. It lists Frank's birthplace as Illinois, although both brothers had been born in Waldo County, Maine. It also had their ages wrong. Their father, an Irish immigrant, had settled on Trout Creek with his six sons and daughter May. Another daughter had been lost to diphtheria coming around the Horn and the mother had died in California.

Mike Mogan established his own ranch on Trout Creek. In his house were people the census taker missed entirely: two daughters of Martha McCloud Mogan by a previous marriage, Mattie and Maggie, and her two-year-old son by Mike, Edward Michael. A daughter, Stella Elizabeth, was born April 21, 1882, but lived only five weeks. They buried her in the Pioneer Cemetery in The Dalles. Shortly after their return from the funeral, Mike rode into Prineville to do some drinking and gambling.

Bud Thompson gave an account of Mike Mogan in his autobiography (published 1912), but he had reason to paint Mogan in the worst possible light. He claimed that the Mogan brothers arrived several years prior to the Vigilante take-over. He said that they had originally called themselves Tom and Frank Page, but, when a man arrived from Nevada who had known them there, they admitted that their actual name was Mogan. Since the entire "Mogan" family, including their father, lived in the Antelope area this seems unlikely. "They were a quarrelsome pair and posed as bad men," claimed Thompson, "and were not long in involving themselves in trouble and were shunned by the better class of citizens." Thompson said that he employed Frank on his cattle ranch, but became dissatisfied and fired him. He said that both "remained in the section, accepting such employment as they could obtain." A 1937 Pendleton newspaper article claimed that for a time James Blakely hired them.

The Mogan men were about six feet tall, with dark curly hair, and very blue eyes. At least one other account describes them as quarrelsome and quick-tempered.

Both Thompson and Blakely believed that the shooting involving Mike Mogan occurred later than it did. Thompson said the fall of 1882; Blakely

George Barnes, in 1880, became Prineville's first lawyer, and an early newspaper publisher. Barnes was shot down in Canyon City in 1911. *Bowman Museum, Crook County Historical Society*

implied 1883. Court records reveal the date as June 1, 1882.

Nor is the reason for a quarrel between Mike Mogan and James Morris ("Morsey" or "Mossy") Barnes agreed upon. Barnes was a son of Elisha Barnes. Thompson claimed that Morsey was 17; the census record says about 21. Thompson also claimed that the trouble had its seed in a lawsuit against Frank Mogan in which Morsey's brother, George Barnes, was the opposing counsel. He said that Mike Mogan began abusing Morsey Barnes to get back at George. "The boy went to his brother and told him of Mogan's conduct," asserted Thompson. "He was told that if he associated with such men as Mogan he must suffer the consequences."

Thompson claimed that young Morsey Barnes went home "and securing an old cap and ball revolver, came back to the street. Mogan began on him again, and after suffering his abuse for some time, drew the revolver and shot him through the chest. Mogan ran a short distance and drawing his revolver, started back. Seeing that young Barnes was ready for him, he turned off, walked a short distance, sank down and died the next day. The affair created some excitement. The boy was arrested but subsequently came clear."

Except for Barnes shooting Mogan in the chest, Thompson's story practically contradicts all other accounts, including the official court records.

One account claimed that during a poker game in Dick Graham's saloon, a man scooped in a $20 pot that belonged to Mogan. Mogan verbally abused the man but otherwise did nothing. This account does not identify the cheat. Later, in the same saloon, Mogan pulled out a $10 bill and asked if anyone could make change. Mosey Barnes gave him $10 in coin, and Mogan took it without giving him the bill. Mosey demanded the money but Mogan ignored him. Later that evening, in a different saloon, Mosey walked up to Mogan at the bar and shot him through the breast.

Shaver's *History of Central Oregon* (1905) said that "Barnes walked up to Mogan and demanded $6 which, he claimed, Mogan owed him, stating at the same time that if he did not pay him he would shoot him. Barnes shot him through the lungs, killing him almost instantly."

Robert Ballou's account in *Early Klickitat Valley Days* (1938) says that Mosey Barnes had put all of his cash into a pot during a draw poker game. Mogan won. Barnes accused him of cheating and tried to stop him from raking in the pot. Mogan slapped Barnes on the face. Barnes left the saloon and returned about an hour later. Mogan was no longer there. Barnes was drinking at the bar when Mogan walked into the room through a rear door, went up to Barnes, and in a friendly joking manner said, "The drinks are on you, Morsey." Barnes pulled out a .45 and said, "Give me back my money, you crooked son of a bitch." Before Mogan could say anything, Barnes shot him in the chest and he collapsed on the floor. Friends carried him across the street to the Jackson House lobby.

James Blakely's account says that Mogan and Barnes were seated opposite each other playing cards in Dick Graham's saloon. They started arguing. Barnes pulled out a gun and pointed it at Mogan. "Why, Mossy," said Mogan in a quiet voice, "you wouldn't shoot me." Barnes shot him. Mogan rose from the table and walked across the street to the livery stable, where he had left his gun. "He started back," recalled Blakely, "but fell down in the street. He didn't die for several days." Blakely said that Mogan told him before his death that Barnes had used Bud Thompson's gun, which he had seen often while working for him. Thompson, however, never mentioned employing Mike, only Frank.

The Ballou account claims that a boy who had known Mogan around the cow camps slipped into the hotel lobby while Mogan was lying there. According to the witness, Mogan spoke in a low tone to friends gathered around him, tears streaming down his face. The boy could not make out much of what was said, but did hear Mogan ask them to summon Martha.

Cowboys galloped in relays the 40 miles to Mogan's ranch on Trout Creek. Martha Mogan got into a hack driven by a cowboy and pulled by a team of sorrels. She arrived at the Jackson House the following afternoon. Men tossed blankets over the sorrels, removed their harness, and led them up and down the street so they could cool off gradually.

Michael W. Mogan died on June 7. His body was taken to the same cemetery where his daughter had been buried a few days earlier.

Although Blakely claimed that Barnes was never arrested (and perhaps never spent time in jail), Bud Thompson was correct in saying that Morsey was brought to trial. A deposition filed more than a year later by the district attorney said that two Linn County witnesses "were present in a saloon in the town of Prineville and saw [Barnes] come into the saloon where Mogan was, and after a word or two saw him draw a pistol and say to Mogan the deceased, 'Give me up that money,' and thereafter immediately fire the pistol at him inflicting upon him the wound from which he afterward died." The deposition states further that Barnes "drew the pistol as [Mogan] was buttoning up his pants and was not making any offensive movement or doing any threatening act toward [Barnes]."

The Wasco County grand jury convened that fall and heard the testimony of witnesses John Combs, Perry Read, Frank Mogan, E.L. Harpool, and Samuel Norman. Combs (himself about 21) was a friend and Read a cousin of James Blakely. Harpool and Norman were the Linn County residents. The district attorney said that William Gird had also been present and would testify to the same facts as the others. The grand jury returned an indictment on September 13 at The Dalles, charging James Morris Barnes with the first degree murder of Michael Mogan. Morsey Barnes had been represented by his brother, George, and H.Y. Thompson.

Morsey Barnes filed a request that the venue be changed from The Dalles to Prineville, citing the great distance between the towns. Barnes feared a trial at The Dalles. Til Glaze liked young Barnes and allowed him to stay on Glaze's ranch at Indian Ford Creek, near what is today Sisters. There Barnes awaited the outcome of events. By the time his case came to trial on September 29, 1883, Prineville had become the seat of Crook County and the trial could be held there. Now represented by Mays Shoater and George Barnes, Morsey pled not guilty. The court chose a jury: J.H. Gray, Columbus Friend, W.T. Vanderpool, Ed Kutcher, Frank Forrest, Z.B. Offrell, J.J. Brown, Harry Thompson, J.B. LaFollette, T.J. Powell, W.W. Dodson, and W.J. Saltzman.

District Attorney M.A. McBride filed a motion the day before the trial was to start, requesting a delay. McBride protested that he could not present the best case against Barnes because the important witnesses from Linn County could not be found. Interested in the business of horse racing, they were apparently at the state fair.

McBride added: "that friends of the deceased have stated to me and I believe these statements to be true that they have been deterred by fear of personal violence from making any very active efforts to hunt up the evidence on his behalf heretofore and that until lately I have been compelled to seek for evidence without any local assistance.

"That I have carefully and diligently sought to bring this case on for trial at the present term but now state that I believe that the interests of justice would be jeopardized and the prosecution of this case be a mere formal mockery if this cause should proceed to trial with all the above witnesses absent."

But the case went to trial. And, on October 1, after two hours of deliberation, jury foreman J.B. LaFollette informed Circuit Court Judge A.S. Bennett that the jury had found Morsey Barnes not guilty.

Was the jury packed with Vigilantes? Or did the jurors believe that mitigating circumstances made it less than murder for Barnes to shoot an unarmed man?

Blakely reported that Morsey Barnes "went crazy and killed himself soon afterward." F.A. Shaver (1905) also later claimed some Vigilantes had "gone insane" and "some have committed suicide." Barnes died in January 1895. On the other hand, his brother George was a part owner of the *Prineville Review*, which published an obituary reporting Morsey's death as being due to apoplexy. Whichever version of his demise is true, merchant Dick LeMert, who decades later owned the Barnes house, liked to claim that some nights Morsey Barnes' ghost made loud noises upstairs where he had hanged himself.

Vigilante boldness increased after the legislature created a new county out of old Wasco. Prineville attorney Frank Nichols had introduced the bill. The county was formed on October 24, 1882, and named after Gen. George Crook, whose Indian campaigns had recommended him for the honor. Covering more territory than New Jersey, the new county included part of present Wheeler and all of modern-day Crook, Deschutes, and Jefferson counties. Over this vast region containing more than 2,000 people, Gov. Z.F. Moody appointed officers to serve until the first election could be held in June 1884. To make the appointments, Moody accepted advice from his friend Bud Thompson.

Sam Richardson had joined Thompson's posse in pursuit of Lucius Langdon. No one is now alive who can say whether Richardson had joined the Vigilantes (Til Glaze, it is worth noting, who also rode with Thompson, did not), but Richardson did become the first clerk of Crook County. The first surveyor was S.J. Newsome, the treasurer of the Ochoco Livestock Association. County treasurer was Horace Dillard, publisher of the *Prineville News*. Soon, Gus Winckler, manager of the Hahn & Fried store and a known Vigilante, replaced Dillard. George Churchill became sheriff. It is now impossible to say why Moody picked Churchill, but fair to point out that no Crook County sheriff ever had more unsolved murders on his watch. The commissioners were two big sheep ranchers, Ben Allen and 44-year-old Charles M. Cartwright. Gov. Moody appointed S.G. Thompson, Bud's brother, as county judge. The county court appointed justices of the peace, constables, and other officials. As Prineville's first justice of the peace it appointed Elisha Barnes.

Benjamin Franklin Nichols, the Prineville druggist and lawyer who introduced the bill to create Crook County, was not a Vigilante. Like his brother-in-law, Til Glaze, he disapproved of them. A native of Clay County, Missouri, Nichols had come to Oregon in 1844 when about 18. He served as the first sheriff of Polk County and later as county clerk before moving to Prineville in 1877. He was admitted to the bar in 1882 and served in the legislature for Wasco County when it included Prineville. When other legislators tried to blackmail Nichols into supporting the very corrupt John H. Mitchell for the U.S. Senate in return for creating Crook County, Nichols held up another bill they wanted until they agreed to support the creation of the new county. Nichols would form a law partnership in 1887 with George Barnes.

Four communities contended to become the new county's seat: Prineville, Mill Creek, Cleek (the Henry Cleek ranch northwest of Prineville), and Mitchell. Not surprisingly, Prineville was the easy winner.

In a letter, a woman living in Crook County related how in early December 1882 a man had been found shot to death in the hills above Prineville. She did not mention his name, but said that he was not known to have had enemies, and no one knew who might have killed him. She also reported that about New Year's, someone fired a shot through a window at a man who lived alone. The man was a suspected Vigilante. Sheriff Churchill started looking for John and Price Thorp in the belief that they might have done it.

At this time, men such as Al Schwartz, David Stewart, Steve Staats, James Blakely, John Combs, and C. Sam Smith might criticize the Vigilantes privately, but their opposition remained individual. No one suggested forming a group to oppose the gang. Those who did speak out did so at great risk. As *Oregonian* editor Harvey Scott would observe later, anyone who Bud Thompson marked for death in three counties was as good as hanged. Initially, Scott appears to have been less critical, judging from his reporting of the 1882 Christmas season bloodshed in Prineville.

Al Schwartz had ranched on Mill Creek since the 1870s, where his neighbor Kate Robbins described him in a letter to her mother as a good neighbor, intelligent, and well-informed. But she had heard from someone that he led a group of horse thieves. He did speak out against the Vigilantes. Schwartz had a wife and three small children. He apparently did not worry much about Vigilantes confronting him face to face, but feared that they might get the drop on him.

One cold December night, he entered Henry Burmeister's saloon. About ten o'clock, Vigilantes playing cards there urged him to join the game. Schwartz agreed. However, he took a chair facing the door with his back to the wall. Unfortunately, the wall had a window. Schwartz himself became all too aware of it when he felt a draft. "Why is that window up?" he asked. "It's cold." He rose and shut the window, then returned to his chair. Just then someone who had been waiting outside fired two shots through the window. One account says that Schwartz, hit twice in the head, died instantly. Another says that he was shot through the throat and carried to the hotel, where he died during the night.

Meanwhile, the Vigilantes had arranged to lure two young men staying on the Schwartz ranch to the cabin of W.C. Barnes. W.C. was Elisha Barnes' second son, the oldest next to George. The boys were Sid Huston, a son of William Huston of Willow Creek, and Charles Luster, a jockey. Neighbor Kate Robbins described Huston as kind-hearted and the idol of his mother, but claimed that he had fallen into bad company. The Vigilantes rode to the W.C. Barnes house, rushed in, and grabbed them. Huston apparently got off at least one shot before being seized. They took the boys to a large juniper tree at what is now the intersection of the Ochoco highway and Barnes Butte Road. There, they lynched them. While the boys dangled, the Vigilantes shot them in the head. Next morning, James Blakely and C. Sam Smith discovered the bodies.

The deputy marshal who had helped guard Langdon at the Jackson House, W.C. Foren, was not seen around town after the lynching of Huston and Luster. Vigilantes said that the blacksmith had been kicked by a horse and was home in bed. They would not allow anyone to visit him. A few days later, the middle-aged father of nine died. Word spread that Foren had been a Vigilante who young Huston had mortally wounded during the attack in the Barnes cabin. Blakely reported seeing a bullet hole in the cabin wall.

Blakely described Schwartz as an outspoken man, who had denounced the Vigilantes for murdering W.H. Harrison. As for Luster, the Vigilantes allegedly paid him to throw a horse race but instead he won. An account published only two decades later claimed that Luster had bet $60 on his own horse and won. The Vigilantes claimed publicly that Luster was planning to steal some horses. They said that he and Huston had confessed before being hanged and even named their confederates, who escaped.

The *Oregonian* reprinted a front page article from the *Times-Mountaineer* (The Dalles) about the murders, based on Vigilante information:

TRIPLE LYNCHING.

ONE HORSE THIEF SHOT AND TWO HUNG AT PRINEVILLE.

The Stock Raisers of Eastern Oregon, Robbed, Forced by Organized Bands of Outlaws to Administer Punishment.

(SPECIAL DISPATCH TO THE OREGONIAN.)

DALLES, Or. Dec. 27—From a correspondence from Prineville dated Dec. 24th. to the *Times-Mountaineer* of this city the following particulars of the lynching in Prineville in Crook county are obtained: For several years the stock raisers of that section and of Beaver creek have complained bitterly of the frequent raids of horse thieves. During the last two years it has been estimated that nearly 500 head of horses have been stolen. About two weeks ago a drove of about thirty head was taken from Prineville past Mitchell and turned over to accomplices in the John Day country. This stealing has been done by organized bands of thieves whose members are scattered throughout Eastern Oregon. Their mode of operations is for the resident thieves to gather up a band of horses, drive them thirty or forty miles and turn them over to their confederates, who in turn would drive them to the next station and so on, while the first would return home and be able to show they had never left the neighborhood. As they are so well organized and so perfectly acquainted with the country, capture and convictions have been almost an utter impossibility. But the stock men it seems have organized little by little and have picked up evidence showing who the thieves were. At last the capture of some of the weakest of the band and a judicious use of the rope has brought out a full confession as to who the members are.

Last night our town was shocked and horrified by the shooting of A.C. Swartz [sic] and the hanging of Sid Huston and Chas. Luster. Swartz and one John Thorp are alleged to have been the leaders of the thieves here. Swartz in some way knew the business had leaked out and he came into town and boasted of his party's strength and said whoever "batted their eyes" he would shoot them. That evening while sitting at a table in Burmeister's saloon he was shot through the neck, his assailant standing outside and shooting through the window. The same night a band of masked men broke into W.C. Barnes' house and captured Sid Huston and Chas. Luster and took them about a mile and hung them to a juniper tree. Huston was also shot once through the head and Luster twice. Who the executioners are is only a matter of conjecture and horrible as it seems the act appears to meet the hearty approval of the entire community. The rest of the band who have so successfully worked this section, John Thorp, Price Thorp and James Townsend, have escaped but the vigilantes are on their tracks and by the time this reaches you their days of stealing may be over.

Thompson's later account of the events of that night strayed even further from the facts: "Along in January, about the 10th, as I remember, a crowd of the rustlers came to town, and after filling up with bad whisky rode up and down the streets, pistols in hand, and declared they could take the town and burn it, and would do so 'if there was any monkey business.' Little attention was paid to them, people going about their business, apparently unconcerned. But that night there was 'monkey business.' Three of the gang were hung to a juniper two miles above town, while another was shot and killed in town. The next morning notices were found posted, with skull and cross-bones attached, telling all hard characters to leave the county. There was then such a higera as has seldom been witnessed. Men not before suspicioned skipped the country. They stood not upon the order of their going, but went—and went in a hurry. Among them was an ex-Justice of the Peace."

"Nothing of the kind had really happened," was James Blakely's observation about Thompson's account. He said that the murders outraged the decent people in Crook County but "most of them were afraid to even talk out loud."

That horse race had rankled the Vigilantes mightily. Aside from murdering the jockey, they took it hard that a certain Hank Vaughan, who had bet on Luster, had won so much money. Vaughan—a tall and finely-dressed professional gambler who had drifted into town a year and a half before—had a wide reputation as

Gambler and gunfighter Hank Vaughan almost died in a shootout with Charley Long after winning money from Vigilantes in a horse race not fixed as well as they thought. *Bowman Museum, Crook County Historical Society*

a gunfighter. He had earned it. He had killed his first man in 1864 at Canyon City, apparently an impulsive (and drunken) act of murder. Vaughan was 15 years old at the time.

A year later, after lawmen from Umatilla County tracked down Vaughan and a friend when they stole some horses, he gunned down the sheriff and his deputy, though Vaughan himself was wounded and his friend—like the deputy—killed. The sheriff survived to testify against him at Auburn, with the consequence that he served almost five years in the state penitentiary. Vaughan never made trouble for lawmen thereafter, but he got into plenty of other trouble, and by the time of his death he would have 13 bullet wounds in his body. The *Oregonian* regularly reported on his adventures; he had become one of the state's celebrities.

There is a theory that Bud Thompson persuaded cowboy Charley Long to get even with Vaughan for the bets. Long has been described as a handsome fellow with a fine sense of humor, whose only previous illegal act had been to bust a fiddle over the head of the man playing it, for which the community was said to have been grateful. At any rate, Vaughan and Long played a card game at Dick Graham's saloon on the Sunday following the race. They later wandered down to Til Glaze's saloon and continued the game. Eventually that afternoon, they argued, walked out into the middle of the floor, and drew their pistols. Long shot Vaughan in the scalp and high in the left breast; Vaughan shot Long three times in the left shoulder. Both men recovered.

Other Vigilante activity became evident. A friendly fellow who had a small ranch near town vanished without a trace. Shorty Davis has been largely forgotten because a more prominent rancher with the same name vanished under similar circumstances 17 years later. Men from Prineville looked for Davis's body but never found it. They had little doubt that Vigilantes had murdered him.

Prineville had become the murder capital of Oregon. The Vigilantes not only controlled Crook County, they also had influence in neighboring counties. They continued to send skull and crossbones notes to people who spoke against them. A house still standing on Prineville's Deer Street has burn marks remaining from when Vigilantes bombed it with dynamite. But some men believed that the situation was becoming intolerable. And some held Vigilante threats in contempt. Til Glaze told Blakely that, if Blakely ever received one of the threatening notes, to bring it to his saloon and they would tack it up and put a hole through the center with the pistol he had used to kill the Whitney brothers in a Dalles gunfight.

RISING OF THE MOONSHINERS
1883–1884

UNTIL DECEMBER 1883, Bud Thompson's involvement in Vigilante murders could not be proved. Although some men insisted that he led the organization, no one outside the Vigilante group—and perhaps no one inside— had seen him kill anyone in Prineville.

That ended the night of December 9, 1883. As usual, conflicting stories relate what happened. Thompson's version was that Frank Mogan bore him a grudge because of Morsey Barnes' murder of Frank's younger brother. Mogan had married his brother's widow a few months after the fatal shooting and had remained in Crook County. In doing this he had shown either more courage or less wisdom than George Langdon, who had left after his own brother's murder. Mike's son was now three and Martha was expecting a baby by

Complaining about the murder of his brother proved fatal to Frank Mogan. *May Smith and Frances Juris*

Frank in August. Although Mike Mogan had been killed a year and a half earlier, a jury had cleared Morsey Barnes only a few weeks before. Frank probably was especially bitter at the time. The recent trial may also explain why both Thompson and Blakely recalled Mike's murder as happening later than it did and close in time to Frank's death.

Thompson said that he was out of town when Morsey Barnes killed Mogan. "The other Mogan brother, however, affected to believe that I had given the revolver to the boy and had told him to use it. I explained to him the absurdity of the charge, proving to him that I was out of town. This appeared to make no difference, he still holding a grudge against me for discharging him. He made many threats against my life, all of which were borne to me. He declared he would 'kill me if he had to lay behind a sage brush and shoot me in the back.' Still I paid no apparent attention to the threats, being satisfied he would never at any rate face me.

"One evening I was called to the store of Hahn & Fried to attend to some business. It was just after dark and while I was there I was notified by a friend that a daughter of Judge Nichols had overheard Mogan tell one of his friends that he had come to town to kill me and would not leave until he had accomplished this purpose. This was going a little too far, and I determined to settle the matter one way or the other at our first meeting. The test came sooner than I anticipated. On seeing me he attempted to draw his gun but was too slow, and fell with more than one bullet through his body."

Thompson was being modest when he said "more than one bullet." He had emptied his revolver into the man.

The front page of the December 12 *Oregonian*, under the headline "Bud Thompson Shoots a Man Six Times at Prineville," related the account given at The Dalles by a stagecoach driver. Saturday night between midnight and one o'clock, Thompson and Mogan "were quarreling in a saloon, and everybody left them to fight it out. Six shots were fired, and when the firing ceased Frank Mogan was found shot through the body six times, either of which would have been fatal. Thompson is under arrest."

F.A. Shaver, in his 1905 history of Central Oregon, said that Thompson and Mogan argued in the saloon. Thompson worked his way around Mogan, drew his gun, and shot him in the back of the head.

Blakely remembered it differently. He claimed to have been in Kelly's saloon that night and witnessed the shooting, although he or reporter Herbert Lundy incorrectly placed the date as December 18. Mogan "was standing with his elbows on the bar and his hands resting against the sides of his face." Thompson entered the saloon and walked up behind him. Before Mogan became aware of his presence, Thompson put his gun to the back of Mogan's neck and fired.

Blakely's 1939 account is almost identical to an account published in the *Oregonian* in 1905 by a Crook County resident who signed himself "Moonshiner." It stated that Thompson walked up behind Mogan, shot him in the back of the head, and then emptied his gun into Mogan's head. Then Thompson got down and beat out Mogan's brains using the pistol butt. Whoever wrote this account, it was not Blakely, who had left Crook County long before 1905.

"I sent for Sheriff Geo. Churchill and surrendered myself as a prisoner," wrote Thompson. "He told me to go home and if he wanted me he would send me word. The committing magistrate, at my request, placed me under bonds to appear before the Grand Jury. The announcement caused an uproar among the throng with which the court-room was packed, and I was compelled to go among them and explain that it was done at my especial request. I wanted the matter to come up in the Grand Jury room and so told the people. The *Oregonian* published distorted and untruthful statements regarding the affair, and attorneys from every part of the State volunteered their services to me free of charge. I wrote to them, of course thanking them, but told them I had no use for attorneys, as the matter would never go beyond the Grand Jury." Thompson said that District Attorney McBride proved to be his strongest witness.

Thompson neglected to mention that Vigilantes packed the grand jury. Even if they had not, few would have dared indict the county's political boss. But B.F. Nichols, the 56-year-old druggist-turned-lawyer-turned-legislator, was game. He filed a deposition the next day charging that Thompson had murdered Mogan. Sheriff Churchill served the warrant on Thompson the same day and took him before Johnny Douthit, the town recorder acting *ex-officio* as justice of the peace. Douthit, originally from Linn County, would soon establish a newspaper in partnership with George Barnes. Thompson asked him for an immediate examination.

What happened next is puzzling. Thompson called four witnesses, among them 22-year-old John Combs. Not only was Combs not under Thompson's thumb, he stood with James Blakely and C. Sam Smith in opposing the Vigilantes.

After hearing testimony, Douthit took the case under advisement until eight o'clock the following morning. At that time he ruled that it appeared to him that manslaughter had been committed and set Thompson's bail at $2,000. Going sureties to guarantee his appearance were Judge Thompson, E.F. Foley of Prineville, and Elisha Barnes.

For "voluntarily and felonously" killing Mogan by "shooting him with a pistol loaded with powder and ball cartridge," Thompson went before the grand jury the following spring after McBride signed an indictment. The state subpoenaed James Cantrell, R.R. Kelly, and Thomas Cross; Thompson subpoenaed John Combs, Lucien Lytle, Joe Mills, and Frank Barnes (another son of Elisha). Other witnesses included E.F. Foren, Martha Mogan, Garrett Maupin, May Mogan, George Churchill, George Barnes, Elisha Barnes, William Prine, C.E. Jenkins, David Prine, John Culver, a Mr. Shelby, William Brown, a Mr. Stuart, James Turner, and A.B. Webdell. Circuit Court Judge A.S. Bennett, the 26-year-old Dalles lawyer who had presided over Morsey Barnes' trial, now presided over Thompson's.

John Combs, a Moonshiner, was a deputy to both James Blakely and Newt Williamson before serving three separate terms as Crook County sheriff. *Bowman Museum, Crook County Historical Society*

On May 18, 1884, Bennett signed an order: "Now came the Grand Jury in the above entitled cause wherein said William Thompson was held to answer for the crime of Manslaughter by killing Frank Mogan and returned 'not a true bill' whereupon it is ordered that same defendant be hence dismissed and his bail exonerated."

Thompson walked free.

Steve Staats fell next. The Staats family information says that he had immigrated to Oregon, that his marriage to Caroline Coffee was the first in Polk County after its organization in 1845, and that his son, William, married Emma Turpin in 1883. Blakely called him a good citizen who had condemned the Vigilantes for murdering W.H. Harrison. He remembered Staats as being an early victim of the Vigilantes, but in fact he may have been among the last.

The Vigilantes murdered Staats at Powell Butte west of Prineville, apparently in mid-January 1884. One of Sid Stearns' boys rode into Prineville with the news. Sid Stearns still ranched at Farewell Bend, where Staats also had land. Stearns later wrote out a letter claiming that Staats had killed himself accidentally. Stearns said that, about four o'clock in the morning while they were looking after their horses, they found the body of his "dear friend" after hearing a gunshot. He told Newt Williamson to remain while he rode into Prineville for a coroner, jury, and physician.

That is not how Blakely told it in 1939. Blakely said that he and Mose Sichel rode to Powell Butte and found that the whole top of Staats' head had been blown off. About 15 to 20 men stood around his body, every one a Vigilante. Blakely became concerned when he noticed how the men were looking at him and talking to one another. He and Sichel quickly left for town.

(Steve Staats' son William survived him. He continued to live on a claim on the east bank of the Deschutes near John Sisemore's Farewell Bend ranch. Staats and Sisemore became fierce rivals and for awhile each had a post office. Sisemore's ranch developed into the village that became Bend, although promoters considered changing the name to Staats.)

One day that winter of 1883–1884, Vigilantes met in a Prineville saloon. Gus Winckler said that if Jim Blakely did not watch his step he would be going up the cemetery hill feet first. Friends of Blakely overheard. When Blakely arrived in town from a trip to Mitchell, they met him. "They sure gave you a good panning at that meeting tonight," they said, and related Winckler's comment. Blakely, Combs, Smith, and the Wagner brothers then burst into the saloon, but found that the Vigilantes had already departed.

The following morning, Blakely strapped on his Colt .41 revolver and went looking for Winckler. He saw him in front of the Jackson House talking to Mose Sichel. When Winckler realized that Blakely was coming after him, he ducked into the hotel and went straight through to the privy out back. Blakely did not lose sight of him, though, and walked up to the privy. "You come out of there," he ordered. Winckler stepped out with his hands up. Blakely forced him to walk out into the street. He told the county treasurer to take the Wednesday stage out of town "because you won't get out of here if you don't." No Vigilantes came forward to defend Winckler. He left town as ordered.

Blakely received an invitation to go down to the Prineville Flour Mill. John Combs and C. Sam Smith received the same invitation. There they found David

C. Sam Smith joined James Blakely and John Combs to provide gun support for the Moonshiners. He later became a sheriff, big rancher, and prominent business leader. *Bowman Museum, Crook County Historical Society*

Stewart, his partner Charles Pett, and a "little preacher" named T. Clay Neese. These men wanted to set up an organization to fight the Vigilantes. They would do their fighting by ballot, at Crook County's first election in June 1884, but everyone understood that force might be needed to carry it off. Blakely, Combs, and Smith agreed to join up. The men formed the Citizens' Protective Union, and devised a cipher to communicate with one another. They chose Blakely as their leader.

Because these men had met at night, the Vigilantes mockingly called them "The Moonshiners." The name stuck. The Moonshiners themselves wore the moniker with pride.

"We worked hard," recalled Blakely, "trying to brace up the backs of folks who had been terrorized for two years by the vigilantes, and it was not long before we had 75 or 80 good citizens in and around Prineville in the Moonshiners."

Blakely mentioned David Templeton and Al Lyle as other Moonshiner leaders. Templeton lived in Prineville, while Lyle organized in the "north end of the county." Merchant Isaac Ketchum is also known to have been a Moonshiner. Not everyone opposed to the Vigilantes joined them. Fear stopped some. Others— Til Glaze for example—chose for their own reasons to stay out of the fight.

The election was scheduled for June 2. The Moonshiners would campaign for candidates who were either members of their own organization or at least opposed to the Vigilantes. Although partisan feelings still ran strong less than 20 years after the Civil War, they would ignore party affiliation. A Moonshiner Democrat would be willing to cast his vote for a Moonshiner Republican running against a Vigilante Democrat. At the time, the idea bordered on revolutionary. But only a Crook County revolution could depose the gang from power.

The Vigilantes hoped to break up the Moonshiners before the election. But George Barnes boasted of the plan, and it came to the ears of Moonshiners. They decided upon a demonstration of force.

They gathered in Prineville, fully armed. Blakely, Combs, Smith, Stewart, Pett, the Wagners, Templeton, Lyle—they were all there, 75 to 80 of them. With Blakely in the lead, they marched down the street to Til Glaze's saloon. The

Vigilantes inside watched the serried Moonshiners approach. The anger and cold determination of the Moonshiners could be seen, for they wore no masks.

Blakely stepped forward and hollered, "If you think you can stop this, come out and try it!"

The Vigilantes stayed put.

Blakely recalled later that the showdown "broke the hold the vigilantes had on the town and range."

No more trouble happened before election day, when the Moonshiners and others drove the Vigilantes from office. Blakely had stood for sheriff as a Democrat against Churchill, who ran as an independent. Although 132 Republicans insisted on voting for John Combs instead of Blakely, Blakely still garnered 380 votes to Churchill's 174. He took office July 7. Churchill, a young man, retired to his ranch at Richmond, where he soon died.

F.A. McFarland took office as county judge. Commissioners were G.L. Frizzell and J.H. Garrett. School teacher W.R. McFarland became county surveyor. A.C. Palmer replaced Richardson as county clerk. J.T. Bushnell became county treasurer, replacing the absent Gus Winckler. M.D. Powell became county assessor, replacing S. J. Newsome who had resigned as surveyor earlier to take the job. Newspaper publisher D.W. Aldridge became county school superintendent. And Ben Allen, the former commissioner, became sheep inspector.

Al Lyle became a state representative, along with William Lewis. The candidates for state senator had been former members of the county court, S.G. Thompson and Charles Cartwright. Thompson, the Democrat, beat the Republican Cartwright, 357 to 322, but it was Cartwright who went to Salem. The Thompsons had decided to quit the country.

According to one account, the Thompson brothers left Crook prior to the election. Other evidence indicates it may have been several months later. A deed at the Crook County courthouse dated October 15, 1884, shows that S.G. Thompson Jr. sold land on that date to Elijah A. "Amos" Dunham for $8,000. While it is possible that Bud and S.G. left separately, it is reported that the brothers slept together in the Dunham barn with their guns handy until they were ready to leave. The Moonshiners did not stop them. Martha Mogan, twice widowed by the Vigilantes (she had buried Frank in The Dalles next to Mike), sued Bud Thompson for damages. A jury awarded her $3,600. Thompson never paid.

Thompson moved to Alturas, California, where he resumed his newspaper career. He occasionally visited friends in Crook County and some members of his family still live here. He died in California in 1934. Unlike the Barneses, who never denied their participation in the Vigilantes even after the organization fell into opprobrium, Thompson joined the many who later claimed to have never belonged. The novelist Dwight Newton found when he visited Alturas that people there venerated Thompson as a founding pioneer. Newton's *Crooked River Canyon*, a fictional account about the Vigilantes, is his most enduringly popular book.

Charley Long also left Prineville. He was later gunned down in Washington state. Hank Vaughan died in Pendleton when he rode his horse onto a sidewalk and the animal stumbled and fell on him. Vaughan remained a celebrity to the end, the *Oregonian* even reporting when he took a job in Baker City selling newspaper subscriptions.

Most men of power involved in the Vigilantes stayed in Crook County. Some of their descendants insisted that the Vigilantes were good because they drove stock thieves out of Central Oregon. Other descendants claim that their Vigilante ancestors had been Moonshiners.

14
AFTER THE REVOLUTION
1884–1888

HE VIGILANTE REIGN and the Moonshiner revolution marched in step with other events.

Prineville had its first big fire on November 10, 1883. It began in the Occidental Hotel's kitchen. The fire spread quickly through the rooms. Volunteers fought the blaze, but soon the entire building was engulfed. The Occidental sat on the corner of Main and Second, and the fire spread up Main, destroying one building after another on that side of the street. The loss of the hotel itself was estimated at $9,000. Other losers included: Horace Dillard, $1,500, for the *Prineville News* building and $400 damage to the *News* office itself; $2,800 damage to a store building owned by Alexander Hodges; Mrs. M.A. Holbert, a millinery; and R.R. Kelly, who lost some furniture in the hotel. Doc Vanderpool lost his drugstore. The *Prineville News* for Saturday, December 8, 1883, mentioned that William Circles had saved several pounds of nails from the ruins of the Occidental.

Just over two months later, on January 19, 1884, a second fire wiped out more businesses. Damage was put at $10,000 in the blaze that destroyed R.R. Kelly's Saloon, Bushnell's harness shop, Wilson's Saloon, Til Glaze's livery stable, and the vacant Selling & Hickley mercantile store.

C.C. Maling's mill must have been humming during this period because construction boomed even without the fires. Sheriff Churchill might not have been busy hunting for Vigilantes, but he was busy with hammer and saw. Alva Tupper may have had something to do with that. Tupper was a sheep thief. He escaped from the Prineville jail by lifting up a floor board and walking away, and then riding out of Crook County. (Tupper's freedom did not last. Eight years after his escape, he was getting married in a distant county when the Crook County sheriff stepped up and arrested him.) Whether inspired by Alva Tupper's escape or some similar incident, the county court sought bids for a new jail. None came in, so it ordered Churchill to build one on land owned by S.J. Newsome. The *Prineville News* reported that he did a good job. Apparently not perfect, though. A prisoner later escaped by removing part of the wall.

The court condemned the Crooked River bridge and asked for bids to rebuild it, while also ordering Churchill to tear up the planks and put up barricades so nobody would try to cross. This time the court received bids. David Stewart and Charles Pett—a carpenter by trade—constructed the new bridge for $200.

A one-story building at the corner of West Fifth and Main streets served as the courthouse. It remained in use until Harley Belknap contracted to build a new two-story wooden one for $5,474. He finished it in a few months. Moonshiner county officials also had the jail removed from Newsome's land to the courthouse block's southeast corner. Months later, on April 6, 1886, someone broke into the courthouse and robbed the safe of $3,308.06. Indignant officials offered a $5,500 reward.

The county court also authorized A.J. Tetherow to operate a ferry on the Deschutes River to aid travel and immigration. The court set the tolls, which ranged from 5¢ for a pig to 50¢ for a vehicle drawn by no more than two horses, mules, or oxen. The ferry began operating in the spring of 1883. In December 1884, Tetherow appeared before the court and asked for help to build a bridge across the Deschutes. The court agreed to pay out $72.61 in county money for materials and to pay the wages and board for a bridge building foreman.

New settlers continued to arrive, among them John Newton "Newt" Williamson. Born in 1855 on his parents' donation land claim in Lane County, Williamson grew to manhood strong, handsome, and eloquent of speech. He attended Willamette University and in 1876 rode a horse over the Cascades into Central Oregon. He did not intend to remain, merely planned a short stay for his health. But remain he did. At the time the Vigilantes came to power, Williamson and his new bride lived in a log cabin near Powell Butte. He worked as a shepherd for Ben Allen, earning $25 a month. He eventually became a partner of Allen's. Whether his own idea or with encouragement from Allen and other big ranchers, in 1886 Williamson ran for sheriff against James Blakely.

Moonshiners had been running the county for two years. There is no hint now of what sort of job they did. Blakely retained the esteem in which people always held him. F.A. McDonald had served only a year as county judge, whereupon C.A. Van Houten replaced him. Van Houten remained until the next election, when Republican W.S.A. Johns was elected.

Central to the mystery about the election of 1886 is the question of what had happened after the Moonshiners seized control of the county in 1884. Blakely, in the account he gave when approaching 90 years of age, said that the Vigilantes ceased to be a force when the Moonshiners took office. "The vigilante gang scattered after the election," he said. "Most of them got out of the county. Some of the sympathizers settled down and became good citizens."

Shaver, whose history was published in 1905, also indicates that the 1884 election forever ruined the Vigilantes. Both Shaver and Blakely separated the Vigilantes from the later illicit activities of the Crook County Sheep Shooters' Association. Indeed, the county court during the Vigilante period had included two of the region's biggest sheep ranchers. "Sheep always crowd you a little," said Blakely, but added that "the sheep didn't have anything to do with the vigilante terrorism."

But novelist Dwight Newton, when talking to Crook County residents in the 1950s, found that they continually referred to the sheep shooters of the early 20th century as Vigilantes. Others noticed the same confusion. And the "Moonshiner" letter of 1905, written during the sheep shooters' rampage, stated outright that the old Vigilantes were still violently active 21 years after the Moonshiner revolution.

According to a 1949 newspaper article, Crook County residents lived for years in terror of secret societies. Rural residents cowered on their isolated ranches, and, depending upon which side they supported, feared that either the Vigilantes or the Moonshiners would ride out of the night. The account claims that the Moonshiners finally destroyed the Vigilantes when one man snuck up to a place where the Vigilantes were meeting and eavesdropped. He took down the names of all the men there and turned the list over to the Moonshiners. The Moonshiners sent letters to everyone on the list telling them that they knew the identities of all the Vigilantes and if they wished to go on living they had better disband. Vigilante activities ceased. And, claimed the reporter, for years after these events men who knew the identities of people in both organizations refused to reveal their names.

Well...perhaps, but it sounds fanciful.

It is true that people for years pointed out one or another community leader as a former Vigilante, and indeed pioneers are still discussed in this manner in Crook County. But the names of the Moonshiners—who wore no masks—were not secret.

No less a source than the official history of Oregon's sheriffs claims that the Vigilantes were intimidated when word reached them that each Moonshiner had been given the name of a Vigilante to kill if there was one more murder in the county. However, this same source claims incorrectly that Blakely did not become sheriff until two years after the Vigilantes were defeated and that his body "bore evidence of bullets that sometimes slowed him down" (Blakely was never wounded in his life).

There are three questions. One, did the Vigilantes disband in 1884 after the Moonshiner victory? Two, did the Moonshiners disband in 1884 because their mission was completed? Or, three, did the two organizations continue to fight each other for years, as several sources claim?

It is certain that the Moonshiners lost ground in 1886. Whether the work of the Vigilantes or other considerations, no one now is alive who can tell us. The election gave Crook County a new judge and two new commissioners. Also, a new sheriff.

"I served two terms as sheriff of Crook county and kept everything peaceful," reporter Herbert Lundy had Blakely say in 1939. "In 1888 I went to ranching in Wallowa county, and served two terms as sheriff there, from 1904 to 1908." Did Lundy misunderstand what Blakely told him? Perhaps, but other, later, accounts based upon interviews with Blakely report the same thing. Perhaps an old man confused what happened in Crook County, where he served only one term from 1884 to 1886, with his later experience as sheriff in Wallowa County.

Certainly the days when men were gunned down in Prineville without fear of punishment had passed. A newspaper editor complained in 1886: "Last night some idiot, who had more ammunition than brains, made night hideous by emptying his pistol several times on the street." Only three years earlier, some people would have trembled in fear at the sound of gunshots in the night.

In any case, the man who had led the Moonshiners to victory and ended the Vigilante reign of terror came to defeat. The popular, intelligent, and eloquent Newt Williamson ran as the Republican candidate against the Democrat Blakely. When the votes had been counted, Williamson had 476 and Blakely 347. A member of Williamson's family claimed in a historical account written almost a century later that Williamson had to "put an end to warring vigilante and moonshiner uprisings." The upset appears to have been a simple Republican victory, not a Vigilante victory. Young John Combs, the Moonshiner who had been deputy sheriff under Blakely, continued to hold the job under Williamson.

Blakely possibly just got in the way of a rising political star. Although Douthit & Barnes hired Williamson in 1894 to be editor of the *Prineville Review,* political activity and developing a large sheep ranch interested him most. Central Oregonians elected him to the legislature, where he became speaker of the house, and then to the state senate. Later he became the first Crook County resident elected to Congress.

After Williamson vacated the sheriff's job in 1888, John Combs took it, defeating Democrat W.A. Booth 502 to 499. Booth took it the next time. But Combs was still in his twenties and would live many more decades. The last had not been heard of this lawman who later declared that in Crook County a sheriff needed not only personal courage but a fast horse.

And Blakely? In 1888 he sold his homestead to his brother-in-law, Kennedy Montgomery, and received another $1,500 from Charles Requa for his big house in Prineville. He headed for the Wallowa country to ranch.

In August 1887 (the same month Binger Hermann became the first congressman to visit Prineville), A.H. Breyman, John Summerville, and Charles Cartwright sought a national bank charter, and received it. They organized the First National Bank of Prineville with $50,000 in capital. The first board consisted of Thomas McClelland Baldwin, Henry Hahn, Leo Fried, V.E. Allen, Mose Sichel, A. H. Breyman, Charles M. Cartwright, John Summerville, Sol Hirsch, and I. Fleichman. Ben Allen became president, a job he would hold for a decade.

This introduces Thomas McClelland Baldwin, better known as "T.M." Born in Cedar Bluff, Iowa, in 1854, he had accompanied his parents to Linn County in 1862. Initially overshadowed by Ben Allen, Baldwin became one of Prineville's community leaders and remained associated with the bank until his death. "There was a beauty about his life which won every heart," the editor of a Prineville newspaper wrote years later when Baldwin died, an unusual aside for an obituary of that period. "In temperament he was mild, conciliatory and candid; and yet remarkable for an uncompromising firmness." In 1917, Baldwin would buy Allen's stock in the First National Bank—50 percent of the total—for $75,000.

When tax assessments were published in 1893, sheepman Ben Allen had the largest personal assessment of any resident, at $30,000. True, the Baldwin Sheep & Land Company—owned at the time by the Van Houtens, John Summerville, and others—was assessed at $70,000, but it was a firm. The biggest assessment, at $400,000, was Cahn & Weill. It is because of the wealth of Cahn & Weill that some area pioneers did not appear among the county's rich. Cahn & Weill was the successor to the infamous Willamette Valley & Cascade Mountain Wagon Road Company.

15

CATTLE BARONS
1862–1890s

MOST CROOK COUNTY RESIDENTS were farmers or stock raisers. The livestock consisted of cattle, sheep, and horses, and often ranchers mixed their stock. Stock raisers built houses, barns, and corrals, but not fences. They bought little of the acreage they used. They ranged their stock on public land. The grass mattered, not title to the real estate under the grass. Farmers did get title and then fenced their land, which blocked off livestock from grass and water holes.

While some livestock firms like Mays & Company and Howard & Stearns prospered, others failed. As in previous and later times, farmers and ranchers scraped by precariously. And even large firms could go broke.

Winter, which was a big inconvenience to town dwellers, often could be financially disastrous and even fatal to stock raisers and other country folk. Climatic change appears to be on a cycle of 400 years cold, 100 years warm. The last warm cycle began at the end of the 19th century, peaking in 1942. During the cold cycle, the still wild Columbia used to freeze over at the place where Bonneville dam now stands, and winters in Central Oregon were much colder and snowier. This translated into heavy losses of livestock during the 1880s.

There had been bad winters before, but few whites had settled in the region and there were few witnesses to the harshness. The first actually witnessed by the pioneers was the winter of 1871–1872, when snow arrived sooner than normal and stayed on the ground longer. It was a very heavy snow, with some drifts ten feet high. Other bad winters followed in 1873–1874, 1874–1875, 1876, and 1879–1880.

The first of many absolutely miserable winters in the 1880s arrived on December 20, 1880. After a hot, dry year, there had been days and days of fog, and then came snow. Settlers expected that it would remain on the ground a week or so, but it did not melt for more than a month. Stored fodder was fed to the livestock, and when warm weather arrived in January they were herded into the high pastures used in summer.

Suddenly, in February, snow began to fall, thick and fast, from the Cascades to the Strawberries and beyond, from above the Columbia to below the Pups. Sheep and shepherds alike were trapped in the high meadows as the snow piled up to almost four feet, and the temperature fell to 35 degrees below zero. Sheep froze to death, and the shepherds almost did the same before they abandoned their charges for lower elevations. The snow and the cold paralyzed everything.

Nothing could move; everything was trapped. People were barely able to leave their houses, but some ventured out to feed animals in the barns. Straw was torn out of mattresses to provide fodder. Livestock caught outside of barns froze or starved to death. Some drowned when they ventured out onto frozen rivers like the John Day where ice broke beneath their weight. More snow fell in March. After it finally melted, the whole region was a scene of devastation and death. Soon ranchers had rail fences everywhere in the region covered with the pelts of sheep whose carcasses had been skinned. There were cattle, horses, and sheep still standing, but only because *rigor mortis* held them up after they had frozen to death.

However, the worst was yet to come.

For many years, the eastern foothills of the Cascades were covered with snags, a grim reminder of the terrible winter of 1883–1884. Snowbound cattle and horses had eaten so much bark off the trees in their desperate effort to reduce hunger that trees had died. Those people who lived through this winter claimed that thermometers froze. It became the winter that all later ones were measured against and found lacking, the winter that pioneers and their descendants always talked about when they were in a mood to reminiscence about hard times. Possibly it was influenced by the eruption of Krakatoa the previous August. Although this mountain was in the South Pacific, it sent so much ash into the air that it interfered with climatic conditions (the explosion was heard 2,000 miles away and the air wave circled the earth four times).

The storm began just before Christmas, 1883. Snow fell heavily, steadily, until two feet stood on the ground. A brief warming front arrived, melting the snow down to several inches, and then it snowed heavily for two days and two nights without stopping. The snow was finally measured at 72 inches—six feet— level on the ground. Accompanying it came bitter cold. For awhile the temperature dropped to 35 degrees below zero. These conditions prevailed throughout Central Oregon, and were as bad in the usually sheltered Ochoco Valley as in the exposed terrain around Camp Polk. Apparently conditions were almost as bad in southeastern Oregon.

For stockmen, it was a disaster. Cattle, horses, and sheep were trapped in the snow. Some could not be found; others could not be reached. Some animals died of starvation, while others froze to death. Some were found and rescued in time. The thaw between the storms, and the fierce cold that froze the melted ice on top of the snow, allowed ranchers in some areas to simply walk their animals to shelter. In the Prineville area, ranchers dug tunnels from their front doors to their barns. But they could not tunnel out to their herds, and throughout Central Oregon vast numbers of livestock perished, while the ranchers and cowboys working in the snow suffered frostbite when trying to rescue them. One shepherd on the Lower Desert, who had thousands of sheep grazing there, lost every single one of them. After March, when the snows finally melted, the entire region was covered with the rotting carcasses of dead cattle, horses, and sheep. Some still stood, frozen to death and standing in *rigor mortis*, exactly as happened in 1880.

Just when everyone assumed that winter was over, a March blizzard struck that brought new deep snow. It remained there a long time, and many ranch animals had to continue to fend for themselves.

Human nature being what it is, people probably believed that the worst they had ever seen—the winter of 1883–1884—would be followed by milder winters. Indeed, there has never again been a Central Oregon winter quite that bad, though several have come close. Alas, for those who breathed a sigh of relief after March 1884, one winter that came closest to being as bad was the next one.

In the 19th century, a "double winter" referred to any winter that had two separate periods of severe cold and heavy snow divided by a long stretch of almost spring-like weather. But in Central Oregon, where several of the 1880s winters were "double winters," the name is usually applied to one in particular: 1884–1885.

Marshall Awbrey had horses grazing on the west bank of the Deschutes in 1884. He rounded them up and drove them to The Dalles. When he was unable to get the price he wanted, he decided to wait until the following year. Awbrey drove the horses all the way back, then turned them out to graze on his ranch along the south bank of the Metolius. Every horse died during the double winter of 1884–1885. The snow in the Metolius area stood five feet on the ground, while eastward at Grizzly Mountain it reached four feet. Any way you measured it, the snow was too deep, and it buried sheep and trapped larger stock.

The losses were not as bad overall as they had been during the previous winter. Partly this was because so much livestock had been killed on the earlier occasion that there had not been adequate time to replace them, so there were fewer to be killed. But this time, because of the experience of the previous winter, many ranchers had better prepared themselves. Some of them had put up hay. Until 1883–1884, it had been assumed that there was no need for hay in Crook County, thanks to its abundant grass. Now ranchers knew better. Also, in the previous winter they may have assumed that a thaw would arrive earlier than it actually did, thereby they delayed too long before making any effort to rescue their stock. Now that they knew what could happen—the bones of cattle, horses, and sheep still covering the region reminded them—they recognized the need to act with speed. However, in some cases disaster was not preventable.

An Agency Plains rancher, A.W. Boyce, had 2,600 head of sheep before the snow began to fall on December 13, 1884. What he did not have was hay. When spring came, he discovered that he now had only 400 head of sheep left alive. Trout Creek rancher Columbus Friend found most of his sheep alive after three weeks, but so numb from the cold that they could not move their jaws. He and Perry Maupin put grass in the mouths of the sheep, then used their hands to work the jaws until the animals could finally begin to chew for themselves again.

Animals that were together in a band or herd, stomping the snow down around them as it fell, eventually found themselves stuck, surrounded by high walls of snow. Horses ate off each other's tails to relieve their hunger. Far south at Wagontire Mountain, the Brown brothers had about 5,000 head of sheep in 1884, but the following spring counted only 700. In the valley where Madras later appeared, many livestock died. At nearby Grizzly Mountain, where James Blakely and his neighbors fought to save their herds, some of the ranchers who had failed to put up hay for the winter lost everything. Others, who had hay, survived with minimal losses despite four feet of snow on the ground and fiercely cold temperatures for five weeks. The stage company replaced its coaches with sleighs.

The thaw that arrived after five weeks gave the impression that the worst was over, but then bitter cold settled in and the thermometer dropped below zero. Where the snow had melted into water, the water became ice. Any livestock surrounded by it were trapped again. Whistling Smith, an old cowboy known throughout Central Oregon, was the shepherd for 2,000 head of sheep belonging to Alonzo Boyce in the Vanora area of the Deschutes. He could not feed the sheep. Having turned his three horses loose, he started out on foot for the Negro Brown Ranch. He never reached the Brown house. Boyce found him in springtime, frozen to death. The three horses were also discovered, dead. The sheep were huddled together, every one of the 2,000 frozen to death.

A couple of years later, during the blizzard of 1887, cattlemen are known to have again cut open mattresses to feed straw to starving cattle. It has been said that about three-fourths of the cattle in the Harney country died during the winter of 1888–1889. No hay had been stored because of several dry years. One writer has recorded how, as a boy when camped by a lake, he found so many cattle skeletons that he could have almost walked along on the bones.

Another double winter, 1889–1890, hit stockmen savagely, especially because almost no hay had been harvested. The first snow and cold arrived in December, then a deep freeze settled over the region in February. The whole region was affected. The notorious cattle king John Devine went broke after he lost three-quarters of his stock in the Harney country, while up north in what later became Wheeler County, the big Gilman-French Land & Livestock Company lost 1,600 head of cattle. In the Deschutes country, ranchers rode out each day to look for cattle that had not yet starved or frozen. If they could be moved, they would try to drive them to a place more protected from the cold. If they were too weak from the cold and hunger, the ranchers shot them to end their misery. Often they would shoot a cow that was standing but had refused to budge, only to discover that the animal was already dead, frozen on its hooves.

A Burns newspaper reported the losses suffered by sheep ranchers in its area: Jackson Chesebro of Glass Buttes lost 2,800 head of sheep out of 3,400; Jim Mackey lost 1,500 out of 4,000; and at Wagontire Mountain, the Brown brothers lost more than 6,000 out of 9,600. One rancher reported how he and his men labored for three days getting his sheep to ground where the snow had been partly cleared. The sheep did well there for a couple of days, but then a hard, cold wind blew steadily and froze them to death.

However, some stockmen were less than annoyed by the losses. Cattle baron David Shirk later observed that the winter weather destroyed almost all of the sheep in the region and a decade would pass before cattlemen were again bothered by them. Shirk said that cattlemen prayed for another such winter to rid them again of sheep.

But perhaps not all cattlemen.

Sidney and Frances Stearns pioneered at both Bend and Prineville while building a cattle empire on the Great Sandy known as the "Triangle Outfit." *Bowman Museum, Crook County Historical Society*

Sid Stearns, one of the Deschutes ranchers who rode out to rescue and shoot stranded cattle, had twin babies at his cabin; they had to be kept between two feather mattresses most of every day to keep from freezing. When Mrs. Stearns wiped off the kitchen table with a wet cloth, a thin sheet of ice formed over the table. Ice also formed atop a milk bucket in the time taken to carry it from the barn into the cabin.

Yet the older settlers could still tell the new arrivals, "You think *this* is bad? Why, you shoulda been here during the winter of '83–'84. Now *that* was really a bad winter!"

Predators were another problem. Although timber wolves were eliminated soon after white people arrived, coyotes and mountain lions remained. In 1905, Paulina rancher Charles Lister was driving a band of 2,400 sheep across the desert when suddenly a pack of coyotes scattered them in every direction. After Lister rounded up as many sheep as he could locate, 600 remained missing. The coyotes had herded them deeper into the desert, to be picked off and eaten at will.

Another difficulty was thieving. Horse thieves, cattle rustlers, and sheep thieves abounded. Even before Central Oregon's settlement got underway in a serious manner, rustlers were a problem in the area between The Dalles and the Metolius. Accounts by early settlers frequently mentioned horse thieves. And while pioneers said that the Vigilantes never really caught a horse thief, they did not deny that there had been horse thieves in the region. The early criminal court records in Crook County cover a multitude of crimes, but perhaps the largest number were sheep thefts.

While local thieves were present, especially when the prey was sheep, the most successful robbers were part of networks that spread over several counties, and perhaps into other states. One outstanding Crook County sheriff, Frank Elkins, rode horseback into Nevada early in the 20th century to pursue a gang of horse thieves. Thieves knew one another. Sometimes they cooperated formally, but often informally as well. For the outlaws, it was better to have connections outside their own locality, because a former owner and his neighbors would probably recognize a stolen animal if it remained in the vicinity of its theft.

To escape identification and possibly arrest, horse and cattle thieves needed to hide stolen stock on an outlaw-owned ranch or in a canyon or other hideaway until they could change the brand. Some rustlers were skilled artists at altering brands, so that the former owner could look at a new mark and not detect the old brand covered by it. In some cases, thieves removed hides rather than changing brands. This happened when the price of hides was high enough to be more profitable than selling livestock on the hoof. Sometimes ranchers discovered that thieves (known as "hide-peelers") had cut the hides off cattle while the poor animals were still alive.

For many years, rumors existed of a huge hideaway in the lava beds of the upper Deschutes country. Many lawmen and range detectives sought this "Robber's Roost," but the hideaway for a long time remained only a rumor to all except those using it, or those who had close connections to those who did. Almost a legend. Finally in 1931, a Bend resident who was associated with the Livestock and Poultry Theft Protection Services of the Oregon Department of Agriculture, discovered the hideout in northern Lake County. There in the middle of the East Lava Beds was a 200-acre meadow that had served as a giant holding pen for generations of cattle and horses stolen throughout Central Oregon. The rustlers had cut a narrow trail through the lava for driving stolen animals to and from the meadow. They used juniper branches to close and hide the entrance. Thousands of head of cattle and horses had passed through the Robber's Roost.

While the lynching of horse thieves was never really as common as western novels and movies would indicate, other, more legal methods were employed. A suspected rustler or horse thief could be told with considerable official or unofficial authority to leave town and never return. Also, branding was used to counter thefts. Bill Brown, a major sheep and horse rancher, branded his sheep on their noses where the mark could not be overlooked or easily altered. He also insisted that people who bought horses with his mark had to live outside Oregon so there could be no confusion later about ownership and so that horses with his mark would not get mixed into the general population of Oregon horses. If someone had a horse with a Bill Brown mark on it in Oregon, and that person was not Bill Brown, the horse was stolen.

Cattlemen branded their animals in more than one place. Indeed, some stockmen branded their cattle on practically every part of the animal that was available to take a hot iron. Another defensive strategy for ranchers was to put horse thieves and cattle rustlers onto their payroll. The robbers tended to handle the stock better than other cowboys anyway, and the ranchers believed that they would not steal from the man who paid their wages. While this was a dubious belief, many big ranchers in particular resorted to this strategy. A biographer of Bill Brown reported that among the well-known horse thieves Brown employed were Jesse B. Bunyard, Cecil Hart, and Punk and Bill Robertson. Brown hired the very skilled horse thief Charlie Couch right out of prison and for four years he became the outfit's buckaroo boss.

Part of the problem the really big stockmen faced was the hostility of farmers, who in most areas were more numerous and therefore comprised most of the jurors. Many stock thieves were sent to prison, but many others, despite evidence of their guilt, were turned lose by sympathetic juries. Stock thieves themselves often sat on the juries.

Robert Mays became Crook County's biggest cattle baron. Accompanied by his wife and two-year-old son, Mays crossed the plains to Oregon in 1852. At first he settled on the west side of the mountains, but in 1862 Mays established a cattle ranch in the Tygh Valley. Over time, he acquired additional ranches at Bakeoven, Antelope, Dufur, and Muddy Creek, as well as buying the toll bridge over the Deschutes from John Todd.

Todd was born in 1830 and spent his youth in Missouri. After working as an army teamster in the Mexican War, he joined the California gold rush. He went to Portland in 1852, and four years later fought in the Yakima War. Following his marriage, he moved into what is now Crook County, possibly before 1860. Todd built a toll bridge over the Deschutes during eastern Oregon's gold rush, but maintenance costs ate up his profits and he sold it to Mays after its second collapse. Todd returned to his ranch at Prineville and brought in Eastern Oregon's first Herefords. He ranched and operated a pack train until 1877, when he paid $60 and two horses to Tom Geer for rights to land near Pilot Butte. Todd eventually had 2,000 head of cattle ranging from the Metolius to Farewell Bend of the Deschutes, the northern ranching boundary of his enemy Joel Allen.

The conflict between Todd and Allen began in 1879. Allen, headquartered at Big Meadows south of Todd's ranch, had his cattle grazing on government land near the junction of the Deschutes and Little rivers when Todd drove some of his own cattle onto the same pasture. Allen ordered him to leave, but Todd would not. Furious, Allen stampeded Todd's cattle. Instead of riding across the desert seeking the scattered herd, Todd sued Allen for the loss. He was awarded $1,000, but never managed to collect it.

Todd built a cabin near the same place he had had his encounter with Joel Allen. The cabin was afterward known as the Dorris cabin, after Todd's cow foreman, Felix Dorris. He then bought a herd of cattle that Barney Springer and Douglas Strope drove across the Cascades that same year of 1879. He hired Springer, and listed his name with the government as the homestead's owner. Earlier Todd had John T. Storrs file on the land. Possibly Todd had exhausted his own right to file on government land. Earlier stockmen had filed claims on the same or nearby land, starting with an anonymous one in 1874. Others who did so were S.S. Splaun and later John S. Martin. The latter sold his claim to Steve Staats and C.B. Allen. Neighboring claims were filed in 1870 by Dee Springer, which went to Tom Geer and then to Todd.

Todd ranged most of his cattle free on public lands all the way to the Metolius, but the Deschutes country was not as good for stock raising as the Ochoco country. He found it necessary to raise hay and other feed for the livestock. Later he bought alfalfa seed from Dr. David Baldwin's ranch on Hay Creek, but he planted it wrong and wound up with hog feed instead of cattle feed.

North of Todd and west of Baldwin lay a great stock empire, the Teal & Coleman Company, headquartered on Trout Creek. The firm was owned by Henry Coleman, his brother-in-law Col. Joseph Teal, and Barney Goldsmith. The foreman was William H. Gates. Coleman, his brother William, and Gates ran the ranch, while Teal and Goldsmith could usually be found in Portland. The outfit arrived in Central Oregon in 1868 when Gates and two other cowboys drove 750 head of cattle down from Washington to the Trout Creek area. Coleman arrived the following winter with more cattle. In their pockets, the ranch owners had a contract with the federal government to supply beef to its army posts in Oregon and Washington. The Coleman brothers and Gates filed land claims and burned down a huge beaver dam to empty a nearby swamp into the creek. Northward, the firm established supply depots in the Tygh, Yakima, and Klickitat valleys.

Teal & Coleman became one of the most important cattle outfits in Oregon. While it did not number as many beeves as Pete French's Harney country spread, let alone the 43,000 head owned by Todhunter & Devine before the killer winter of 1889–1890, in the 1870s it was a giant by outback standards. The big difficulty the firm faced was how to dispose of its stock, which became too large for the limited needs of Oregon and Washington. They drove thousands of cattle to the railheads in Cheyenne and Council Bluffs. In 1878, two Texans came up and bought 5,000 head, which they themselves drove out.

The downfall of both John Y. Todd and the Teal & Coleman empire began in 1880 with one of the most famous cattle drives in the history of the West, and easily the most famous in Oregon's past. Teal & Coleman decided to drive a herd to Cheyenne, Wyoming. As trail bosses they recruited E.O. Grimes of Prineville and John Y. Todd. Todd and other cattlemen combined their own herds with Teal & Coleman's for the drive that began at Prineville on June 14, 1880. The size of the herd is uncertain. One source said that the whole herd numbered 3,000 head. Another said that Todd and Teal each put in 3,000 head, for a total of 6,000, although this included the cattle of neighbors as well as their own. Todd took the lead with his herd, moved from the Deschutes through Prineville, then Henry Coleman followed with the herd he had assembled along the banks of Trout Creek from its vast ranges that stretched for hundreds of miles around. They moved southeast, the way other Teal & Coleman drives had done, but there was trouble all along the way. Blackleg infected the herd, and many of the cattle died of disease.

John Y. Todd, toll bridge builder and livestock baron, owned the site of Bend before losing his range empire in one of the West's most infamous cattle drives. *Bowman Museum, Crook County Historical Society*

When they reached Cheyenne, Todd turned all of the cattle over to John Teal and began the long ride home to Farewell Bend. Teal formed a sales company to dispose of the assembled stock, the John T & Co. He then sent the cattle down to Kansas to be fattened on the grass-rich plains. There, many were lost when they crashed through ice on a frozen river. Alice Farrell in *Jefferson County Reminiscences* (1957) says the river was the Missouri, but most other sources claim it was the Platte. The drive became a disaster for everyone involved, though for awhile only Teal & Coleman knew it. Todd learned what had happened only later in the spring when he rode down to Cheyenne to talk to Teal.

Whether or not they realized it immediately, they were broke.

Todd owed money for cattle that he had contracted to buy to include in the drive. Also, the smaller ranchers, whom he had persuaded to include their own stock, needed to be compensated for their losses. He sold all his remaining cattle to Breyman & Summerville for $15,000. Nor could he save his Farewell Bend Ranch. In the summer of 1881, he sold it to John Sisemore for about $1,400. Sisemore had entered the cattle business in California with $32,000 in gold dust that he had taken out of a placer mine on South Humbug Creek. Todd was left with only a claim to a small amount of land on Squaw Flat, until a Portland friend gave him enough money to re-establish himself as a rancher near Prineville.

Teal & Coleman fought the lawsuits filed by the small ranchers for recovery of their losses. The case went all the way to the U.S. Supreme Court. Eventually, the big outfit lost and was forced to sell its Central Oregon holdings to raise the money necessary to settle all the claims against it.

Meanwhile, John Sisemore, having bought the Farewell Bend Ranch from Todd, became a major figure in the Central Oregon cattle scene. The year he bought the ranch, Sisemore went to retrieve his stock pastured near Fort Klamath. With three men, he began driving them up to his new ranch. They had not gone far when a blizzard hit. The cattle were scattered, and Sisemore stood to go broke before he got started. However, he obtained help from the Klamaths, and the Indians and cowmen together successfully rounded up most of the stock. After wintering the herd near the fort, the next spring Sisemore tried again, and this time the herd reached their destination.

Sisemore's immediate neighbors were William H. "Billy" Staats, Sam Collins (three miles north), and Sidney Stearns. The former had homesteaded his place in 1879. As mentioned earlier, Staats and Sisemore became rivals. Both men had a post office and a hotel. Staats' post office was called Staats, as well as the hotel, but the latter was better known as the Deschutes Hotel. Sisemore's post office was originally intended to be named Farewell Bend, after his ranch, but the Post Office Department shortened the name to Bend. From that time forward, some people, especially old-timers, called the settlement growing up in the vicinity Farewell Bend, while others called it Bend.

Sidney Stearns homesteaded in a one-room log cabin on the riverbank north of present-day Pioneer Park. The cabin measured 18 by 25 feet and had two windows. About this time, a woman planted an orchard on the site of Pioneer Park, but it is uncertain whether this was done by Sam Collins' wife Mary or by Sidney Stearns' wife Frances. Eventually Stearns moved to a place a few miles south of Prineville and established a ranch, whose range covered most of the area between the town and present-day Bowman dam, as well as having holdings at LaPine.

Also settled in the Bend area was a Mississippi family named O'Neil, but they worked for Sisemore. As for John Sisemore himself, he lived on the ranch year-round, even while his family commuted between it and their original place in Jackson County. In winter, the several ranches at Farewell Bend were snowbound and isolated from the world. In this they were like the ranches and homesteads throughout Central Oregon. Sisemore acquired additional land in the locality, and his cattle grazed on the upper Deschutes with those of Jack Pelton and Bill Brown.

A year or two before Sisemore sold his ranch, he built a bridge over the Deschutes. The writer Phil Brogan claims that the bridge was 285 feet long and that Sisemore, as a Crook County district road supervisor, collected fees to pay for its cost. Author Joyce Gribskov, however, says that the bridge was 386 feet long, and that Sisemore sold it to the county for $386. In 1904, Sisemore sold the Farewell Bend Ranch to Dr. W.S. Nichols, an Oklahoman, for $6,000.

Nichols sold off the timber to the Pilot Butte Development Company and planted the remainder of the land with a large orchard of apple and other fruit trees. It was a typical ambition, on a bigger scale, for people moving into Central Oregon at the time, and it produced the typical results: except for 2,000 strawberry vines, all of the plants were killed by winter freezes.

James Blakely, the Moonshiner leader, was another cattle baron. His holdings were scattered across all of the modern counties of the region, though his headquarters was at Grizzly Mountain. For example, in about 1880 he grazed roughly 800 head in the Madras basin for several months. He also bought a 160-acre homestead at Black Butte that his friend Til Glaze used as a summer cabin.

One of the most famous Central Oregon ranches of olden and modern times is the G.I. Ranch in southeast Crook County, halfway between Bend and Burns. After Miller & Lux took over the big Todhunter & Devine and other ranches, owner Henry Miller put them under the management of John Gilchrist. In the late 19th century, Gilchrist acquired the ranch lands that became known as the G.I., which was named for him.

William "Billy" Foster was about 23 in 1871 when he arrived in the Ochoco Valley. He and his brother lived in a juniper log cabin a short distance from Crooked River. In time, Foster moved into the Bear Creek country and soon had land and cattle stretching from Suplee and Paulina to Farewell Bend. He married Mary Allen, a daughter of Ben Allen. In May 1890, Billy Foster was drowned in Crooked River about ten miles northwest of Prineville while fording it on horseback during flood season. A stable hand found his body. The Foster family moved away, but many years later his eldest son Carey returned.

These early cattle barons did not luck into their success. It took a lot of hard work under harsh conditions. One early rancher said that those who succeeded did so by camping under the juniper trees in all seasons and all weather, and spending almost every day sitting in the saddle. They became tough, leathery men, and dangerous to cross. Their prejudices were aimed strongest against people who they believed threatened their economic livelihood, principally sheep raisers and homesteaders. They tended to be active in their community, but their view of progress was mitigated by the impact it might have on the open range, on which they themselves depended. They did not want to buy land, believing it made much more sense to graze their cattle on grasslands that had no value except as range. They did not know that grazing damaged the land because of their failure to move cattle from season to season. In Europe and the East, where they had become adults and learned their business, such precaution was unheard of; the soil in those places, however, was very different than in the dry West.

Cattlemen from throughout Central Oregon came together for big spring roundups. Bill Hanley, a later Harney country cattle baron who became famous throughout the region for his civic and political activities, described an 1882 roundup at Wagontire Mountain. Here stockmen gathered for a week, holding bucking contests, horse races, sheep lassoing competitions, and target-shooting at deer. Hanley rode over via Silver Creek, where he was joined by Ike Foster of the big, tough Hardin & Riley outfit headquartered in California, and together they continued to the mountain. Gathering there, said Hanley, were 30 or 40 vaqueros from the big cattle ranches of Summer Lake, Goose Lake, Chewaucan, Silver Lake, and the Crooked River and Beaver Creek areas.

Sometimes buyers arrived at a cow town or even at a particular ranch to buy stock, but usually ranchers had to drive their cattle to market. Mention has already been made of Marshall Awbrey's horse drive to The Dalles and, of course, the disastrous Teal & Coleman drive to Kansas. The closest markets were Prineville and The Dalles, where cattle would be bunched and taken to bigger markets. But if a rancher wanted to exclude the middleman, he himself and his employees would drive stock directly to the bigger markets. This is what Teal & Coleman did, and what James Blakely did.

From Central Oregon, the markets included the Willamette Valley, the Okanagan villages of British Columbia, Idaho's Orofino mines, California towns, and the big mid-western markets at Cheyenne, Council Bluffs, and so forth. Unlike Texan cattlemen, who followed established trails such as the Chisholm and the Goodnight-Loving, the Oregon trails were no beaten-down paths. Cattle ranchers would simply set off across country, leasing grazing land along the way. If all went well, they would get the best prices by going directly to the buyers. But often then, as today, they arrived to find offered prices too low to cover the costs of the cattle, feed, and wages. Strength and money were often less a determining factor in success or failure than mere circumstances.

Cattlemen had it hard.

Sheepmen had it hard, too, and had the additional aggravation of hostility from the cattlemen.

16

SHEEPMEN
1868–1898

ELISHA BARNES, E. Johnson, and W.H. Marks drove the first band of sheep into Central Oregon in 1868. Elisha's son George lamented the results at a later date:

"I have a painful recollection that the sheep had the doubtful honor of having the first case of scab in the settlement, though at that time we did not know what it was. We thought it was the mange, the same disease that the hogs have in the Willamette valley, and we lost all our wool and nearly all our sheep before we learned what ailed them. Greasing the measly things with a bacon rind did not cure them, and some of us retired from the business with disgust. Why, the scab is a native of this section. I have seen the coyotes perfectly naked with it; the rim rocks had it; the sage brush had it; it was in the grass, in the rocks, in the air and our sheep caught it and caught it bad."

From this dubious beginning, the Central Oregon sheep industry became one of the most profitable endeavors for ranchers. Ben Allen became the richest man in the region from his sheep business, which he began soon after his arrival on Allen Creek in 1871. Many ranchers operated a mixed cattle-sheep operation, rather than having all sheep or all cattle. Even the firm that became the region's largest, the Baldwin company at Hay Creek, had cattle as well as sheep. In early times the big cattlemen and the big sheepmen were often the same persons. Only in time did the hostility between "beef raisers" and "wool growers" reach such intensity that it became violent. In 1890, a pound of wool sold in Prineville for 12 to 15 cents. It remained about the same in 1900, then rose, peaking at 28 cents a pound in Bend in 1920.

Shepherds came to Central Oregon from France, Spain, Scotland, Ireland, and Wales. Most in the northern part of the region were from Scotland, while the Basques were most numerous in the southern area. Central Oregon became one of the few places in America with a Basque jai-alai ball court. Early 20th century Burns had three hotels—the Commercial, Plaza, and Star—that were owned and operated by Basques and patronized mostly by Basques. Basques were also employed in northern Central Oregon by the big Morrow & Keenan ranch. The shearers were often Mexicans, who visited shearing sheds and pens on an annual circuit. Except for the ranch headquarters, the sheep camps were isolated, lonely places. The sheep needed large amounts of land to graze upon, and shepherds kept them moving through the grass all day long and tried to protect them from coyotes and other predators at night. Supplies for the shepherds and sheep would

Baldwin Sheep & Land Company mercantile store, Hay Creek. The wagons are hauling wool. *Oregon Historical Society 26551*

be delivered from the ranch, which in turn obtained them in great bulk during shopping trips to Prineville or The Dalles.

The wool sheared from the flocks was originally sent to The Dalles, often via Prineville. Almost all the outback's wool eventually found its way to Moody's warehouse in The Dalles. Getting the sheep to The Dalles was a difficult task. Sometimes, in fact, it was fatal. A former employee of Bill Brown's large operation related how the shepherds would drive the animals north from Brown's ranges in Crook, Harney, and Lake counties via Powell Butte to Prineville. From there they headed northwest toward Sherar's Bridge. That meant going into Cow Canyon to reach the Deschutes, and reaching the bridge meant braking the wagons with poles as they went down, inching their way over the face of the nearly perpendicular side of the canyon. Often, he said, men were killed in the canyon, because the slightest mistake or mishap would send men and teams with their wagons hurtling over the narrow grade to almost certain death.

In later times, after the Columbia Southern Railroad penetrated the region, wool was taken by wagon to the railhead at Shaniko. For awhile, Shaniko became the largest wool shipping center in the United States. The sheep themselves were driven to market in much the same way as cattle. Divided into bands and driven by mounted herders, sheep were moved across the southern pastures of Central Oregon to Nyssa, and across the Snake to points east. Many were driven to Wyoming, and some as far away as Nebraska.

The richness of Central Oregon's pastures soon attracted sheepmen from the Willamette Valley and the Pendleton country; not to settle, but simply to have their flocks graze on the open range. These transient sheep, rather than the resident bands, caused the greatest resentment among cattlemen.

Meanwhile, some resident sheep made some resident ranchers quite prosperous.

Shorty Davis, who arrived in Prineville in 1881, about two years before the other rancher of that name disappeared, found work as a shepherd. He gave his name as Elias Davis and said little else about himself. He never revealed where he came from or anything of his past. His employer paid him once a year, in sheep. Davis worked hard, saved his pay, and eventually bought a place on Eagle Creek, about 16 miles southeast of Prineville. Acquiring three quarter sections, he allowed his sheep to range far in the area. Davis prospered, but never married. A short man with a large head, described as resembling a dwarf, by 1895 he had a nice house and one of the county's best sheep ranches.

When merchants Hahn and Fried departed for Portland in 1890, they incorporated their ranching interests as the Prineville Land & Livestock Company. Ben Selling and Julius Durkheimer held minority interests. The partners left ranch operations to managers, although in 1893 Henry Hahn did appear in Prineville to deny a newspaper report that a labor dispute had been settled with Winchesters.

Started on a small scale, the Prineville Land & Livestock Company—or Muddy Creek Ranch—acquired at least 36,000 acres of land in Crook, Jefferson, Wheeler and Wasco counties, and leased additional Crook County land from the Hahn & Fried Investment Company. It also ranged livestock on public land. At its peak, the firm had about 800 head of cattle (at first predominantly Herefords) and 12,000 sheep. Muddy Creek Ranch later had one of the first Polled Angus herds in Oregon. The sheep wintered near Clarno and summered on Summit Prairie. The ranch grazed cattle close to homesteaders, which led to trouble.

The region's largest sheep ranch had its origins in 1873 when a practicing Boston physician, Dr. David W. Baldwin, established the Baldwin Sheep & Land Company on 160 acres of land at Hay Creek. He bought registered Spanish Merinos in Vermont, where he had raised sheep earlier, shipped them by rail most of the way west, and then drove them overland 1,000 miles. While practicing medicine in Central Oregon—sometimes riding 150 miles to care for an injured or sick patient—Baldwin built his ranch into one of the most impressive sheep spreads in the United States. It expanded across thousands of acres, made possible in part by buying up adjoining homesteads and unused tracts nearby. Baldwin also raised the first alfalfa ever grown in Central Oregon, soon harvesting 2,500 tons of it seasonally, which supplemented the fodder his stock enjoyed in the form of tall bunch grass growing on government land.

In 1884, after his health failed, Dr. Baldwin sold the company to C.A. and J.P. Van Houten, H. Loneoy, John Summerville, and others. John Griffin Edwards bought a half interest in the company in 1898, and went on in 1905 to buy out almost the whole firm by acquiring the interests of his principal partners, J.P. Van Houten and State Sen. Charles Cartwright.

"Jack" Edwards already had been called the "Sheep King of America." Born in Wales in 1855, he immigrated to America as a teenager. He clerked in a store until he became the operator of a coal delivery business in Salt Lake City. He went to Wales for a visit, and after he returned to America he acquired the Circle-O Ranch near Rawlins in 1879. This effort to become a cattleman was defeated by a severe winter and the outbreak of a Ute war. Edwards volunteered as an army scout in the conflict. In 1885, he returned to the cattle ranching business, but soon decided that more money could be made by growing wool. To the fury of his neighbors, he entered the sheep business. For awhile there was violence, but Edwards and the cattlemen came to terms. Before homesteaders filing claims on the open range took the fodder needed for his woolies, Edwards was the largest and most famous sheep raiser in the United States, with 100,000 head. Seeing no way to survive in the face of the homesteader invasion, Edwards in 1898 bought his half-interest in the Baldwin Sheep & Land Company—better known as the Hay Creek Ranch—and also purchased the Oregon King Mine.

Mr. and Mrs. John Griffin "Jack" Edwards at the Hay Creek Ranch. *Bowman Museum, Crook County Historical Society*

Baldwin Sheep & Land Company shearing plant, Hay Creek. *Oregon Historical Society 26552*

He eventually expanded the Hay Creek Ranch to cover 27,000 acres of deeded land. Additional acreage was leased from private or public sources, and his 50,000 sheep roamed widely over the open range for many miles across three modern counties. Edwards himself traveled worldwide in an effort to make his ranch renowned for its quality and innovation.

He bought Rambouillets from the French government and two estates in France, then cross-bred them with Spanish Merinos and Delaines to produce a new breed called the Baldwin. Weighing up to 200 pounds and thickly fleeced, it produced more wool and more mutton than other breeds. Meanwhile, Edwards' acquisition of 800 Rambouillets, paying up to $2,000 for each ram, gave him the largest purebred Rambouillet flock in the world. He also kept flocks of purebred Spanish Merinos and Delaines.

Edwards paid top dollar for prize-winning sheep in the United States and Europe, and he sold only the rams, not the ewes. He was very conservative in selling his sheep. He installed a shearing plant, the first ranch to do so, and it sheared 42,000 sheep during the first year. The ranch sold about 500,000 pounds of wool annually.

Self-sufficiency was a goal for all the isolated ranches of Central Oregon and few if any achieved it better than the big ranch at Hay Creek. Edwards kept a gardener on his payroll to raise fruits and vegetables to be consumed at the ranch, sheep camps, and neighboring farms. The tops of the early alfalfa crop were cut and used in salads at the cookhouse and ranch house. Edwards seldom had to buy hay despite his operation's large number of animals because the ranch grew its own, harvesting about 6,000 tons every year. The famous sheep ranch also had one of the largest cattle herds in the region, 1,500 to 2,000 head. Dr. Baldwin's large house became a general store, owned and operated by the ranch. Its customers mostly consisted of employees and settlers from neighboring farms and ranches.

Most neighbors were people who had filed homestead claims, which they proved up and then sold in a few years to the Baldwin Sheep & Land Company. While proving up their claims, the settlers worked for the Hay Creek Ranch as shepherds or shearers.

Baldwin's original house became available for use as a store because Edwards had a new, three-story home built after he married an English socialite. He had hardwood floors installed, but he feared that the house would be too cold for her, so he had wagons go up to The Dalles for more hardwood lumber. After it was nailed down on top of the other hardwood floor, Edwards was still worried, so the wagons went back to The Dalles and a third layer of hardwood went down. The Edwardses entertained European nobles and such American notables as Sam Hill and Edward H. Harriman there, but Mrs. Edwards found life on a desert ranch rather tame after her years in England.

The Edwardses were also very hospitable and generous to their neighbors. Appeals for help in a time of need never went unheeded, and the Hay Creek Ranch enjoyed a better reputation among homesteaders than other large ranches. Neighbors of the Hay Creek Ranch included, among others, the Parrishes, Pridays, and Thompsons.

Orlando Parrish settled north of the Hay Creek Ranch in 1876. His mother-in-law was Elizabeth Sager, whose young brothers had been murdered during the Whitman Massacre of 1847. The Parrish house became a well-known stage station. Neighbors were customers of its thriving fruit and vegetable gardens.

The Pridays settled on land that had once been part of the Teal & Coleman empire. Albert Priday was born in England in 1847 and immigrated in 1880. Along with his brother-in-law, William Morris, he established a sheep ranch adjacent to the Hay Creek Ranch, but later he moved to Trout Creek. Albert expanded his holdings from his headquarters at Cross Keys, but never became a big rancher himself. However, one of his sons, Leslie, who had been born in Gloucestershire in 1877, bought out the other heirs after his father's death. He then expanded these holdings into a very big ranch, finally owning 80,000 acres of land and leasing 40,000 acres more. He sold the Priday Ranch in 1945 and died in Redmond a decade later.

The Thompson brothers—S.G. "George," William "Bud," and Duovery, lived in the Hay Creek area only briefly, in the early 1880s. George became the first judge of Crook County by gubernatorial appointment, and Bud, of course, became the most infamous of the Vigilantes. It is not known now whether the Thompsons raised sheep or cattle, but Amos Dunham, who bought three of their six ranches, was a sheepman until he sold his place to the Baldwin company in 1902.

Another big sheep outfit on Trout Creek, near Ashwood, was the Tom Hamilton ranch. Hamilton, arriving in 1874, was the first rancher to introduce blooded stock there, both Shorthorn cattle and sheep. At its height, the outfit ran 7,500 sheep as well as a couple hundred cattle. Also on Trout Creek, occupying the old home ranch of unlucky cattleman Henry Coleman, was Bidwell "Bud" Cram. A Texan by birth, he had accompanied his family to Oregon and they operated the toll gate in Cow Canyon for awhile. Bud worked on the Mays and other ranches until he got enough of a stake to buy the old Coleman place. Eventually the Cram Ranch grew to cover 20,000 acres.

The most famous sheep rancher in Central Oregon was Bill Brown of Buck Creek, Paulina, and Wagontire Mountain. At his peak, Brown owned 22,000 sheep, upwards of 10,000 horses, 34,220 acres of land—and controlled another 100,000—all enclosed in ranches in Crook, Harney, and Lake counties, with woolies grazing in Grant County and mustangs running free with his brand in Deschutes County. Brown considered himself a Crook County resident. While his headquarters was on Buck Creek, he was sometimes listed in government documents as Bill Brown of Paulina, but usually as Bill Brown of Fife. The range that he controlled was about the same size as modern Crook County.

William Walter "Bill" Brown saw himself as a Crook County sheep rancher but others considered him the "horse king of America." *Deschutes County Historical Society*

William Walter Brown was born in Wisconsin in 1855, and accompanied his family to Oregon City when he was 14. After attending the California State Normal School in San Jose, he entered the sheep business with his brothers at Wagontire Mountain. The first winter, they camped between a mountain outcropping and their fire, and it was miserable. The next winter, they survived in tents and had a camp stove. Over time they managed to gather enough logs to build themselves a little cabin. But then the bitterly cold winter of 1884–1885 killed 3,300 of their 4,000 sheep. Brown's two brothers wanted out, but he did not.

They sold him the enterprise on his promise to pay them when he had the money in hand.

His neighbor Joe Foster filed claim to a meadow that Brown had staked and posted but not yet fenced. Foster's shepherd, 31-year-old Johnny Overstreet, moved a flock of sheep there in April 1886. Brown ordered him to leave, but Overstreet refused. What exactly happened next is disputed. What is known for certain is that words were exchanged between Brown on the one hand, and Foster and Overstreet on the other. Mrs. Martha Foster later testified that from a distance she saw three men and heard four shots. One man screamed, one man fell, then one man ran toward the Foster cabin and one ran toward the Brown place. Overstreet had been carrying a .38-caliber Smith & Wesson pistol, Brown a 45-60 caliber Winchester rifle. Investigators later found the pistol with three empty chambers, and three rifle cartridges lay 18 paces from the dead body of Johnny Overstreet. Some claimed that Overstreet fired at Brown three times before Brown took serious aim. But there are many versions in many different accounts.

About a dozen buckaroos went looking for Brown, planning to hang him. Thomas Jefferson Shields, later to become Harney County's first judge and at the time of the shooting the justice of the peace for the district, accepted Brown's surrender, then tried to get him to safety. He took Brown to the cabin of Alfred O. Bedell. When the buckaroos trailed Brown to the cabin, Bedell stepped out and told them that he, his sons, and Brown were all armed, but if they wanted Brown they could try to take him. The men rode a short distance away, talked it over among themselves, and departed. Bedell took Brown to Canyon City, the seat of Grant County. There, in November, Brown pled not guilty to a charge of first degree murder. Apparently the grand jury did not indict, because the case was dismissed in April 1888.

Brown's success came in fights against cattlemen, the elements, and four-legged predators. Decades later, guests in his big house on Buck Creek would be jolted from their sleep by the nightmares of their host when he cried: "Coyote! Coyote!" Yet it was less for his toughness that Brown was known than for his eccentricity.

Even in his late seventies, he would work all day and after supper walk the 20 miles from his Gap ranch to his Buck Creek house. He did not swear, smoke, chew, drink, gamble, use slang, or engage in sexual intercourse. Totally honest, personally austere, he accepted others as being the same until they proved otherwise, which they frequently did. Famous were his checks, written on anything available, from a piece of hide to the back of a can label, honored at the banks in Prineville and Burns.

Stories about Bill Brown's eccentricity became famous in his lifetime, covering everything from how he nibbled on strychnine to build up a resistance to the poison that he always carried in his pocket for coyote control, to how he bought his own saddle horse several times from the thief who stole it. Obviously many of these tales, including these two, were false. But there were enough tales that were true—for example, how he always wore shoes without strings (to avoid being tangled in the stirrup) instead of boots—to give credibility and wide circulation to the false stories. Brown, who became famous as the "horse king of America" but concentrated his attention on sheep, remains even today a legend on the Great Sandy Desert. Stories of Bill Brown are told there with the frequency that "Jack" stories are told in eastern states and rural Britain.

One story related to the sheep business is true, but does not concern Bill Brown. It concerns a missing livestock inspector.

It happened in the spring of 1889. Crook County stock inspector George Nutting went up to Antelope on an inspection trip soon after his appointment on April 9. He wanted to check sheep for scabies, which was prevalent at the time. He inspected 64,000 head belonging to Baldwin Sheep & Land and rode into the Trout Creek district. Nothing more was heard from him. After he had been gone for two weeks, county Judge John C. Sumner asked George Dodson to go up and look for him.

Dodson inquired at the sheep camps if anyone had seen Nutting. He traced him from a camp on O'Neil Creek, where Nutting had stayed several days during a rain storm, to the house of Tom Jones, where Nutting had left his horse, saddle, bridle, and equipment. Dodson learned that he had walked by foot to the ranch of Phil Brogan, where he inspected one band and left to inspect another, planning to return and give Brogan a permit to move his sheep. Dodson found only Mrs. Brogan and a small girl at the Brogan cabin. Dodson spent three days in the vicinity looking for Nutting, then went to the house of Knox Huston on Upper Trout Creek and secured his assistance.

According to a later newspaper report: "When they returned to the Brogan ranch, Brogan was at home. As soon as they approached within hailing distance, Brogan and Huston began to abuse each other roundly and Mr. Dodson says he began to wonder if he had improved matters, but soon saw that it was merely the good-natured railery of frontier acquaintances. Huston then mentioned Nutting in a casual way and Brogan promptly began to abuse Nutting for his failure to return and give the permit for the movement of Brogan's sheep. Huston then told Brogan of the fears for Nutting's safety and Brogan at once apologized for his remarks, told them what he knew and gave every aid in the search. Mr. Dodson went as far as the Schrum [sic] ranch on Cherry creek, visiting every cabin and sheep camp, but was unable to gain any trace of the missing inspector after he had left the Brogan home."

After a week, Dodson and Huston gave up. Dodson reported to Judge Sumner. Sheriff Combs or someone else organized a posse that included Sumner and rode to Trout Creek. Guided by Dodson, the posse examined every place Nutting had been and questioned everyone who had spoken with him. But they could not find him. It appeared that on May 10, 1889, he had vanished from the face of the earth.

Well known and respected in the upper Crooked River country where he ranched on Newsome Creek, Nutting had entered the Antelope area as a stranger and therefore without enemies. Because the range war between cattle and sheep interests overrides other memories of the period, people later tied his disappearance to the quarrel. In fact, an Australian ex-convict may have murdered him.

People recalled Nutting's disappearance 34 years later after Idaho police arrested a man for murdering a Nampa crossing guard on the Oregon Short Line. Someone accused Kenneth McClellan (aka McClean, McClellahan and McLennan) of also being Nutting's murderer. Recollections by oldtimers pieced together the story of McClellan's life in the Antelope area.

They said he had arrived from Australia and lived amid the Scots who had settled near Antelope. He shot a man named John Moran, for which he spent time in the state penitentiary. Oldtimers recalled that he could not get along with anybody, and Newt Williamson said that drink especially made him quarrelsome. McClellan got into a row with Pat Kelly, a shepherd for Phil Brogan at the Long Hollow camp. Kelly beat up McClellan. The next day, friends found Kelly's body in bed, where he had been murdered in his sleep. Everyone believed that McClellan did it, but no evidence could be found to bring him to trial.

Precisely why McClellan would have killed Nutting was not explained. It was said, however, that at Antelope, McClellan belonged to a local vigilante group, the Kim Kem Komrad.

George Nutting's body has never been found.

17

CROOK COUNTY WAR
1898–1916

Main Street, Prineville, ca. 1909, looking south from the north edge of town. *Bowman Museum, Crook County Historical Society*

THE CENTRAL OREGON RANGE was becoming crowded. The 1890 U.S. census showed that Crook County had 23,000 head of cattle and 249,000 sheep, Wheeler County 27,000 sheep. The 1910 census revealed Crook had 31,000 head of cattle and Wheeler 14,000, and Crook with 256,000 sheep and Wheeler 15,000. Yet there was even more overcrowding than these figures indicate. An enormous population of transient sheep occupied the region's pastures during the warm months. Wherever a cattle raiser grazed his herd on public land it was afterward acknowledged as his range by other cattlemen. Cattle ranchers throughout the West observed the system. But not sheep raisers.

Cattle and sheep ranchers had clashed all over the West. The history of these conflicts, and the reasons for it, can be found elsewhere. Here, the only causes that need to be mentioned, other than the widespread belief among cattlemen that sheep damaged the range, are the regional ones that led to America's last great range war.

The rich grasslands of the Cascades, Ochoco, and Blue mountains proved ideal for livestock. Sheep raisers in the Willamette Valley and northeastern Oregon began driving their flocks there each summer. Not a few hundred sheep or even a few thousand, but hundreds of thousands of sheep, year after year. They drove thousands down the dusty streets of Prineville while disgusted cattlemen watched from the sidewalks.

The Crook County Sheep Shooters Association was organized beneath this tree six miles from Paulina. *Jno. D. Guthrie and Ochoco National Forest*

It infuriated cattlemen that sheepmen ignored their grazing rights and ran the "woolies" onto their range, sometimes right up to their front doors. Sheepmen dismissed the protests. They said that everyone had a right to use public land regardless of who had arrived first. The law said the same. That the transient sheep raisers did not have to pay local taxes also annoyed cattlemen. These sheepmen had no local responsibilities. And sometimes they set fire to the range when they left. Once lush pastures had begun to disappear because of overgrazing.

Finally, in late July 1898, the cattlemen acted. About 30 of them met under a large yellow pine on Wolf Creek, six miles from Paulina, to talk things over. Present as guest speaker was a certain Mr. Snodgrass, representative of the Izee Sheepshooters Association in the South Fork John Day country. Snodgrass told the ranchers how to organize, how to bury shepherds and camp tenders if they were killed, and how, if a member of their own group were slain, to take the body home for burial without revealing how he happened to be killed. The Paulina ranchers responded favorably.

They decided to establish "deadlines," boundaries across which sheep would not be permitted. They had no legal right; it was public domain. With their livelihoods at stake, they did not care. Any sheep crossing a deadline would be killed and the shepherds punished. If necessary, they would kill shepherds as well as sheep. They organized the Crook County Sheep Shooters Association. Crook County residents afterward remembered them as the Vigilantes. Whether this was because the old Vigilantes led the group, or because local residents later confused the two groups, can no longer be ascertained.

Dorothy Lawson McCall in *Ranch under the Rimrock* (1972) claimed that when she arrived in Crook County the bridge over Crooked River sometimes had as many as six bodies dangling from its beams. But Warren Glaze told historian Frances Juris that the only man ever lynched on the "Hanging Bridge" was W.H. Harrison during the Vigilantes' reign in 1882. Contemporary complaints focused on sheep shootings, not murders.

Records relating to the Crook County War disappeared from the courthouse the same way historians shortly after 1900 discovered old Vigilante records missing. Moreover, fear of the second group of vigilantes lasted decades. A half century later, Dwight Newton planned to write a novel about the range war but upon visiting Prineville discovered that people would not talk. A radio series about Crook's history also skipped the range war after the producers were warned not to mention it. It is not surprising, therefore, that the conflict's history is sketchy. The new vigilantes hid their identities better than the old Vigilantes. Nor did a James Blakely later relate their story, naming names and describing incidents. Their identities remain as mysterious at the beginning of the 21st century as at the beginning of the 20th.

They rode at night, their faces blackened and masked, spreading terror and death. When the Crooked River men ranged into other counties, allies there assisted them. The Crook County War involved Grant, Wheeler, Harney, and Lake counties as well as old Crook. The masked riders gunned down thousands of sheep, burned barns, corrals, and haystacks, and defied anyone to stop them from enforcing their own brand of range justice. They killed sheep by shooting and stabbing, by driving them over cliffs, and by bunching them so tightly that they suffocated one another. Oregonians outside the region expressed outrage, and state officials threatened dire consequences, but the slaughter continued.

Jack Edwards spoke out on behalf of his fellow sheep raisers, but not because he himself suffered. Located in the county's sheep center, Baldwin Sheep & Land Company never received a visit from the masked cowboys. Other ranches and sheep raisers did not escape so easily.

Like Edwards, Shorty Davis raised cattle as well as sheep. But Davis was recognized primarily as a sheepman. In the summer of 1900, neighbors heard his cows and calves bawling. They investigated, and discovered that the cattle and sheep had not been watered. What they did not find was more interesting. They did not find Shorty Davis.

He was missing. So were his horse and saddle. No one knew how long Davis had been gone.

Men searched for him across Crook County. They asked officials in other counties to look for him, too. No possibility existed that he could have decided to ride away and disappear; his huge head and small body made it impossible for him to go unnoticed. Before long, word leaked that cattlemen had hired a man to murder Davis because they wanted his grazing lands. But a $3,000 reward for the recovery of the little man's body and the identity of his killer went uncollected.

Several seasons passed in relative quiet. It did not last.

Lake County sheep shooting, 1904. *Oregon Historical Society 12192*

In February 1903, Monroe Miller was corralling some of Bill Brown's sheep in Riddle Canyon, near Hampton Buttes. The work done, dusk setting in, Miller went into his tent, pulled off his shoes, and started a fire to cook some grub. Suddenly, rifles began firing and sheep began bawling. Miller rolled out the back side of the tent and started running barefoot across the desert. He did not stop until the next morning when he arrived at Brown's Buck Creek house, about 20 miles from the camp. Brown later discovered that he had lost 487 sheep.

That summer, Crooked River men rode down into Lake County and massacred 2,400 sheep at Benjamin Lake. Their campaign in Lake County continued into 1904. Masked riders used guns, clubs, and knives to attack Guy McKune's 4,000 sheep at winter's end, and in June they burned Charles McKune's sheep corrals in Thompson Valley. Popular Silver Lake merchant Creed Conn foolishly told people how he had sold bullets to some cowboys before a big sheep massacre. Vigilantes burned his freight wagons in reprisal. Then people heard that state investigators would travel to Lake County to interview Conn.

On Friday morning, March 4, 1904, Conn ate breakfast with several people and walked down to his Silver Lake store. After speaking to his clerk, he went to the post office, then strolled up the dirt road. Witnesses saw him walk about a half mile west, stop, look back toward town, and then again turn up the road. That was at 7:30. Minutes later, a man who lived farther up the road heard a pistol shot from the direction of the Silver Creek bridge. He assumed boys were hunting and paid no attention.

No one missed Conn until noon Saturday when his clerk finally gave the alarm. More than 50 men began searching the area. When they could not find Conn, they assumed that he had committed suicide and that Silver Creek had carried away his body. Men in a boat dragged the creek, but found nothing. For days, posses rode out looking for Conn's body.

Only after a month had passed without a trace of him did people begin to voice suspicions that cattlemen might have murdered him. Finally, a cowboy for the ZX Ranch walking along the bank of Bridge Creek, 150 yards above the bridge, found the body. To many it seemed strange that the body could have remained unseen so near the public highway while posses scoured the area.

Two bullets were found in him. The *Oregonian* reported that either would have been fatal, therefore at least one of the shots could not have been fired by Conn. He had been murdered. But the cattlemen and cowboys who comprised the coroner's jury declared his death a suicide. Lake County residents did not believe it. They offered a $2,000 reward for the arrest and conviction of the murderer. Sheepmen organized for their own defense. Everyone started carrying a gun.

A firm 40 miles south of Silver Lake lost 2,300 sheep in one night. That was in May. By month's end, newspapers were reporting that it had been the bloodiest season yet for sheep shooting.

Up in newly organized Wheeler County, several killings were recognized as being related to the range war. For example, Bert Strychnin "accidentally" shot Billy Wilson near Deep Creek, where Wilson's body got itself buried under a mound of rocks. In May 1904, after a dozen cattle belonging to Sigfrit Bros. died near the Canyon City road as a result of poison, five men rode at night to a sheep corral belonging to Butler Bros. of Richmond. They arrived about three hours after midnight. They proceeded to shoot 106 sheep and wound many others that had to be killed later by the owners to put them out of their misery.

The closest sheep shooting to Prineville in 1904 came on Mill Creek. Masked riders gunned down 65 of Allie Jones's sheep and threatened to return if he did not move his remaining stock.

The Antelope Wool Growers Association added $500 to the state wool growers' reward for the arrest and conviction of sheep killers. The same association appointed a committee to ride into the Blue Mountains to negotiate range lines with cattlemen. The committee members returned and reported success. A Prineville newspaper lauded this spirit of conciliation. Its editor foresaw "the time when these two industries will move side by side and with the utmost good fellowship."

Several weeks later, about 20 masked vigilantes with blackened faces rode out of the timber onto Little Summit Prairie and across to the Horse Heaven Creek range. James Keenan, a principal in the big Morrow & Keenan ranch that straddled Willow Creek below Grizzly Mountain, had believed the Horse Heaven area to be outside the deadline. However, when he had moved his valuable flock of 2,400 Shropshires there, he had taken no chances, driving them at night and avoiding corrals. Keenan afterward had returned to Willow Creek with most of his Basque shepherds, leaving one shepherd behind to watch over the band. The vigilantes rode up to this man and ordered him to raise his hands. They tied a grain sack over his head and bound him against a tree. They then spent two hours shooting 500 Shropshires worth $7,000. Big money in that day and place. About the same time, ten masked riders with blackened faces gunned down 100 sheep on Mill Creek. They scattered another 100 that owner U.S. Cowles of Hay Creek never found.

Not only were cattlemen attacking sheepmen; the latter were beginning to fight one another for a share of the range. Thus it happened in April 1903 that two ranchers quarreled over Wheeler County range, fatally. In the John Day country, about 15 miles above Spray, a fellow sheepman gunned down James Jones. The *Prineville Review*, normally circumspect about harm done to sheep ranchers, headlined this report that did not involve a cattleman: "MURDERED IN COLD BLOOD."

"Since the recent slaughter of 1,000 sheep in Crook county," editorialized the *Grants Pass Courier*, "the big excitement over the range war has been keen in eastern Oregon. The cattlemen are aggressive and seem determined to create a reign of terror. While such methods as the slaughter of sheep certainly cannot be condoned, the cattlemen should not be judged too harshly by those who do not understand the situation and who have never seen the devastation which sheep can cause in a country where they are ranged. Sheep and cattle cannot mix and the only way to preserve peace is to have the sheep confined strictly to certain areas."

Many believed: "No cow will graze where once a sheep has trod." Not until years later did agriculture experts discover that sheep grazing on a pasture improved the soil for cattle.

Local editors had to be careful what they printed. Prineville remained a cowtown. Many residents were retired cattle ranchers or owned cattle ranches outside the community. But Crook County also was home to important sheep ranchers such as Jack Edwards and Newt Williamson. Some prominent families, such as the Listers and Dunhams, owed their livelihood to the woolies. In 1900, sheep accounted for $256,000 in sales in Crook County, while cattle produced only $31,000 and horses $23,000. The *Prineville Review* expressed its opinion by discussing the situation in Lake County, not Crook: "The sheep destroy the range, it is true; but again, while destroying the range they also bring in immense sums of money annually to the county, which fact any right minded citizen will appreciate."

The *Crook County Journal* in July 1904 took aim at a woolgrowers' association $1,500 reward for information leading to the arrest and conviction of sheep shooters. The *Journal* declared that "the spite embodied in the proclamation is wrong" and continued:

"On the face of it there is an open dare that the sheep belonging to the members of this particular association, have a right to the territory in which they are now stationed, and that none shall question that right under penalty. There is too much in evidence the spirit that 'might makes right' with no thought given to the sacrifices made by the Crook County stockmen in order that the nomadic herds might have summer feed. And wouldn't the same ends have been met, wouldn't existing conditions have remained a trifle less strained if this association, instead of offering a reward for information leading to the arrest of anyone found guilty of injuring the property of its members, had offered that amount of money for information leading to the arrest and conviction of any of its own members found grazing his herds outside the territory which the Crook County stockmen in their generosity had granted him."

Far from the danger, the Salem *Statesman* attacked the "utter brutality of... deliberately murdering innocent animals in order to punish their owners" as "too fiendish to be properly characterized."

The 1905 sheep killing season began New Year's Day. Six masked riders with blackened faces tied and bound a shepherd on Grindstone Creek and then began gunning down sheep belonging to Fred Smith of Paulina. They killed 500 and scattered 300 more. At Izee, Owen Keerins' sheep on Morgan Creek and Keerins Bros. sheep on Swamp Creek died mysteriously. Fear spread that the cattlemen had begun to use poison.

With the state's attention focused on Crook County, a local resident wrote to Oregon's largest newspaper in 1905 to elaborate on the situation. First he reviewed the history of the original Vigilantes. Then he connected those vigilantes to the new vigilantes:

"A number of the original Vigilantes...together with other lawless characters, now form...the Sheep Shooters' Organization. These men are a power in county politics, and many of the lawabiding citizens of the county are afraid to report what they know, for fear of losing stock, or even their lives.

"Houses and haystacks have been burned and stock killed and the losers are powerless to either prevent these outrages or secure redress. Why? One reason is that witnesses are afraid to testify to what they know, and jurors, if they are not already under the influence of this criminal element, are unwilling to bring in a verdict of guilty on the same ground.

"Violation of the law is and has been so common in this county that very little notice is taken of minor crimes. Gambling is so common that a conviction could not be secured, even in the most fragrant cases.

"The gambling element predominates in county politics to such an extent that it virtually controls all the offices, and it is among this element that one finds remnants of the old Vigilantes....

"Sheep killings have been frequent, but no arrests have been made, even when in at least one instance very strong circumstantial evidence was offered a certain official; said official making the statement that the party under suspicion was equally as good a citizen as the informant [who] lost property at the hands of the sheep-shooters.

"The mysterious disappearance of 'Shorty' Davis was another coup of the Sheep-Shooters' Organization, and there is yet more to come.

"There are good citizens in this county who are eking out an existence in fear and trembling who would welcome a change; others, more fortunate, have sold their belongings and left for civilized climes."

He signed the letter "Moonshiner."

With such a signature, the letter could have been dismissed as anonymous and therefore worthless, but its publication by the *Oregonian* and other newspapers gave it consequence. Also, the little evidence available supports many accusations made by "Moonshiner."

But not the accusation that the old Vigilantes had taken control of the county government. Judge Well A. Bell, a lawyer who arrived after Bud Thompson's departure, had married Effie Vanderpool, a granddaughter of Moonshiner David Templeton. Templeton served as a county commissioner from 1898 to 1902. Sid Stearns and Mark Powell were the commissioners when the letter appeared. Rumor claimed a Vigilante past for Stearns, but proof is lacking. Powell may have been a Moonshiner. He replaced S.J. Newsome, a Vigilante, as county assessor in the 1884 revolution. The sheriff, C. Sam Smith, had accompanied James Blakely and John Combs to the Prineville Flour Mill where they, Stewart, Pett, and Neese had organized the Moonshiners.

Terror enforced silence. In 1967, the *Central Oregonian* published an interview with Lorene Lakin, then about 85 years old, in which she recounted a girlhood incident when she and her parents went for a picnic west of the Maury Mountains. Walking back to their mining claim, they saw four cattlemen at a shepherd's cabin. They smelled blood, and then saw the slaughtered sheep that covered acres of land. The Lakins and the cattlemen greeted one another, tensely, while the family walked past. The Lakins remained silent about what they had seen after they returned to Prineville, fearful that if they talked they would be murdered. They learned that the cattlemen had driven most of the sheep off a steep ridge at Sheep Rock, then shot or slit the throats of the remainder. The bodies of the shepherd and his dogs lay in their midst. Mrs. Lakin did not name the murderers; she merely said that they had grown old and died of natural causes in Crook County.

National attention focused on the Crook County War after the *Oregonian* published a letter dated December 29, 1904, signed by the "corresponding secretary" of the Sheep Shooters. Newspapers throughout the United States republished the letter, taking it seriously although the tone suggests satire.

Its author told the *Oregonian* that the association had authorized him "to notify the *Oregonian* to desist from publishing matter derogatory to the reputation of sheep-shooters in Eastern Oregon. We claim to have the banner County of Oregon on the progressive lines of sheep-shooting, and it is my pleasure to inform you that we have a little government of our own in Crook County, and we would thank the *Oregonian* and the governor to attend strictly to their business and not meddle with the settlement of the range question in our province." The letter continued in the same style and stated (probably accurately) that the association had killed 8,000 to 10,000 sheep that year and planned to do better in 1905.

At least one historian has claimed that the letter came from a Newsome Creek area cattle and sheep rancher named Roscoe Knox. Whoever the author and whatever his motive, the letter stirred up such outrage that it forced the state government to take stronger measures. The legislature made it a felony to kill someone else's sheep, and authorities increased the rewards for the arrest and conviction of sheep shooters.

The federal government took more effective action. Disagreement about who should be allowed to graze on various tracts of the public domain had caused most of the trouble. In 1902, the Theodore Roosevelt Administration created the Blue Mountain Forest Reserve in order to protect timber and to control rangelands. Comprised of federal lands in Crook, Baker, Harney, Malheur, Umatilla, Union, and Wallowa counties, it covered 3,053,178 acres. The government soon reduced the reserve to 2,813,769 acres to prevent timber thieves from using about 200,000 acres of it as federal "lieu land" in exchange for much less desirable state acreage. (The profitable trading of state acreage for federal forested lieu lands was the actual reason why Oregon's congressional delegation wanted the reserve in the first place. Improprieties soon led to convictions for corruption; see Chapter 19). Cattlemen petitioned the government to set aside the entire reserve for cattle and horses and to keep sheep out. A Department of Interior agent reported to his superiors:

"It is apparent that a few interested persons who have engaged in public land matters such as dealing in lieu scrip, securing fees, etc., have persistently endeavored to arouse sentiment against the reserve by dealing to the less informed ranchers and others, fanciful tales of wrongs to be inflicted upon the people by an unwise and oppressive government. Among the small stock owners there is now but little opposition to the reserve, the consensus of opinion being that 'the range conditions can be made no worse than they are,' and that they have confidence in their government to do what is best for them. Any action which will exclude the migratory herds of sheep from the mountain range will be approved by the local cattlemen and miners."

The government withdrew from entries another 62,480 acres of land located 12 miles west of the Blue Mountain Reserve around the Maury Mountains. An Interior Department agent who examined it recommended that 51,360 acres be made a permanent reserve. "The entire area has been over-grazed by sheep, cattle and horses and the springs seriously injured in many places," he reported. "A

bitter conflict exists between the sheepmen and cattlemen." He said that "sentiment is generally favorable to the creation of the reserve, though the cattlemen,
who are now in control of the range, fear that sheep may be permitted to graze
on lands which they claim for themselves alone." He recommended that both
reserves be placed under the same management.

On April 1, 1906, to stop the Crook County War, the Interior Department
created the Western Division of the Blue Mountain Reserve and the Maury
Mountain Forest Reserve. A.S. Ireland became forest supervisor of both reserves,
with the first forestry office located inside his Prineville house. His principal task
would not be timber sales, but the settling of grazing disputes by allotting pasture
lands within the forest. U.S. Chief Forester Gifford Pinchot's assistant notified
him on April 11 of the grazing fees for cattle, horses, and sheep, and the seasons
each stock would be permitted on the range. The reserve would be open to all
stock that had grazed there earlier, provided owners made application and paid
the fees. Ireland divided the Western Division into ten grazing districts, estimat-
ing that during the first season they would have to accommodate 340,000 sheep
and 20,000 horses and cattle.

At first, it went badly. At the end of the grazing season, the Western Division's
Grazing Advisory Board passed resolutions complaining about Ireland's management. This in turn led to a Prineville meeting of dozens of forest users in January
1907 to readjust the district lines. Committees of six to eight users drew new
lines, with cattle and sheep raisers equally represented. Ireland himself presided
over the meeting. He decided to abandon division boundaries by sections, replacing them with a more practical division by topographical features. Both cattle and
sheep ranchers came away satisfied with Ireland. The chief of the federal Office of
Control had attended the meeting and reported that several prominent sheep and
cattle ranchers in attendance had told him that "at the time the Blue Mountain
Forest was created a sheep and cattle war of more serious character than any ever
occurring before was impending, and that the creation of the Forest was all that
prevented it."

For 1907, the government permitted 247,004 sheep and 32,170 head of
cattle and horses to graze in the forest. The following year, to stop overgrazing,
they cut this number to 152,500 sheep and 17,900 head of cattle and horses.
The reductions hurt stockmen. Jack Edwards, for example, originally received an
allotment in the Blue Mountain Reserve for 40,000 sheep. Despite all his clout
and lobbying in Washington, it was cut to 18,000, and then reduced another 30
percent. In 1910, believing it now impossible to profitably raise sheep, he sold
his ranch to Portland capitalist L.B. Menefree and *Oregonian* publisher Henry
Pittock. Edwards moved to Portland and became an artist.

The last big slaughter of the range war occurred east of Fort Rock. Phil Barry,
a shepherd for Parker & Green, moved a flock of 2,200 sheep there in April 1906.
Masked riders appeared and told him to move the sheep off the range. Barry had
recently arrived from Ireland and did not take the warning seriously. A fortnight

later the masked riders returned. They drove sheep over a cliff and shot others, killing 1,800.

As time passed, sheep shooters slaughtered fewer animals. They still shot a few, though.

Range violence would continue sporadically until Congress passed the Taylor Grazing Act in 1934. For example, the April 6, 1910, issue of the *Bend Bulletin* carried this news item: "Last Saturday evening George Estes of Prineville shot and killed A.F. Randall on the range near the county seat. Randall worked for Allie Jones, whose sheep, it is alleged, were trespassing on the range rented by Estes, despite the latter's repeated warnings that he would protect his rights. But five minutes were required for the coroner's jury to reach a verdict of justifiable killing, exonerating Estes from blame." And, in April 1915, masked riders killed 30 sheep belonging to Isadore Meyers of Paulina.

The last significant act of the war occurred in 1915 when Newt Williamson prosecuted two men who had burned down his shearing plant. The *Madras Pioneer* responded to the jury's verdict of guilty by noting: "This is the first case in Crook County where a sheepman has had sufficient courage to endeavor to cause the punishment of those committing depredations on his property." It praised Sheriff Frank Elkins for helping to bring the culprits to justice.

There had been a successful prosecution earlier in Wheeler County. This occurred after a shepherd, who had hidden when five night riders approached, witnessed the massacre of 1,000 sheep belonging to Tom Fitzgerald. It was the largest single slaughter of sheep in Wheeler County. The Woolgrowers' Association paid out a $2,500 reward on top of a $1,000 reward put up by the Wheeler County court for the arrest and conviction of the killers. They were tracked down by range detective Jesse Selkirk. A jury convicted a man and his sons of the crime, but then the wife and children of one of the sons wound up on county relief.

Late in 1916, cattlemen and sheepmen sat down together at the Pilot Butte Inn in Bend to discuss their differences. Those present reached an agreement for livestock grazing in the Great Sandy Desert regions of southern Crook County. They agreed that the Bend-Burns road would be the boundary, cattle grazing north of the highway and sheep to the south.

With the big slaughters over, the government counted the reserve a success, and began to pay more attention to forestry than peacemaking. In 1908, it had divided the Blue Mountain National Forest into several smaller forests. The Western Division became two new forests: the Malheur, headquartered in John Day, and the Deschutes, based in Prineville. In 1911, 819,030 acres from the Deschutes and Malheur national forests were designated to form the Ochoco National Forest, headquartered at Prineville.

Hotel Oregon originally was the Poindexter (opened 1901), which boasted of having "no Chinese cooking," and service by a "White" staff only. *Bowman Museum, Crook County Historical Society*

18

EDWARDIAN AGE
1890s–1910s

THE POPULATION OF THE DALLES in 1900 was 3,542. It remained the big town in Oregon between the Cascades and the Blue Mountains. Farmers and ranchers from Crook County and throughout the outback continued to send products there, no longer to be placed aboard OSN steamboats, but loaded onto cars of the Oregon Railway & Navigation Company, by then a subsidiary of the Union Pacific. Large warehouses owned by the Wasco Warehouse Company and former Gov. Z.F. Moody abutted the rails on the east side of town, and wagons, boats, and railroad cars were unloaded or loaded continuously hour after hour, day after day. Activity increased as rails spread out of The Dalles to Condon in 1904 and Dufur in 1905.

Steamboat traffic had not vanished entirely. Local businessmen, led by Robert Mays and the banking French brothers, organized a steamship line to preserve the traffic, called The Dalles, Portland, & Astoria Navigation Company but popularly known as the Regulator Line. It built two sternwheelers at Portland to carry passengers and freight up and down the Columbia. It forced the Oregon Railway & Navigation Company to hold its rates lower than it might have otherwise. This benefited the whole outback as long as The Dalles remained the region's shipping hub.

Much of this community where Central Oregon residents took their produce was new. The old wooden town that had grown up from the Indian trading center disappeared during a series of devastating multi-block fires in the late 19th century and a big summer flood in 1894. The latter wiped out much of the town when the Columbia rose 40 feet above the low water mark and cut off The Dalles from the outside world. Water reached the second floor of the Umatilla House. Because of the fires, businessmen rebuilt their stores with brick. Although Baker City, Prineville, Burns, and other large towns in the outback boasted a few brick buildings, none had as many as The Dalles.

The Dalles also had more and a wider variety of businesses than other outback towns. In addition to more than its share of restaurants, mercantile stores, saloons, real estate brokers, bakeries, milliners, wool buyers, auction rooms, tailors, and pawn shops, it was the home to a packing plant, flour mill, brewery, coal yard, corset company, sarsaparilla soda works, salmon packing plants that caught fish in big wheels in the river, and several hotels, including the nationally famous Umatilla House. The latter was a three-story building with 141 rooms. It had all the elegant woodwork and decorations of high-end Edwardian hotels, and the railroad and the stage companies had depots inside. Its stately rooms, fine meals, and drinks were among the best that could be found between the Cascades and the Rockies, certainly much better than anything in Crook County.

Much of the wagon traffic from Crook County into The Dalles ended in 1900. It was on May 13 of that year that the Columbia Southern reached Shaniko.

The announced intention of the men who had organized the Columbia River and Southern Railroad in 1896 was to build the line from Biggs on the Columbia down to Prineville. There was the usual excitement about this prospect in Crook County. Time and again hopes had been raised that a line would be built into the area, and time and again these hopes had been dashed.

However, the continual construction of rail lines along the Columbia and throughout the entire West maintained the impression that this development would happen eventually. After all, Central Oregon had many resources being hauled to market by wagons that could profit any railroad willing to take away the business.

The Columbia Southern bought second-hand rail from the Oregon Railway & Navigation Company and began laying it south from Biggs in the summer of 1897. Going through Wasco, Moro, and Grass Valley, it reached a location near the southern end of Sherars road in 1900. Here the railroad could gather up the farm and ranch products from both sides of the Ochocos, carried there over the Prineville and Canyon City roads. While the railroad owners continued to promise that they would soon extend their line to Prineville, in fact there was no reason to do so. The livestock that formerly had been driven to The Dalles, as well as the wagonloads of wool and other agricultural products, would now be collected at the new railhead and sent over their meandering line.

All they needed at the terminus was a town. The French brothers and other Dalles businessmen joined with W.H. and Laura Moore of Moro to plat a townsite on a flat, barren parcel that had no natural geographic assets to recommend it. The nearby town of Shaniko, seeing its opportunity, bodily moved onto the site from its old cross hollows location. The railroad established its headquarters in this dreary setting.

Shaniko boomed. Its population grew into the hundreds. The Columbia Southern Hotel served guests going to and from the outback. Receiving business from every small sheep rancher as well as such giants as Jack Edwards and Bill Brown, Shaniko became one of the biggest wool shipping centers in the world. Thousands of head of cattle and horses also were shipped out from there. A town that had been little known even to its Central Oregon neighbors became a famous community in the outback. People throughout the region were continually on the roads to and from Shaniko.

The old Scherneckau store was not part of the new town. In 1887, Scherneckau's bookkeeper, William Farr, had bought the store from him and paid Richard Watson of Fossil $450 to move it to Antelope, incorporated the previous year two miles west of Howard Maupin's old stage station. By that time the town had gaslight street lamps. The community had its origin in 1879 when Amos Carter built a hotel at the junction of two busy rural roads. Soon he added a tavern. Before long, four large hotels graced the town, along with three saloons, two mercantile stores, two livery stables, two blacksmith shops, a newspaper, drug store, stationery store, other businesses, churches, six fraternal societies, and a Christian Temperance Union.

Most of the Antelope business district was destroyed on a warm July night in 1898 after a blaze spread from a bowling alley to neighboring buildings. The fire did not destroy many private houses, but it burned out more than 20 businesses, many outbuildings, wooden sidewalks, large patches of grass, and other property. Only five businesses were left standing. The businessmen who had lost their commercial properties remained optimistic about Antelope's future. Most rebuilt their stores within months. The town's population in 1900 was 249. Had Shaniko not been located so close by, drawing off commerce and people, Antelope's population likely would have been much larger.

Meanwhile, Col. T. Egenton Hogg's Oregon Pacific Railroad, which had played so significant a role in originally causing people to move into the region, had progressed eastward from Yaquina Bay. As mentioned earlier, in the summer of 1881, 1,400 men began work building the railroad that Portland businessmen continued to fear. Four years later, when the firm's trains began running from Corvallis to the Bay, residents of Albany raised $400,000 to help Hogg cross Santiam Pass. Another four years saw the tracks reach Idanha, but that was as far as it went. The colonel had done himself proud, in the face of skeptics and the hostility of the state's business elite, putting down 143 miles of track, but he just did not have the cash to complete the job. In 1890 his company defaulted on interest payments and went into receivership.

The railroad changed ownership several times during the next few years until it was snapped up by Wall Street rail stock entrepreneur Edward H. Harriman, who turned around and unloaded it on the Southern Pacific Railroad—which he controlled—for $750,000. Hogg, meanwhile, lost everything, and those who had invested in his railway at the outset and contributed to its building received nothing. And, of course, that particular railroad never reached Crook County.

Had Hogg succeeded, perhaps a north-south railway route never would have extended below the latitude of Shaniko, but with the vast timber resources waiting in the Deschutes and Ochoco forests, that seems unlikely. People in Prineville were beginning to wonder, but had not given up on getting a railroad beyond Shaniko.

By 1900, Prineville had 656 residents. Within ten years, the number shot up to 1,042. Already the biggest town in Central Oregon, its bright future as the region's commercial center was accepted as fact. Of course, lack of a railroad could kill even a town as important as the seat of huge Crook County.

It had three churches (Baptist, Presbyterian, and Methodist) and five saloons. Also, five boarding houses, five lawyers, four general stores, three drug stores, three livery and feed stables, three lumber yards, three physicians, two variety stores, two meat markets, two jewelers, two barber shops, two hotels, two public halls, two dentists, a flour mill, grocery store, restaurant, brewery, planing mill, and a red light district. The latter consisted of three houses on the north bank of Ochoco Creek. The first Chinese man to enter Prineville had been stoned, but now it had a Chinatown. Some were irritated by that.

Ben Allen had bought the old Jackson House, now renamed the Prineville Hotel. He hired two Chinese brothers to run it, Ah Doon and Moy Doon. Ah Doon had been the first Chinese man really accepted by local residents, thanks to his excellent cooking. *Ochoco Review* editor Johnny Douthit published a humor piece that he called "Ah Doon and Ah Ben." However funny it struck others, "Ah Ben"—rather, Ben Allen—was not amused. He found Douthit and beat him up. Ranchers called upon Allen at the bank and told him to fire the Chinese. Allen said that keeping them helped his business and changed the subject.

Ah Doon boarded the stage-coach for The Dalles on the first leg of a trip to San Francisco to buy merchandise. On the road, four masked riders stopped the stage. Three dismounted, dragged Ah Doon out of the coach, and cut off his queue. They told him that if he ever returned to Prineville he would be killed. Ah Doon was wild with fury. He continued his journey and returned with the merchandise. Ah Doon remained in Prineville until about 1898, a partner in business enterprises with Moy Doon and Wah Tye. Then he sold out and returned to China, where he became an importer and wholesaler of American merchandise. Another Chinese merchant, Ng Ah Tye, owned the popular Japanese Bazaar store.

One man saw the hostility directed toward the Chinese as a business opportunity. Perry Poindexter was about 22 in 1880 when

N.A. Tye owned the Japanese Bazaar in Prineville, next to the First National Bank at Third and Main streets, and became a leader of the community's small Chinatown. *Bowman Museum, Crook County Historical Society*

he moved to Prineville from his native Eugene. He worked in a stable and courted the restaurant cook. He married her, and in 1888 opened his own restaurant. "Absolutely no Chinese cooking" he advertised, and customers were served by "White Waiters." In 1901, he opened the Hotel Poindexter on the east side of Main Street between Third and Second. A good hotel, but not in the same class as Mary McDowell's.

After Mrs. C.E. McDowell took over the Prineville Hotel, she decided upon a complete renovation. In fact, a whole new hotel. The new Hotel Prineville would have a lobby and bar made of tile and marble—the best east of the Cascades. Lavish tiles of four colors and a Grecian border would go on the floor, and as a newspaper reported: "There will be a six inch dark blue vein Alaska marble base around each room with marble plynth blocks," and the lobby would have a marble counter, Circassian walnut woodwork, and a frescoed ceiling. The saloon and cardroom woodwork would be finished in oak with decorated walls and ceilings. The lobby and bar would be lit by elaborate chandeliers of the latest pattern and design. The old Jackson House would become an annex. Construction of the red brick building began by 1906, personally supervised by Mrs. McDowell.

Prineville's most important businessman at the time was George McIntire "Mack" Cornett. Born in Kentucky, Cornett arrived in Oregon while still a youth and herded sheep in the John Day hills. He worked on several ranches until 1886 when he bought a stagecoach. He drove the 200-mile route from Shaniko to Silver Lake, allegedly the longest continuous line in the United States. Cornett had an eye for opportunity, worked hard, and was all business.

Eventually he employed dozens of men, owned 360 stage horses, and more than 100 vehicles. From the hub at Prineville, more than 500 miles of stage lines went to Shaniko, Burns, Sisters, Crook, La Monta, Mitchell, Paulina, and Bend. After the rails reached Shaniko in May 1900, Cornett coaches picked up the mail and distributed it throughout the region. Drivers often came from Cornett's native state, and soon Crook County had a big Kentuckian population. It included the colorful Kentuck Ledford, who married Jennie Williamson, the congressman's daughter, and became Prineville's postmaster.

Cornett replaced stagecoaches with automobiles when they became available. Automobile companies believed it an excellent endurance test for their vehicles to be put on Mack Cornett's stage line in Central Oregon. He also diversified, investing in farms and ranches, a big mercantile store in Prineville, and a sawmill. and he became vice president of the Crook County Bank.

Cornett had a big house built for himself at 331 West First Street. Two and a half stories, with a basement besides, it had a reception hall, 32 x 15 foot living room, 22 x 14 foot dining room, buttressed stairway, brick fireplace with a tile hearth, plate-glass mirrors, and a basement washroom and laundry. On the second floor was an enameled bathroom. Everything else was built of fir, stained

G.M. Cornett mansion, seen here shortly after construction, was the grandest house in Prineville, suitable for the poor shepherd boy who became a rancher, stage line operator, banker, and lumberman. *Bowman Museum, Crook County Historical Society*

in golden and Flemish oak. The whole place was steam heated. The house cost Cornett between $6,000 and $10,000.

Down the street from Cornett's mansion, another banker built an equally imposing home. T.M. Baldwin's house was constructed in 1907, a two-story structure with a basement and stone foundation. Measuring 41.6 x 38.6 feet, it had broad porches on the north and east sides, a 16 x 24 foot living room,

The Thomas M. Baldwin mansion, shown here ca. 1909, was later bought by the Stearns cattle family as a townhouse. *Bowman Museum, Crook County Historical Society*

Band concert at the east-side entrance to the Crook County Courthouse, 1910. The side entrances were removed during 1941 remodeling. *Bowman Museum, Crook County Historical Society*

casement windows and glass doors that opened onto the porch, a 25.9 x 9.8 foot hall that separated the living room and library, a 20 x 13.6 foot dining room, and a fireplace. The kitchen containing drawers, cupboards, and sinks was near the boiler room and refrigerator room, and had both wood and gas ranges. The big bedrooms on the second floor had doors that opened onto balconies. The bathrooms and closets were also on the second floor. The basement contained the hot water heater and fruit and vegetable cellars as well as a billiard and smoking room. The interior was hardwood throughout.

Culture had arrived. There were balls, musicals, and a literary society. Men joined the Prineville Band that Til Glaze and five other settlers had started in 1880. Til's son Warren was one. Til Glaze was killed in a Burns gunfight in 1894, but Warren remained in Prineville and taught children to play the violin, piano, and other musical instruments. In 1924, he organized the Crook County High School Band. It is perhaps the only high school band in America that can trace its origins back more than a hundred years to a violin-playing, gun-fighting saloon-keeper. Special events such as the Independence Day celebration, the Fireman's Ball, weddings, and religious celebrations called for dances and music. School events, such as drama presentations, debates, or other oratory, drew parents and

The mansion belonging to Prineville businessman and rancher Charles M. Elkins, shown here ca. 1909, later became known as "the green house" because of its color. *Bowman Museum, Crook County Historical Society*

well-wishers. Horse racing and faro perhaps remained more popular than church activities (the Prineville Jockey Club leased the racetrack about this time). And, of course, there came many visiting lecturers and politicians.

Socially prominent people from Boston, New York, and Chicago bought Crook County ranches. Portland real estate dealer Spokes Wheeler persuaded New England bluebloods that they would enjoy living amid juniper and sagebrush with coyotes and rattlesnakes. His first sale was to rich young Tom Barnes of New York, who had run away to San Francisco to marry an actress. Douglas Lawson, son of Copper Trust founder Thomas Lawson, bought a ranch near Post. Others who arrived included the Hoelschers from Chicago, Kellys from Philadelphia, and Howards from Santa Barbara. Hal McCall, son of the governor of Massachusetts, received a ranch on Crooked River as a wedding gift from Thomas Lawson, his father-in-law. Thomas Lawson McCall, who would be Oregon's governor when Prineville celebrated its "centennial" many years later, attended Crook County High School from the McCall ranch.

A lass who came down from the Yukon had less social prominence, but greater fame: Katherine Rockwell. During the Klondike gold rush, she had been a dancehall girl in Dawson. Men praised her beauty far and wide. They called her "Queen of the Yukon," "Belle of the North," and any number of sobriquets. She is best remembered as Klondike Kate. Miss Rockwell first saw Central Oregon around 1910. She fell in love with the area and traded some land in Seattle for a homestead one mile northeast of Brothers. She remained there in a shack, working her farm and entertaining visiting cowboys, until she married Floyd Warner in Prineville. Warner, scion of a local ranching family, served in the Great War and afterward bought a Prineville restaurant on the west side of Main, just south of Ochoco Creek. He and Kate lived above it until he divorced her and moved to western Oregon to get away from her.

Other Crook County women founded an Equal Suffrage Club. Men gathered one day in 1906 to fill a school board vacancy. Before they could nominate anyone, 16 suffragettes walked in and demanded to participate. The women—all taxpayers—included the wives of David Stewart, S.J. Newsome, Hugh Lister, Dr. Horace Belknap, Jack Shipp, and other community leaders. Wilda Belknap led them. The men tried to ignore the interruption, and nominated M.E. Brink to the vacancy. The women thereupon nominated Effie Bell, granddaughter of David Templeton and wife of the county judge. The men decided to bow out gracefully. Brink withdrew in favor of Bell and the men unanimously elected her to the board.

Statira Biggs, niece and law partner of Marion R. Biggs, was appointed Prineville's city attorney on July 6, 1915, after incumbent T.E.J. Duffy became the first judge of the 18th Judicial District. Miss Biggs apparently performed well because in January 1916, Mayor David Stewart and the common council reappointed her. She held the post until August, when she left town for health reasons.

Crook County also had a female postmistress at the booming town of La Monta. In fact, Kate Helfrich named the town. Born in the Antelope Valley of Colusa County, California, in 1870, Katherine Helfrich was left motherless at the age of nine. When her young mother was dying, she had Kate pledge to always be a mother to her little sister. Kate helped raise her sister and brothers. Somewhere she learned to be a newspaper typographer. She arrived with her father and siblings in Crook County in 1896. They settled in an area filling with homesteaders who believed the land fertile. The Helfriches maintained an orchard.

Chosen postmistress, Kate named the post office—and thus the town—La Mont, in reference to Grizzly Mountain that stood above the community. But postal authorities would not allow it. So she added an "a" and on September 7, 1898, became the first postmistress of La Monta. Later, the *Prineville Review* and *Crook County Journal* at various times employed the vivacious and attractive Miss Helfrich as a typesetter. She also wrote editorials. In 1902, the *Deschutes Echo* proprietor contracted with her to manage its plant in return for half the profits, less $20 a month to him for editing. She moved to Bend. The *Echo* prospered on land notices, and Helfrich began spending time in Portland's Imperial Hotel looking for prospective land buyers. She also wrote fiction, some of which was published in the *Sunday Oregonian*.

Jack Shipp first rode into Prineville without a horse. Born in England in 1858, he accompanied his parents first to Canada and then to Portland. Young Jack became a fancy cake decorator and baker, but his father's trade as a cabinet maker appears to have been his meal ticket. He became a building contractor, entering Central Oregon in the 1890s when he won the contract to erect the first Warm Springs Reservation school. Hardware store proprietor and rancher Charles Elkins asked Shipp to build him a house in Prineville. Shipp rode his bicycle over from Warm Springs in 1897. He remained. In time, he became owner or part-owner of a bicycle shop, sawmill, and shingle mill. Shipp built some of the biggest and nicest houses in turn of the century Prineville, including T.M. Baldwin's.

Shipp's big houses had wiring. In 1906, Stephen Yancey freighted down a power plant from The Dalles. It took him five trips to bring in all the parts of the 160,000-pound plant, and then everything had to be assembled. But when that was done, Prineville had electricity.

Towns elsewhere in America had boomed after oil discoveries. Men first sought oil in Crook County late in the 19th century, and found some near Mitchell early in the 20th. Traces found in Marks Creek encouraged several oil companies to look there and near Barnes Butte in 1901. No oil was found.

Of course, the area had its share of problems: crimes, arguments, political disputes, and money quarrels. While the Williamsons, Baldwins, Stearnses, Listers, Cornetts, Elkinses, and some others lived well in comfortable houses, hundreds continued to merely scrape by—doing backbreaking work for meager wages. No Prineville business firms went broke before the turn of the century, but there was fire and flood. The meandering Crooked River often overflowed its banks. Typhoid from the river, when its summer waters were stagnant, killed people living nearby.

Disaster struck Prineville on a beautiful April day in 1903. A stranger rode into town. He went to the Hotel Poindexter, where he had a meal in the dining lounge and rented a room. The man stayed the night and left town the following morning. Afterward, few doubted that the stranger had brought smallpox to Prineville. (Actually, the incubation period for smallpox is two weeks, so he was not the source.)

It actually started at Shaniko's Columbia Southern Hotel. Several men arrived with a sick companion. They told people that the ill man had come into contact with poison oak. Apparently they realized he had smallpox and feared that if it were recognized, they would be held in quarantine at the hotel. After leaving their friend, they fled town. By the time the local physician identified the disease, members of the hotel staff, guests, and Mack Cornett's stagecoach drivers had been exposed. Stagecoaches carried the disease to Prineville.

It began the night the stranger slept in town. The waitress who had served him, Miss Rhonda Claypool, and a young daughter of hotel guests, Miss Laney

Katherine "Kate" Helfrich warned Prineville
residents about a growing smallpox epidemic.
Frances Juris

Boyd, first became stricken. Guest Kate Helfrich, who had recently begun negotiations to buy the *Deschutes Echo*, warned that the girls had smallpox. Their families and hotel proprietor Perry Poindexter denied this; an oculist, Dr. Taggart, ridiculed it. Helfrich stood her ground. However, although she herself had never been vaccinated, she nursed one of the victims before leaving for Portland. Dr. Van Gesner later diagnosed smallpox. The girls recovered, although Miss Claypool's father died during the epidemic.

The disease spread from the Poindexter. A man who lived in a little house next to the hotel was among the first to die. Perry Poindexter and his son Ralph fell sick, but recovered. Authorities removed those with the disease or suspected of having it (a scarlet fever epidemic also raged) to a two-story white house on the east end of town, a "pest house." Guards took position at the roads into town to prevent anyone from entering or leaving. Prineville remained under quarantine for six weeks.

Officials closed the schools and ordered children kept home until the epidemic ended. They also ordered that dogs running loose be shot on sight. Robert Harrington, the town marshal, took charge during the emergency, although he himself contracted the disease. He ordered that if anyone had reason to leave home, they must walk down the middle of the streets.

Vaccine arrived from Portland. Officials assembled the town's

The "pest house" was the most feared place in Prineville in 1903 when this photograph was taken. *Bowman Museum, Crook County Historical Society*

children outside Dr. Gail Newsom's office in a line down Main Street. The line proceeded through the office, with Dr. Newsom vaccinating every child.

Officers patrolled the streets day and night, discouraging unnecessary movement and making sure that no one violated quarantines. They permitted no public meetings or church services. People entering town after authorities eased restrictions were escorted to the drug store or express office to be fumigated. The officers also fumigated the mail. Only one of the doctors, J.H. Rosenberg, caught the disease, and he recovered.

Authorities condemned contact between people as dangerous. To obtain food, people hurried out of their houses and placed boxes in the street. Ed Harbin had survived smallpox as a child and had immunity, so he picked up the boxes, filled them with groceries, and delivered them. Businesses quit at 7 p.m., saloons removed their chairs and card tables to discourage loitering, and some stores shut their doors for the duration of the epidemic. Barbers closed their shops, depriving men of haircuts and shaves.

Ed Harbin, 1903, kept housebound residents fed during the smallpox epidemic. *Bowman Museum, Crook County Historical Society*

Officials issued daily reports. They even described how much of a patient's body was spotted. Newspapers kept people informed of the latest cases.

Authorities also opened a special graveyard. They wrapped the coffins in sheets soaked in formaldehyde, to keep the germs inside, and took them by wagon to the waiting graves. Few lingered while diggers lowered the eerie white coffins into the earth.

Dr. Woods Hutchinson, the state health officer, followed the disease from Shaniko to Prineville. He urged everyone to be vaccinated. In his report regarding Prineville, Hutchinson noted: "A young ranchman, Percy Davis, and an oculist, Dr. Taggart, nobly volunteered for the purpose of nursing the patients," and later called Taggart "the brave volunteer nurse." At Portland's Imperial Hotel, Miss Helfrich read about Taggart's nobleness and steamed. Being proven right gave her no comfort. Terrified, she consulted one of Portland's best physicians, took folk and other remedies, and spoke anxiously with John Combs and other people from Crook County staying at the Imperial. A severe headache sent her into near panic, but the doctor reassured her that she did not have smallpox. Nevertheless, she slept with the light on so that when she awoke from her smallpox nightmares, she could see that she had only been dreaming.

Finally, the epidemic ended. People came out into the streets again, and dogs roamed without danger from Marshall Harrington's gun. The churches and schools reopened, the card tables were unfolded, and barbers stropped their razors.

In addition to the human cost, the epidemic had hit hard financially. In April, the town had paid only $146.15 on bills incurred during the previous month. But in June, when the charges from physicians, druggists, and nurses arrived, the outlay came to a whopping $4,554.51.

The proprietors of the Poindexter later renamed it as the Hotel Oregon. The "pest house," however, had no formal name that could be changed, and retained its infamous moniker forever.

In Portland, meanwhile, Kate Helfrich had relaxed enough to help a visiting lumberman celebrate his birthday out on the town. In a letter home, she told about the excursion: the Chinese pillow she had bought; the books and magazines she had accumulated to read; the "bad" girl she had met at a variety show the lumberman had taken her to and how she would put the girl into one of her stories; how some men would probably head into Central Oregon to file land claims (fear of smallpox had turned them back after setting out earlier); and her plans to buy the *Deschutes Echo*. By the time the letter to her "Little Sis" arrived, pretty Kate Helfrich was dead of smallpox and buried in Portland's Lone Fir Cemetery.

19

PROSECUTIONS
1902–1913

IN THE SUMMER OF 1902, a man arrived in Prineville looking for timber. Stephen A.D. Puter operated as an agent for big Eastern timber companies. He would locate prime government forest land, hire people to enter claims for it under the Homestead or Timber and Stone acts, receive the titles from these people after the claims had been approved, and transfer or sell the land to the timber companies. It was illegal and everyone was doing it. Nobody did it bigger than Puter, soon to be notorious as the "King of the Oregon Land Fraud Ring."

Puter found 20,000 acres of federal land laden with very tall yellow pine 30 miles south of Prineville. The trees measured about three feet in diameter. Puter got a local man to gather people interested in making claims, then had everybody go out into the forest so that they could swear under oath that they had been there.

In his tell-all autobiography published in 1907, Puter recalled the expedition from Prineville: "The concourse of vehicles resembled a Sunday turnout in Golden Gate Park, San Francisco, only of course the equipages were not quite so swell. Some had light buckboards, others good-appearing buggies, while express wagons and heavy farm traps of all sorts were in evidence, making an imposing spectacle as we sauntered leisurely through the beautiful timber, with its picturesque surroundings."

Puter had these accomplices file on 108 quarter sections (160 acres each). He noted: "The 108 people whom I filed on these lands were all from Crook county, mostly residents of Prineville." Remembering that Prineville had a population of 656 people in 1900, the scale of the swindle can be appreciated.

After returning to town, Puter visited the office of the local U.S. land commissioner, lawyer Well A. Bell, who told him that the 108 filings had been duly recorded. Federal regulations required Puter to file legal notice of the claims for nine weeks in the nearest newspaper. Bend was nearer to the claims than Prineville. Almond C. Palmer, a Prineville lawyer and former U.S. land commissioner, established the *Deschutes Echo* there to profit from the requirement. Puter said in his memoirs that the *Echo* became a hugely profitable newspaper. Palmer split the profits with the plant manager, typographer Kate Helfrich.

Just like a gold rush, there came a rush of "dummies" for big Eastern timber companies, sometimes 100 to 150 in one train. Recalled Puter: "Every vehicle or animal procurable was…pressed into service to supply the abnormal demands, and the hotels in Prineville and Shaniko were overflowing with guests.

All summer long, in fact, the dusty roads between Shaniko and Bend were lined with travelers, and it was soon evident that a large proportion of them were under contract to convey whatever timber rights they might acquire to syndicates of Eastern lumbermen."

Fraud operators mostly sought state school lands. When Congress organized Oregon Territory in 1848, it had reserved sections 16 and 36 in every 36-section township for the territorial government to perpetually support public schools. If someone had already settled within one of these mile-square sections, the territory (later the state) could select an equal amount of federal acreage as compensation. The state could also take these "lieu lands" if the federal government included the two sections in Indian, military, or forest reservations, or if someone had filed a mineral claim upon them.

In 1887, the Oregon Legislature ordered the newly-created State Land Board to sell all state lands. Incredibly, in a time of fast rising land values, it mandated that they be sold for $1.25 an acre—an amount less than they were already selling for. Puter and others used false applicants and forged applications to claim the newly surveyed school sections and trade them for valuable federal forest land. Some men filed phony homestead or other claims and later relinquished the land to the fraud operators. Midwestern lumbermen bought forest land from the fraud operators or hired their own phony homesteaders. Oregon politicians took bribes to expedite the process and block investigations.

Creation of the Warm Springs Indian Reservation in 1891 included 36,643 acres of school sections inside its boundaries. Only the State Land Board knew the location of the school sections, but that presented no obstacle for land thieves, because the Board's employees had their own racket: in return for hefty bribes, they identified the school sections. Sometimes different land thieves found themselves fighting over the same section because unscrupulous crooks at the State Land Board had sold the same locations several times.

The fraud operators had so much influence that they spent only $1,400 convincing the federal government to create the Cascade Forest Reserve, a 30 to 40-mile-wide belt of land running from California to Washington. Their object was not to preserve forest. It was to create a government reservation containing 190,000 acres of unsurveyed school sections for phony homesteaders to claim and then exchange for lieu land. Puter's group persuaded the government to create the reserve, but another group of land thieves snuck in ahead of them and filed on 40,000 acres of school sections.

Land thieves also devised the Blue Mountain Forest Reserve. While they promoted it as a method of preserving forests, and while the government saw it as a way to stop the Crook County War, the fraud operators sought another 200,000 acres of school sections.

President Theodore Roosevelt appointed Francis J. Heney as a special prosecutor to investigate the land frauds and prosecute those responsible. Heney

Appointed special prosecutor by President Theodore Roosevelt to investigate land frauds, Francis J. Heney struck fear into the hearts of many Crook County residents. (Drawn in federal court by artist Harry Murphy of the *Oregonian*)

secured the conviction of Puter. The "King of the Oregon Land Fraud Ring" discovered that his friends would not step forward to post his bond and that his accomplices pretended not to know him. On the floor of the U.S. Senate, Senator John H. Mitchell of Oregon denounced him. Furious, the proud thief began to name names and explain the frauds to Heney and Secret Service detective William J. Burns.

Meanwhile, some in Congress advocated changing the land grant laws in order to stop the frauds. Congressman Newt Williamson, however, opposed repealing the Timber and Stone Act (which allowed claims of up to 160 acres, at $2.50 per acre). The law was seldom violated in Oregon, he said, and there would be some fraud under whatever law existed. Therefore, he opposed a bill that would authorize the government to sell timber instead of granting it, because poor people could not compete with moneyed speculators and big timber companies.

Shortly afterward, when the government suspended the regional inspector of forest reserves and looked for someone to replace him, Williamson

Newt Williamson came to Central Oregon for his health and remained to become a sheriff, state legislator, and U.S. congressman before his conviction in a land fraud case. (Caricature by Harry Murphy, cartoonist for the fiercely anti-Williamson *Oregonian*)

recommended to President Roosevelt his former deputy sheriff, John Combs. In April 1904, the *Deschutes Echo* reported opposition that arose to the nomination:

"It now appears that some Prineville republicans have been 'knocking' Combs to the Interior department, until it is doubtful whether he will get the place. The people who are knocking Combs are using the same brand of tactics as was used in the late republican primaries in Prineville. There is one republican coterie in Prineville that is trying to force Williamson to select persons for federal appointments from its rank. These people are Williamson supporters when there is something to get at. At other times they are indifferent. There has been no small amount of trickery in the late republican primaries, and the fight that is being made against Combs shows how little one republican faction is."

After Prosecutor Heney had heard Puter's information and gathered other evidence, he went to the grand jury. On February 1, 1905, they indicted Senator Mitchell and others. This was shocking news, for the Mitchell machine had controlled Oregon politics for decades. Later, they indicted Congressman Binger Hermann. On February 11, they also indicted Congressman Williamson for conspiracy to suborn perjury. Except for Senator Fulton, they had indicted the entire Oregon congressional delegation; the state was ridiculed nationwide for its political corruption. The grand jury indicted two other Crook County residents along with Williamson: Dr. Van Gesner and Marion R. "Dick" Biggs.

Born in Missouri in 1864, Biggs graduated from the University of Missouri and became a lawyer. He arrived in Prineville in 1889, where he became a partner of George Barnes. Biggs moved to Burns to handle the firm's business there. After they dissolved the partnership, he became a Harney County deputy sheriff and later a U.S. marshal. After his marriage in 1894, Biggs returned to Prineville and resumed the practice of law. For awhile he was in partnership with his niece, mentioned earlier. In 1903, when Judge Booth resigned, Gov. George F. Chamberlain appointed Biggs as county judge. Biggs held the post for a year; his job as federal land commissioner proved more profitable.

The government charged that Williamson, Gesner, and Biggs had conspired to suborn perjury by hiring 45 people to file fraudulent applications on federal land in the Horse Heaven country 20 miles east of Prineville. The odd sections in the area almost all belonged to the Williamette Valley & Cascade Mountain Wagon Road Company, while the even sections remained mostly unentered and unfiled-upon before July 1902. After people entered the lands, they transferred title to the firm of Williamson and Gesner. Trial was at the U.S. District Court in Portland.

Prineville Review editor A.H. Kennedy spoke for many Crook County residents in claiming that Williamson was being unfairly treated. Kennedy noted that all of the men indicted were foes of former Gov. Moody and that Williamson and Hermann were being attacked by the "city journals" in what had "all the earmarks of political jobbery." The *Review* said that the scandal was "making mountains out of molehills."

The government also indicted Williamson, Mitchell, Hermann, and three other men in the Blue Mountain Forest Reserve case.

The grand jury handed down indictments in a separate case against a group that included prominent Crook County residents in May 1906. The government charged that rich Wisconsin timbermen had conspired to steal an immense amount of federal forest land in Crook, Lake, and Klamath counties. Federal agents arrested the Eastern leaders of the alleged plot—F.W. Gilchrist, Ralph E. Gilchrist, Patrick Culligan, James G. MacPherson, and Herman W. Stone—and went after several Oregonians, including five Prineville residents: Charles M. Elkins, John Combs, Judge M.E. Brink, Donald Steffa, and Thomas H. Watkins. The grand jury also indicted Ben Allen, who had moved to Portland. Elkins, Combs, and Allen were partners in Elkins & Company of Prineville, which the government alleged had furthered the Gilchrists' scheme.

Writing at the time, Puter said: "Elkins & Co., charged with being closely allied with [the Gilchrist group] in the conspiracy, are men well known throughout the entire state. The firm's business is money lending and general financial business. The company is said to have put up large amounts of money and to have otherwise assisted in the plot." In Prineville, the Elkins firm was known best as a downtown hardware store. Charles Elkins had married John Combs' sister Amanda. However, Elkins was also involved in banking. The government accused Almond C. Palmer of using his job as U.S. land commissioner to assist in the acceptance of fraudulent proofs and illegal filing of claims. It charged Brink with using his power of attorney in the same manner that Palmer had done as land commissioner. Puter does not identify what role Steffa (the editor of the *Crook County Journal*) or Watkins (a partner in Watkins & Erickson) were alleged to have had in the conspiracy.

The prosecutors charged that the Gilchrist group had used more

U.S. Senator John H. Mitchell presided over a corrupt political machine to which many Crook County Republicans gave allegiance until it came crashing down in land theft investigations. The allegations damaged many, and destroyed Mitchell. (Harry Murphy drew this ink portrait during the senator's trial in Portland) than 400 claims taken under the Timber and Stone Act to steal 201,600 acres of federal land bordering on the headwaters of the Deschutes River. Excellent yellow pine stood upon the tract.

Williamson testified only briefly in the Horse Heaven case. He denied knowledge of a conspiracy to suborn perjury and stated that he had never before met two of the men who had testified to making false entries for him. The public sympathized more with Williamson than the others, and saw the Horse Heaven case as merely a rancher seeking to expand his holdings. Other ranchers used similar tactics.

Twice the jury deadlocked. The government sought a third trial, which began in August 1905. In an editorial, the *Prineville Review* accused special federal prosecutor Heney of trying to intimidate witnesses. "Whatever is in the wind," it declared, "it must be something in connection with the Wiliamson-Gesner-Biggs persecution on trumped up charges, and it is the belief of those who think much about it that the witnesses will be handled with out gloves in the sweat box when Mr. Heney again takes hold of them. He realizes only too well that his is a lost cause, and it is irritating."

The *Oregonian* charged that witnesses from Crook County feared revenge. Indeed, the government indicted Sheriff C. Sam Smith for attempting to intimidate witnesses in the Williamson case. When news reached Portland that the barn of witness Wilford Crain had burned down six miles from Prineville, the *Oregonian* reported: "The news of this fire and the knowledge of its incendiary origin, coupled with things that have gone before, has thrown the witnesses from Crook county into consternation so great that only by the greatest efforts on the part of the government have they been kept in the city." In fact, Crain's barn still stood and the fire had actually burned down a shed on Ralph Porfily's ranch.

"The Push Club held an indignation meeting Saturday evening," reported the *Prineville Review* on September 14, "and passed a resolution condemning the *Oregonian* for the scurrilous and libelous article appearing in its issue of the 4th. The people of this city and county are greatly wrought up over the bitterness shown by the Portland paper for Crook county since the trials began, simply because it is patent that we do not want to see our friends convicted when we believe they are innocent, and no opportunity is lost to hand us a bunch of slanderous lies dipped in wormwood...It pictures the inhabitants of Central Oregon as a band of cutthroats, against all semblance of law and order and not at all entitled to human consideration any more than a lot of bobcats; and all because Crook county has a congressman."

The Citizen's Business League (or "Push Club") declared that the *Oregonian* article was "wholly false and malicious" and "was purposely intended as a detriment to Crook county, its business interests and associations, and was directed against the society of the county in general." The league said that the shed, jointly owned by Crain and Porfily, only covered several tons of last year's hay. Porfily said he believed that transients had accidentally started the fire.

The *Oregonian* and Crook County leaders continued to spar. A few days after the resolution, testimony came out at the trial that *Oregonian* editor Harvey Scott had threatened to dig Williamson's political grave two years earlier when Williamson—then a state legislator—refused to support Scott for U.S. senator. Although Scott did not print that part of the testimony, pro-Mitchell newspapers throughout the state did. As late as mid-December, the *Oregonian* noted: "The way for Prineville to 'square' itself with the public is to make life safe and liberty secure within its boundaries. Then it will have no reason to complain of the 'misrepresentations' of *The Oregonian*."

In the midst of the trials, word leaked that one witness had information about the 1900 disappearance of Shorty Davis. Well A. Bell, now deputy district attorney, rode to Portland to interview Christian Feuerhelm, who told him that the man who had murdered Davis had regrets and had related details about it to Feuerhelm. The murderer, he said, had dumped Davis' body into an 85-foot-deep well and then dropped the rancher's horse down on top of him. Bell returned to Prineville, where he announced that officials now had all the information they needed to recover the body of Shorty Davis.

County authorities rode to a dry well near the Davis ranch. Men had dug it to a depth of 60 feet 20 years earlier and abandoned it when no water entered. Earth and stones had gradually been filling it in, so that it was only 35 feet deep. The authorities lowered some men down into the well who dug down six feet and found bones. The bones were too small for a horse or man. They belonged to a dog that had fallen into the well in 1895 and been shot when he could not be saved. The searchers continued to dig. They reached the bottom without finding more bones.

Shorty Davis remained missing.

However, the publicity stirred up by the search aroused the interest of Hood River lawyer A.J. Derby. He began trying to discover the true identity of the tight-lipped rancher. The search took years and led to the Ottoman Empire. Eventually, Derby learned that Davis' real name had been Leonidas J. Douris. He had been born to a Greek family in the Balkans province of Montenegro, part of the Ottoman Empire, and had five brothers living in Europe. One of the brothers, Constantine, acting for the family, made the long voyage from Athens to Prineville to claim the Davis estate money held by Oregon, worth between $75,000 and $100,000. Because of Davis' unique physical appearance, Constantine Douris easily proved that Leonidas Douris and Shorty Davis was the same person. Leonidas Douris had changed his name to escape other Greek immigrants in California who continually borrowed money from him and never repaid it. In May 1907, the state awarded the money to the Douris family.

At the federal courthouse, meanwhile, after three months spent in three trials, a jury finally reached a verdict. It had deliberated from 5:20 p.m. until almost midnight. The court summoned the defendants and their lawyer into the courtroom. The *Oregonian* reported:

Defense attorney "Mr. Bennett was the first to arrive upon the scene and in silence took his place at the long table where he has labored for three times to clear his friends and neighbors from the taint of crime. Mr. Williamson came in with the iron set mask of his face as calm, as expressionless and as gray as it has been during all the long strain of the trials. Dr. Gesner, like a white haired shadow, slipped into his accustomed place and nursed the cane upon which he has leaned during all the trial.

"'Have they agreed?' Mr. Bennett asked, and, as no one seemed to know, settled back in his chair solemn-faced and sad.

"Judge Hunt came in, took his place upon the bench and waited for the jury to file in, while the big clock filled the silent room with its beating.

"The 12 men slipped through the door and into their seats silently, while the court addressed them.

"'Gentlemen, have you reached a verdict?' the question came, and without a word, John Bain, the foreman, arose and handed the sealed envelope to the aged bailiff, who tottered across the few feet intervening and handed it to the judge.

"As the harsh rasp of the tearing paper struck the silent room it seemed to arouse spectators who had sprung from nowhere and they leaned breathless to the front waiting for the word.

"Mr. Bennett shifted in his chair and clasped the sides of the table with nervous hands, but the rest of the men sat as though carved in stone, their eyes alone moving as they followed the fingers of the Judge.

Dr. Van Gesner was a respected Prineville physician who was convicted with Newt Williamson of illegally acquiring public lands in the Horse Heaven district. (Caricature by Harry Murphy)

"The folded paper was handed to the clerk…to be filed, after which it was read aloud, while the listeners hung upon the words…As the reader pronounced… 'guilty'…the defendants shrank as from a blow, while Mr. Bennett grasped the table until his knuckles were white and tense. He seemed to be the worst hit of all, and gazed dumbly at the clerk and then at the Judge, as though he could not believe the evidence of his ears."

The *Prineville Review* of September 28 announced the verdict to Crook County residents: "Will Wurzweiler, who is on his way to Portland, 'phoned up this morning from Shaniko that the jury in the Williamson case had brought in a verdict of guilty some time last night. The news has cast a gloom over the entire city, as the defendants friends, who are numerous, had thought the verdict would be about the same as the previous ones. It is to be regretted that this verdict was rendered, as thereby a Congressman—the only one Crook county has ever had—is cut off from the public usefulness and the way is paved for still further wrecking the Republican party of Oregon upon the rocks of factionalism....

"Notwithstanding the conviction of Messrs. Williamson, Gesner and Biggs, their friends in Prineville will be glad to grasp their hands in welcome when they return. Conviction of irregularities in acquiring lands necessary to carry on their business in this county carries with it no stigma except in the *Oregonian* and the minds of federal officials, and the defendants will be none the less popular through out the district because of such conviction."

A couple of weeks later, Williamson, Gesner, and Biggs returned to the courtroom for sentencing. The *Prineville Review* reported:

"When the time came for the judge to impose sentence, Judge Hunt asked Mr. Williamson to stand up. With his hands in his pockets and with no change in color, looking the Judge squarely in the face, the congressman stood ready to hear his fate.

"Judge Bennett [objected] that [Williamson] was a member of congress and that imposing of a sentence would interfere with his attendance in Washington and violate his constitutional rights. The objection was over ruled."

When the judge asked if Williamson had anything to say before he pronounced sentence, the newspaper reported proudly that: "There was no whimper of mercy from Newt Williamson. He answered in a firm voice, grimly, without shifting his position: 'I guess it's all been said, Judge.'"

Hunt told him that the "same good faith, honesty and fair dealing should pervade every dealing in the matter of public lands as should every purchase of private property, between man and man. This, and this only—no more, but no less." He sentenced him to ten months in the Multnomah County Jail and a $500 fine.

Marion R. "Dick" Biggs served ten months in the Multnomah County Jail for his involvement in the Williamson land frauds, but returned to Prineville to serve a dozen years as Crook County judge. (Sketch by Harry Murphy)

The judge went easier on the frail Gesner, not because his guilt appeared less, but because a long period in jail might endanger his life. Hunt sentenced him to five months, but imposed a $1,000 fine.

Because Biggs failed in his public responsibility as a land commissioner, Hunt gave him the same sentence as Williamson.

A reporter who interviewed Williamson found him resigned:

"I could not expect anything less after having been convicted. I have no criticism to make of the judge because of the sentence." But then Williamson added in a bitter tone: "I might say that women and children may now come out from hiding. Williamson has been sentenced; they will be safe now."

Williamson echoed Mitchell's claim that the whole thing was dirty politics by Democrats and anti-Mitchell Republicans. Prominent Republicans, in fact, were delighted to see Heney smash the corrupt machine. The *Oregonian*'s Harvey Scott said later that the convictions had "revolutionized political affairs of the state." They had. The Mitchell machine that had dominated Oregon politics for 35 years collapsed after the senator's conviction and death.

The prosecutions resulted in the convictions of a U.S. senator, a U.S. congressman, the U.S. attorney for Oregon, the Oregon surveyor-general, and three legislators. Hermann, who had been the commissioner of the General Land Office in Washington before he became a congressman, was tied up in court for years, and Senator Fulton, the only member of Oregon's delegation who was not indicted, was defeated in the Republican primary as a direct result of the frauds. The government removed from office the U.S. marshal for Oregon and federal officials in Lakeview and La Grande.

Mitchell appealed his own conviction for taking bribes. The appeal was never heard. A few months after his conviction, Mitchell visited a Portland dentist to have some teeth extracted. He sank into a diabetic coma after the operation and died. Normally the U.S. Senate would send a delegation to a colleague's funeral and adjourn its session for the day. For Mitchell, they gave no such honors.

Williamson, who has the dubious distinction of being the only Crook County resident named in Carl Sifakis's *Encyclopedia of American Crime*, fared better. He carried his appeal to the U.S. Supreme Court. It overturned his conviction in January 1908. The Interior Department had stated that purchasing land from entry makers before the final entry constituted a criminal act, but the court ruled that the department lacked authority to make such a statement. Heney had decided not to prosecute Williamson in the Blue Mountain Forest Reserve case, believing that the other sentence would be punishment enough. The government could have retried Williamson on other aspects of the Horse Heaven case, but decided not to do so. It did allow the charges to hang over his head for another eight years. They were dismissed in 1913. Biggs and Gesner served their full sentences.

Crime historian Sifakis noted that in 34 land fraud cases, the government secured convictions in 33. But, he added, in later years some of the prosecutions were found to be corrupt and tainted by politics. Secret Service detective William J. Burns had allegedly intimidated witnesses into giving perjured testimony. In 1911, the U.S. attorney general reported to President Howard Taft that Burns had stage-managed the jury selection, but Sifakis adds: "there is little doubt about the guilt of most of those charged in the land frauds."

In Crook County, however, the *Prineville Review* editor's prediction came true: people did not hold the convictions against the three local men. Dick Biggs would later be elected and re-elected as county judge, holding the post longer than any other man up to that time. Williamson, on the other hand, never again held an elective office, but President Warren Harding appointed him Prineville postmaster and Republicans often consulted him.

20

BEND BECOMES A TOWN
1902–1914

OVERSHADOWED THOUGH IT WAS by many other outback communities, by the century's turn Bend was about to become a town. Homesteaders attracted by cheap land opening up in Central Oregon patronized the small one-store-with-post-office communities they found on the Great Sandy. Bend, being close to vast forest lands and thus to many settlers sitting on timber claims, had more than the usual share of customers. Business at John Sisemore's store increased as the area's population grew.

Among the earliest settlers was an Ohio widower with two sons who homesteaded on Little River south of the Farewell Bend Ranch in 1870, Jackson Vandevert. They persuaded Jackson's brother, William, to move up from Texas with his own family. William's family arrived with a horse, cow, and wagon, and, after staying the winter on Powell Butte, bought the Scroggins homestead next to the William Vandevert place, complete with blacksmith shop, for $600. The Vandeverts stayed to become one of the area's most prominent and respected families.

Meanwhile, John Sisemore's neighbor, William Staats, had been busy, prompted perhaps by his hotel's flourishing business. Before the end of 1902, he platted a townsite right next to Bend for a village he called Deschutes. Perhaps it would have become the big town on the river were it not for a rich Eastern capitalist with an infatuation for irrigation.

One day word spread through the vicinity that a strange visitor had arrived. A Michigan native who had acquired great wealth and traveled extensively in Europe and the Orient, this little fellow had arrived at the Staats place with his wife and an attendant in a wagon with a house atop it. Alexander Drake was his name, and though he was a friendly sort of fellow, he was ambitious, stubborn, and powerfully influenced by the big, progressive ideas of his age. This short, quiet man focused almost

In developing Bend from a farming hamlet into an industrial town, Alexander Drake plotted to split Crook into three counties. *Bowman Museum, Crook County Historical Society* entirely upon business, and would do more than anyone else to elevate Bend from an isolated hamlet at the edge of the forest into the biggest town in Central Oregon, overtaking Antelope, Shaniko, and finally Prineville.

Drake had been approached by someone aware of his interest in irrigation, Charles C. Hutchinson, who had organized the Oregon Development Company in 1898 to file reclamation claims along the Deschutes. The following year, having inadequate money, he wrote to Drake in an effort to interest him in the project. He described to him in the most positive terms the great profits that could be reaped from such a development. Drake, who was in Spokane when he received the letter, decided to travel down to Central Oregon to see for himself what the area offered.

Drake had originally intended to go farther south. His wife, a modest woman whose father had been a preacher with a large family, wanted to remain at least for the night where they had paused, on the Staats place. Drake consented. Their attendant, Charlie Cottor, rode over to the William Vandevert ranch seeking to replace their horses with fresh stock. Vandevert rode to the Staats place to discuss the deal and discovered that Drake was the same man he had guided during a hunting trip in Arizona a dozen years earlier. This unexpected welcome further strengthened the Drakes' positive impressions of the vicinity. Soon he decided to remain and to put into use the irrigation knowledge he had gained studying European water projects while touring the continent.

Irrigation was all the rage in Central Oregon because arriving homesteaders found their new farms dry and because entrepreneurs saw ways to reap profits using new reclamation laws passed by Congress. One of Drake's companies later acquired real estate under the reclamation laws for $1 an acre, dug a ditch to the land in order to qualify it as irrigated land and secure the title, and then sold it for $40 an acre. However, all of these projects were vigorously opposed by ranchers. They did not want more homesteaders moving into the area and fencing off water holes and the open range.

Drake received half the stock in the Oregon Development Company as well as its presidency in return for his promise to provide Hutchinson with the money that he needed. However, after Drake paid for surveys, he suddenly seized complete control of the company and ejected Hutchinson. His victim fought back and formed the Oregon Irrigation Company in 1901. Drake, meanwhile, formed the Pilot Butte Development Company. Hutchinson and Drake then filed new water rights claims, seeking some of the same land to reclaim and sell. But Drake had the advantage of deep pockets. Hutchinson was seen both in Bend and in Washington, D.C., as a speculator; Drake as a substantial businessman. Drake won the battle when the Department of Interior recognized Drake's claims and ruled Hutchinson's invalid.

The Pilot Butte Development Company began to dig canals off the Deschutes to reclaim 84,000 acres south of Bend under the Carey Act. In 1904, its claims and those of the Oregon Irrigation Company were consolidated into a new firm, the Deschutes Irrigation & Power Company, headed by banker W. Eugene Guerin. It began digging ditches to irrigate 25,000 acres, which by June 1904 opened up 200,000 acres for sale to settlers. Early the next year, however, the company got greedy. It decided to cut the pay of its employees from $2.25 to $2 a day. Almost immediately 200 employees quit. They went to work on other reclamation projects at Klamath Falls and elsewhere, and others threatened to walk off as well. To get the project going again, the company had to reinstitute the previous pay scale.

Working with other well-heeled investors between 1902 and 1904, Drake platted the town of Bend and started the Bend Townsite Company. Most stock in the latter was held by Drake and his wife. It acquired land for new additions using the reclamation laws, took up some timber claims, and established a small sawmill. Again, these efforts were not ubiquitously appreciated. Opposition developed to Drake's projects among some existing Bend residents, and sometimes fistfights broke out between these people and Drake's employees.

Drake himself bought land throughout the immediate vicinity, including the Staats place that had been his original camping spot. Rich Easterners moved to Bend based upon Drake's reports of its attractions and potential. Some had become his friends during earlier travels to Europe and Japan. These people settled next to one another in a park area soon known to locals as "Millionaire's Row." Wall Street, for years the main north-south road in Bend, received its name from a 3½-foot rock wall that bordered Drake's lawn above the street. It was on this street that Drake established one of the town's most famous businesses, the Pilot Butte Inn.

The Inn went through several versions, though it remained the principal hotel in Bend during the many decades of its existence. The one that Drake built in 1902 on the east bank of the Deschutes was a two-story building with only four bedrooms in addition to a dining room and parlor. The outside walls were unbarked pine, while the inside was covered in maroon-painted burlap. Rustic furniture sat atop Oriental rugs, and beneath lanterns that Mrs. Drake had bought in China during a visit. Drake hired two women from Prineville to run the inn, which they did until he sold it in 1905 to A.C. Lucas.

By 1903, Bend had a population of 258, with three general stores, three hotels, two meat markets, two small sawmills, and two saloons, among other establishments. When the Independence Day celebration was held there, 300 people showed up from across Central Oregon to watch foot, bicycle, and horse races, bronco riding contests, two nights of dancing, and a Bend-Prineville baseball game. A parade formed at the Pilot Butte Inn and proceeded down Wall to Franklin streets, over to Bond, and then north to Minnesota. The Declaration of Independence was recited and $50 worth of fireworks set off. At a second big

Independence Day celebration held in 1907, a barbeque served up 3,000 trout, pre-caught in the Deschutes during the days preceding the event and kept in ice.

But the big year for Bend and for Alexander Drake was 1904. It was then that W.E. Guerin organized Bend's first lending institution, the Central Oregon Banking & Trust Company. Its operating capital was shipped by rail from Portland to Shaniko, then driven to Bend accompanied by an armed escort. In the fall, the new Deschutes Telephone Company linked Bend to the Prineville line. This firm was reorganized the following year as the Pioneer Telephone & Telegraph Company, and it strung lines to Rosland [LaPine] and Sisters. It installed a 20 drop switchboard the year after that. Alas, reaching any telephone outside Central Oregon still depended upon the attention of the Prineville postmaster, who was also the telephone operator, and who often would leave the Bend line open while he busied himself in the post office or tended to private business affairs elsewhere. However, Drake's big victory came on December 19 when residents voted 104 to 3 to incorporate Bend as a city. Upon learning the results, the Bend Coronet Band marched to the house of A.L. Goodwillie, the new mayor.

Aided by the related factors of irrigation, the influx of homesteaders to the vicinity, and the promotions of Alexander Drake, Bend continued to boom during the year after its incorporation. About $100,000 worth of new buildings were put up, including the second version of the Pilot Butte Inn, a couple of sawmills, a Baptist church, a couple of saloons, and several other businesses. A fire department was established in late July after a blaze a few weeks earlier at Oregon and Bond streets burned down Hugh O'Kane's saloon and almost reached other buildings before volunteers managed to stop it.

However, one scheme for boosting the new town failed, except to fix Bend's place in history as the home of America's "first intercity bus." Officials of the Deschutes Irrigation & Power Company decided it would be good public relations to have an automobile meet the train at the Shaniko railhead and bring dignitaries or settlers directly to Bend without subjecting them to the inconvenience of a long, dusty ride on one of Mack Cornett's stagecoaches. The firm paid William A. Gill of Portland's Gill Engine & Machine Company to build a vehicle for them by March 1905. The vehicle he produced was a four-cylinder, four-seat automobile that weighed 6,800 pounds and had solid rubber tires. The Shaniko-Bend Stage Company was set up to operate this intriguing machine, but did not operate it long. It bounced along wildly on its rubber tires at 8 mph over the rough roads between Shaniko and Bend for only a few weeks, before the damage sustained by machine and passengers prompted its early retirement and an end to the whole scheme.

Although Indians still wandered into Bend each fall to sell huckleberries and leather crafts, Drake's town was growing fast. His Pilot Butte Development Company began building a power plant on the Deschutes in 1909, and in November of the following year electricity lit up 40 houses and businesses. The town council placed an order for 10 arc lights to be installed on the business district's corners. In 1911, the company transferred its water rights to Bend Water, Light & Power Company. It was this latter firm, in 1909, which laid the foundations of one of Central Oregon's most beautiful urban locations when it built a dam on the Deschutes just south of the Pilot Butte Inn, creating Mirror Pond.

By 1909, Bend had two banks. The first was owned by Alexander Drake, A.L. Goodwillie, and J.M. Lawrence. Goodwillie had been a Chicago banker, and Lawrence was the editor of the *Bend Bulletin*. They in turn sold it to John Steidl and J.E. Sawhill in 1907, who renamed it the Central Oregon Bank. A couple of years later the Independent First National Bank opened with Charles S. Hudson as president.

Some of the land sold by Drake's companies prior to 1907 was foreclosed in that year, when a stock market collapse set off an economic depression that lasted until Woodrow Wilson became president. Drake himself also acquired land far from Bend, including ranches covering thousands of acres. Eventually, in the 1920s, after Bend had become Central Oregon's biggest town, he retired to Pasadena.

The Bend library began in 1908 when women in and near the town organized the Ladies' Library Club in the house of Mrs. J.E. Sawhill. By raising money from dances, dinners, and other events, they hoped to establish a public library. Eventually they had enough funds to buy 50 books, and to subscribe to 17 magazines and 5 weekly newspapers. The women also donated 38 books from their own private libraries, and the *Bend Bulletin*'s J.M. Lawrence allowed them to use a small corner in his building as their facility. Miss Mary Coleman became the first librarian. That was the same year that the Bend High School was built.

The 1910 census revealed that the population of Bend had more than doubled, to 536, since Alexander Drake arrived at the Staats place in his wagon house. For all that, in 1910 Bend was not the largest town in future Deschutes County. Its neighbor six miles down river, Laidlaw, had that distinction.

The beginning of Laidlaw can be traced to 1893 when William A. Laidlaw and two partners formed the Three Sisters Irrigation & Ditch Company. In 1902, it joined forces with the Columbia Southern Irrigation Company to develop acreage under the auspices of the Carey Act. The firm began irrigating land, and sold it to settlers through a Portland company. Many long-time Central Oregon residents left other areas to move there. William Laidlaw, meanwhile, decided to build a town to serve the settlers and, of course, to attract still more. In 1904, he filed a plat for the town of Laidlaw. A post office was established the following year after businesses began to arrive.

William Laidlaw became the secretary of the Laidlaw Banking & Trust Company, housed in the same building as his irrigation firm. He believed that when the Corvallis & Eastern Railroad arrived, the town would boom and overtake Prineville to become the region's metropolis. Had the railroad entered Central

Oregon from the west, as Col. Hogg and others believed that it should, William Laidlaw might have been right. The town of Laidlaw, not Bend, was best located to be the railhead on such a route. Indeed, even after the rails approached from the north, some people believed that the builders would go to Laidlaw. Had that happened, Bend probably would have died.

The presence of three grocery stores, besides other businesses including a lumber and shingle company, reveals Laidlaw's early prosperity. A.P. Donahue founded a newspaper there in 1905 that attracted 600 subscribers. The *Chronicle* was a four-page weekly, not untypical of other Central Oregon newspapers of its era, except for its large circulation. But everything depended upon the irrigation project and the arrival of a railroad.

The irrigation project was a resounding failure. Thousands of acres received irrigation, but settlers on many thousands more who had been promised water never got any. In 1911, the state stepped in, seized the assets of the Columbia Southern Irrigation Company, and renamed the firm (now a government enterprise), the Tumalo Irrigation Project. The legislature authorized an expenditure of $450,000, principally to build a dam and reservoir in the Bull Spring basin. This was done, and water rose behind the dam to a level of 35 feet. And then the level began to drop down again. Lava fissures beneath and around the reservoir provided tiny cracks for any amount of water to escape. Efforts by engineers to plug the leaks failed. The basin, in fact, was a giant sinkhole. Finally in 1914, the state had to write off the project as a complete loss.

Everybody lost. Most of the farmers who had moved to the Laidlaw vicinity never received water. Small farmers in California who had bought $1 million worth of bonds, believing in a guarantee by the state of Oregon, found their investment virtually worthless and the state's guarantee little better. The state itself was out of pocket for its efforts to save the project. As for William Laidlaw, he saw the ruin of his project and the renaming of his town to Tumalo.

21

THE EAST LEAVES, THE WEST GROWS
1880s–1910s

As the end of the 19th century approached, residents of northeastern Central Oregon had decided to separate from Crook County. Neighbors who were within the boundaries of Grant and Gilliam counties likewise were unhappy. This area was separated from the remainder of Central and Eastern Oregon by mountains. The inhabitants had close ties with one another, but it was physically difficult to maintain connections with the three different county seats. In wintertime, C.P. Bailey, an early Baptist minister who served the area from his usual base in Prineville, had to leave his horse somewhere along the road and hike to his Mitchell congregation on snowshoes. For local residents, difficult trips had to be taken to Prineville, Canyon City, or Condon every time that a deed needed recording. Moreover, despite its predominant character as a cattle-raising district, the larger mountain community began to develop its own infrastructure.

Newspapers indicate the autonomous character of this locality. Despite the small population and the isolated geography, several newspapers served the community at various times during the 19th century. The first of these was the *Fossil Journal*, established in September 1886, which lasted until it merged with the Condon *Globe-Times* to become the *Times-Journal* in September 1975. Founded by lawyer H.W. Hendricks, it became an institution in the area over its long life, and its eventual passing was much regretted.

None of the other newspapers had such staying power. The only other Fossil newspaper, established in 1905 as the *Central Oregon Star*, blazed out after only three months. The only Spray newspaper, the *Courier*, was born in 1902 and continued to be published for many years, but finally fizzled out during the 1920s. Mitchell had three newspapers over the years, two of them drawn off by the magnetic financial attraction of Prineville. The *Mitchell Monitor*, debuting in 1894, lasted four years before it was moved to Prineville. Next was the *Mitchell Sentinel*, founded in 1904, which was published until it folded in 1925. The final entry, the *Wheeler County Chronicle*, established in 1929, was also later moved to Prineville.

Oddly, this area had one feature of which no other Crook County community could boast: steamboats. Charles Clarno built the first in 1889, naming it the *John Day Queen*. It was destroyed in 1899 when swept from its moorings. Undaunted, Clarno in 1905 built another, the *John Day Queen II*. About 40 feet long and 10 feet wide, the *Queen* operated as a ferry and cruise boat for about 14 miles up and down the John Day River. Clarno, a son of cattle baron

Andrew Clarno, operated the boat personally, standing in a three-by-three feet pilothouse. The community of Clarno served as his headquarters. Alas, the steamboat had a short life. In 1909, Clarno decided to take it up to the Columbia, then steam to Portland to have it renovated into a luxury boat. On the way north, while being pulled over the waters by men with ropes, the boat wrecked on the Clarno Rapids.

A much more common mode of transportation was stagecoaches. The line pioneered by Henry Wheeler in 1864 continued to run coaches from The Dalles via Sherar's Bridge, and on to Canyon City; the eight stations he established to serve his vehicles became the nucleus of several communities. Outlaws continued to prowl the region. One such, his face concealed by an oatmeal-sack mask, stopped the stagecoach to Canyon City two miles below the summit of Farghers Canyon on an August afternoon in 1891. He took five mail sacks, but rode away without harming the driver or passengers.

Mitchell and Fossil became the large towns in the vicinity, but Mitchell had a problem its first settlers had not anticipated. The town's location in the Bridge Creek canyon subjected it to flooding that was sudden and violent.

On Election Day 1884, residents were alerted to this danger in the worst way possible. Nearby ranchers and their employees were in town to cast ballots. The day was sultry, and early in the afternoon great black clouds began to bank up to the southwest. When the black mass rolled above, fierce winds suddenly roared through town, accompanied by a plethora of cloud-to-ground lightning flashes. Hail pelted down, as people ran for cover and animals bolted for parts unknown. Almost instantly, Bridge Creek rose to the top of its banks, and only minutes later spilled across the countryside. Boulders were rolled across fields, haystacks floated away, and houses were surrounded by the rampaging waters. Some houses were swept away entirely. Mild little Bridge Creek had become a very big and violent river, 300 feet wide and an incredible 30 feet deep.

One of the flood's victims, a woman who lived five miles below Mitchell and who, with her three children, had been surprised by the rising water, was later found 14 miles from her house. Not all of the victims were killed by water; some of the livestock perished from lightning strikes. Before this, many ranchers had built their houses and barns in the valleys of Bridge Creek and other streams fed by mountain waters. But in 1884, they began learning how swift and violent the flash flooding could be in eastern Central Oregon. Mitchell's residents, however, refused to be driven off. They looked at the empty lots where houses once stood and decided to rebuild. (The Mitchell flood provided a backdrop for Dwight Newton's 1981 novel, *Disaster Creek*.)

Fossil's history was less dramatic. The town was incorporated in 1891, with the first mayor being the rancher upon whose land it stood, Thomas Benton Hoover. By the early 1900s, it would have three general stores, a bank, flour mill, drug store, jewelry and optical shop, and livery stable. The Fossil Fire Company was formed in 1901 with 34 volunteers. By 1905, Fossil had a population of 800 people, roughly the same number as Prineville. And, like Prineville, in 1905 Fossil was a county seat.

As noted above, by 1892, many people in the northeast corner of Central Oregon wanted to form their own small county and avoid the long journeys to Prineville, Condon, and Canyon City. A campaign was launched to take parts of Crook and Grant counties and establish a new county seat at Mitchell or Waldron. The effort came to naught, but the discontented residents persevered. They tried again three years later, seeking to form a new county. Again, they failed, but again persevered.

Leading the charge was a 30-year-old shoemaker's son who had been born and raised in Scotland, James Simpson Stewart. Trained in his native country as a journalist, he had arrived in Fossil to work as a *Journal* reporter. He became its editor in 1890 and in that capacity crusaded vigorously for the creation of a new county. Against the opposition of people at Condon in particular, Stewart editorialized continuously about the benefits that a new county would bring, and did not allow the two defeats to discourage him.

Stewart's most important ally became R.N. "Mose" Donnelly of Richmond. He had been elected as a Grant County representative to the legislature. In 1899, Donnelly introduced a bill in Salem to create a new county from parts of Crook, Grant, and Gilliam. Over the fierce opposition of the town of Condon in Gilliam County, Donnelly managed to get the bill through, and on February 17, 1899, the new county came into existence. It included 2,500 people spread across 1,656 square miles and possessing about $1 million in taxable property. It was named Wheeler County, in honor of pioneer stage operator Henry Wheeler.

William W. Kennedy, a school superintendent in his early sixties (a graduate of California's State Normal School in San Jose) became the first county judge. Other officials appointed by Gov. Geer included commissioner Eugene Looney, clerk George O. Butler, treasurer George S. Carpenter, school superintendent O.B. Mills, and stock inspector Frank Peaslee. Fossil became the temporary seat, and Stewart crusaded strongly to win that distinction for it permanently. On June 4, 1900—the 16th anniversary of the political triumph of the Moonshiners—an election was held to determine where the permanent Wheeler County seat should be located. Twickenham received 267 votes, Spray 82, but Fossil triumphed with 436. Seven months later, the county court accepted a $9,025 bid from A.F. Peterson to build a courthouse.

Henry Wheeler, the county's namesake, founded one of its big ranching enterprises. He formed a partnership with Daniel M. and Joshua W. French, well-known bankers at The Dalles, but later sold his interest to D.E. and J. Wood Gilman. This firm, the Gilman-French Land & Livestock Company, later owned 38,120 acres of deeded land, including the Corn Cob, Prairie, Sutton, Hoyt, and O.K. ranches.

On the west side of the Central Oregon region, people were settling on land very different from that found in Wheeler County. When two former North Dakota schoolteachers arrived in Crook County, they asked someone at the Deschutes Irrigation & Power Company where would be the best place to buy land under the Carey Act. The parcel recommended to them was 20 miles north of Bend next to the right-of-way for a planned canal (and also near the route of a proposed railroad, never built). Frank and Josephine Redmond acquired 80 acres of land at the place mentioned, and pitched a tent.

Many homesteaders lived in tents after their arrival in Crook County. New-comers would live on isolated homesteads in these flimsy accommodations until lumber became available from one of the area's few sawmills or they could afford to buy wood and nails, and possibly hire labor, to build something better. Some-times, entire hamlets were composed temporarily of tents. During the homestead boom era from the late 19th century until the First World War, it was common to see families living on the Great Sandy Desert in tents in the same way that contemporary Arabs were living in tents in the Sahara.

A problem faced by desert dwellers was the lack of water, even along the right-of-ways of irrigation canals. For a year after their arrival, the Redmonds had to haul water to their homestead in wooden barrels from Cline Falls, six miles away. Friends arrived before irrigation water did. The Ezra Eby family, former next-door neighbors of the Redmonds in North Dakota, bought 80 acres of land nearby. Then B.A. Kendall, also from North Dakota, pitched a tent and built a barn on 80 acres of land that he had bought. William Buckley, Frank McCaffery, and Z.T. McClay were others who moved there with their families before the irri-gation canal was completed. By 1905, the town of Redmond was well started.

In 1906, the canal company sent water through the canal, and in the fol-lowing year a well was drilled at the town. A 10,000-gallon tank was installed in 1910. That was the same year the town was incorporated (recording a population of 216) and when the Redmond High School was built. The first meeting of the town council convened in July, chaired by Mayor F.M. White and attended by councilors Frank McCaffery, M.E. Lynch, H.E. Jones, G.W. Wells, Guy E. Dobson, and Dr. J.F. Hosch.

Close friends Dobson and Lynch had only just arrived in town from Port-land. Dobson had mentioned to Lynch that he planned to open a bank in Red-mond, and Lynch said to let him know if the area looked promising. If it did, he said, he and his partner J.R. Roberts would go there and build a store. In 1910, they did. Within a few years, the Lynch & Roberts Department Store was also operating a profitable mail order department that posted catalogs all over Central Oregon, even beyond the Mauries.

By the time Lynch & Roberts opened its door there were many other busi-nesses in Redmond. Among the most important was the Redmond Hotel, owned by Rowlee and Whitted, built in 1905. It was the town's first frame building. The second, erected that same year, was a mercantile store, Ehret Brothers. Other businesses established before the town was incorporated included a brickyard owned by the Advance Construction Company of Portland, a two-story building put up by J.S. Jackson that housed a furniture and hardware business, Harry Gant's Redmond Livery Barn, two newspapers (the *Oregon Hub* and *Redmond Spokesman*), and two banks, one established by G.L. Ehlers in 1908 and Guy Dobson's Redmond Bank of Commerce, which opened in 1909.

By 1911, in addition to the above businesses, Redmond had three saloons, another hotel, three restaurants, two feed stores, three blacksmith shops, four confectionaries, two lumberyards, two drug stores, two transfer lines, two barber shops, two meat markets, two hardware stores, another mercantile store, five real estate agencies, two bowling alleys, two billiard halls, and other businesses, as well as professional people, including four lawyers, two dentists, two photographers, and two doctors. Also, Redmond had developed an impressive number of public facilities and civic organizations. It had a skating rink, brass band and orchestra, public library, reading club, fire department, commercial club, ladies auxiliary to the commercial club, basketball team, social dancing club, four fraternal clubs, and five church organizations. It also had a city water plant, electric light system, and telephone office.

An early event in Redmond's history was a clash of church and state, or at least of a churchman with local government officials. In 1912, the town's Methodist preacher, J.M. Crenshaw, informed Gov. Oswald West that councilor H.E. Jones was holding poker games in a rear room of the Redmond Hotel. West was no figurehead governor; he was probably the most proactive of any of Oregon's chief executives. Only a month earlier, he had warned that if Central Oregon towns continued to flaunt the state's laws he would send in the militia to enforce them. West now sent an undercover agent to Redmond. The agent sat in on a game, then arrested Jones and another participant, town marshal Z.T. McClay. West demanded their resignations, and received them. Later, local residents became so fed up with Crenshaw's admonitions that the community drummed him out. He sued 15 residents for $50,000 in retaliation, but received a judgment for only $4.13.

West's threat had not been an idle one. The following year he warned city officials in the Snake River community of Copperfield to suppress lawlessness there or he would use the militia to do it for them. Basically, it was the same message he had sent to Redmond. Copperfield's officials ignored him. After he heard that there had been illegal drinking and gambling in Copperfield during Christmas, West sent his 25-year-old secretary and a half-dozen militiamen by train to Baker County. With a large crowd watching, the secretary, Miss Hobbs, presented the town council with a letter from West demanding their resignations. When they refused, the militiamen stepped forward and arrested the officials. They then posted "closed" notices on the businesses around town. Before that day, Copperfield had been a booming town with two hotels and a school, as well as plentiful saloons and casinos, but it never recovered, and died.

Just west of Redmond, the road past old Camp Polk became a heavily traveled route after 1880. Numerous immigrants from the Willamette Valley came this way into Central Oregon, while eastern Oregonians visiting friends or kin on the west side went the opposite direction over the same route. Cattle bound for the new ranches of Central Oregon had often been driven past of the old camp. Later, it was great flocks of sheep—tens of thousands of them—driven by valley woolgrowers to summer grazing lands in the Cascades and points east, then returning to the Willamette Valley in the autumn before the first snow. Salt for the sheep and supplies for the shepherds were driven over the same route on pack horses all during the summer.

People began to settle near the Samuel Hindman ranch (established ca. 1870)—so many that in 1883 they established a school, which in a couple of years had about 30 pupils. In the summer of 1888, a post office was installed at John J. Smith's store. Smith asked his customers to suggest a name. Jacob N. Quiberg proposed that they call the community Three Sisters. Smith sent this name to the Post Office Department, which promptly struck "Three" and accepted Sisters. Smith remained postmaster for a decade before he sold his homestead and post office to Alex Smith, who in turn sold a half-interest to his own brother Robert, who became the new postmaster. They moved the post office into a new, larger store that they built nearby, sharing space there with a dance hall. It was these same brothers who, in July 1901, platted the town of Sisters.

Late in 1904, the *Prineville Herald* described Sisters as having a hotel, saloon, livery barn, large school building, blacksmith shop, real estate office, and two stores—one owned by Smith and Wilt and the other by Alex Smith. Four miles west of town on the bank of Pole Creek stood W.T.E. Wilson's sawmill. Six years later another Prineville newspaper would report that there were three sawmills within a five-mile radius of Sisters producing lumber for homesteaders and for use by the railroad in bridge building.

For several years the community had no church. Once a month, the Rev. C.P. Bailey of the Prineville Baptist Church rode over and conducted services in the Sisters school. John Dennis donated two town lots at the corner of Main and Spruce for a church, apparently sometime during or after 1912 when he built the Hotel Sisters. A Presbyterian church went up on the lots and the Rev. Ralph Towne preached from its pulpit.

The year 1912 was especially significant for Sisters. Dennis built his hotel that year, and the town got a two-year high school. It and the lower grades were all housed in a two-story, six-room building. George Aitken arrived in town that year from Baker City and became the proprietor of the drug store, which housed a soda fountain and the post office, and his wife became the postmistress as well as the librarian. Aitken briefly published a newspaper, the *Sisters Herald*. Although

Aitken was principally known as a small village businessman with a knack for making delicious ice cream, in later years he would emerge as a civic leader whose influence extended far beyond his own community. That year, too, John Wilt sold his 320-acre ranch west of town to John Allen, who the next year sold it to Meredith Bailey. His wife, Maida, a former librarian at Stanford University and Reed College, would later become one of the area's most prominent citizens.

In a precursor to the now widely known Sisters Rodeo, in 1914 the town held a three-day-long fair and race meet that drew hundreds of spectators from all over Central Oregon as well as 150 Warm Springs Indians. Small though it remained, Sisters was already an important town in the region, showing a talent for projecting its influence beyond its size and attracting people of skill and ability.

Nearby, Culver was a town that traveled. It moved twice. Also, it underwent several name changes. Prior names were Haystack, Opal Prairie, and Perryville. It acquired its final moniker when O.G. Culver became the postmaster in Perryville, where he ran the general store. The Post Office Department listed the name as Culver. This community, later to be remembered as Old Culver, soon had a hotel, boarding school, barber shop, blacksmith shop, and general store as well as a school. Dr. W.H. Snook arrived from Sherman County about 1902 and practiced there for a couple of years until he filed on a homestead just south of Madras.

Culver moved again in response to rumors that a railroad would be built through Opal Prairie. In order to be on the line's route, residents picked everything up and moved five miles west to Dan Swift's homestead. This was the final move, and the railroad did find the town there. Electricity arrived about 1905 and a telephone line to connect Culver to Prineville. By that time Culver had two hotels, two churches, two general stores, as well as a lumberyard, weekly newspaper, drug store, and grain warehouse. O.G. Culver remained as the postmaster of New Culver until his death in 1939.

In the area that later became Jefferson County, many small hamlets came into existence as an increasing flood of homesteaders arrived in that and neighboring localities. As in the other areas, the people who settled in these hamlets hoped and often believed that their communities would survive, prosper, and grow large. Most of the hamlets, here as elsewhere, died. A few survived. Of these, Madras became the most successful.

About 1887, Orla Hale entered the basin that later became the site of Madras. He took up land and increased his ownership to include 1,400 acres of the best real estate in the locality. Other people were also attracted to the area, and the population grew. In 1904, John Palmehn filed a plat for a town called "Palmain," but postal officials said it might be confused with Parmen or Palmer. Finally, the name Madras was chosen. For many decades there has been a dispute about how this choice was arrived at. One version is that the town was named after a piece of Madras cloth in a store; the other that its first postmaster, Max Wilson, suggested it be named after the famous city in India. The second version is probably correct. According to the *Madras Pioneer* of February 2, 1905, when the community's founders were very much still around: "The famous city from which our town has derived its name is the third city in India."

Gradually the new town grew, its economy based on ranching and farming. By December 1909, a Portland firm advocating investment in the new community declared that it really did exist: "You can find Madras on your map." Less than a year later, Madras was officially incorporated, in March 1910. Early businesses included two general stores, a couple of saloons, a blacksmith shop, and other firms. The Madras Milling & Mercantile Company, owned by Max Putz, Henry Dietzel, and Simon Peter Conroy, operated both a general store and a flour mill that produced several brands of unbleached flour.

Three physicians took up residence early: Dr. W.H. Snook, originally from Sherman County via Old Culver, who started the town's first drugstore and became something of a local institution for almost a half century; Dr. T.A. Long, like Snook a farmer and drugstore owner, originally from Missouri; and Dr. Homer D. Haile, from Oneida, New York, who was said to have been a superbly skilled and intelligent physician when sober. Telephone service in the basin was established on the line from Shaniko to Prineville. Early churches included the First Baptist (1905), United Methodist (1907), and St. Patrick's Catholic (1911). The first one-room school in the basin had been established in 1902, with Charles Crowfoot as teacher. A second room and another teacher were added in a couple of years, a third room in 1908.

Smallpox broke out in Madras in 1909 and again in 1911. Unlike the great Shaniko-Prineville epidemic of 1903, however, both of these outbreaks were contained and neither took more than a couple of lives.

About 25 miles south of Shaniko and 40 miles north of Prineville, a town suddenly sprang into existence on the banks of Trout Creek in 1898. The community of Ashwood grew up in what previously was sheep pasture. Valuable ore had been discovered in the area as early as 1884 by Whitfield T. Wood when digging a well. Wood organized a mining company, but a later discovery that led to a boom was as accidental as his own. A shepherd was minding sheep on the Jones ranch in 1896 when he picked up some float quartz that he took home and had assayed. It held a rich deposit of gold and also some silver. The Oregon King Mining Company was created to develop the resource, selling stock to several people, among them Whitfield T. Wood. Eventually others became principals in the enterprise, notably Hay Creek Ranch proprietors Jack Edwards and Sen. Charles M. Cartwright.

Cartwright was sued by Thomas J. Brown of Roseburg, who in 1897 had discovered quartz while he was herding sheep on Trout Creek. Brown had named his own claim the Oregon King, but Cartwright had claimed the same deposit. Meanwhile, news of the Oregon King discoveries led to a gold rush in which

Wool buyers at Shaniko in 1910. *Oregon Historical Society 21067*

hundreds of prospectors took up claims along and beyond Trout Creek. Other notable mines included the Morning Star and the Red Jacket.

The Brown lawsuits and other litigation forced the closure of the Oregon King, and court action dragged on for many years, even decades. Occasionally a break would come in the legal action and the Oregon King would reopen, only to be shut down again by a new lawsuit.

It has often been noted that the prospectors seeking gold and silver along Trout Creek cast aside a valuable red ore found there in abundance: cinnabar. Meanwhile, the influx of prospectors to Trout Creek meant a new town emerging on both banks in 1898, with a post office opening the same year. Ashwood was a combined name referring to Ash Butte and founder Whitfield T. Wood. James and Addie Wood platted the 15-block townsite on their homestead in June 1899. A school went up in 1900, and the following year Max Lueddemann began publishing the weekly *Ashwood Prospector*. Other businesses included two hotels, saloons, and stores, and for awhile it was a major Central Oregon town. Ashwood benefited because the Trout Creek gold rush occurred simultaneously with the dramatic increase in the region's homesteading activity.

Meanwhile, no hopes for railroads, gold, or industrialization motivated Indians on the Warm Springs reservation to invest, promote, or scheme. The tribes' members basically went about their traditional activities—growing crops, raising sheep, fishing, collecting huckleberries, herding cattle, and the like, while the federal government pursued its national program to assimilate them and other Indians into the mainstream of American culture.

The first boarding school had been established at the agency in 1874, and the Simnasho boarding school in 1881. Students from the reservation began to attend the Salem Indian School in the 1880s. After the Simnasho school burned down in 1895, the Bureau of Indian Affairs built a new boarding school a couple of years later.

The first missionary appointed to the reservation, the Rev. R.N. Fee, had arrived with his wife in 1878 after previously working on the Nez Perce Reservation. The Nez Perce War, one of the few if not the only war in which a great number of settlers and other white Americans sympathized with the Indians instead of the cavalry that chased them, had been fought the previous year. Fee, a United Presbyterian, arrived at Warm Springs the same year a typhoid-malaria epidemic devastated the tribes. Another four years passed before the first church building was erected.

While agriculture, supplemented by the hawking of huckleberries and leather crafts, remained the foundation of the reservation economy, the lumber production that in Central Oregon had begun at the agency remained a major contributor to the local economy. A sawmill was built on Mill Creek in 1880, and the Seekseequs and He-He sawmills were built in 1915.

By that time, the government had given all the Indians new names—"American" names.

22
HOMESTEADERS
1890s–1920s

"S OMETIMES NOW,** when the jets thunder over my home in Portland and break the sound barrier with a terrible blast," Isabel McKinney told the *Oregon Journal* in 1960 (and quoted by Thomas Vaughan, 1981), "my thoughts go back to the log cabin on the edge of the desert, the sage with its pungent odor, the cowboys who always managed to drop in just at mealtime, the sheriff on his galloping horse, ever searching for his man, the purple sunsets, and the lonely howl of a roving coyote."

People had been homesteading in Central Oregon ever since the first white settlers arrived. The cattle barons usually got their start by filing a homestead claim. After five years of occupation and making "improvements," a claimant was granted ownership to the land by the government. Homesteaders, however, also could "pre-empt," gaining title to their homestead earlier by paying $1.25 per acre. Congress in 1909 extended the amount of land that a homesteader could claim from 160 acres up to 320 acres. This revision of the Homestead Act encouraged more people to take claims, and these people were further encouraged by the promotional campaigns of the railroads and their economic allies.

The railroads had good reason to promote homesteading. In order to encourage the building of railways, the federal, state, and local governments had granted

Central Oregon stages at the Hotel Shaniko. *Oregon Historical Society 56059*

large tracts of land to the railroad companies. Most railroads were built for the specific purpose of obtaining these grants, exactly as the earlier road promoters had laid their trails to collect similar grants. However, the land by itself had no use to the railroads: these companies did not grow crops or harvest timber.

The profit came not from owning the land, but from selling it. After it was subdivided and sold, the railroads made money shipping the products of the buyers, whether it was produce grown by new farmers or lumber cut by new saw-mills. The more produce, the more lumber, the more commodities to ship, the more profit for the railroad. It therefore became advantageous for the railroads to sell not only their own land, but to have other vacant acreage near their tracks filled in with farmers, mills, or other shippers. The revisions of the Homestead Act, the disappearance of available land elsewhere in the country, and the arrival of the railroads in Crook County happened at the same time. This set the stage for a boom in homesteading.

The railroads, and land promoters who were tied to them, as well as other developers whose interests were in reclamation, real estate, or other associated enterprises, promoted Central Oregon throughout the United States and in foreign countries. The region was described in advertisements as a fertile land of great opportunity. Fruits and vegetables thriving on the very best land in the region were shown to prospective settlers as typical of what could be grown every-where in the region, and then shipped profitably to markets over a railroad that was projected to be built from The Dalles all the way to San Francisco. Aiding the efforts of the promoters was a statement by agricultural experts in the General Land Office in Washington, D.C., that the Great Sandy Desert was suitable for dry farming.

Railroad agents known as "locators" haunted trains throughout America, approaching travelers to pitch the opportunities abounding near Bend in Cen-tral Oregon and showing pictures of marvelous fruits and vegetables that they claimed had been grown there. In actuality, 19th century homesteaders in Crook County looked forward to their trips to the Willamette Valley in part because they could stock up on fruits and vegetables, but the potential suckers had no way of knowing this. Other "locators" were on the spot in Crook County to act as real estate brokers who would select the best possible land for a potential settler willing to pay them $100 for their expert opinions. Some agents of the railroads hid their affiliation, pretending to be independent, while they too tried to attract people to the Great Sandy.

Other land companies also became involved. The activities of Alexander Drake have been mentioned. The big California ranching empire of Miller & Lux got involved by buying the old Central Military Road Company grant in central and eastern Oregon, dividing it up into 20-acre parcels, and then selling it. Eventually, much of this land would become county property when absentee owners failed to pay their taxes.

And so, people from California, Portland, Chicago, Germany, and numerous other places arrived to stake claims in Central Oregon. They were taken out by locators to land that in summer was tall with bunch grass, where they were told that as soon as the acreage was plowed or as soon as the projected new irrigation canal was dug, they could plant almost any crop imaginable. And they bit. Many, many came, and bought. In 1890, there were 622 farms in Crook County. In 1910, a scant 20 years later, Crook and Wheeler counties had a total of 1,742 farms. Ten years after that, despite a marked decline in the land boom and the abandoning of many homesteads, there were 2,243. This was all good news to the railroads, irrigation companies, and real estate promoters.

But not everyone was cordial to the homesteaders. Most ranchers did not welcome them. Indeed, some ranchers bitterly hated them. Homesteaders were taking public domain that had been used by stock raisers to graze cattle, sheep, and horses. Even if homesteaders did not plant crops or put up buildings, or have dogs that harassed or even killed range stock, they fenced in their new land to keep out free roaming livestock. Sometimes, a man riding over open country to town found on his return trip, later the same day, that his route was blocked by a new fence. Cattle, unused to fences, occasionally became entangled in them and were cut up.

Ranchers told some homesteaders to leave, or else. They also might continue to graze their cattle on land that now was included in a homesteader's new claim. If a fence had been put up and the rancher believed his stock had a right to be on the inside because of prior use, he might cut down the fence to let his herd in. Some homesteaders became so frustrated by this behavior that they finally gave up and departed. The Prineville Land & Livestock Company was notorious for grazing its sheep on homestead lands. Fights erupted. The Muddy Creek region was frequently the site of conflict. In 1900, a Prineville Land & Livestock shepherd named Breuner gunned down homesteader Tom Reilly on a ridge north of Black Rock in a range dispute.

Not all of the big stockmen were as hostile to homesteaders as the Muddy Creek outfit. In the Pony Butte district near Ashwood, many homesteaders survived only because of help extended to them by the biggest stock baron in the vicinity, Thomas Hamilton. The homesteaders there referred to him as "Uncle Tom" in a kindly way, and to his wife as "Mother Hamilton." But people like Thomas Hamilton, and local sheep baron Jack Edwards too, were the exception.

As much as many ranchers hated homesteaders, the latter also despised the big stockmen. Even before they arrived in Central Oregon, many homesteaders already had formed a deep and bitter resentment of the ranching class. Homesteaders huddling in tents and rough-lumber shanties on the Great Sandy and Lower Desert especially resented the rich ranchers living, what the homesteaders perceived, as lives of ease in fine, big, painted houses in Prineville and the Crooked River country.

The most famous Oregon cattleman at the beginning of the land boom was Peter French down in Harney County. French was also the rancher most bitterly hated by homesteaders. The day after Christmas, 1897, French was helping his vaqueros move cattle into a corral. Suddenly, homesteader Ed Oliver appeared on a horse and charged the unarmed French, who he shot in the head. Oliver then fled, and French's unarmed crew did not pursue him. Later it was widely rumored that a group of homesteaders had drawn straws to determine who would kill French. Oliver was later arrested, but a jury of homesteaders found him not guilty.

Cattlemen in the Harney Valley and elsewhere claimed that homesteaders had formed secret societies to kill livestock, burn hay, and commit other financially damaging acts against ranchers. As early as 1883, the *Oregonian* was reporting that buyers could not find herds to buy in Oregon because homesteaders had broken up the open range. The article noted that the only parts of the state where great droves of cattle still fed on the open range was in Lake County and the areas around Prineville. A few years later, a Prineville newspaper editor would comment upon a cattle drive through town as a nostalgic sight, although thousands of sheep passed through annually. Wild and isolated Prineville (still two days journey by stagecoach from The Dalles) had become settled.

Homesteaders thought it ridiculous that a man would wish to deny thousands of acres of land to his fellow human beings so that he could keep cows on it. On the other hand, cattle barons appeared to be contemptuous of poor people; their actions suggested their belief in a greater worthiness of cattle to occupy land rather than human beings. The homesteaders' viewpoint is illustrated in a 1902 history of Grant County by C.H. Voegtly:

"But the settlement of the country has indirectly as well as directly, affected the interests of the stock king in Grant County. The Walla Walla country, which now produces its millions of bushels of wheat annually, was formerly a vast stock range. The same was true of the Pendleton country, the Palouse country, in fact, of all the old settled communities of the inland empire. Stockmen have retreated before the advance of civilization and their field of operations has ever been narrowing, until now the remaining ranges are greatly overcrowded. Disputes and even feuds have already arisen and the end of the troubles between the different interests cannot be foreseen. Cattle and sheep men encroach upon the rights of the settler or the miner and the result is a damage suit. They encroach upon the supposed or understood rights of one another and disputes are the outcome, too often ending in the use of firearms either against the offending animals or the men who have charge of them. All classes of residents are united in opposition to foreign sheep and cattle…driven in from adjoining counties to spend the summer in Grant county and eat out its substance without paying any taxes to the exchequer. To remedy the evils and prevent trouble various measures have been introduced in Congress, among them being bills providing for the leasing of public lands to stockmen. The leasing system…has been generally considered as likely to conserve the interests of the large stockmen to the detriment of the farmer and small cattle raiser and the general welfare of the country, hence has been bitterly opposed by the masses. The conclusion of the whole matter is not far to seek. The stockman himself must become a home builder. He must reduce his herds to such numbers as can be supported by his own proper holdings and such public lands of no value to agriculture as lie adjacent to his home and can be controlled by him, through his ownership of water rights. Such land as is arable must be cultivated intensively and such domestic animals as he keeps around him must be improved so as to yield a greater profit per head than did the range stock, valuable only for their hides and flesh."

Such arguments failed to impress cattle barons who warned (to general amusement) that if the encroachments continued there might come a day when poor people in America would not be able to afford beef. Merchants favored the homesteaders because their greater numbers meant more customers, more money. Public opinion also favored the homesteaders. Crook County supported stockmen more than most areas, but even here many believed that the day for such enterprises had passed. A few stockmen agreed. Mays & Son did, and sold its remaining 2,000 head of cattle at The Dalles for $30,000. But most stockmen held on, intent upon passing down to their children what they believed to be theirs.

A pattern developed for these homesteaders. A family would file on 160 acres of desert that looked like pastureland. They would build a one-room shack with a lean-to bedroom using rough lumber from a Grizzly Mountain sawmill. They hauled water daily from the nearest well in a canvas-covered barrel, until they dug a cistern. They worked very hard clearing their land of rocks, sagebrush, and juniper. After several years of insufficient rain to grow seeds into crops, they would give up and abandon the homestead.

Moist summers with many thunderstorms, and cold, wet winters with great accumulations of snow, helped the land promoters between the years 1902 and 1913. Homesteaders arriving during the early part of this period in particular could not be blamed for believing that this was the norm. But it was not the norm. At Bend, twice the average normal precipitation fell in 1907, and other years during this period also saw very high amounts of snow and rain. When they had settled in, though, the homesteaders quickly discovered that little water was immediately available. Getting water became one of the great hardships of their lives.

During the years of the land boom, homesteaders were daily on the move throughout Central Oregon, fetching water. Some hauled water 12 miles from its source to their farms. Some men, such as John Isham, Frank Loveland, and Fred Waymire in the Madras basin, dug good wells. Others drilled down 1,000 feet without encountering a trace of liquid.

Homesteaders without their own wells—and that was the majority—had to get water from a neighbor's well or from rivers or railroad tanks. Sometimes, a homesteader's wife or a son would make the long trip to water over narrow, dusty desert roads, while the homesteader himself remained on the farm ripping up sagebrush and junipers. Sometimes, the homesteader himself made the journey at night after a day spent working in his field. Once there, if it was a well, he had to wait in line behind other farmers to reach the hand pump and fill his barrel. Other homesteaders had to go over one of the tight little trails down into the Deschutes canyon, then turn around and begin the long, sometimes dangerous, ascent. Sometimes, for those going down to the Deschutes or living in the Great Sandy's drier areas, a homesteader might spend an entire day getting water. Some used huge tanks, others a multitude of barrels, wash tubs, or any other available containers.

Once they had a temporary supply of water, homesteaders were frugal about using it to avoid making any more long, dreary, wearing journeys than were necessary. Water was usually kept in one or more barrels. Barrels could leak, and water could evaporate or slosh out if carelessly left uncovered or dipped into. Barrels also could become a breeding ground for mosquitoes and cause typhoid and other diseases. Each bucket of water was used several times before being emptied onto flowers by the door or given to the animals. A homesteader, his wife, and all their children bathed in the same water, the man getting it fresh (unless it had already been used to wash the dishes) and the youngest boy getting it when dirtiest. No drop was wasted. Homesteaders put barrels under the eaves of their cabins and barns to catch rainwater. Cisterns helped preserve water, but drawing water from them to supply livestock every day was work. Little wonder that the most interesting subject to these people was irrigation.

Clearing land was the other backbreaking task that every homesteader faced. Imagining the day when his farm would be covered with lush wheat or other grain, a homesteader first had to rid it of sagebrush, junipers, and rocks. Sagebrush proved most difficult, its deep roots preventing even teams of horses from pulling it out. The most efficient method of extracting it, unfortunately, was to use a grub hoe rather than a mule or horse, which meant aching muscles for a man. Plentiful rocks lay atop the thin ground over thick lava beneath it; homesteaders also wrestled with removing these. Many such rocks were used to build walls along property lines or other borders—walls that can still be seen snaking across the desert today.

If the planted wheat came up, it had to be threshed. Some threshing machines were used by a whole community. The neighbors worked together, and each man in turn had his wheat threshed. Other machines were taken in a circuit around a locality. Ed Kutcher and A.P. Clark, for example, hauled threshing machines around, accompanied by a work crew of more than a dozen men and a cook wagon. A homesteader who paid for threshing supplied the operator with hay for the horse teams, sacks for the threshed wheat, and wood for the fireboxes.

In past times, stockmen had come to Prineville to buy enough supplies to last them a year on their isolated ranches. The newly arriving homesteaders, however, could get most of what they needed at numerous small communities that sprang up on the deserts to serve them. Supplies and merchandise mostly came down by train to Shaniko, and then were transferred to freight wagons to be hauled to Prineville for distribution, or hauled directly to general stores and stage stations in the little desert hamlets. Later, after the railroads reached further south, Bend replaced Prineville as the main distribution center, although supplies now could also be acquired at Madras, Redmond, and other communities along the tracks.

No longer did pack trains struggle over the mountains; no longer did a single misstep send a freight wagon, driver, and horse team hurtling down into Cow Canyon. But costs remained high. Shipping by rail was expensive, and the freighters hauling goods from the depots to hamlet stores or directly to farmers also charged whatever the traffic would bear. The homesteader, already strapped, found the cost of living on his desert farm high. Still, he seldom had to ride all the way to Prineville.

La Monta, ca. 1909, when residents could still believe that it would become one of the important towns of Central Oregon. *Bowman Museum, Crook County Historical Society*

23

FARMING TOWNS
1890s–1920s

THE INFLUX OF HOMESTEADERS led to growth for many existing small communities and the establishment of numerous new ones. Today it is difficult to appreciate how widespread these hamlets were, scattered amid the forests and across the Great Sandy and Lower deserts. Some of the hamlets survive today, but most have vanished.

An atlas, published in the 1940s, identifies the communities along the Prineville to Maupin railway lines as Wilton (approximately five miles west of Prineville), McAllister, Gateway, South Junction, and North Junction. East of the tracks, but within the boundaries of Jefferson and Wasco counties, were Grizzly, Hay Creek, Ashwood, Antelope, and Shaniko. Today, Wilton and McAllister are forgotten, and O'Neil remembered principally as a siding. In homesteading times, the brothers O'Neil had a general store at the site. Oddly missing from the map is Lone Pine, still a community on Crooked River that was originally homesteaded by Dr. James R. Sites. His ranch received its name from a single pine that stood above the junipers. Nearby, also along the Crooked River, the hamlet of Forest grew up around the 1,200-acre Frank Forest ranch. Forest operated a store that sold goods to nearby homesteaders, in much the same way Bill Brown did at Buck Creek and Jack Edwards at Hay Creek.

Opal City was named after a small section of the Crooked River called Opal Springs, where, until it was ruined by dynamiting in the vicinity, very smooth opal-shaped stones were found. Abe Merchant filed the first homestead claim in the area in 1894, but it was not until 1909 that four partners incorporated the Opal City Land Company with $25,000 capital to develop an old 160-acre homestead. It boomed, at first as a tent town, in the style of Madras and so many other desert communities that were born after the railroad arrived in 1912. The Wilson family opened a restaurant, while the Dee mill at Grizzly sold rough lumber for houses and other buildings. To supply its water storage tank, the railroad drilled a 1,600-foot-deep well.

By the time the 1940s atlas appeared with Opal City but without Lone Pine, Opal City was nothing but a section of crested wheat grass owned by the federal government. Drought in the 1920s drove out the farmers, and the government later bought the land. However, it was easy for anyone in Central Oregon to identify someone who had been born and raised in Opal City because the railroad's well, from which the homesteaders took drinking water, contained a mineral its users never suspected of being present: fluoride. It turned the children's teeth brown, and the condition was permanent.

La Monta also did not appear on the 1940s map, though a few years earlier local homesteading activity had made this desert community a thriving little town. Jerry Achey first homesteaded in the area in 1883, and Col. Smith settled nearby in 1887 on his Rimrock Springs Ranch. Smith irrigated 40 acres of alfalfa with water from the springs. Bill Rodgers had the first post office in 1890, when the community was called "Desert." When the post office closed in 1892, the postmistress was Lizzie Pringle.

In 1896, however, a new post office was established, this time at the Helfrich farm, with pretty young Kate Helfrich as postmistress. To her went the honor of naming the new post office, and with it the community it served. As related in Chapter 18, she initially named it "La Mont" after nearby Grizzly Mountain. Postal authorities disallowed it, however, saying it sounded too similar to existing towns. So she added an "a" to "Mont" and inadvertently gave linguists ever after something to complain about. The post office would move frequently before rural delivery began, usually housed in a La Monta general store or Walt Rice's drugstore.

Surrounded by dozens of 160-acre farms growing wheat, oats, barley, and rye, and with many houses boasting gardens outside their back doors that grew watermelon, squash, corn, beans, and other vegetables and fruits, the town gave every impression of being permanent. The grange hall—the first in all of Central Oregon—had more than 100 members. A stage stop was located just south of town on Joe and Rosie Weigand's ranch.

Businesses in La Monta included a general store, dry goods store, one or two saloons, a livery barn, drugstore, blacksmith shop, telephone switch board, and dance hall. A schoolhouse was built in 1901, and also was used as a church and Sunday school. The town had its own baseball, football, and basketball teams as well as a literary society. Popular here as in many homesteader communities on the Great Sandy were rabbit drives, or bunny bops. More about that later. In 1910, La Monta also had an oil well, drilled by rancher Frank Forest and Frank Loveland on the Taylor Place. Like many other such efforts in the region, it created a great stir and caused many acres of land to go under lease for oil exploration, but produced no oil.

The drought that killed Opal City did the same to La Monta. With the rains and heavy snows gone, farms became unproductive. In 1934, the federal government bought up the land. Today, the ground upon which La Monta once thrived is part of the Crooked River National Grassland.

Nearby was Grizzly, with a ball team that played against both La Monta and Culver. This community could trace its origins back to James Blakely's arrival not far away in the 1860s. Ranchers had resided in the Grizzly Mountain locality ever after, with about 150 families living around the town of Grizzly.

The community started in 1900 when Ed Wills built a store here, which included a post office, plus a large dance hall on the second floor. The store became the center of most community activities. Wills sold out in 1913 to John Lewis. A fire destroyed the business, but Lewis replaced it, although the new building was smaller. A big stage station stood nearby on the former Henry Cleek ranch; Morrow & Keenan bought it in 1900. In the early years, some homesteaders were able to keep their land and even bought more acreage after the style of such big outfits as Morrow & Keenan and the Hay Creek Ranch. Then drought settled over the region; most of those who had remained sold their farms and went elsewhere to seek employment.

The Ashwood vicinity experienced an influx of homesteaders that lasted from about 1908 until 1925. Pony Butte and other neighborhoods became thickly-settled. Other parts of the northeast country, such as Donnybrook and Antelope, saw their own populations increase.

West of the Deschutes and south of the Metolius, on the section known as the Lower Desert, more new communities came into existence. Lower Desert lands looked good during the very wet years of the early 20th century. No sagebrush or juniper grew there, but rather lush bunchgrass as high as a man's belt. Homesteaders began streaming in about 1908 or 1910, and the soil at first did not disappoint them. A local newspaper in March 1911 reported that settlers had planted orchards and were growing bountiful crops of potatoes, onions, corn, other vegetables, rye, wheat, timothy, clover, and alfalfa.

This led to the emergence of two communities at opposite ends of the desert, both founded in the early 1900s. Rancher Nick Lambert established a mercantile business to serve homesteaders. Soon, a Mr. Ransom started a blacksmith shop, there was a postmistress, and a barbershop opened. This was Grandview. Settlers built a school here, which in its heyday had as many as 75 pupils. The other community was started on J.T. Monical's land and called Geneva, in honor of the postmaster's wife. Settlers established a school, which eventually had as many as 40 pupils. It also was used for church services. Just as ranches such as Morrow & Keenan and Hay Creek acquired homesteads in their vicinity, the big ranches near the Lower Desert bought up acreage abandoned by farmers, who were driven out by drought.

The Cove, homesteaded by Clark Rogers in 1879 and traded for a house in Prineville to T.F. McCallister in 1888, was sold intact to William Boegli for $10,000 in 1905. Boegli had been adopted by the McCallisters the same year that they acquired The Cove. A 12-year-old orphan from San Francisco, he grew up to become a teacher, school superintendent, and first judge of Jefferson County. Boegli did not divide and sell the land, but kept it intact until 1941, when he sold it to the state highway commission for $16,000. The state converted the property into Cove Palisades State Park.

Several hamlets emerged with the arrival of the railroads in 1910–1911. Gateway, near the Jefferson-Wasco line, was one. It was born when the rails reached the site in 1910, and the town-to-be was named by a railroad water-pumper. A traveling salesman opened the first store, and the second built there included a post office. One building at Gateway served as a saloon during the evenings and weekends, and as a school for about a dozen pupils on weekdays.

A couple of railroad depots were built on Agency Plains. The area had good pasture for livestock, until homesteaders arrived and began stringing fences. Agency Plains was about 15 x 8 miles in size; Little Agency Plains to the south, 12 x 3 miles. The Oregon Trunk built a railway depot with a water tank, named Mecca, on Agency Plains in U.S. Cowles' alfalfa field. Attracted perhaps by the increasing numbers of homesteaders, and by the section hands the railroad housed near the depot, Will See built a store there and later added a house and grain warehouse. The Mecca post office was started in September 1911, and operated until the railroad was removed in 1924.

Another depot on Agency Plains was built on land belonging to G.A. Paxton and named after him. The Paxton place later had a grain warehouse. South of Agency Plains, the railroad established a station at Vanora, named in 1911 for resident Ora Vantassel. In addition to Vantassel's house and grain warehouse, Vanora consisted of a post office, saloon, school, and two stores. Vanora is best remembered today for a single incident that took place when its baseball team was playing the Warm Springs Indian team. A thunder storm came up and everyone scampered for cover. A hired man and three girls ran beneath a large juniper tree, where a team of horses hitched to a buggy were tied. A bolt of lightning hit the tree, killing the horses, and knocking the four people unconscious. Dr. Snook was summoned from Madras. He helped revive the four people, who all survived. The Vanora community, however, died in 1923, after the railroad was abandoned.

The town of Metolius, which still thrives today, began when Volney Williamson bought two homesteads secretly, hoping to profit from the impending arrival of the railroad. Indeed, he laid out and named the town. The area had been settled earlier by German Methodists, after they read an article about it in a German magazine.

Also surviving today, and indeed growing vigorously, but far from the railroad, is the community of Powell Butte, located southwest of Prineville. The town was named for the nearby buttes, the namesake of pioneer settler John Powell. Homesteaders moved into the area early in the 20th century, relying on dry farming, and hauling water from the Vandevert and a few other ranches that had readily available sources. In 1908, the Central Oregon Irrigation District ran a flume from the Deschutes River to Powell Butte, and the situation improved. In March 1909, a post office was established, with Moses Niswonger as the first postmaster. At that time, the town was about two miles south of where it stands today. J.E. Beckman later ran the post office in his hotel, and then Elof Johnson had it across the street in his store. In the 1920s, the new state highway bypassed Powell Butte, and Johnson decided to move his store two miles north to be on the route. The remainder of the town followed. By 1936, the population of the Powell Butte community was about 600.

Paulina had been founded in 1870, and its post office was established in 1880 with John T. Faulkner serving as postmaster. Livestock baron Bill Brown sometimes listed himself as a Paulina resident. Cornett had a stage station there, but the big businesses in the early 20th century were the Paulina Cash Store, operated by Lee Miller and George Ruba, and the Hotel Paulina, built by Elmer Clark in 1906. The hotel had a lounge, dining room, and kitchen on the first floor, and eight bedrooms upstairs. While a few homesteaders filed for land in the vicinity, the Paulina area remained a ranching district.

Post lies between Paulina and Prineville at the junction of the Crooked River and Newsome Creek. It is often assumed that the hamlet received its name because there was a post office there. Many small hamlets had little more than a post office, so it would seem logical enough that one such place might have such a moniker. In fact, Post was named for Wallace and Walter Post, who homesteaded there in 1886. Later homesteaders settled nearby, and patronized the Post store while they retrieved their mail from the Post office.

Many small communities developed in what is today Deschutes County, especially after the great homesteader onrush began about 1910. Some of these, notably LaPine, survive today, while others have disappeared without a trace. Not all hamlets were in the desert. Cline Falls was located near cascades of the same name. An early Prineville dentist named Cline settled there in 1891. At its peak, the community included two hotels, several stores, a school, jail, livery stable, post office, and newspaper.

Pringle Falls was an old stock-grazing area originally called Warm Springs. Homesteaders began arriving about 1911, and by the following year so many were present that a school district was formed. A community hall served the people at Pringle Falls, but never a store or post office. Now nothing remains of the once flourishing little community except abandoned cabins and crumbling old windmills.

LaPine was founded about 1910 by a speculator named Morrison, who planned to start a 28,000-acre irrigation project. Morrison's agent, Alfred Aya, mapped out a townsite that envisioned a hotel, stores, and other buildings. It was even sited on the projected route of the Oregon Trunk Railroad. The promoters began advertising LaPine's future prospects and even people already living in the vicinity took the bait. A few miles south stood the little town of Rosland, founded 30 years earlier by Frank Bogue and his son. Believing that the future lay with LaPine instead of their own community, the residents of Rosland moved their town to the new site. The Bogue store and Grandma Beasley's hotel were placed onto large carts and drawn by horse teams all the way to LaPine. Homesteaders were attracted to LaPine, too, but the irrigation scheme failed because Morrison had not secured enough water for so much land, some of which already had been taken by prior water rights claims. Also, the Oregon Trunk stopped up north, at Bend.

Homesteaders continued to move into the locality, however, and the LaPine Townsite Company continued to sell lots to would-be residents. Aya remained, and when a bank opened in the town in 1914 he became its president. E.N. Hurd established the *LaPine Intermountain* newspaper in 1911, and it lasted until 1934. At one time when LaPine's population was 40, the *Intermountain* had a circulation of 627. Glen Roper attached a saloon to Mrs. Beasley's hotel, and John Masten's sawmill provided settlers with lumber for houses and other buildings. By 1915, LaPine had 600 people, and when U.S. Highway 97 was routed through it, the town's future became more secure.

Many of the homesteaders coming after 1910 located claims in the Great Sandy Desert between Bend and Burns. Consequently, some hamlets emerged there. Millican, named for a homesteader, became one of the most famous little towns in Oregon, while remaining the smallest. It was a little store that housed a post office. Fame came in 1940 when *Ripley's Believe It or Not* identified it as the smallest post office in the entire world. At the time, Billie Rahn was the postmaster and sole resident of Millican.

Further down the Bend-Burns road, about 55 miles east of Bend, C.H. Coffey filed a homestead claim in 1913. Ray and Elizabeth Markham came along soon after and staked their own claim to land nearby, and then built a store. A post office was installed inside the store, and the town was named Brothers, allegedly because many of the settlers there were brothers of other settlers. A school was built later.

Next down the road was Hampton. In 1910 a hamlet with only two houses, Hampton eventually had a post office, store, lumberyard, schoolhouse, and a couple of dozen houses. The dry climate drove out most of the farmers and left the land for cattle grazing, but the hamlet still exists today.

Nearby was Halfway, located 75 miles east of Bend in the Hampton Valley. It began in 1910 when the Brookings family settled there. Observing the perpetual stream of homesteaders passing by, the Brookings decided that they could turn a good penny by converting their house into an inn. They called their ten-room facility the Halfway House, from which the hamlet took its name. Bert Meeks bought it in 1918. Author Joyce Gribskov (1980) noted that among the guests staying at Halfway House at one time or another were Idaho's Sen. William Borah, opera singer Madam Schuman Heink, and baseball player Christi Matchinson.

Another nearby hamlet was Rolyat, which was "Taylor" spelt backward. In 1910, its school had nine pupils. A couple of years later, the women of the community formed a literary society. Despite these early indications of a town a-borning, Rolyat vanished entirely.

Also close by was Imperial, a town promoted far beyond any semblance of its actual status or prospects. It came into existence about the same time as the neighboring communities but had speculators behind it. Based on brochures advertising Imperial—showing pictures of long, straight streets, fine buildings and water fountains, and palm trees—lots were bought by people throughout the United States as well as Canada, Australia, England, and China. The actual town, in 1913, consisted of a couple of stores, an unoccupied real estate office, a dance hall, post office, blacksmith shop, and two houses. Later, a schoolhouse, barbershop, and shoe store were added. Imperial's population reached 125 before it vanished from the Great Sandy.

Social life for the isolated homesteaders was actually richer than it is today for average Central Oregon residents. People visited one another. They knew one another. A farmer's wife living at La Monta would be on friendly or unfriendly terms with practically every other woman in the Grizzly Mountain locality, but also would know women living in other areas. They met at dances, pie and basket socials, church, school programs, fairs, literary society meetings, community picnics, rabbit hunts, sewing bees, and in stores. Men became acquainted at county fairs, horse races, barbershops, baseball games, saloons, hotels, and when doing agricultural and herding jobs. People greeted one another, talked, and exchanged news and gossip. Everybody knew everyone's views and business.

They actively sought one another's company. A dance at a Grandview house or a hall in Culver or Metolius might attract friends from La Monta or Madras. A baseball game in Prineville could draw people from Paulina, Redmond, Laidlaw, Silver Lake, Madras, or Powell Butte. An Independence Day celebration in Bend might bring participants from Madras, Prineville, La Monta, Paulina, Silver Lake, LaPine, Culver, or Pringle Falls. A school spelling bee in Fort Rock in Lake County might draw friends and relatives of some of the parents of the young participants from Laidlaw, Powell Butte, or Cline Falls. Life on the desert was not boring. People worked actively to keep it interesting, and, living in the time they did, they knew how to do it.

Most of the schools often doubled as community halls and churches, and were usually one-room affairs. Teachers were boarded in local homes and earned minimal salaries. In Crook County, a female teacher who married would lose her job, since she now had a husband to support her. The job then would go to some young maid who needed the money.

Male teachers were not uncommon and often were necessary to control the tough, unruly boys. A boxer named Andrew Larson was hired as an instructor by the La Monta school board after children there ran off a couple of predecessors. He took control swiftly by applying a leather harness strap that he carried in his pocket. Children often walked or rode horseback many miles to reach school. Fairview school in Jefferson County was a one-room schoolhouse with as many as 32 pupils. A big barn stood next to it for the students' horses. Some of the children rode as far as seven miles to reach the school, and then seven miles home. A former pupil of the Grandview school remembered attending in snowy, very cold weather. However, many schools in Central Oregon operated only in the warm months of the year, from late May until early autumn, because winter snow was a danger to children when traveling several miles to and from a schoolhouse.

Warm Springs Indians frequently visited the hamlets and homesteads. They sold huckleberries picked from below Mount Jefferson, leather crafts, and wicker baskets. They roamed far and wide across the region, bartering with ranchers on the Metolius, housewives in Bend, and store owners in Paulina. Their trade was two-way, and some merchants and settlers numbered Indians among their regular customers. Bands of gypsies were less common, but they, too, wandered through Crook County.

No homestead was without its milk cow and chickens, and many a home-steader's wife had a garden. Basic staples were purchased in the little hamlet stores. Meat and potatoes were the standard dinner fare, with beans, cottage cheese, and home-churned butter spread over homemade bread. Coffee was ground in the home coffee-grinder. Settlers also made their own soap, lye, and vinegar, and butchered their own cattle, pigs, sheep, and chickens. Unless, that is, a predator killed them first.

The great predator was the coyote, enemy to the homesteader's chickens as well as the rancher's sheep. After the wet years passed, and people realized that their farms were worthless, coyotes became a meal ticket for some homesteaders. Men earned income and perhaps fed their families by trapping coyotes; they received a bounty of five dollars for each coyote, and could command an equal amount for the pelt. Other predators of chickens were bobcats and cougars.

The animal that caused homesteaders the worst problem was the lowly rab-bit. He ate their crops. Not all, but a great part of it. Farmers might lose a quarter of their crop to this animal. Rabbits were everywhere. Thousands and thousands of them. No homesteader on his own could hope to stay their appetites or rid his fields of them. For that reason, homesteaders joined forces and held big rabbit drives. They would spread out and move across a large patch of desert, making noise to flush out rabbits and drive them in front. Homesteaders clubbed any rabbits in reach. Rabbits escaping the advancing line of homesteaders met either a net spread across the desert or other club-wielding people closing in from another direction. Normally, hundreds of rabbits were killed at one time, and in one drive in Jefferson County, 1,500. Although drive after drive was held across Central Oregon, and homesteaders were joined by club-wielding townspeople and Indi-ans, the rabbits continued to roam through the crops, eating.

24

LAND BUST
1910s–1920s

COMMUNICATIONS IMPROVED in Crook County as elsewhere after the century turned. Mail was no longer an occasional affair, delivered by a friendly Indian, or on a stagecoach that arrived in Prineville only three times a week. Except for Sundays and six paid holidays (not including Christmas), the mail was now delivered every day.

Telephones, too, had arrived, although not everybody could afford one. Unlike television later, which spread through the lower income groups first and then up to people with higher salaries, the telephone was first adopted by businessmen, professionals, and the more prosperous ranchers and farmers. Rural areas received phone service after towns such as Prineville and Bend did; lines reached Trout Creek by 1904; Paulina, 1909; and Agency Plains, 1911. Operators were necessary to make the connections, and often became well known to users. On the fragile line running through Paulina and Suplee, the operator for years was wheelchair-bound Johnny Morgan, who had been paralyzed as a teenager. When the South Fork and Beaver Creek began to thaw, Paulina area ranchers now were able to telephone stockmen farther down the Crooked River, warning them that the stream soon would be flooding. It gave Prineville area ranchers a few days to move their livestock to higher ground.

As noted, many of the homesteader-patronized hamlets had newspapers. One of these became significant for reasons no one reading it at the time could have imagined. In the summer of 1892, E.M. Shutt launched the *Antelope Herald* at the southern edge of Wasco County, and with some breaks managed to keep it going for 33 years. The significance of the newspaper came not so much from anything it published or from anyone who owned or edited it, but because of the boy who worked there after school, setting type and sometimes acting as a part-time reporter.

Harold Lenoir Davis, born four years after Shutt launched the paper, was a son of the Antelope school principal. The Davis family eventually moved up to The Dalles in 1908, where Harold went through high school. After service in the Great War and doing various small time jobs, he became an assistant to his father, who had become the Wasco County assessor. Harold eventually became a professional writer of articles and short stories, and in 1929 started contributing to H.L. Mencken's *American Mercury* magazine. Then, in 1935, Davis won the Pulitzer Prize for his novel about Oregon, *Honey in the Horn*. The book focused on Oregon's working class and its disadvantaged people, with a very accurate portrait of the life and death of the Central Oregon homestead boom. It was not a popular book in Oregon, especially among business and community boosters. Davis later wrote *Beulah Land* (1940), *Harp of a Thousand Strings* (1947), *Distant Music* (1957), and *Kettle of Fire*, published in 1959 just a year before his death. *Honey in the Horn* is generally regarded by literary critics as the best novel ever written by an Oregonian.

As the climate became drier, and the unsuitability of the Great Sandy and Lower deserts for farming became ever more evident, the railroads tried to prevent a mass exodus of homesteaders. Their goal, after all, was not merely to dispose of their land grants, but also to ship in supplies for a growing population while hauling out agricultural produce. The railroads urged homesteaders to adopt summer fallowing and other more rational and sustainable farming techniques. But these homesteaders were the same people who had believed they could farm in the desert. Selling them on scientific methodology was no easy chore, and most homesteaders refused to adopt new techniques. Those who did, however, produced more abundant crops than their stubborn neighbors.

Farmers had been misled by promoters, and by the untypically wet weather that made the land seem more fertile than it truly was. Starting in 1912, the climate became drier, more typical of Crook County's usual weather. Dry, and very cold in winter. In summer, blistering hot. And sometimes, freezing at night and sweltering during the daytime. Gardens not killed by late frosts were broiled. The sun burned up many of the crops that rabbits and grasshoppers had not already consumed, crops that had just managed to survive the frosts of a short growing season. All of these problems, as well as high freight charges, the difficulty of transporting water, higher debts to banks for seed and other farm supplies, and the loneliness of desert nights, led to discouragement and sometimes to breakdowns in health.

After a few dry years, people abandoned their farms. Pine mills in Bend, established after the arrival of the railroads, gave them an escape, since the sawmills needed laborers. Some homesteaders sold their land to neighbors, or to one of the big ranches, while others simply walked away. A few may have paid their annual property taxes to keep their titles valid, but most abandoned their homesteads completely. They then took jobs in Bend, living in new shacks owned by the timber companies. Others did not seek mill employment, but went to Portland or larger cities to work in the war industries after America entered the Great War in 1917.

Left behind were the old homesteads. The gardens and fields that once received such loving attention and hard work now vanished beneath the blowing dust of the Great Sandy and Lower deserts. Buildings and other improvements remained behind, silent evidence of what had happened. Small one- and two-story houses, the latter often tall and narrow, stood abandoned: ugly houses all, consisting of unpainted rough-hewn lumber, standing with busted doors squeaking in the wind, and with faded, cheap, torn curtains blowing through broken windows. Nearby, rock-lined wells filled with blowing sand, dilapidated windmills squeaked in the wind, and drooping fences and basalt walls bordered on nothing—no trace of crops or fruits, only the blue-gray sage and the gray-green juniper.

Normally, when a business goes bust, the evidence of the failure vanishes swiftly. If a merchant goes bankrupt, within months his store will be reoccupied, and the merchant's house, if lost to the bank, is resold. But the homestead boom and bust left plenty of evidence scattered across the region. Even today, generations later, some of these abandoned homesteads remain visible.

What was accomplished? For the homesteaders whose dreams were blown away by desert heat and unproductive land, little or nothing. For the land, well… junipers were cut down, sagebrush pulled out, and rocks moved and stacked. In the regional economy, the ranching industry was damaged with the fencing of the range, but the new timber industry benefited. When sawmills were built in Bend, there was an adequate supply of cheap labor readily available.

James J. Hill was the most famous man in Central Oregon when he drove the "golden spike" at the end of the railway he built to Bend. *Bowman Museum, Crook County Historical Society*

25

ARRIVAL OF JIM HILL
1908–1911

EDWARD H. HARRIMAN, the Wall Street mogul who dominated transportation in California by controlling the Southern Pacific Railroad, had visited Crook County. He was a guest of Jack Edwards on the Hay Creek Ranch, and stopped in Prineville in September 1907. While in Crook County, he declared: "You people will never see a railroad through Central Oregon. There is not enough tonnage to justify one."

What Harriman did not know was that a few years earlier a man calling himself John F. Swanson had stayed for several days and nights at the J.P. Hahn Hotel in Madras. Swanson traveled all over the region, extolling the area's beauty while taking photographs. What no one knew, and thus what no one could inform Harriman of, was that Swanson was really John F. Stevens, an engineer for Harriman's hated enemy, James J. Hill.

Central Oregon's desperation for a railroad had grown. From a mild longing, the desire became a great hunger. Residents gave ear to every rumor of interest by distant railroad moguls. Reaching Prineville still meant a long stagecoach or automobile trip from Shaniko. The stagecoach to Shaniko ran at night, so that passengers and freight could catch the morning train. Coming or going meant a 12-hour ride over roads that were either dusty or muddy but always bumpy. Roads reached Prineville from The Dalles via Hay Creek, from Sisters, from Fort Klamath via the Deschutes, from the Wagontire area, and (two) from the Upper Country. In 1904, Crook County had 750 miles of public roads, only 10 miles of them surfaced with gravel.

This interest in a railroad rose above simple concerns about inconvenience. It cost more money to get livestock and crops to market without a railway, leaving Crook residents less competitive than ranchers and farmers in other regions. And despite the interest shown by Midwestern timber companies in Central Oregon forests, it meant no big sawmill would be built there.

When the Columbia Southern Railway reached Shaniko in 1900, its owners had promised to extend the line to Prineville. Year after year, they announced they were about to start construction, but they never did. The cost would have been great. Central Oregon's principal product—livestock—could be driven to the railhead anyway, so why bother? Either way, they would make money, and it was logical to make it in the cheaper way.

In 1908, some Prineville businessmen took matters into their own hands. David Stewart joined with stagecoach tycoon Mack Cornett, banker T.M.

Baldwin, hardware store owner Charles M. Elkins, and former county judge W.A. Booth to incorporate the Central Oregon Railroad. They planned to run an electric road from Shaniko to Bend, and then over the desert to Prineville. But they failed to raise enough capital.

In 1910, Louis Hill, the son of James J. Hill of the Great Northern Railroad, arrived in Central Oregon. He had a stake in the area. That same year, he and St. Paul lumbermen John E. Burchard and W.P. Davidson organized the Oregon & Western Colonization Company. The colorful Harney County cattle baron Bill Hanley, a friend of James J. Hill, had a share. The firm bought the 800,000-acre Willamette Valley & Cascade Mountain Road grants. Although attracted by the 178,000 acres of timber included within the grants, the purchase also made them landlords to many unhappy tenant farmers. Reversing previous policy, Hill and his partners began selling the farmers their land. They also gave away a block of lots in Prineville for the biggest baseball field east of the Cascades, named Davidson Park in honor of company president W.P. Davidson. About 660,000 acres of the grants were rich agricultural lands, and 140,000 acres contained 4.5 billion feet of pine, fir, and cedar.

Hill, with Hanley at his side, toured the region in a new Studebaker "40." They went over the rough trails that Central Oregonians called roads, helped by guides, and the visit caused a big stir among the locals. It was while this tour was underway that the *Oregon Journal* announced that a St. Paul corporation headed by Hill had bought the old wagon road company. Thus it created much interest when Hill declared in Prineville that he did not "see how it would be possible for a railroad to come within 18 or 20 miles of Prineville and stay out of it." Both C. Sam Smith and Newt Williamson held private conversations with him. They said later that Hill had virtually promised that a branch line would be built.

By then, a main railroad was already on its way, though its eventual destination would surprise everyone. James Jerome Hill had become very interested in Central Oregon a few years earlier. The Canadian entrepreneur was a financial legend. Starting life in the traditional way for such men—with nothing—Hill had built up a vast railroad empire in the West. Now in his sixties, he was saluted by an admiring public as "the Empire Builder." At a time when Americans viewed capitalists with awe and loaded them with praise, few inspired more awe and praise than Hill. It was also the age of muckraking and populism; in the West, farmers named one hated weed "Jim Hill Mustard." He had, however, retained the common touch while building a fortune worth more than fifty million. He controlled the Great Northern, Northern Pacific, and Burlington railroads. But this did not satisfy him. He wanted to enter California. A monopoly over transportation there belonged to a man with as much determination and even greater power than Hill: his old enemy, E.H. Harriman. Looking at the map of Oregon, Hill believed he saw a way to tread upon Harriman's turf.

In 1908, an obscure railroad called the Oregon Trunk announced that it would build a line to Bend. This aroused suspicion in Central Oregon. Such promises had been heard before. And why the little village of Bend? Why not the metropolis of the outback: Prineville?

On Wall Street, one man thought he knew why. Harriman too could read a map. Anyone seeking to tap Central Oregon's wealth would build to Prineville. The only reason to build a railroad to Bend was because it would be the most direct route to San Francisco—into Harriman's domain. Harriman believed the Oregon Trunk was a front for Hill.

Hill's ownership became widely rumored and then accepted as fact. He admitted it in August 1909. "JIM HILL IS COMING!" read the big letters in a Prineville newspaper. Not as the headline for a news article or editorial. No, a local photographer used the words atop his advertisement. Neither the photographer nor his advertisement had anything to do with Hill. But nothing would draw more attention to the promotional piece than those words. When Hill celebrated a birthday, a local newspaper reported on it in a lengthy front page article. Perhaps nothing in Central Oregon history created as much sustained excitement as the coming of Jim Hill. Few conversations failed to touch upon the subject of Hill or railroads. The industrial revolution would arrive. People would prosper. The region would boom.

Meanwhile, E.H. Harriman had died, but his heirs were ready for bear. They organized the DesChutes Railroad to stop the Oregon Trunk. Both railroads hired construction crews and prepared to race each other to Bend. The DesChutes Railroad filed for rights-of-way conflicting with the Oregon Trunk's and its lawyers marched into court with a plethora of lawsuits. But Hill had been careful to record all of his rights-of-way. The Harriman lawyers lost.

Before October 1909, almost 2,000 men were working on the railroads in what one newspaper headlined a "TITANIC STRUGGLE FOR POSSESSION OF DESCHUTES." Newspapers carried columns of news about the battle, week after week, and soon the entire country had reason to watch. The last great American railroad war had begun.

The Oregon Trunk would be built by the contracting firm Porter Brothers, the DesChutes Railroad by Twohy Brothers. Most of the laborers were immigrants from southern Europe. The average worker was paid 20 to 30 cents an hour. The Harriman forces went down the east side of the Deschutes Canyon, the Hill forces down the west. Hill's people even worked at night. Dynamite blasting began on the Columbia and continued all the way up the canyon. When it started, thousands of wild geese that roosted at night on Miller's Island in the Columbia fled to the island's eastern edge and stopped flying to the wheat fields bordering the Deschutes.

Violence erupted between the rival crews. Teamsters hauling supplies were doped, made drunk, shot at, or had boulders dynamited into their paths. Stewart

H. Holbrook recorded in *The Age of the Moguls* (1954) that down the Deschutes Canyon: "Shovels, crowbars and pick handles were used for close fighting. Men were killed. Several warriors narrowly escaped death when great boulders suddenly came rolling down the steep grade."

Boulders could be dynamited into the path of the other firm's rails or even into the camp of the opposing crew. One came hurdling down the canyon wall and smashed a railroad car into kindling. The crews on both sides had men hidden above the canyon to spot where their adversaries stored their powder. When such a cache was located, a squad of a half-dozen or so workers would sneak over and detonate the explosives. This created delays because of powder shortages. Holbrook also reports that armed guards lay flat on hilltops, ready to shoot in case of any suspicious movements below.

The adversaries also employed less potentially lethal tactics. Harriman's construction boss, George W. Boschke, had built the great sea wall at Galveston, Texas. While racing down the Deschutes, Boschke received a telegram supposedly wired from Galveston: "Come at once. The sea wall has broken." Boschke remained, believing Hill's forces had sent the wire to trick him. They had.

Late one night in February 1910, the U.S. land commissioner in Madras, Howard Turner, was awakened when a group of men arrived in an E.M. & F. motorcar. When he opened the door to let them in, he discovered he had three important visitors: James J. Hill's son, Johnson D. Porter of Porter Brothers, and Oregon Trunk land agent Matt Clark. At their request, Turner accompanied them and the driver to his office to draw up the papers necessary for filing on 40 acres along the Crooked River, using Northern Pacific Railroad script, so they could build a railroad bridge across the stream. Turner then watched as the group set off through the stormy night in their open top automobile to drive over the rough, deeply-rutted, dirt road to The Dalles. He learned later that somehow they had reached the district land office in The Dalles a few minutes before it opened. They recorded their claim. An hour later, several of Harriman's agents arrived at the office to file for the same ground using Union Pacific script; too late.

The attraction of the land in question was that this was the narrowest place on the river in advance of the projected railroad route (located two miles below Trail Crossing). The steel bridge built there by the Oregon Trunk in 1911 would be 330 feet long and 304 feet high. The crews erected and placed the north half first. Then they lowered equipment and other steel bridge parts down to the river, took it across the water, and drew it up with cables to the south side; the laborers had to descend down the canyon wall to the river using a 300-foot-long rope ladder. After the south span was built, the two halves were bolted together, forming the third highest railroad bridge in the world and only the seventh of its sort in existence.

Madras became the common goal of both forces. The Porter Brothers built south to Mecca, then Vanora, and across the Agency Plains to Madras, while the Twohy Brothers went down to Gateway, then Paxton, and then Madras. Hill spent $10 million to get to Madras; the Harriman forces $8 million over an easier route.

Even before the Porter Brothers crews reached the Crooked River and the bridge that they were building there, they needed to get over a smaller obstacle: Willow Creek. This was a significant barrier. To get across, the Hill forces erected a trestle 1,050 feet long and standing 250 feet above the ground. Hill's crews reached the south end of Agency Plains in August 1911. A few months later they installed a 65,000-gallon water tank near their new depot, and allowed farmers to tap as much water as they could haul away in wagons. This was great public relations, and Hill's people were better at it than Harriman's.

As the crews approached Madras, the town's population rocketed to 3,500; another 3,000 or so also were located in the vicinity. The town hired two tough characters as police officers, but they wound up non-fatally shooting each other. For awhile, Madras became a rollicking fleshpot filled with cussing, rough laborers, foremen, and teamsters crowding into 13 saloons. A boom town spirit prevailed, and apparently some of the local developers let it go to their heads. The Madras Townsite Company allegedly tried to charge the Oregon Trunk an unreasonably large amount for a right-of-way through town. Hill's men balked and instead secured a right-of-way just west of Madras.

Oregon Trunk Locomotive No. 702 reached Madras on February 15, 1911, greeted by a crowd of 6,000 men, women, and children. After James J. Hill's car came to a stop, complete silence followed; no machinery creaked, no person spoke, no dog barked. Suddenly the crowd exploded into cheers. Railroad laborers, townspeople, homesteaders, and visitors from neighboring communities went into an ecstasy of celebration. A more formal celebration followed, for which $1,500 had been raised locally. The town had appointed S.J. "Beany" Sellers head cook for a very big pot roast. "Beany," who was normally a saloonkeeper, had his work cut out for him, but met the challenge. Most everything served—potatoes, beans, and beef—were roasted in the ground, and there was a lot of it, too. "Beany" served two tons of beef and 900 loaves of bread. Railroad executives from Chicago, St. Louis, St. Paul, and other cities addressed the crowd. Optimism prevailed.

An unexpected benefit of the railroad came a few months later. Land commissioner Howard Turner of Madras talked Al G. Barnes into bringing his circus into Crook County. The whole show was shipped over the Deschutes railway to Madras. The town contributed by providing 40 horses to pull wagons, as well as strengthening bridges for elephants and making other preparations. About 4,000 people, some of them from as far away as Lakeview and Burns, attended Central Oregon's first-ever circus performance on May 11, 1911.

The railroads were built mostly to haul freight, not passengers, and in Central Oregon the principal freight was agricultural. To store grain for shipment, the company built large warehouses at Gateway, Paxton, Madras, Metolius, Culver, and Opal City. Another benefit was the system of supply roads that construction crews used to haul freight to their railroad camps. These were good, professionally built roads, in sharp contrast to the rutted wagon trails that had evolved from old Indian paths, the prevailing highways in Crook County at the time. The railroad later granted these roads to Jefferson and Deschutes counties and the public used them for many years.

The older Columbia Southern route to Shaniko had only six miles of level line, with the remainder of the tracks either ascending or descending, and it had 198 curves. But the first big Central Oregon train wreck occurred on Hill's newer Oregon Trunk. It happened in Wasco County, about 22 miles north of Sherar's Crossing. The train derailed on an only "semi-" ballasted road bed and fell into the Deschutes. Among the six people scalded to death from the locomotive's steam was the engineer. The coroner's jury ruled that members of the train crew had caused the accident by their negligence.

The Harriman outfit's DesChutes Railroad bought an option for a right-of-way through a ranch that lay on the Oregon Trunk's route to Bend. The Hill lawyers went to court, arguing that the rancher's ownership of the land was not valid. But the court ruled for the rancher, and Hill's route to Bend was blocked.

Disappointed, Hill compromised. Negotiations produced an agreement that the two lines would connect at Metolius. Hill would build to Bend, but no further, while the DesChutes Railroad would stop at Metolius and have the right to use the Hill tracks.

They also agreed that any income received from construction of a branch line to Prineville would be split evenly between the two railroads. Considering that livestock would be trailed to the existing railhead from Prineville and points east no matter how far away the railhead remained, this killed any incentive for constructing a branch line. It had cost Hill $16 million to build the railroad from the Columbia toward Bend and would cost hundreds of thousands more for anyone to build from the main line to Prineville.

In Prineville, emotions were mixed. While pleased that Crook County would finally have a railroad, people were disappointed that it would go along the Deschutes instead of to the center of the county, where government, business, and population were focused. However, without notice, the president, general manager, legal counsel, engineers, and other top men of the Harriman lines in three big automobiles entered Prineville at five o'clock one August afternoon. This produced excitement, and a flurry of questions were directed at the visitors. Everyone wanted to know: would a railroad be built to Prineville? The executives spoke glowingly of the vicinity's beauty and bounty, and then they departed.

But as the rails continued to advance toward Bend, Prineville residents became increasingly apprehensive. In the winter of 1910-1911, local businessmen had decided to organize a company that would either promote Prineville to the railroad builders, or build a railway themselves. Behind the scheme were T.M. Baldwin, C. Sam Smith, and H.A. Kelley. The latter, having a degree from the Massachusetts Institute of Technology, had been a civil engineer for the Oregon Trunk. In January 1911, they incorporated the Prineville & Eastern Railroad Company for $100,000. Among the stockholders were David F. Stewart, Mack Cornett, Charles M. Elkins, W.A. Booth, G.N. Clifton, and T.H. LaFollette. Although some were suspicious of Baldwin's motives—fearing the group planned to secure city land for free and then sell it—voters approved a franchise allowing the firm to operate a railroad within the town and build a depot.

Nothing came of it. The Prineville & Eastern made some surveys, but it could neither attract railroads nor raise enough money to lay its own tracks.

Even after the rails reached Bend, Prineville's efforts to save itself from being overtaken by the upstart village on the Deschutes did not end. The Prineville Commercial Club appointed T.M. Baldwin, C. Sam Smith, Charles M. Elkins, and John R. Stinson as a railroad committee to explore ways of getting tracks laid to town.

In less than a year, it appeared that Prineville would get its railroad. H.P. Scheel, owner of the Hercules Sand Stone Company of Tenino, Washington, offered to finance and build one in exchange for a $75,000 bonus. Led by Baldwin, the town secured land for the tracks and a terminal, some of it donated by the Oregon & Western Colonization Company. Copper Trust founder Thomas W. Lawson of Boston also became involved in promoting the idea. The $600,000 projected cost of building 31 miles of track did not detour Scheel. In December 1913, he incorporated the Metolius, Prineville & Eastern Railroad Company and announced that construction was imminent. A few months later the scheme collapsed for reasons never made public. The town returned the donated land.

Meanwhile, on October 1, 1911, James J. Hill drove the "golden spike" at Bend. For two days, between 1,500 and 2,000 people celebrated—everything from a parade to a downtown pillow fight. Every hotel and rooming house was booked, every cafe crowded. People throughout Central Oregon and beyond were there. Most came to celebrate the arrival of the railroad and all that it represented for the future; some simply turned up for the fun and excitement of the celebration; and a few wanted to see the dignitaries, notably the famous Mr. Hill. Almost 300 people arrived on the first train to reach Bend, the majority of them from Portland and Seattle.

A parade got the festivities going, led by several automobiles decorated with bright banners and streamers. Then came a couple of stagecoaches, a bandwagon, and various other wagons, including water wagons, fire-wagons, hay wagons, and about every other sort of transportation. Children paraded down the street with their school classes; women paraded on horses; cowboys drove cattle down the street. Other activities included foot, horse, and canoe races, boxing matches, a baby show, a football game, lectures, and a dance. Horses in the bucking contest refused to buck, but judges handed out prizes anyway to the cowboys who came closest to getting them to do so. Bend's mayor presided over the official dedication, and James J. Hill drove the golden spike. After he finished, men pulled out the spike, which was turned over to the Bend Commercial Club. Many speeches were delivered, many predictions offered. It is doubtful, however, that any of the prognosticators topped the prediction that Hill himself made the following year, when saying the population of Central Oregon would be 300,000 in five years, and top a million within a decade.

The benefits began immediately. Most, as will be shown shortly, went to Bend, and somewhat to Redmond and Madras. But smaller communities also profited. However, for some Central Oregon communities, the arrival of the railroad was disastrous. Deschutes, always the competitive neighbor of Bend, was fatally wounded. Laidlaw, which many had expected to be what Bend now was, instead became the village of Tumalo. Rosland-LaPine wilted on the desert because the railroad stopped at Bend.

It was reminiscent of what had happened to Antelope a decade earlier. In 1900, Antelope had a population of 249, but its vitality was gutted when the rails of the Columbia Southern reached Shaniko. The latter, of course, then became the most important town between The Dalles and Prineville.

Shaniko and Prineville: one had a railroad, the other had long wanted one. When the rails reached Bend, both of these towns—until 1911 the most prominent and necessary marketing centers in Central Oregon—were profoundly affected. When news had reached Shaniko that the first shipment of the Oregon Trunk's construction equipment had arrived in Grass Valley, a wild celebration ensued. Shaniko, whose own prosperity came from a railroad, thought of railways in positive terms and wished other Central Oregonians well. But dissenting voices were raised. Several warned that a railroad penetrating farther into Central Oregon than Shaniko meant that Shaniko itself would not survive as the region's railhead. Why would a rancher, living 20 miles from Bend, drive his stock all the way to Shaniko if he could drive them the much shorter distance to Bend? It would save him time, energy, and money.

These warnings came true. Shaniko went bust. Almost overnight, people and businesses that had patronized the town stopped coming, going instead to Bend, Redmond, Madras, and other siding sites along the new lines. Shaniko's freight yards, loading sheds, and warehouses became as empty as its big hotel and restaurants. Business died. People were forced to look elsewhere for their livelihoods. The population shrank from 495 in 1910, to 175 in 1920. Shaniko was on its way to becoming Central Oregon's most famous ghost town.

Prineville, too, faced a challenge.

26

BEND'S GIANT MILLS
1915–1916

AS OBSERVED EARLIER, the first Central Oregon sawmills had been established at Warm Springs and Mill Creek, with the latter being a community facility. The first commercial sawmill was built by the English immigrant Charles C. Maling on upper Willow Creek. This steam-operated mill supplied local lumber needs for most of the region.

In about 1890, Mrs. Maling's brother, a Mr. Dee, joined with a man who had accompanied the Malings over from England, Charles Durham, to locate a second mill, south of Blizzard Ridge on a tributary of Trout Creek. Durham and Dee also became partners in a mill on Grizzly Mountain. Durham and U.S. Cowles had a mill on Foley Creek, later moved to the Deschutes.

Another mill was built on Grizzly in 1903. A certain Mr. Hawkins put it on the mountain's west slope, but did not operate it long. He sold to Guyon Springer, William Peck, and Henry Window, and they ran it until 1910. Sam Compton may have had a mill on Grizzly for awhile, and, much later, in 1919, Harry E. Blackwell had one on the same mountain. A sawmill owned by a Mr. Fronhoffer was built on Coon Creek, a tributary of Willow Creek. Jack Dee, the son of Durham's partner, bought the Maling mill with Sam Compton in 1912.

Meanwhile, over in the Deschutes country on Awbrey Butte, John Steidl installed a water-powered sawmill in 1902. Steidl had the mill shipped from his home town of Bimidji, Minnesota, to Shaniko, and then freighted to Bend. This mill, known as the Steidl-Reed Mill, burned in 1910.

The early sawmills supplied local needs, and no lumber milled in Crook County was shipped out of the region until the railroads arrived. Rough hewn lumber from the Grizzly mills in particular went into ranch and homestead buildings, from Shaniko to Silver Lake, from the Cascades to the Ochocos. But everyone knew that there was a greater treasure waiting to be tapped: the Ochoco and Deschutes forests, which could feed several giant commercial sawmills for many years, shipping lumber to points outside the region and employing thousands of people.

As the chapter on land frauds showed, timber interests were already investing in Crook County. This process was accelerated after the railroad arrived in Bend, with Louis Hill and the Oregon & Western Colonization Company promoting timber holdings in the region to Midwestern lumbermen.

The acquisitions record is rather murky, but a number of transactions are known. The A.J. Dwyer Pine Land Company bought 46,000 acres in the

Deschutes country at an early period. Anthony J. Dwyer, like so many of these incoming lumbermen a native of Minnesota, had moved to Oregon in 1906, and began buying and logging timberlands in the Portland area. S.S. Johnson, a timber buyer from Minnesota who had relocated to California, bought the bankrupt Dwyer holdings, which were then organized under the name, Deschutes Lumber Company. Eventually Johnson's company increased its holdings to 60,000 acres.

Another early investor was A.T. Bliss, who in 1905 sold the 8,400 acres of timberland he had acquired to the Irving Family Investment Company. Irving had a total of 20,000 acres of timberland, according to one source. The Alworth-Washburn Company acquired 35,000 acres. The Scanlon-Gipson Lumber Company got 10,000 acres. The Mueller Land & Timber Company of Davenport, Iowa, in 1901 acquired about 20,000 acres in the Deschutes valley. F.W. Gilchrist of Michigan had 85,000 acres, and R.E. Gilchrist about 60,000 acres. The Bend Timber Company acquired the land belonging to Irvine and then another 15,000 acres.

The first mill installed at Bend was a portable that the Pilot Butte Development Company freighted down from The Dalles and set up above the Deschutes. The firm used it to produce lumber for making irrigation flumes, until the mill burned in 1908. The Bend Company mill that replaced it also burned, in 1915. Other early Bend area firms were the Griffin, Anderson Bros., and McNaught and Girtson mills.

About 1910, A.O. and D.E. Hunter acquired the properties of Alexander Drake. Like Drake himself, the Hunters wished to enhance their investments by increasing development around the area. They were well aware that, for any entrepreneur or company owning substantial interests in a locality, any general improvements would increase their overall business. Soon after their acquisition, they met Clyde McKay, who was visiting Bend while preparing ground for a sawmill south of town on behalf of his employer, the Mueller Land & Timber Company of Iowa. The Hunters told McKay that they wanted sawmills located in Bend. McKay, who had been looking at a site 20 miles south, thought that locating in the Bend neighborhood would be a better investment; that is, if the Mueller company could combine its efforts with another, larger timber company. McKay followed up on his idea, making five trips to Minneapolis to see executives at another firm that had been buying timberland in the Bend vicinity, the Brooks-Scanlon Lumber Company.

Joe Scanlon of Brainerd, Minnesota, had begun buying timber near Bend after he first visited the area in 1898. Scanlon was a partner with Dr. Dwight Brooks and H.E. Gipson in the Scanlon-Gipson Lumber Company, which owned a mill at Cass Lake, Minnesota. In 1901, the firm changed its name to Brooks-Scanlon. By that time, Scanlon had bought two 16,000-acre tracts near Bend. Brooks-Scanlon built a big mill at Cloquet, Minnesota, and intended to

The Brooks-Scanlon sawmill was built when Bend still remained in Crook County. *Bowman Museum, Crook County Historical Society*

establish a huge paper mill in British Columbia. Indeed, the firm was expanding rapidly in many directions when McKay came calling in 1910.

In 1911, the Bend Company was organized to buy the Drake holdings, including the remaining town lots, the office building, the sawmill with its timber inventory, and the Bend Water, Light & Power Company. Clyde McKay became the new company's vice president and general manager. By then, the railroad was no longer a distant dream, but a reality that gave a firm like Brooks-Scanlon the ability to ship lumber and other timber products out of Bend. While the Mueller and Brooks-Scanlon firms made their plans, another company also was well along in the planning stage: Shevlin-Hixon.

Thomas L. Shevlin Jr. was best known for his football days at Yale, where he played end. He had spent six months in the Bend area in 1906. Thus, he was very familiar with its timber resources a half dozen years later when he became head of the family business upon the death of his father. By that time, the Shevlin family already had bought large tracts of timberland near Bend. Tom Shevlin was responsible for seeing that the investment was expanded and developed. In 1915, Shevlin bought the Deschutes Lumber Company. John E. Ryan, who represented S.S. Johnson's company, announced in May that Shevlin-Hixon would build a huge pine sawmill in Bend on the west bank of the Deschutes. Processing 80 million board feet annually, it would employ hundreds of workers earning an average wage of three dollars a day. Residents of Bend, and indeed people throughout

Crook County, were ecstatic that at long last the region would have a big mill. Later in the year, the new Shevlin-Hixon Company bought 35,000 acres of timberland from the Bend Company.

On August 18 of the same year, Dr. Dwight Brooks announced that the Brooks-Scanlon Lumber Company would build a sawmill on the east bank of the Deschutes in Bend. Indeed, its mill would be directly across the river from the Shevlin-Hixon mill. It would have a box factory and logging spurs into the woods. These plants would be the two largest pine mills in the entire world.

Tom Shevlin never lived to see his mill built. On December 29, 1915, the 32-year-old businessman died of pneumonia in Minneapolis. Frank P. Hixon, a LaCrosse, Wisconsin, banker associated with the Shevlins, became president of the firm, while a Shevlin cousin, T.A. McCann, became superintendent of its West Coast operations.

Central Oregonians watched in fascination as these two huge plants went up on opposite banks of the river. The companies employed hundreds of construction workers. They were bringing the industrial revolution to Central Oregon. Nothing like it had happened before in the region, and nothing quite the same would happen again. The previous pattern in the arrival of any commercial firm had been for it to begin small and then gradually grow, and not to arrive as full-grown giants.

Shevlin-Hixon sawed its first log on March 23, 1916; Brooks-Scanlon on April 22, 1916. Shevlin-Hixon's plans called for employing 700 men cutting 80 million board feet a year; Brooks-Scanlon's for 500 men producing 50 million

The Shevlin-Hixon sawmill was one of the two largest pine mills in the world, both of which were located in Bend. *Bowman Museum, Crook County Historical Society*

board feet per year. But the plans of both firms were quickly amended. The timber supply was bountiful, and with the Great War raging in Europe, the American economy was making a good recovery from the recession of 1914. Strong demand existed for lumber. (Shevlin-Hixon would soon decide to build a second mill almost as large as its first. This would raise the firm's overall production to 110 million board feet a year.)

The Shevlin-Hixon plant covered 200 acres. Besides the 54 x 180 foot steam-powered sawmill, the facility included 30 dry kilns, electric-powered planing mills, two dry sheds (one covering 78,368 square feet), an electric stacker, an unstacker, a machine shop, a blacksmith shop to tend to the big draft horses used for logging and yard work, a powerhouse, water tank, sash factory, box factory, warehouse and yard, fuel storage tanks, a pumping station, barn, office, two skidders, a roundhouse for the locomotives, 50 logging cars, a locomotive gear train, other railroad equipment, and additional buildings. Burners that stood 150 feet high consumed the debris from the mills, including bark and sawdust. Smoke from these burners lay over the town and drifted out across the desert, depositing half-burnt ash on everything downwind for many miles. The burners were fed day and night, without pause, and were the mill's main source of pollution.

The barn housed the horses, and in the early days both companies owned many draft animals. Draft Shires weighing almost a ton were used for logging in the woods. Individually or in pairs, and with heavy chains attached to their halters and other rigging, they pulled logs through the woods. Their work was hard, and they did not last long. Other horses were used to move lumber in the mill yard.

For employees, 10-hour shifts were common and could be extended to 16 hours. In the mid-1920s, a mill worker's pay was 60 cents an hour. Each shift could produce 150,000 board feet a day. Thirty-five percent of production was shipped out rough, with the remainder remanufactured on site as finished lumber, sash, windows, or boxes. About 900 people worked in the Shevlin-Hixon mill. Seven oil-burning Baldwin locomotives linked the mill to the company's four camps, where hundreds of more men were employed. Shevlin-Hixon rented and showed motion pictures, had a 40-piece band, and published a company magazine, *The Shevlin Equalizer*.

Brooks-Scanlon also had four logging camps, which shipped logs to its mills on 15 miles of private railroad. In Bend, the company had a planing mill with very modern and fast machines, dry sheds, a dipping tank, machine shop, automatic sprinkler system, box factory, private fire department, and roundhouse. It, too, published a company magazine, *Pine Echoes*.

For decades, most of the log hauling done for the two giant mills was by timber railroads. This is where Bend had an advantage over Prineville. Prineville lay many miles from the Ochoco's forests, making it too expensive to log in the mountains until logging trucks replaced trains. Bend, on the other hand, was situated adjacent to the Deschutes' forests, and no great distance to the first timber. As lumberjacks moved out from Bend, they laid down tracks to haul out the moveable camps and to haul in cut timber to the mill. After an area was logged, tracks were pulled up and laid out in a new locality. A few main lines ran from the mills, sometimes extending 50 miles from Bend. In the 1920s, these would cost up to $50,000 a mile to lay, preceded by surveyors and engineers and using second-hand, top-quality rail bought from major railroads that recently had refurbished their own tracks. From the main line, spur lines snaked out into the forest on routes selected by logging foremen; the subsidiary tracks were made of a lower grade steel. The Brooks-Scanlon logging railroads extended almost as far south as the Fort Rock Valley and as far north as the head of Fly Creek, a tributary of the Metolius. The Shevlin-Hixon rails extended into Klamath and Lake counties.

The logging camps could have larger populations than some small but well-known Central Oregon towns. Indeed, they were mobile communities. The buildings were moved from location to location on flatcars: bunkhouse, cabins, community store, cookhouse, commissary, church, school, shower house, and dining room. Just as in the homesteader communities where many of the lumberjacks came from, the schoolhouse also was used for community events, such as Halloween and Christmas parties, dances, and the screening of motion pictures. The companies paid workers in scrip that was negotiable in the commissary to purchase groceries and other goods. Trains brought in tank cars, which were hooked up to standing pipes in the camps for distributing water. Residents carried water from the distribution pipes to their cabins in buckets.

Families moved together from one location to another, part of the same mobile camp, like groups of gypsies. They all knew one another, and cooperated in establishing new camps and helping out during emergencies. The camps moved about once a year, with cabins placed on flatcars and hauled to new locations. Families sometimes had two cabins, which were bolted together while in a camp but could be separated for moving. When arriving at a new location, the first things put up after the unloading of the cabins were an outhouse and clothesline for each family. Families also dug root cellars to store fruits, milk, cheese, and other perishables.

The beginning of this industrial revolution occurred while Bend remained in Crook County. Only briefly, however, did Crook County itself benefit from the two largest pine mills on earth. Soon, the mills would be within the limits of a new county, Deschutes, and Crook County again was without a large timber industry. The loss of this part of the county began when Bend area residents discovered that Crook County officials were planning to build a new courthouse.

27

THE WEST SECEDES

1907–1916

WESTERN COUNTY RESIDENTS expressed outrage about plans for building a new courthouse in Prineville (finished 1909) when their own area lacked good roads. They staged a protest meeting at Forest, and Charles Benson of Bend and others obtained an injunction against the courthouse project from a judge in The Dalles, on the grounds that it would incur new indebtedness. The judge ordered that new debt for the courthouse be limited to $5,000. Consequently, the Crook County court again asked for bids. For the same plans, the accepted bid came in $25,000 lower. This fed suspicions that county officials had struck a private deal with contractors.

In January 1907, Alexander Drake had launched a new effort to break up the county. The scheme had been plotted in secrecy, and only when the western residents prepared to petition the legislature did people in the eastern section learn of it. The divisionists wanted to create two new counties, Jefferson and Deschutes, taking almost everything west and north of Prineville. The legislature shot down the proposal, and also a movement to create another new county out of Western Crook called "Nesmith."

In 1910, Redmond residents proposed creating one big new county called Deschutes to include both Bend and Madras with the seat in Redmond. Bend and Madras businessmen joined Prineville leaders to defeat the proposal.

The road issue continued to rankle the westerners. Eastern residents voted to defeat a 1913 proposal to issue $200,000 in road bonds. A report from Bend appeared in the *Oregonian* on November 13, stating: "It is already evident that there will be opposition to a heavy levy for road work on the part of residents in the East Side districts…and it is equally certain that the West Side territory will be well represented by those favoring good roads, at whatever cost, for sentiment in the region now served by the railroads, and settled chiefly by newcomers, is distinctly at odds with the 'old timer' sentiment of the remote stock districts."

After the rails reached Madras, Redmond, and Bend by 1911, the western section boomed with new businesses and population, while points east experienced little growth. Jim and Louis Hill had urged lumber friends to invest in Central Oregon even before the rails reached there. Minnesota lumbermen bought timber as early as 1898. Conservationists were speaking grimly of a U.S. "timber famine," and Chief Forester Gifford Pinchot announced that by the 1920s the entire timber supply of the United States would be sawed out. Timber barons looked to Oregon for the trees the conservationists claimed did not exist.

When western county residents learned of the plan to build this courthouse, they seceded from Crook to form Jefferson and Deschutes counties. *Bowman Museum, Crook County Historical Society*

And then in 1915, of course, came the announcements by Shevlin-Hixon and Brooks-Scanlon.

Divisionists again proposed to create two new western counties, and would support each other against the eastern county residents opposed to division. But the political lines actually became non-sectional. One Prineville newspaper opposed division, but the other favored it. Opponents claimed that division would increase the costs of local government, result in lower school standards, and cause all of the old county indebtedness to fall on the Prineville locality. One newspaper observed that the big taxpayers opposed it: "Apparently in an effort to fool somebody, a lot of half baked estimates of setting up and operating new counties have been industriously circulated by the divisionists. Any cause that resorts to such methods is UNSAFE and should be let alone." The proposed new county lines had been drawn in secret without public consultation, and besides, the anti-divisionists said, one county made a better impression for the region than three.

In the November election, however, Jefferson County emerged, while Deschutes went down to defeat. Opponents of division disputed the election results creating Jefferson, but the state supreme court upheld the voters' decision.

The rapid population increase in Bend and Redmond, which were still in Crook County, of course, began to alarm many people, as the county's western portion became more heavily populated than the eastern. If Crook remained undivided, westerners might move the county seat to Bend. Consequently, division suddenly became popular throughout the county. Deschutes County finally emerged on December 13, 1916. By 1920, Bend would have a population of 5,415, while Prineville limped behind with 1,104.

People in Portland and mapmakers back East barely noticed; even after World War II, national maps often showed Prineville standing alone in Central Oregon. Prineville residents never forgot that their town had once been the metropolis of the sagelands. When its business or political leaders compared the community to someplace else, they compared it to Bend. Long after Redmond also overtook Prineville in population, they still saw Bend as "the other" important Central Oregon town.

John B. "Jack" Shipp was an English-born fancy cake decorator who arrived in Prineville on a bicycle and stayed to build the new courthouse, elegant churches, and such grand houses as the Baldwin mansion. *Bowman Museum, Crook County Historical Society*

The courthouse project that had initially spurred the division fight was completed in May 1909. Salem architect W.D. Pugh designed the stone structure, and Wright & McNeely of Portland contracted to build it. Judge Bell ordered that the cost not exceed $40,000. The Portland firm built only the basement and three flights of steps before it defaulted. That is when the former English fancy cake decorator stepped forward.

Jack Shipp agreed to finish the job. He made minor design changes. Shipp or (more likely) the original contractors placed the basement at ground level instead of subterranean as designed by Pugh. Probably the high water table mandated this. Even today water can be found near the courthouse at a depth of five feet. Shipp made the clock tower wider than Pugh's design and placed a flagpole atop it instead of the statue Pugh had envisioned. No framing plans for the courthouse have been found. Apparently Pugh left it to Shipp for such details as how to attach the clock tower to the building.

The basalt stones that formed the walls came from a quarry west of town. Shipp used rock from the same quarry in other buildings, including his own house. He had to exceed the project's budget because the contracts and specifications failed to list all costs. He contracted with a Portland firm for the stonework and had other contractors do the wiring, heating, and plumbing. For interior paneling and fixtures, Shipp used local pine lumber, which he stained to look like oak. The interior walls were pine covered with plaster, looking like it was 16 inches thick. Containing about 5,000 square feet of space, the building had three floors, an attic, and a three-story clock tower, making the seven-stories-high structure the tallest in Central Oregon.

Four and a half feet of cornice, frieze, and architrave graced the upper level. The eight-ton, four-faced, clock tower stood above barred windows. (Generations of local children have believed that the barred windows held prisoners behind them.) Three huge stone stairways led into the building. Even today, the 2,268-square-foot circuit courtroom on the third floor, with its elevated judge's bench and oak-stained wainscoting and banisters, is praised by lawyers as one of the most handsome in Oregon.

Shipp brought it in for $48,591. He paid $725 for the four-faced clock tower, and the main entrance and outside doors cost him only $6. A rail fence and trees surrounded the courthouse. (In 1941, the county court decided to remove the two big stone side entrances to create more office space.) The whole county government moved into the building: the courts, county departments, school superintendent, jail, sheriff, and library.

The creation of Jefferson County raised problems for Crook, not least the county court's political legitimacy. Judge Guyon Springer had taken office in 1913 but lived in the north portion of the county, which became part of Jefferson County. And Springer was controversial.

In 1914, he had summoned an outside auditor to review the accounts of every county department. Accusations had come from the north country— Springer's base—of corruption afoot. Without the support of commissioners R.H. Bayley and Willis W. Brown, he hired A.M. McE. Ball to audit the books. Ball examined everyone's accounts, from the school superintendent to the county surveyor. Especially of interest: a "Haynes 40" automobile purchased for $2,400, and allegations by a disgruntled former deputy against Sheriff Frank Elkins.

Elkins had courage and diligence. He would arrest the men who burned down Newt Williamson's shearing plant. Later, despite public outrage in Bend and threats of lawsuits, he shut down the Bend stores, groceries, bowling alleys, and billiard halls that remained open on Sundays in violation of state blue laws, and ordered his deputies to arrest any businessman who defied those laws. He also busted up the most notorious gang of horse thieves ever to operate in the region, at great personal risk, following one trail all the way into Nevada. He reported in February 1914 that he had received 127 criminal complaints, resulting in 52 arrests and 18 people sentenced to the penitentiary. He noted, too, that for three months the jail had stood empty, while the previous winter there were 8 to 12 inmates. (This was temporary: the following August, the circuit court would have a heavy docket that included three new murder cases.) Most people liked their sheriff. Judge Springer did not, and the Ball audit brought the conflict into the open.

Sheriff Frank Elkins, pictured here with his wife, enforced the law vigorously, to the fury of horse thieves, Bend businessmen, and the Crook County judge. *Bowman Museum, Crook County Historical Society*

On February 11, while Elkins was out of town, Ball went into the sheriff's office and removed the tax rolls. He took them upstairs to the lawyers' smoking room to do the audit. When Elkins returned, Deputy Van Allen told him what had happened. Elkins went home assuming that Ball would return the rolls to the sheriff's vault for the night. But the next morning, he found no books in the vault. Ball had left them upstairs. Elkins had the janitor use a pass key to open the smoking room door and he then took all of the rolls to the vault except those Ball was working on. He later told Ball that, because they were a public record, under state law the rolls could not be removed from the sheriff's office in the manner Ball had done.

He offered Ball the use of an adjoining office. Ball rejected it, declared that the sheriff had acted illegally in removing the books during an audit, and demanded their immediate return. Elkins refused. Ball then told Judge Springer about this encounter. Because District Attorney Willard H. Wirtz was absent in Salem on county business, Springer consulted local lawyers. Each confirmed the sheriff's words, which was not at all what the judge wanted to hear. Springer then got in touch with Circuit Court Judge W.L. Bradshaw, who refused to order the sheriff to give up the rolls, and then Governor Oswald West, who declined to get involved. Springer hired Portland lawyer Bert Haney to give an opinion. Haney also said that Sheriff Elkins was right, and billed the county $100 for the opinion.

Ball, meanwhile, concluded that various department heads had improperly charged items to the county. Furious county officials retorted that Ball did not know what he was talking about. Ball criticized the surveyor, for example, because he had charged both his per diem salary and mileage when he took a trip, but all county surveyors in Oregon did the same. The officials discovered that Ball had been in Oregon less than a year and had never before audited a county's books.

Referring to the county high school's agricultural course, Ball declared: "We do not believe your county has reached the stage of advancement when this department should be maintained, and would suggest that you make an investigation in order to ascertain the number of pupils who are taking this course, and whether the number warrants your Honorable Body in continuing this department. We believe the cost per capita is too high to warrant its continuance."

When the *Crook County Journal* reported on the controversy and quoted the above, the editor could not restrain himself. In the middle of the news story, he raved: "Ye Gods! What is the man thinking about? He has passed judgment on something he acknowledges he knows nothing about…Too high, forsooth. Had this high brow expert been called here when there were only six high school students enrolled in the lean-to of the old First National Bank building we wonder what he would have advised? He did not know that there were 38 students enrolled in the agricultural department that he wanted abolished. From our lean-to school of a few years ago we have now a high school that is second to none in the state…This year 125 boys and girls are in attendance."

County officials appealed to the state insurance commissioner, charged by law with all such investigations, to examine their books. Prominent citizens from Prineville, Bend, Redmond, and Laidlaw met in the courthouse in March, examined Ball's work, and adopted a resolution declaring that the investigation "chiefly actuated by political malice, is incompetent, is arriving at no beneficial results and is clearly a waste of money." The court fired Ball. Springer's investigation had cost the county $1,060.75.

The insurance commissioner sent over two auditors to examine all the books. They reported in March that there was no evidence of wrongdoing by county officials. They found the books in order. However, in the future, county departments would have to obey state financial laws applicable to public agencies, which they had previously neglected to do.

A year later, the county court of Springer, Brown, and J.F. Blanchard instructed District Attorney Wirtz to sue former commissioner R.H. Bayley for refusing to account for $30,800.66 placed in his charge for road repairs. At the same time, however, Wirtz prepared a lawsuit against Springer and Brown. When Jefferson County had come into existence, both of these court members lived there, and Brown continued to do so. On January 8, 1915, Springer and Blanchard appointed H.J. Overturf to replace Brown, but Brown refused to vacate his seat. The disputed seat fell almost two years later to E.T. Luthy in the 1916 election.

Springer's case was more complicated. Prior to the governor's proclamation affirming Jefferson County's creation, Springer had announced that he would move to Prineville, and he did. Before Wirtz could sue to oust Springer, state Attorney General George M. Brown sustained Springer's right to hold the office. Brown, a Republican, said that the Democrat judge had fulfilled his residency obligation when he moved.

In May 1917, men circulated recall petitions against Springer and Blanchard. The petition said Springer was actually a resident of newly created Jefferson County, that he had missed court sessions, that he had allowed the commissioners to spend large amounts of money contrary to law, and that he had let contracts without competitive bidding. Springer denied every charge. He had sold his Jefferson County holdings and was living in Prineville, had missed only three days of court in four years, had let no contracts without competitive bidding, and the expenditures for road improvements that one commissioner had handled without bonds had been done over his objection and vote.

Judge Nathan Wallace oversaw the formation of Oregon's first county-unit school district. *Bowman Museum, Crook County Historical Society*

Meanwhile, the Prineville *Central Oregon Enterprise* published an article on May 24 attacking Springer. Springer sued for libel. Nathan G. Wallace, a lawyer who had married a granddaughter of David Templeton and would himself succeed Springer, represented him. Springer sued newspaper publisher A.M. Byrd, Oregon & Western Colonization representative B.F. Johnson, lawyer Jay Upton, and ranchers Stephen W. Yancey, J.W. Stanton, and George H. Russell Sr. Springer charged that the five men had formed a conspiracy in mid-May to remove him from office by libel, slander, and defamation.

Dozens of witnesses testified. Springer asserted that the recall campaign had focused more on his private life than his public work. He sought $50,000. But the jury found for the defendants and he received nothing. The recall effort never came to a vote. (Later, defendant Jay Upton in 1923 became the only Crook County resident ever elected president of the Oregon senate.)

The western rage over Crook's failure to spend for roads proved ironic. Crook invested more in its roads than the new counties. In 1919, for example, Crook had 1,050 miles of public roads, Deschutes 1,650, and Jefferson 1,550, but Crook spent $134,165.50, Deschutes $32,778.47, and Jefferson $25,000. Crook issued bonds to its legal limit of $220,000 for road construction.

Crook County received matching money from the state on one project. Only a single state highway existed in the reduced Crook County when the state Highway Commission was organized in 1916: the McKenzie, running from Eugene to Dayville. The state now designated the road between Prineville and Paulina as a state highway, and put up money to help surface it. Crook residents voted the road bonds for the same purpose, but federal officials looked at the map and refused to help, saying that it looked to them as if the road went nowhere. By 1919, an 18-foot-wide stretch was surfaced for 31 miles between Prineville and the Shorty Davis Ranch. It cost the county $102,912.27; the state $204,087.73.

Three years later, the state removed it from its system and instead adopted the Prineville-Lakeview Road (on which Creed Conn had taken his fatal walk in 1904 during the Crook County War) as a state highway. They abandoned the Lake County portion in 1928, but the section of this rough, unpaved road between Prineville and Highway 20 remains a state highway to this day. For years called the Bear Creek Highway, it is now Highway 27. In 1922, the state renamed all of the McKenzie Highway east of Madras as the Ochoco Highway.

A state maintenance report for the Ochoco Highway that year stated that "maintenance has consisted chiefly of ditches, widening of fills...Constant maintenance has been necessary on the Ochoco Highway between Prineville and the Wheeler County line owing to the large number of stock which are driven over the road from Grant and Wheeler Counties to be shipped to market from Prineville." After noting that the heavy rain of a water sprout had damaged the road in June 1921, the engineer reported that a camp had been "established near the summit near the Wheeler County Line for general maintenance purposes and, in addition, it's expected the highway can be kept clear of snow during the winter months."

Crook, Jefferson, and Deschutes counties shared one last struggle. Rabies in 1916 led to a savage war between man and beast. Central Oregonians for years had heard coyotes throughout the night but rarely saw them. Coyotes hid well. Only when rabies caused the animals to ignore caution did people learn just how large the coyote population was. Coyotes attacked any human or animal unfortunate enough to encounter them.

A mad coyote's bite could doom a victim to agony. A few people could be rushed to Portland for treatment. Generally they died anyway. For many years hydrophobia had no cure. When one was found, the pain it induced sometimes killed a patient. People in Central Oregon had to practice ceaseless vigilance. A man could be working, a woman hanging her wash, or a child playing in the yard, when suddenly a snarling coyote with a foamy mouth would spring from the nearby woods or prairie. Rabid coyotes and mountain lions slaughtered sheep and cattle. At night a family might listen while an infected coyote or cougar wandered around in the yard outside their home. A hound that rose and fought to defend its master later would be rewarded with a bullet in the head.

Coyotes came out of the hills to attack cattle in the presence of cowboys and wage fierce fights with dogs. They chased people into their houses. Men found themselves gunning down coyotes in the main streets of Central Oregon towns. At least one school had to close so that children would not have to venture across open country to attend class. Livestock, dogs, and wild animals that coyotes bit became infected and died. The dead bodies became a common sight and familiar smell. Rotting carcasses covered Central Oregon. No place was safe. One woman near Prineville was forced to flee out of her kitchen when a crazed mountain lion crashed through a window.

First Prineville depot, ca. 1925, facing McKay Creek Road where it becomes Main Street.
Bowman Museum, Crook County Historical Society

28
PROGRESSIVES
1916–1922

MERICANS ENTERED the 20th century optimistic. Technology and science would solve whatever Theodore Roosevelt and Woodrow Wilson had not. People dismissed as timid those who warned of dangers ahead.

The progressive spirit was manifested in Crook County when residents took actions that forever changed the area. They reformed, consolidated, and built, laying the foundations for an industrial future. The great miscalculation of developers David Stewart, T.M. Baldwin, and others was how long it would be before that industrial future arrived.

Stewart had been at the forefront of developments since his arrival. In 1910, for example, he had joined with W.A. Booth, Warren Brown, and Mack Cornett to form the Cove Power Company. Its authorized capitalization became $100,000. It and other Central Oregon power companies were taken over by the Des Chutes Power Company in 1913, which in turn was acquired in 1926 by the Deschutes Power & Light Company, which in 1928 was purchased by Inland Power & Light Company, which in 1930 was bought by Pacific Power & Light Company.

What role Stewart played in any particular event—whether organizing the Moonshiners or reappointing Miss Biggs as city attorney—is obscure. He preferred partnerships. Yet things happened when he was around. As mayor, in March 1916 he noted the poor condition of the Crooked River Road, declared martial law, and took every male citizen of Prineville into custody to repair it. Stewart ordered the women to provide refreshments.

The Moonshiner mayor refused to concede that loss of the county's western and northern regions would reduce his town to a rural backwater. A bright future lay ahead if only people took bold steps to secure it. The town and county had problems, but also resources. Stewart, Baldwin, and their ilk believed that the potential outweighed the difficulties.

February 1916 was not the beginning—there had been talk about a railroad and an irrigation district before that month—but that was when the talk became action. Farmers had long believed that they could reap a bonanza if the areas just east and north of Prineville were irrigated. No irrigated land existed in the Ochoco and McKay valleys, only 12,000 acres of dry farms. In 1915, a state inspector investigating the feasibility of constructing a dam on Ochoco Creek reported favorably. Farmers voted 51 to 17 to build. On February 5, 1916, they formed the Ochoco Irrigation District (O.I.D.). They elected as board members

David Stewart, John Grimes, T.H. LaFollette, F. Fred Hoelscher, F.T. Slayton, D.P. Adamson, and later, Marion Biggs. Their first priority was to raise $1.1 million in construction bonds.

During the Prineville Common Council meeting on February 24, someone suggested that the city use municipal bonds to finance the building of a railroad from the main line to town. The bonds would raise money to hire contractors. After the contractors had finished the railroad, the town would sell or lease it to a big railroad corporation or other private company. City Engineer H.A. Kelley projected the cost of laying 19 miles of track between Prineville and the Oregon Trunk at $213,000. It would prevent Bend and Redmond from eliminating Prineville as a distribution center and encourage timber companies to build sawmills in Crook County.

Mayor Stewart believed that the projects would be mutually supportive. Dam contractors shipping in equipment could pay railroad rates instead of much higher wagon rates. Later, the new farmers and ranchers of the irrigated Ochoco and McKay valleys would ship produce and livestock to market at the lower rates.

Engineers found the only viable location for the dam 6 miles east of town. Construction of a 125-foot high dam would cost $360,000, and store 47,000 acre-feet of water that would allow the O.I.D. to irrigate 23,000 acres, bonded at $47 per acre. Canals would carry water from Ochoco and McKay creeks to lands previously without irrigation, two-thirds of it already occupied by farmers. Much of the acreage belonged to the Oregon & Western Colonization Company. The main canal would be 22 miles long, with a 3,000-foot tunnel, a 1 mile long flume, and 3 miles lined with concrete. The main laterals would have a combined length of about 100 miles. The dam and canals would be built simultaneously. At the dam site, workers would pump water up the hills on both sides, then let it wash down the rocks and earth; one of the world's rare hydraulically filled dams, it would create a lake 4 miles long.

After farmers voted 56 to 28 to approve the bonds, the editor of one local newspaper interrupted the news report to prognosticate: "Cattle and sheep feeding will increase greatly, the value of the alfalfa grown [here]…and favorable weather conditions having already created a demand for hay that can scarcely be equaled. The possibility of a sugar beet plant, which could be maintained with a small part of these lands in beets, seems to be brighter all the time…Those who have started the development of this project are entitled to much praise and consideration, and as the work progresses we believe that all apparent opposition will be eliminated, and the development will thus be measurably abetted."

The O.I.D. retained Clark Kendall & Company of Portland to sell the bonds and employ a reliable contractor. The firm hired Twohy Brothers of Portland.

Meanwhile, voters in town on March 28 approved a $100,000 railroad construction bond measure by 355 to 1. W.P. Davidson declared that the Oregon &

Western Colonization Company would buy the bonds if no one else did. No one else did. Davidson reneged.

Town leaders believed that the terms of five percent interest for ten years made the bonds unattractive. They revoked the first offer and issued $100,000 worth of 30-year, six percent bonds. Keeler Brothers of Denver bought them in December. The city would still need an estimated $125,000, but could borrow it.

Unfortunately for both projects, in April 1917 the United States entered the Great War. Since 1914, Crook County residents had followed the conflict in the newspapers. America's entry came as no surprise. Forty-one locals enlisted before the draft became law in June. The first draft number drawn in Washington, D.C., included Portland lawyer David Pickett, a Crook County High School graduate. The government conscripted more than 400 Crook County men between 21 and 30 years of age. It arrested and tried those who failed to register.

In February 1918, the transport ship *Tuscania* was torpedoed off the Irish coast. Crook County men were aboard. All but one was rescued. News of the sinking jarred the community.

In a time of wartime shortages, local newspapers told residents how to save flour by substituting potato patties for bread. Dr. J.H. Rosenberg, E.J. Wilson, and Harold Baldwin formed a committee to sell Liberty Loan Bonds. Prineville, with a war bond allotment of $50,000, became the first town in the state to over-subscribe its assigned amount. A parade in September 1918 to honor the mothers, sisters, and wives of soldiers drew a large crowd. Each mother wore a star for each son serving in the military. Mothers of sons who had died wore gold stars.

South of Paulina, Bill Brown was making big money from the war. Buyers for the U.S. military had bought draft and saddle horses during the Spanish-American War in 1898. Having bred his Oregon mustangs with English Shires and French Percherons to increase their strength, Brown's horses were ideal for pulling artillery. Horses he had purchased for $3 to $10, were sold for $80 to $100. Buyers from the British government also had come to Central Oregon at the turn of the century to purchase horses for the Royal Army in the Boer War (1899–1902). Now, during the world war, buyers representing the armies of the United States, Britain, Canada, and France appeared at Brown's horse auctions, which were held at various corrals on his ranches. Thousands of Bill Brown's horses were sold at premium prices. By the war's end, he was one of the richest ranchers in the state.

From one end of Central Oregon to the other, most people did what they could to support the war effort. A Red Cross sewing circle met twice a week in Paulina, for example, to sew khaki sweaters and other items for soldiers, while in Jefferson County, farmers from the Mud Springs valley rode into Madras every evening to stand guard over the little town's wells and warehouses, protecting them against German saboteurs. Red Cross activities extended across the region. The Red Cross circle in Shaniko produced 148 pillowslips, 115 hand towels, 63 sheets, and 23 pairs of pajamas. To conserve meat, the federal government proclaimed that people should have "meatless days," which annoyed the region's ranchers.

Meanwhile, Prineville continued to build its railroad, but with wartime inflation and men absent in training camps and at the front, unanticipated problems arose. First, money. Unable to borrow the additional $125,000, the common council had to issue more bonds. In December 1917, residents voted 202 to 14 to approve issuance of $100,000 worth of 20-year bonds at six percent. Again, Keeler bought. But it was not yet enough. In September, the council had to go to the voters for $85,000 in bonds. Voters approved 127 to 9. Keeler bought. Finally, in March 1920, they had to issue another $100,000 worth of bonds. To cover interest and make payments on the principal, the town doubled its taxes.

Contractors began rail construction on May 30, 1917. It would take them three months to complete the line to Prineville. Farmers supplied labor, ranchers provided wagons, and housewives made noontime lunches to keep down costs. Contractors used local workers whenever possible.

From Prineville Junction on the Oregon Trunk south of Redmond, the rails extended to O'Neil, then McAllister, then Wilton, and finally into the northern edge of Prineville. The town built a depot, office, and shop at the northwest corner of Laughlin and Main, and livestock pens north of those facilities. For years, cattle and other livestock would be the big outbound item. The town also built a two-story train station at Prineville Junction and sidings at O'Neil and Wilton. (Later, it agreed to build a siding on Elliot Lane opposite the Vice ranch in return for land the Vices provided for a highway widening project. The railway tried to renege, and in 1946 a court ordered the siding built. It was, but later the railway tore it out again. Forty years after the court order, rancher Jack Vice was still asking the railway commission to obey it, to no avail.)

Freight service began in September 1918; passenger service in April 1919. Most outbound freight was cattle, with sheep and some horses and grain. Inbound freight was half as much as outbound and consisted of merchandise, gasoline, processed wood products, flour and feed, coal, and automobiles. In 1920, the line carried 15,213 passengers.

A manager oversaw railway operations—the first was E.J. Wilson—and answered to a Prineville Common Council commission. The first commission consisted of T.M. Baldwin, E.J. Wilson, and Dr. C.E. Edwards. Baldwin died soon after the railroad's completion. On January 12, 1919, while attending an Oregon Irrigation Congress meeting in Portland, a heart attack killed him in his Imperial Hotel room. His daughter found him the following morning.

Death by that time had become all too familiar, and not merely because of the war. The great influenza pandemic was spreading full force throughout Europe and America, and Central Oregon did not escape. Many people in the region died from it, which worldwide took more lives than the war itself.

On November 11, 1918, word came that an armistice had been signed in Paris. The *Crook County Journal* described what happened in Prineville: "Promptly at noon all bells in the city were started ringing, automobiles and various vehicles raced through the streets with cowbells, tin cans and every kind of noisy device dragging behind, anvils were brought into the square beneath the flag pole and fired until they were hot, and the image of the kaiser was pulled to the top of the flag pole by the neck.

"Starting at six o'clock in the evening, an automobile parade that extended through the city, and in which cars were four abreast, was preceded by the band and a torch-light procession through the streets and to the ball park, where a huge bonfire was lighted and the kaiser burned in effigy."

Mayor Stewart read a telegram announcing that no more draft calls would be issued. Loud cheers greeted this news.

Meanwhile, construction continued on the Ochoco dam, with hundreds of men working on the project. But relations between Twohy Brothers and the O.I.D. deteriorated. Twohy sued the O.I.D., landowners sued Twohy, but the work continued. In autumn 1921, they finished, and O.I.D. delivered the first water in 1922.

Engineers discovered seepage of 19,000 gallons a minute. How safe was a dam that leaked 27 million gallons a day? Some people believed not safe enough, and some were so worried that they camped every night on Ochoco Heights. Family campfires and lanterns illuminated the hillside above town during an entire summer.

The Oregon & Western Colonization Company already had been promoting the benefits of the Ochoco project to would-be farmers. Many bought dry farms in the Ochoco and McKay valleys. Not only near the dam, but miles to the northwest of Prineville. Now they waited for water to come through the canals. Water came, but not enough. Not nearly enough; the engineers had miscalculated. The O.I.D. could serve only a third of the land projected for irrigation. Families gave up and left their farms, and the O.I.D. defaulted on its bonds.

Progressives also changed the school system. It had come a long way from the first log cabin school on Ochoco Creek in 1868, yet the same basic organization remained. A profile of the county education system can be found in the superintendent's *Annual Report of 1899*, reprinted by Irene Helms in her 1980 history of the early schools. Just before the turn of the century, the superintendent reported 780 children aged 4 to 20 enrolled in 47 Crook County schools, taught by 23 male and 44 female teachers; 20 students attended a private school taught by 2 male and 2 female teachers. But 414 children aged 4 to 20 did not attend school. The public schools operated four months each year, on average. The superintendent received $300 a month, male teachers $41.65, female instructors $34.60.

In 1904, Crook County built a brick high school across the street from the three-story Prineville Public School. Costing $20,400, it had a basement and two stories, a bell tower, and 12 rooms, including office and library. Attendance was not mandatory. The region's best students entered much as high school graduates today can enter (but are not required or entitled to enter) a community college.

Courses taught at CCHS before 1916 included Latin, French, Spanish, botany, oration, physics, shop, math, library, ethics, salesmanship, occupations, plant husbandry, home management, military training, band, Red Cross, woodwork, sociology, Caesar, Virgil, typing, business forms, commercial law, bookkeeping, commercial geography, political economy, history of education, art, penmanship, orthography, metal work, forestry, orchestra, foods, American problems, shorthand, mixed chorus, journalism, choir, mechanical drawing, dramatics, chemistry, and Greek, Roman, and European history.

Each school had its own district; the 47 districts of 1899 became 72 by 1908 and 101 in 1914. Each district had a board and levied taxes. But many failed to levy the taxes, and the county court did it based upon the levy of the previous year. The court supervised all school districts through the superintendent. School matters both petty and major drained the court's time and energies. An entry in the Commissioners' Journal for May 7, 1914, for example, records: "Now on this day it is ordered by the Court that J.E. Meyers, County School Superintendent be authorized to purchase an International Dictionary, and said dictionary shall become the property of the School Superintendent's office." At the other extreme, in 1911 the court had to levy taxes for 5 districts that failed to do so, in 1912 for 15, in 1913 for 23, and in 1914 for 25.

Community leaders proposed combining all the school districts into one county-wide district. Nothing like this had been done in Oregon. Responsibility for the schools would be removed from the county court and placed under a county school board. The superintendent would answer to this board rather than to the county court. Voters approved the proposal on September 8, 1921, by 265 to 137. The Crook County Unit District became the first county school district in Oregon. Its first budget in 1920–1921 was $60,684.47.

State and county money, federal forest reserve fees, and special tax levies financed the district. The board determined how much money the district would need for the coming year, then levied the amount needed above the federal, state, and county monies. Until March 1931, when the legislature limited automatic tax increases to six percent a year without voter approval, the board could levy whatever it wished.

The budgets remained pretty much the same during the "twenties." In 1922–1923, the total budget came to $58,652.51, of which $26,627.65 had to be levied; in 1925–1926, $60,289.12, with $29,505.62 levied; in 1930–1931, $65,350.41, with $36,392.67 levied. A financial statement for 1927–1928 showed $5,342.16 cash on hand, $1,492.92 received from the State School Fund, $17,236.94 from the County School Fund, $30,161.64 from the County Unit Special Tax, $11,679.52 from the State Elementary School Fund, and $498.72

from Forest Reserve rentals. The superintendent received a salary of $2,400 a year, the two principals (Prineville Public School and CCHS) $3,225, teachers $32,101.37, janitors $960, and clerk and stenographer $1,200.

A salary schedule adopted by the school board in April 1922 authorized salaries for teachers without experience at $85 a month, $100 for teachers with one year of experience, and $105 for more experienced teachers. Each teacher also received an additional $5 a month for janitor work; 28 teachers were listed that year, 34 the following year, and 30 in 1930. In the latter case, 23 were rural, 7 in Prineville. In 1924, board minutes listing 31 teachers noted that two received $130 per month, two $127.22, four $122.22, ten $115, four $110, five $105, and six $90. The informality of the times comes across in a notation that school #32 had no teacher, the reason being "uncertain—may be closed."

Katherine "Klondike Kate" Rockwell lived in Crook County after the Yukon gold rush ended, operating a café in Prineville before moving to Bend. *Bowman Museum, Crook County Historical Society*

29

BOOMING BEND AND ITS NEIGHBORS
1920s–1930s

ROM 1910 TO 1920, the population of Bend increased from 536 to 5,415. It was easily the fastest growing town in Oregon. Bend had the appearance, as well as the sounds and smells, of the boom town it had become. It was filled with rushing people—construction workers, lumberjacks, homesteaders, promoters of every sort, gamblers, prostitutes, teamsters, confidence men, carpenters, salesmen, and the flotsam and jetsam of such fleshpots, as well as horses and mules pulling wagons and rigs. Dust hung over the town all day when it was not raining, and during the rainy days the unpaved streets became deep, muddy mires. The whinnying of horses, the clang of wagon team bells, the grinding turns of wooden wagon wheels, and the occasional chugging of the rare automobile, filled the air. Alcohol flowed freely and public drunkenness was common. The town had 12 saloons by 1912, besides liquor served in bordellos and gambling dens.

When the Pacific Telephone & Telegraph Company took over the local Pioneer Telephone & Telegraph Company in 1916, Bend had 24 telephones in service. By the end of the next year, it had 313. By 1924, there were 1,250 telephones in town and 165 on nearby farms.

Businessman Clyde McKay, lawyer Harvey DeArmond, and young newspaper publisher George Palmer Putnam guided the community's development during the early years. Putnam, who had arrived by stagecoach in 1909, was an heir of the G.P. Putnam's Sons book publishing family and later married aviatrix Amelia Earhart. As publisher of the *Bend Bulletin*, he set a precedent for its proprietors, having a powerful influence in the community. This was never true of Prineville or other outback towns, although Harvey Scott had done the same with the *Oregonian* in Portland. Robert Sawyer, hired by Putnam and later succeeding him, would continue to guide the town, as would Sawyer's own successor, Robert W. Chandler. Putnam worked to resolve conflicts between the irrigation companies and area farmers, canvassed in Salem to create Deschutes and Jefferson by splitting up old Crook County, and acted as a lieutenant to Gov. Withycombe. He became mayor of Bend at age 24.

Klondike Kate also moved to Bend after the sawmills caused the town to boom. For a time, she had operated a hospital and surgery in Prineville. In Bend, she nursed convalescents at her small house near St. Charles Hospital.

The St. Charles Hospital began on New Year's Day 1918, when the Sisters of St. Joseph took over a hospital near Mirror Pond. Bishop Charles Joseph O'Reilly of the Baker Diocese had been the primary force in getting the Sisters moved into Bend. The hospital, used for emergency cases only, had been operated by James D. Donovan and his wife. Hardly had the Sisters taken over before the 1918-1919 influenza pandemic struck. It killed many people in Central Oregon and strained Bend's little medical community. The hospital continued to be inadequate after the pandemic, and expansion was deemed a necessity. A new building was erected in 1921. This hospital, constructed of brick, was named St. Charles in honor of Bishop Charles O'Reilly.

Although the two big sawmills and affiliated interests dominated Bend, a variety of other businesses appeared. From 1912 to 1920, five motion picture theaters opened: the Star, Dream, Grand, Liberty, and Capitol. The Liberty Theater, built on the west side of Wall Street by Monty O'Donnell, later became the Tower, Bend's premier and longest-lasting cinema. In 1913, businessmen organized the Deschutes Power Company to acquire and consolidate all the other power companies in the region. It soon took in the Prineville Light & Water Company, Cline Falls Power Company, and the Crook County Water, Light & Power Company. Clyde McKay, who during the 1920s became the principal stockholder of the Bend Company, in 1917 founded the Central Oregon Abstract Company.

In 1925, after the Independent First National Bank closed its doors, the executives of the two sawmills became concerned that the loss of Bend's only lender would have a detrimental effect on their own interests and the whole community. Three years later, no one else having acted to replace the shuttered institution, they joined forces to establish the Lumberman's National Bank. The new firm then purchased the Central Oregon Bank assets. The lumber executives turned to their native Minnesota for a man to manage it, banker Frank McGarvey of Minneapolis.

R.E. Hufferschmidt and C.J. Dugan started the Bend Iron Works in 1916 as a foundry, and pattern machine and repair shop, for Brooks-Scanlon and Shevlin-Hixon. Covering three acres with shops and warehouses, it became the most technologically advanced foundry in Oregon during the 1920s. Its two dozen employees eventually produced machine parts for many other outback sawmills, and also for municipalities and railroads.

Joyce Gribskov (1980) mentions several early important businesses at Bend. These included the Pioneer Soda Works, which bottled ginger ale and soft drinks during the 1920s; the Bend Woolen Mill, where 25 knitters produced worsted men's clothing for lumberjacks as well as other garments from 1923 until the firm was wiped out by the Great Depression; and the Central Oregon Cigar Factory on Bond Street, which competed with two small Prineville cigar factories. The Kirtsis brothers built the region's first motel cabins, the Bend Auto Court, near Pioneer Park. Later renamed the Bend Riverside Motel, it attracted such media stars as Jack Benny, Clark Gable, Bing Crosby, and Gary Cooper. It may seem odd that Hollywood luminaries would stay in motel cabins in a mill town, but even while the big smokestacks released black and gray fumes into the blue sky, Bend was becoming noted for its nearby resorts.

Ovid and Helen Evans helped spark Bend's identification with outdoor recreation. Ovid, a millworker, in his spare time established a sporting goods store on Third Street. Helen ran the store during the day; Ovid in the evening after working at the mill. They opened in 1936 as the Great Depression waned. Later, they built an addition for firearms and motor repair. However, it became famous throughout the West for supplying the sport of fly fishing. From the beginning they had tied their own flies, selling them retail in their store and wholesale to other Central Oregon sporting goods stores. The Evans Fly Company rose to the top of the industry, and their advertising slogan, "When Evans makes 'em, the fish take 'em," was known to fishermen all over the Pacific Northwest.

While most towns looked upon the cutting of trees within their community as a sign of progress, Bend residents sought to preserve their town's natural beauty. They opposed the removal of tall ponderosa pines. Another visual attraction in the community was the Pilot Butte Inn, which became a Bend landmark for decades. A member of the Brooks family built the third edifice of that name in 1917, moving the second inn to have borne the name up the street and renaming it the Colonial Inn.

The third building was modeled on a Swiss chalet, with stone on the first story exterior and rough-hewn square pine timbers on the second and third stories. Brooks provided rooms for 100 guests, but expansion in later years included

The Pilot Butte Inn, Bend, ca. 1930. *Oregon Historical Society CN 017271*

200 additional rooms. Rock gardens and plants decorated the rear yard, while the front faced Wall Street and the south overlooked Newport Avenue. Also in the rear was a 6½ x 17 foot quarter-inch-thick plate glass window from France that gave diners a pleasant view of the river and the distant forest and mountains. Indoors, the lobby was smaller than the huge lobby of the Ochoco Inn at Prineville, but outshined the other hotel with its oil paintings and other artsy decorations. It outclassed the other Bend hotels, which in addition to the Colonial Inn included the Bancroft, Bend, Cozy, Altamont, and Downing.

However, Bend's quality business was a small restaurant that opened in 1919. Martha Bechen and Maren Gribskov, with degrees in home economics from Oregon Agricultural College, had experience in preparing and serving food. They had wanted their own cafeteria, and when they saw Bend during a vacation they decided it was just the place. They rented an old restaurant on Bond Street across from a livery stable, cleaned it up, bought new furnishings and dishes, and opened on September 9, 1919, as a cafeteria, with breads, casseroles, and salads. Originally they called it the O.I.C. Cafeteria. It became popular immediately, especially with singles looking for a place to socialize. It later was expanded into catering, moved several times, and wound up in 1936 in a new building overlooking Mirror Pond. The owners changed the name that year to the Pine Tavern (although no liquor was served). It became the most popular restaurant in Central Oregon, partly because of the cooking but also because of the excellent location—within walking distance of the Pilot Butte Inn, the Tower Theater, and the park. Diners could watch ducks and swans on the pond while they ate. It was a dining experience unavailable anywhere else in North Central Oregon.

Not everyone benefited from the Bend boom. While Bend merely drew off population from most nearby towns, it killed its old neighbor, Deschutes. Fred Stanley owned the three-story Deschutes Hotel, the town's center. Other businesses included a golf club, telephone company, the Central Oregon Irrigation Company, and the local office of the Oregon Trunk Railroad. New businesses chose to locate in Bend rather than Deschutes, but events in the 1920s hastened the latter's decline. The recession of 1926, added to other financial failure, led to Stanley's suicide in 1927. The county seized his hotel and other property in 1931 for unpaid taxes. The Central Oregon Irrigation District moved to Redmond.

Redmond lagged far behind Bend in population growth, although it almost caught up to Prineville by 1930. In 1920, it had 585 people, but faced a challenge because it had failed to become the seat of Deschutes County. Also, Bend businessmen wanted to move the county fair from Redmond, asserting that it should be held in the county seat. Redmond residents feared such a loss. Believing it would be harder to move the fair if the physical assets were more substantial, in 1920 Redmond residents spent time and money improving the grounds. Bend boosters continued to seek its removal anyway. Soon Salem was dragged into the tussle. Early in 1921, the legislature officially designated Redmond as the fair location.

As was the case with Bend, the railroad and then the timber industry created prosperity for Redmond. Though this did not cause a Bend-style boom, it did underpin the local economy. The Redmond wood industry began in 1920 when the Tum-A-Lum Lumber Company built a planing mill. Sawmills at Sisters had been trucking rough timber to the Redmond railroad station for shipment to The Dalles; Tum-A-Lum established the Redmond Pine Mill to plane the lumber first. The mill employed 20 men until it went bust during the depression of 1921–1923, but the plant facilities remained. A decade later, Charles Sine and A.E. Rell refurbished it as a box factory, named Redmond Box. Buying lumber from Dant & Russell's Grandview mill, they employed 36 people making wooden boxes there for several months, until the cash and orders ran out. The Redmond Dairyman's Bank bought its assets in 1933 for $1,500 at a sheriff's sale, which it then sold to Dant & Russell.

In the very depths of the Great Depression, Dant & Russell reopened the plant as Redmond Box and Lumber under the management of W.L. "Pop" Forsythe. Within months, Forsythe had 55 men working there. The 1930 population of Redmond had reached 994, with the mill being the town's biggest and most vital employer. On May 23, 1935, however, the mill was completely destroyed by fire, along with three warehouses and four boxcars. Redmond residents were scared, not only because of the potential elimination of jobs, but also the loss of money the workers spent locally. Business leaders joined forces to buy 33 acres of land from a neighboring farmer in order to give the mill room for expansion. After the insurance money came in for the destroyed mill, Dant & Russell rebuilt it with both a planing mill and box factory. Most of the lumber came from mills in western Deschutes County. The facility employed 100 men by the end of 1935, and eventually 150.

During the short period between the end of the Great Depression and the beginning of the recession of 1937–1939, two other timber firms relocated to Redmond. The Tite Knot Pine Mill of Sisters moved its planing operation there in early 1937. It also built a dry kiln and warehouse, and hired about 60 men. Shortly afterward, Metropolitan Lumber Company of Milwaukee, Wisconsin, announced that it would move its Portland subsidiary, Ponderosa Molding, to Redmond.

One entrepreneur emerged in Redmond with no ties to timber or agriculture. A native of South Bend, Washington, 29-year-old Otto Houk in 1919 used money he had saved while working in a shipyard during the Great War to start a Ford automobile dealership. A superb salesman of a popular product, he prospered. He and his partners—two brothers and a son-in-law—expanded into related businesses, including a Firestone tire store, a Standard Oil agency, and an insurance office. Houk expanded his car dealership to Bend, Prineville, and Condon.

However, the Redmond area business that attracted the most attention was a unique one established by a Danish immigrant. Rasmus Petersen arrived in

Central Oregon in 1906 after stops in Iowa and Washington state. He homesteaded on the desert between Bend and Redmond. In winter, when he could not farm and had time on his hands, he began building miniature Danish houses and castles using the rocks on his farm, putting them out in his yard. Neighbors came to admire his excellent craftsmanship. Needing cash to build more miniatures, Petersen put a box at his front gate for donations. People who came to see his creations would drop a few coins in the box.

When Petersen started making more money from his donation box than from crops, he sold most of the farm to concentrate on the miniatures. These he began to organize into an elaborate rock garden, with the stone houses, and rock castles and walls spaced across a large part of his yard. He paid for especially beautiful stones that were brought in, and explored Central Oregon looking for obsidian and other rocks that he needed for his structures. Petersen also traveled to the American Southwest to gather rocks of a different sort. He laid out the garden across several acres of his property, and landscaped the areas between with grass and plants. Eventually, Petersen's Rock Gardens became a major Central Oregon tourist attraction. It was written up in newspapers and became the subject of cinema newsreels. Petersen worked in his garden even into his old age, and media attention made him famous throughout the United States. In fact, in foreign countries people read about him and saw film clips of him at work. Central Oregonians routinely took visiting friends and relatives to the rock garden.

When Petersen died, his family continued to operate it, including a small shop where they sold thundereggs and other souvenirs, but they did not keep up the garden as well as Petersen had, or add to it. Still, with the rock garden's greenery, castles, minimized Statue of Liberty, and strolling peacocks, Redmond had something that no other Pacific Northwest town could equal.

Meanwhile, in Deschutes County's third most important town, the Sisters Commercial Club in 1922 formally established the Sisters Rodeo, the "Biggest Little Show in the World." From a modest beginning, the rodeo became the best known in Central Oregon.

In general, though, the 1920s were a tough decade for Sisters. Like Prineville and Madras in the same period, it was raked by fires. The first occurred on May 11, 1923. Most of the town's residents were away watching races in Redmond when a fire broke out at a commercial garage. The blaze spread rapidly to other buildings, as only eight or ten men remained in Sisters to fight it. They carried water 200 yards from an irrigation ditch to douse buildings as yet untouched. The flames raced eastward through ten buildings before reaching the Hotel Sisters, a $6,000 building owned by John Dennis. There the firefighters stopped the flames after a long, frantic battle using wet sacks. The buildings beyond—the Hotel Gist, the Hardy Allen garage, and the Leithauser general store—were spared as a result. Meanwhile, hundreds of spectators from Bend and Redmond went to Sisters to watch the fire, believing at first that it was a forest fire. The heroine was Mrs. George Aitken, who saved the post office records from the Aitken's drug store before it burned, as well as all the mail. Damage from the fire was $25,000.

The second fire, starting in the late afternoon of September 11, 1924, in a defective flue at the Hotel Gist, destroyed that part of the little town the first fire missed. Aided by men from Bend and Redmond as well as Deschutes National Forest employees, the people of Sisters fought it, but it took out everything until it reached the Hotel Sisters. Again, the hotel caught fire, but it was saved this time by people dampening down the walls with water and wet blankets and quilts. Among the buildings lost were the Hotel Gist, the Hardy Allen garage, and the Leithauser store. Total damage caused by the east side blaze was exactly the same as the west side fire: $25,000.

Thanks to the booming timber industry of the 1930s, however, Sisters became the fifth largest town in the region, behind Bend, Prineville, Redmond, and Fossil. It had a larger population than either Mitchell or Madras. During the economic resurgence between the Great Depression and the 1937–1939 recession, all the sawmills in the Sisters area operated at double shifts and the town's population reached 440.

The timber industry at Sisters has a long history, and while it never reached the level of Bend and Prineville, for several decades it provided the area with most of its income. The first area mill established in the 19th century was the Stanton plant near the Graham corral west of town. Later sawmills included the Cox mill about 1890 on the Edgington ranch and later on Pole Creek, a mill at Melvin Butte in 1902, a mill at Plainview in 1906, a mill near the Lazy Z Ranch in 1908, Joe Duckett and Everett Ashmore's mill in Sisters in 1910, a mill at Indian Ford in 1912, another at Plainview in 1918, the Spoo mill at Camp Polk in 1928, and the Hitchcock mill at the Sundown Ranch northwest of Indian Ford in 1934. The Dow and Floyd Dobkins mill was destroyed by fire in 1936. A small sawmill at Grandview led to some unusual improvements for the whole community. Dant & Russell needed to get lumber from the Grandview mill to Redmond, so it built nine miles of new road as well as a good bridge over Squaw Creek.

Two major timber families appeared at Sisters: the Spoos and the Johnsons. Edward Henry Spoo, born in St. Cloud, Minnesota, in 1888, drove trucks as a young man while living in Sisters. In 1923, he entered the sawmill business four miles southeast of town with a facility that cut 25,000 board feet a shift. He bought timber from local farmers and the Bureau of Land Management for 25 cents per thousand board feet, logged it himself, and employed two dozen men at the mill. The lumber went to Brooks-Scanlon and to local retail outlets. After four years, he moved the mill to the site of old Camp Polk on Squaw Creek, expanded the capacity, and increased the number of men working at the mill as well as the logging crews. In 1938, the firm, now bearing the name E.H. Spoo & Sons Lumber Company, built a large new mill a half mile north of Sisters that employed

100 people while Edward's son Willis took over management of the Squaw Creek mill. The Spoos began to relocate away from Sisters a couple of years later when they sold their big mill to the C.G. Hitchcock Lumber Company of Kennewick, Washington. The Spoos moved to the Clay Shown ranch, eleven miles east of Mitchell, where they built the big Mitchell Pine Lumber Company.

The Hitchcock company got its start in the area when it built a sawmill on the Sundown ranch in 1934, having until that year operated a mill near LaPine bought earlier from Claude McCauley. This mill was later resold to the Welch brothers, who relocated it to John Day. The original track of timber that Hitchcock bought came from timber buyer Col. S.O. Johnson.

The Johnson family's involvement in the timber business dated back to 1893, when a 26-year-old Canadian timber faller named Samuel S. Johnson established the Johnson-Wentworth Lumber Company in Cloquet, Minnesota. A year after its purchase by the Weyerhaeuser Timber Company in 1902, he moved to northern California, where he became manager of the McCloud River Lumber Company. Johnson also bought tracts of timber in Oregon prior to his death in 1905, including the land that A.J. Dwyer had bought earlier in the Bend area prior to his company's bankruptcy.

Johnson's eldest son, Col. S. Orie Johnson, succeeded his father as manager of the McCloud company, but quit after four years and became an independent timber buyer. Although he continued to live in Berkeley, California, much of the timber he bought was in Central Oregon, including about 40,000 acres near Sisters. In 1934, the colonel's 23-year-old son, Samuel S. Johnson, graduated from the forestry school at the University of California-Berkeley, and his father sent him to Central Oregon to oversee timber holdings there. Sam Johnson lived for three years in the Hotel Sisters, and had an office on Cascade Street with three or four employees. The Johnsons established about a half dozen independent sawmills in the Sisters vicinity before World War II, and obtained a half-interest in the Tite Knot Pine Mill, which had been built four miles south of Sisters by Bert Peterson. In 1937, Tite Knot moved its planer to Redmond, and five years later the partners moved the sawmill there. The Johnsons, meanwhile, sold their remaining Sisters area timber to the U.S. Forest Service.

Bert Peterson died at Redmond in 1944. Col. S. Orie Johnson would continue to live in Berkeley, until his death in 1952. By then, two of Central Oregon's leading lumbermen were well established at Redmond in the partnership of two men: Philip Dahl and Sam Johnson. Dahl had been born in 1910 in Spokane, educated at Klamath Falls, and after leaving high school had worked for the Weyerhaeuser Lumber Company until he accompanied his mother and stepfather to Sisters in September 1933. Dahl took over management of the Tite Knot Pine Mill upon Petersen's death.

Johnson spent World War II in the U.S. Army Corps of Engineers buying lumber from Pacific Northwest sawmills for use in the Pacific Theater. While living in Portland at this time, he met naval lieutenant Elizabeth A. Hill, who had a master's degree from Wellesley. They married in 1944 and moved to Redmond three years later.

A key development in the Deschutes country during this period was the emergence of a new town. It, too, owed its life to the timber industry, but unlike Bend and Sisters came into existence to serve the interests of a specific firm. The Gilchrist family has been mentioned earlier. Frank William Gilchrist had timber interests in Maine, Mississippi, and Minnesota when, after the turn of the century, he began buying timberland near LaPine. His agent, Joe Haner of Bemidji, Minnesota, moved to Prineville, where he established the Crook County Abstract Company, and then to Bend in 1914 and LaPine in 1926. Frank Dushau, a Gilchrist timber buyer, bought more tracts in the LaPine vicinity during frequent visits to Oregon, and Haner oversaw much of the family's holdings as well as those of the Albert Washburn Company and the Fremont Land Company. By 1937, the Gilchrists owned 85,000 acres of timberland in Central Oregon.

Frank William Gilchrist left the timberland to two nephews, W.A. and Ralph G. Gilchrist. A grandson, Frank William Gilchrist, moved to Central Oregon from Michigan to oversee a mill to cut these holdings after the family's timber at Laurel, Mississippi, was sawed out. He brought with him more than two dozen managerial employees from Laurel, who helped operate the new mill. They dammed the Little Deschutes to form a mill pond, and built an eleven-mile-long railroad called the Klamath Northern to link the mill to a new Southern Pacific line between Eugene and Klamath Falls. Eventually the Gilchrist Timber Company had 250 laborers, logging and milling the firm's private holdings. These, as well as the administrative people, lived in a company-owned town, called, of course, Gilchrist. It was located in northern Klamath County, about halfway between Chemult and LaPine on Highway 97.

Hotel Prineville was said to be fireproof until it burned down during the 1922 blaze that destroyed much of the town's business district. *Bowman Museum, Crook County Historical Society*

30

A SMALL, RURAL COUNTY

1920s

VIGILANTES, MOONSHINERS, and those who had stood aside during the long-ago conflict had grown old. Prineville's founder, Monroe Hodges, died in 1905. George Barnes raised the ire of a man in Canyon City in a property dispute. As Barnes prepared to climb into his automobile there one day in 1911, the man shot him dead. Ben Allen collapsed and died in the lobby of Portland's Imperial Hotel in 1917. His successor, T.M. Baldwin, died in the same hotel two years later. C. Sam Smith sold his 8,300-acre ranch to George Russell of Tacoma before dying of apoplexy in June 1920 at age 62. David Stewart died in 1923, about age 70. Sid Stearns in 1923, age 71. His family incorporated their business as the Stearns Cattle Company, for years one of Crook's most visible firms. The pioneers were passing from the scene. In the future people would begin calling someone a pioneer if he or she had been born early into one of the settler families.

New people became the community leaders. Men such as Robert Lister and Harry Stearns took their places on the school boards and in the livestock associations. Lawyer Lake M. Bechtell replaced Statira Biggs as city attorney and later became mayor and district attorney, while lawyer Marion "Dick" Biggs became leader of the local Democrats (serving on the party's county committee for more than 50 years), and Carey Foster and Ben Groff went onto the county court. Foster was a son of cattle baron William "Billy" Foster and grandson of Ben Allen, while Groff arrived new to the county to haul supplies to crews building the Ochoco dam. The first woman elected to a county office, Nora Stearns, became county clerk in 1928.

Hugh Lakin, originally of Minnesota, arrived in 1909 with timber cruisers employed by Shevlin-Hixon. He married Lorene Winnek in 1912. Her father had a drug store on the southeast corner of Third and Main. Lakin bought a confectionery. Fire destroyed it. In 1916, he started Lakin Hardware. He expanded his business into eight eastern Oregon retail stores and a wholesale hardware supply company.

Arthur Bowman arrived in Prineville in 1908 to work for an abstract business. Born in Kansas in 1882, Bowman had earned a law degree at the University of Washington. He became justice of the peace in 1915. For years the local Republican headquarters was inside his stone building at Third and Main. He tried to attract oil companies into the region, have the Ochoco Highway made into an important road, and worked with LaSelle Coles and others to get a dam built on the Crooked River.

The Michels became one of Prineville's most popular families. Isadore and Blanche Michel opened a grocery store after they arrived in 1900. Their sons Arthur and Sylvain were in school when their father died. Arthur, practicing baseball with the CCHS team soon afterward, was called into the principal's office. School officials, family friends, T.M. Baldwin, and Judge M.E. Brink, told him that he was old enough to run the store, so he should get his books and leave school. He did. Sylvain, on the other hand, graduated in 1917 and fought in France during the Great War.

Prineville had a movie theater prior to the Great War. In 1910, the Lyric opened (across from the later Pine Theater) in Til Glaze's old opera house as a vaudeville and motion picture theater, usually showing several short silent features each night. Other entertainment included a bowling alley dating perhaps to 1887, and a huge, covered skating rink that was built on the east side of Deer Street in 1907, but which collapsed under a heavy snow in December 1919.

The town's population rose from 1,042 in 1910 to 1,144 in 1920. Not being on the railroad's main line meant slower growth. All of Crook County in 1920 had 3,424 people; this 1:3 town-to-county ratio has continued. In 1920, Crook County had 50,908 sheep, 36,249 cattle, and 9,636 horses. Its 12 manufacturers employed only 38 people, and it remained a rural agricultural county untouched by the industrial revolution. After the rails and big sawmills caused Bend to boom, people in Portland viewed Deschutes County as urban, Crook as the place where the "cowboy" part of Oregon began. Prineville indeed called itself the "Cowboy Capital of Oregon."

A front page newspaper article in 1922 announced that a radio was being installed in a downtown office. The antenna was being put up, declared the excited reporter, and soon folks would be able to hear concerts from as far away as Chicago and Detroit.

After Prohibition became the law in Oregon in 1916 and the entire United States in 1919, Central Oregonians who maintained their old thirst and had the knowledge to make their own means of satisfying it set up stills. The first moonshine produced in the region was for local use. As demand increased in the cities, though, Central Oregonians sought to fill it.

Central Oregon became the moonshine capital of the Pacific Northwest. Men built stills in obscure spots in the rough country around Bend, the Metolius region, Prineville, the Ochocos, and the John Day. Lake Bechtell tried to enlist the support of local churches in a war against moonshiners. A succession of Crook County sheriffs, including Olie Olson (1920–1924), Stephen Yancey (1924–1928), W.S. Ayres (1928–1931), and Ben Groff (1931–1938), militated against them. (The term of former "Moonshiner" John Combs, who staged another comeback in 1918 and served as sheriff until 1920, had ended just when sheriffs began fighting the new moonshiners.)

The sheriffs fought a losing war. Every night the countryside around Prineville would light up with the fires of whiskey stills. Trucks from Portland and Seattle rumbled over the rough dirt roads to take deliveries. Farmers, unable to make money from the sagebrush-laden land they had been talked into buying, put groceries on the table by selling moonshine. And, when a well-dressed city man arrived in an expensive automobile at a hotel, well, people could just assume that he was a city bootlegger come to buy.

In the Bear Butte hills, a youth leading a packhorse in 1926 came upon a dugout hidden behind junipers in a gully. He investigated. Three state revenue officers were hiding inside because they had learned the dugout housed a still. They shot the youth dead. An inquest in Prineville exonerated the revenuers. A fortnight later Crook men dynamited the building in Bend where the officers were staying. They were not killed.

Sheriff Stephen Yancey arrested most of the big local moonshiners at one time, anticipating that it would diminish or end the illicit business. But moonshine seemed as plentiful as ever. Later, he discovered that one of the prisoners had whittled a broom handle into a key for the jail door. Unlike sheep thief Alva Tupper, who four decades before slid under floorboards to escape, this fellow had not fled the county or even the building. After the deputies and other courthouse employees went home each night, the prisoners unlocked the jail, went to their stashes, delivered orders, and then returned to the courthouse and locked themselves back in the jail before county employees arrived in the morning. Yancey ended the practice, but nothing stopped the flow of Central Oregon moonshine during Prohibition.

Stills cooking mash in a canyon outside Shaniko, or in a lava bed south of Bend, or in an abandoned homesteader's cabin near Antelope might seem unattended, but a moonshiner was watching from a safe distance until the hour when the batch was ready. People approaching a still who were not recognizable as lawmen were often warned away by a rifle shot. Few moonshiners were foolish enough to get caught, although a couple of prominent resort proprietors on the Metolius had that experience (the arresting officers helped them bring in their sheep before hauling them off to jail). One way lawmen sometimes tracked down careless moonshiners was by noting their purchase of key ingredients, such as molasses, at local stores. At Deschutes Junction, someone noticed mash running down the outside wall of a boarded-up irrigation office and called police. Lawmen raided the building but not before someone tipped off the moonshiners, allowing them time to truck out the booze before the officers arrived.

A famous man visited Central Oregon's small towns in mid-1920; William Jennings Bryan had been the Democratic candidate for President three times, and served as secretary of state under Woodrow Wilson. On Friday, July 9, a committee met the 62-year-old orator at the Madras train station and escorted him to Prineville. He spoke to community leaders during a luncheon in the Prineville

Hotel, then to a thousand people under a Chautauqua Association tent. Bryan also addressed a Chautauqua meeting in Fossil.

Minutes before midnight, May 31–June 1, 1922, a fire broke out in an empty building at Fourth and Belknap. The ten-room building had been the old school, and later an apartment house, but had stood vacant for ten days because the Prineville common council had condemned it as unsafe. An alarm was raised. Volunteer firemen arrived and pumped water onto the flames. For awhile it appeared they could contain it. But a strong wind blew in and carried burning shingles to the Jackson House, used as an annex to the new Hotel Prineville. The old hotel caught fire. From there, the flames spread across the alley to a new 50-room hotel. Mary McDowell, just days earlier, had rejected a $50,000 offer for her fine building, and because a contractor had assured her that it was fireproof, she had never wasted money insuring it. Despite the valiant efforts of the firefighters, it burned to the ground in half an hour.

The wind-whipped fire spread from the hotel to the Hamilton Livery Stables and across the street to Pete Seggling's Pastime pool hall and Harvey Cyrus's jewelry shop. Firefighters managed to save the Elkins Motor Sales Company and in doing so protected other frame structures on the north side of Third Street. That, together with a shift in the wind, prevented the fire from jumping Third and burning buildings on the south side.

Instead, it jumped Main Street. The big Cornett & Company mercantile store, which also housed the post office and the Ochoco National Forest headquarters, became engulfed. Soon most businesses north of Third were ablaze. Fire spread through a building owned by Mrs. Mona Shipp and occupied by J.A. Stein & Co. mercantile and the Prineville Bakery, to buildings owned by Mrs. Maling-Walker and occupied by plumber T.J. Minger, the telephone exchange, Lakin Hardware, Joe Gerardo's Prineville Meat Market, DesChutes Power Company, and Staley & Staley, as well as the Michel Grocery Company, Central Oregon Hardware Company, Dr. Tackman's dentistry office, R.L. Schee's real estate office, J.A. Gillis' tailor shop, a shoe shop, a newspaper building, a house, and a creamery building. Firefighters had only two trucks. Calls for help went out over the wires.

Firemen and equipment arrived from Redmond, Madras, and Bend. Riding down the grade they saw enormous dancing flames lighting up the night inside the guts of the community. When they arrived downtown they found danger, confusion, and ghastly heat.

Exploding ammunition in the two burning hardware stores kept everyone ducking and diving for cover. Utility poles that had burned at the base crashed across the streets, hindering the firefighters. Art and Sylvain Michel climbed onto their grocery store and chopped holes in the roof to release the flames inside. The fire burned Art's hands and gutted the store. A big timber knocked one firefighter unconscious. Future Oregon senate president Jay Upton fell through a trap door at Lakin Hardware onto a coil of rope, so he grabbed the rope and fled.

Sparks rose into the sky, floated on the wind, and rained down on Prineville. People climbed atop houses with garden hoses and doused their roofs. When firefighters ordered one man and his two daughters to evacuate, the man argued until a fireman slugged him in the jaw, knocking him unconscious, and removed everyone. The house burned. Elsewhere, efforts to save Dr. Belknap's house also protected other homes in the vicinity.

They pumped the city well dry, but the fire continued to spread. Town officials decided that their last hope of stopping the flames was dynamite. They lit off explosives on Main between Fourth and Fifth streets. About seven o'clock in the morning of June 1, the fire finally was brought under control. Mary McDowell stood in the smoke in front of the bank looking across the street at the rubble that one day earlier had been the finest hotel east of the Cascades. Tears streamed down her face.

The total loss exceeded $350,000, with only about $80,000 insured. The fire had been so hot that strings of melted glass were picked up a half mile from the blaze. How did it start? Theories abounded. One, that cigarette stubs discarded by boys loitering in the vacant buildings caused it. Another, a defective flue in the old school building, although the building had been empty for days. Dr. C.S. Edwards, Fire Chief George Holmes, and a local black man (unnamed in contemporary accounts) were all credited as having raised the alarm. The black man said that he heard a door slam in the locked school building just before he noticed flames. For this and other reasons, Mayor Will Wurzweiler believed that the fire had been incendiary and offered $1,000 of his own money for the arrest of the culprit. Although Sheriff Olie Olson arrested a former resident in Bend who had talked too much about the fire, the man's alibi checked out. Nobody was ever convicted of setting the blaze.

Two days later, a flue overheated and started yet another fire, this one in a building owned by Jack Benton. It completely destroyed the structure. Firefighters saved the adjoining buildings, the Mutual Creamery and a restaurant operated by Klondike Kate, but both structures suffered water damage.

Thieves pilfered some of the burned businesses, and the American Legion established a watch. Six men patrolled from sundown to midnight, six others from midnight to dawn. The Lyric Theater offered free tickets to people who had lost property in the fire. A representative of the Cary Safe Company of San Francisco arrived to assist in opening safes that had melted shut.

Every merchant announced plans to rebuild. In the interim, businesses moved into temporary accommodations. The manager of the DesChutes Power Company opened an office in his automobile. Postmaster Newt Williamson relocated the postal services in a vacant Masonic Hall room. R.L. Schee moved into Arthur R. Bowman's abstract office. J.A. Stein & Son moved to the *Central Oregonian* office. Art Michel, while helping feed people left without shelter by the hotel's destruction, reopened his grocery store in part of the old Claypool building, with Lakin Hardware in the other half. Michel did not allow the disaster to stop him from marrying Kit Love that month. J.A. Gillis moved his tailor shop into Dick Biggs' law office. H.F. Hatch, formerly with Cornett & Company, announced that he would open a new store in the Curtis Building. Central Oregon Hardware moved into the Owl Garage, and T.J. Minger and Clyde Hoover into Mike Trapman's old carpenter shop. Joe Gerardo announced before the second fire that he would move into the Benton Building, occupied by Mrs. Chapman's millinery store, and Mrs. Chapman would move her store temporarily into her house. Richard Spallinger planned to build a new building on Main Street, and Robinson and Clifton said that they would put up a new structure on Main, south of the First National Bank.

While Mrs. Mary McDowell sought money for a new hotel, men cleared away the debris. A carnival played that summer on the lot where the hotel had stood. The Prineville Hotel Company's directors announced plans in September for a new building on the same site. The biggest yet, it would have 64 rooms above a big lobby, a dining room, and eight store spaces for lease. Inspired by Spanish California architecture, it would measure 120 x 240 feet and be "as near to fireproof as it is possible to build in this locality."

It became one of the most beautiful hotels in Oregon, with a dome and an iron-grilled balcony. A garden court with fountain, flowers, and shrubbery fronted the building. Sidewalks bordered the court on three sides, and the hotel's

The Ochoco Inn, seen here soon after construction, was one of the most distinctive buildings in the outback and for years housed the Oregon Cattlemen's Association as well as many businesses and professional offices. *Bowman Museum, Crook County Historical Society*

long, inlaid porch was on the fourth side. Concrete floors, steam heat, every room an outside space each with a closet and washstand, 26 showers, and 8 bathtubs made it modern by 1923 standards.

The lobby, with terrazzo magnatile floors similar to those in the Imperial Hotel in Portland, had a natural red stone fireplace in the east wall. Its woodwork included walnut finish, and a chandelier hung from the paneled ceiling. Shades made of Australian police cloth hung above its mission windows. Entering the front glass doors, one would find the telegraph office to the right and doors leading into a sunken dining room to the left. The dining room, with white enamel walls and hardwood floor, could accommodate 200 people. The front desk and office stood at the lobby's rear. Stairs rose on each side of the desk to the well-lit second floor foyer.

The company asked for suggestions for a name; these included Hotel Prineville, The Pioneer, Rimrock Inn, Juniper Inn, Pioneer Fountain Hotel, The Oriental, Blue Mountain Inn, Oregon Trail Lodge, Ochoco Beauty, Casa Grande, Oregon Villa, Central Oregon Hotel, Oregon Palace Hotel, Ochoco Palace Hotel, Takena Inn, and Menepa. "Takena" is an Indian word for "meeting place," "menepa" an Indian expression for "beautiful." The Portland Chamber of Commerce recommended The Ochoco, while local petitioners promoted Ochoco Inn. The company chose Ochoco Inn. It opened for business on August 19, 1923.

Meanwhile, the town had another problem. No major railroad expressed an interest in buying the Prineville Railway, and other businessmen failed to make good on their offers. The town was stuck with owning and operating a white elephant. And it lost money. Competition from automobiles and buses for passenger service and trucks for freight already had driven the railroad into the red.

In 1925, railway manager C.W. Woodruff joined with Arthur Bowman and Hugh Lakin to incorporate the Prineville & Southeastern Railroad Company. They planned to build a railway from Prineville to Lakeview and Burns, and asked the common council for a one-year option to lease the Prineville Railway and operate it as part of their road. Council members doubted that the new road would ever be built and rejected the request, by a vote of three to two. And, in fact, it never was built.

The town railroad continued to bleed red ink year after year. Prineville became so desperate that it almost would have given the thing away—but not quite. It became clear that the City of Prineville Railway had been built too soon. The town and the county, which had entered the 1920s with such high optimism, began to stagnate. They had become a remote, rural place, secondary in importance to Bend and Deschutes County.

After Prineville rebuilt, nothing much new or unique happened. The rumors continued; mostly about sawmills because everyone could see that Crook County would have much to offer in the lumber industry. Yet the sawmill builders stayed away. Other rumors involved oil exploration. Still others declared that Crook

County could become one of America's great sugar producing localities. Agricultural experts confirmed that the soil would grow sugar beets and there were recurring stories that one or another businessman planned to build a beet processing plant.

Racial relations reflected state and national attitudes. Prineville's small Chinatown was gone, and the Japanese had been driven out. No Chicanos lived there. Blacks had resided in the county for years, but they, too, disappeared. Prineville became so all-white that for decades it was widely believed, although incorrectly, that the town had an ordinance barring blacks from living within its limits. Not until the 1980s did blacks move back into Crook County.

Prineville had become a typical rural Western town. People went about their business and little changed. The town neither prospered nor suffered, neither grew nor shrank. Merchants sold the same sort of goods to the same people day after day and week after week, while the same clubs and churches held the same functions week after week and year after year. It was a stable society with infrequent crime, where residents knew one another. In short, the sort of place from which ambitious youths yearned to flee and to which rat-race weary city dwellers desired to escape.

31

SLOW LANE OF THE ROARING TWENTIES
1920–1929

ANOTHER REMOTE, rural county, Jefferson, got a rocky start. Three days before Jefferson would come into existence on January 1, 1915, the county officials appointed by Gov. Oswald West met in Culver. Judge William Boegli and commissioners John M. King and Roscoe Gard needed to select a county seat. Almost always in new counties, such a selection became a contest between towns and hamlets. Sometimes it became a fight. For Jefferson, it became the latter.

The court voted 280 times before the three-way tie was broken, with Boegli for Culver, Gard for Madras, and King for Metolius. Finally, King voted with Boegli for Culver. The people in Culver built a courthouse and the new county officials moved in. But it did not end there.

Madras residents put the county seat location issue on the ballot at the next election. Madras won. Culver residents sued in circuit court. Crook County Judge Guyon Springer, whose home had been in Jefferson County before the division, issued a temporary injunction to delay moving the new seat until the lawsuit could be heard. Judge T.E.J. Duffy heard the case, then ordered the seat moved to Madras in accordance with the election results.

Angry Culver residents vowed to pursue further legal action to stop the move. But Madras residents, on the advice of their Portland attorney, W.S. U'Ren, struck first. They drove to Culver on New Year's Day 1916 in a caravan of wagons, sleighs, and automobiles. Arriving just when the courthouse opened, as planned, they began taking everything from the building that could be moved: records, furniture, safes. The district attorney, W.P. Meyers, warned them that if they continued he would have all of them sent to the penitentiary. U'Ren, hearing this, yelled: "Go to it, boys. I will defend you."

The movers continued their work. The district attorney's wife began listing the names of the movers. But there was little else the Culver residents could do. After the sleighs, wagons, and cars had deposited all the items in Madras, which took several trips, the books and other materials were divided among the officials' houses, which would be the temporary offices, except that the clerk's office was put in a small building owned by Dr. Homer D. Hale and the sheriff's office in what had until recently been the White Elephant Saloon.

The anger in Culver remained fierce, and relations between the two communities continued to be acrimonious for many years. When Madras tried to have a new courthouse built, Culver residents said they would not approve tax money

"Old Scout," here in front of the Opera House Café in Prineville, beat "Old Steady" in a 1905 race to the Lewis and Clark Exposition in Portland. These were the first motorized carriages to cross the continent. *Bowman Museum, Crook County Historical Society*

to build another courthouse when a new one was already available in Culver. The town of Madras wound up laying out $9,500 to build the city hall that became the new courthouse for Jefferson County.

Before the courthouse went up, some residents decided that they wanted Jefferson County to have a public library. About two dozen people met to get the project launched, and by October 1916 the library was ready. The county school superintendent, Lilliam Ramsey Watts, had his office at the Odd Fellows Hall, and agreed to let the library share the space with him. It was later moved to the new city hall/courthouse until the library received its own building in 1920.

The year 1924 was a time of fires in the county. A big flour mill at Metolius burned, although no one could agree if the cause was a malfunction in the elevator, or the explosion of the moonshiner's still hidden within the facility.

But the bigger blaze was in Madras. The fire burned along both sides of Fifth Street destroying the First National Bank, a drugstore, theater, abstract office, pool hall, confectionery store, butcher shop, two saloons, two restaurants, two rooming houses, as well as other buildings. The heroine of the hour was Mrs. Julie Hobson-Dussault, the telephone operator, who stayed at the switchboard while flames spread across the roof above her until the line went out. People from Redmond and Prineville rushed to Madras to help fight the blaze, but the firefighting equipment sent from Bend arrived too late to be of any help.

A year later, over at Ashwood, Jack Edwards reopened the litigation-besieged Oregon King gold and silver mine. He sank the shaft to 600 feet before a new lawsuit closed the mine again.

Like Crook County, Jefferson muddled along through the 1920s. Unlike Crook, it had some appearance of progress because it was not looking back upon a brighter past. One thing that impeded Jefferson more than Crook, however, was the fierce winters of that period.

They began in late 1919 with a season that residents long remembered as the "Winter of the Blue Snow." On December 8, snow began to fall in Jefferson County, and at an hour after midnight, December 9, in Deschutes County. A precipitous temperature drop accompanied the snowfall. By the evening of December 10, snow on the ground in Bend was 38 inches deep. Soon, snow accumulations reached four feet in Bend and Madras, and almost the same depth in Prineville. The temperature continued to drop until reaching 47 degrees below zero. The result was chaos. Especially in Bend. Ice blocking the dam killed the water-produced flow of electrical power into town. Shevlin-Hixon and Brooks-Scanlon had to close up after their logs became frozen in the river. People scrambled to save themselves from the cold, while men fought against freezing temperatures and snow to get the power going again.

All of the communities in North Central Oregon became isolated and snow-bound. Even in-town pedestrian traffic was hampered. Schools closed. Ranchers and farmers struggled to save their livestock. The name applied to the snow arose because the bitter cold gave it a blue tint. Fortunately, the storm was of short duration. A chinook blew off the Cascades, and by New Year's Day most of the snow had melted.

The following year, in mid-September, an early winter storm in the Cascades froze sheep to death. Snow drifts trapped shepherds and huckleberry pickers below Mount Jefferson.

In the winter of 1921, the temperature again dived, to 45 degrees below zero in Jefferson County. Snow accumulated to a depth of four feet.

The winter of 1924–1925 left snow drifts on McKenzie Pass three to six feet in depth until almost summer. This was discovered in late May when about 200 American Legionnaires from Bend, Prineville, and Redmond, wishing to open the pass before the state Legion convention began at Prineville in June, tackled the project of clearing the road. They gave up. Even in the automobile age, it sometimes became very difficult to enter Central Oregon.

In 1905, the toll collector for the Willamette Valley and Cascade Mountain Wagon Road had been confronted by a problem that no toll collector before had faced in Central Oregon: two Oldsmobile horseless carriages whose drivers were bound for the 1905 Portland World's Fair arrived. The collector had no idea what to charge them. Motorized carriages were not on his price list. Finally, believing the noise from the vehicles resembled those of hogs, he charged the rate normally assessed to a pig.

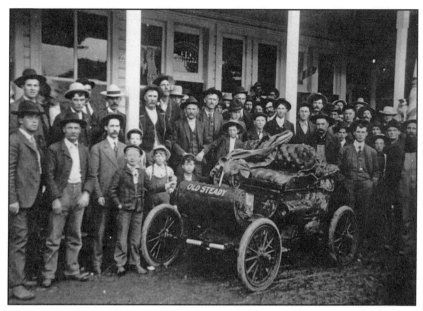

Mud-splattered "Old Steady" parked in front of the Poindexter Hotel. Note the absence of women and girls in the crowd. *Bowman Museum, Crook County Historical Society*

The first car owned by anyone in the region was a high-wheeled Holsman that the Deschutes Telephone Company bought for use at Bend. But it had to be driven in. The best route was from the north, carrying fuel in five-gallon tins along the way. The driver left The Dalles for Bend one day in 1906, traveled down Rattlesnake Canyon to Moro, and on to treacherous Cow Canyon, which he reached during the night. Easing down the narrow road, the fenders on both sides of the car were ripped up so badly by rocks that, when the driver reached the Heisler stage station on Trout Creek, they were removed.

Keith Snyder (2004) reports that by 1910 there were more than a dozen automobiles in Crook County, including Cadillacs owned by David F. Stewart, T.M. Baldwin, C.E. Edwards, and C.F. Smith. Other cars included three Fords, three Reos, two Mitchells, three Overlands, two Buicks, a Marion Flyer, and a Pope-Toledo. Ray and Hammond formed the region's first motorcar stage line. Their cars ran between Bend and Portland. Because only wagon roads crossed the mountains, they had to go through The Dalles.

The federal and state governments gradually replaced many of the old wagon roads with modern highways suitable for automobile traffic. A four-horse team with two logs—as long as a wagon was wide—was used in 1911 to clear a trail from Bend to Gap Ranch, and in 1917 it became part of U.S. Highway 20. The George Jones' road to his dairy ranch east of Bend became the main route to Prineville, and was paved in 1949. The Columbia River Highway reached The Dalles from Portland in 1915, and was paved within the decade. To reach Portland via The Dalles, however, Central Oregonians still had to risk their necks in Cow Canyon. So, in the early 1920s, the state assumed ownership of the Cow Canyon road, re-graded it, and made other improvements, so that by the end of the decade there was a good route from The Dalles via Dufur all the way to Klamath Falls, and no tolls. The state, along with Jefferson and Deschutes counties, also built a highway bridge over the Crooked River near the railroad bridge. It was the highest bridge in Oregon and so beautiful that it helped make the Crooked River gorge a tourist attraction. It eliminated the necessity of using the old narrow, twisting, and sometimes lethal road to Trail Crossing, which was abandoned.

In the early 1930s, construction began on a highway through Santiam Pass. On May 15, 1936, when the roadway opened between Belknap Springs and Clear Lake, the event was celebrated in Sisters, with businessman George Aitken hosting civic leaders from Bend and Eugene. Already an attraction for outdoorsmen, Sisters became the "Gateway to the Cascades" because of its location on the shortest ground route between Portland and Bend. For decades it would remain mostly a place to stop for a meal during a long trip, but by the end of the 20th century its location would be key to local development as an upscale community and tourist draw.

Meanwhile, a different sort of road was being extended from Bend. In 1927, the Interstate Commerce Commission granted the Great Northern Railroad permission to extend a line of the Oregon Trunk from Bend southward. James J. Hill's dream would be realized long after the pushy old tycoon had been molding in his grave. Construction crews began extending the line to Bieber, California, which would allow a direct connection from The Dalles to San Francisco via Madras, Redmond, and Bend. The first train to head south over the new rails left the Bend depot on May 1, 1928.

This transportation expansion through the region did not benefit everyone. As usual, there were losers as well as winners. Putting U.S. Highway 97 through Cow Canyon cost Antelope business and population. And nothing could save the great orchards of Dufur after the unusually wet period on the desert came to an end. Apples grown there each season remained small, unlike those in the splendid orchards of Hood River, Wenatchee, and the Yakima Valley. The Dufur Orchard Company could no longer compete, and lost money. Too much money. The Northwest National Bank of Portland foreclosed on its land, pulled out 400,000 trees, and replanted the soil in wheat. The town of Dufur sustained a hard blow economically, and the French & Company Bank in The Dalles went under. The Gilman-French Land & Livestock Company, a separate entity, survived, and Fred Wilson of Pendleton later bought it for $262,500.

Shaniko's decline continued, but it had not yet become a ghost town. The rails still reached it, and some shipping was done in and out. During Prohibition it developed into a moonshine center. The canyons around Shaniko were ideal for hiding stills. But when the town was cut off from the rest of the world on December 26, 1937, after a westward-moving blizzard left it snowbound, it did not arouse much concern elsewhere in the outback. Shaniko remained snowbound (with rare visits courtesy of snowplows that opened the road for a few hours only) until late in March 1938.

Between the world wars, nearby Wheeler County grew but very, very little. The county's population had risen from 2,484 in 1910 to 2,791 in 1920, but gained only 8 people during the next decade. Fossil's population rose by 19 from 1920 to 1930, to 538, while Mitchell's fell by 13 over the same period, to 211.

The Fossil Telephone Exchange received a franchise for telephones in Fossil in 1913, the same year that the town opened its first movie theater. A paved road went down in 1916. The following year, the town opened a public library with an impressive 600 books. James Simpson Stewart, Cottonwood Creek farmer and *Fossil Journal* editor, led the successful struggle to get the Ochoco highway routed through Wheeler County. Had the effort failed, the county might have become one of the most isolated places in America.

In 1920, banker W.W. Steiwer died, and his widow, Annie, became president of the Bank of Fossil. It had capital and surplus of $105,000. It was unusual, then, for a woman to have a bank account; almost unheard of for a woman to be a bank president. But she did a much better job than many of her male contemporaries. She managed the bank successfully through the Harding depression, the Coolidge recession, and the Great Depression. In January 1937, the First National Bank of Portland bought the sound Bank of Fossil as its 32nd branch.

Another bank had been organized in Wheeler County a week after the end of the Great War. The Mitchell State Bank, with L.L. Jones as president, E.R. Laughlin as vice president, and Fred Anderson as cashier, had start-up capital of $25,000 in November 1918. It would not, however, survive the Great Depression.

Perhaps the best measure of progress in Wheeler County came in 1923, when the first radios appeared. Two were plugged in at Fossil, one at Spray.

As happened after the Gilchrist Timber Company moved into upper Klamath County, the locating of a lumber mill in Wheeler County led to the founding of a new town. E.D. Wetmore had acquired a large amount of timber east of Fossil and organized a new firm, the Kinzua Pine Mills Company. "Kinzua," a Seneca Indian word meaning "the place of many fishes," was the name of a community in Warren County, Pennsylvania. Wetmore put a small mill on Thirtymile Creek in Lost Valley, about eight miles east of Fossil, and began cutting timber in 1927. Meanwhile, he built a large sawmill, with a cutting capacity of 100,000 board feet daily, a planing mill, and a 24-mile-long railroad spur to the Union Pacific line at Condon. The company would do their own logging, at first relying on spurs built from their railroad line, and later with trucks.

To provide housing and services to the workers, Kinzua Pine Mills built a company-owned town that eventually overtook Fossil as the largest community in Wheeler County. Its population would reach 700, as the mill and factory employed up to 330 workers. Starting in April 1928, the company railroad provided passenger service. The Kinzua post office also was opened in 1928. The town itself had a church, elementary school, emergency clinic staffed by a registered nurse, a combination department store-grocery store, community hall with restaurant, tavern, barbershop, library, the post office, meeting rooms, and 125 houses. The firm also provided its employees with trout lakes and membership in a company-owned public golf course. For the employees' children, it built a scout meeting house and camp.

Wetmore had hired Nate Coleman of the Giles Coleman Lumber Company of Omak, Washington, to build the mill. Coleman wound up owning it. He hired his son Joe as general manager, son Carl as woods boss, and son A.B. as mill manager.

Smaller sawmills also were established in Wheeler County. Robert Brown had one on Rock Creek, for example, and there was also a firm called the Chee Lumber Company during the 1930s.

Shades of the Civil War era, butternut ugliness also penetrated Wheeler County, but it had spread all over Oregon, indeed all across post-Great War America. The population of the United States rose from roughly 106 million to 123 million between 1920 and 1930. In the middle of that period, about 1925, it is estimated that membership in the Ku Klux Klan stood at about 5 million. By advocating for Protestant conservative political and religious values, donations to charity, patriotism, and opposition to Catholics, Jews, blacks, and immigrants, the KKK had emerged as a powerful political force throughout America. The 1923 Oregon legislature, whose senate president was Jay Upton of Prineville, was controlled by the KKK. Two years earlier, the Klan had organized chapters in Fossil and Condon. One source says that the chapters lasted for more than a decade, although another asserts that the Fossil group held together for only a few months. In September 1923, the Bend Ku Klux Klan chapter erected a cross atop Pilot Butte, which was set afire during an elaborate ceremony.

The spread of the Klan across America did not happen without opposition. The Veterans of Foreign Wars, American Civil Liberties Union, American Federation of Labor, and even the ultra-conservative American Legion condemned the KKK. Exposure of the methods used by Klan leaders to extract money from the membership, combined with the conviction of the KKK Grand Dragon of Indiana for a savagely brutal rape-murder, helped turn more Americans against the organization. Negative incidents also occurred in Oregon. For example, editor George Putnam of the Salem *Capital Journal* and others militated against the Klan, when, it was reported, the organization had received support from power companies anxious to avoid a Democratic tax proposal aimed at their profits. In contrast to the Salem newspaper, the Prineville *Central Oregonian* endorsed Ku Klux Klan membership as patriotic.

In late fall 1925, Klansmen paraded one rainy Saturday night down Prineville's Main Street. Led by a fiery cross and a white-sheeted horse, 53 masked "knights" marched to the Odd Fellows Hall, where they held an initiation rite and then dined.

But the tide had turned. The exposures and the Indiana scandal repelled even many reactionaries. Klan membership across Amerca fell to 2 million in 1926, to less than 350,000 in 1927. In Central Oregon, the KKK disappeared as a political force.

32

OFF THE BEATEN PATHS
1910s–1930s

N 1920, there were 2,243 farms in Deschutes, Crook, Jefferson, and Wheeler counties, in 1940 only 2,018. The number of cattle declined from 82,000 head in 1920 to 57,000 in 1940, sheep from 186,000 in 1920 to 159,000 in 1940. Much of this decline came from the disappearance of those last impractical homesteaders who had tried to grow cereals in the desert. However, some was related to the general decline of farms and ranches nationwide as the market for beef and wool softened and as the U.S. became increasingly urbanized.

The lifestyles of people living on farms and ranches did not change much between the wars unless they were in areas accessed by electrical or telephone lines. They did travel into town now in automobiles and trucks more often than in buggies and wagons, and, of course, there were bigger towns to visit.

Bill Brown entered the 1920s a rich man, the "horse king of America." He and others could still acquire some of their stock without cost by rounding up mustangs on the Great Sandy. One technique used by the buckaroos was to fan out and sweep across the desert from Bend to the Crooked River, driving mustangs they encountered in advance, and sometimes capturing as many as 200 head, which they would then break and sell. The Oregon Humane Society estimated in 1925 that there were still 100,000 wild horses on the Great Sandy.

The Hay Creek Ranch that Jack Edwards had sold in 1910 proved hardier than the sheep king had believed. It was still in business in 1927 when receiving national attention for doing business with Joe Stalin. The Soviet Union wanted to upgrade the quality and quantity of the mutton and wool of the sheep grazing on the Steppes. Russian experts toured Great Britain, France, and the United States, looking for sheep that could achieve these improvements using a cross-breeding program. The sheep they saw on the Hay Creek Ranch in Jefferson County were the best they found anywhere in the world. The Soviets paid top ruble to buy 10,000 sheep. They were shipped out of Madras in November 1927 in two trains of 27 cars. Alas, the plan, like so many Soviet plans, failed to take into account human nature and immediate needs: peasants killed and ate all the sheep within a few months of their arrival.

Not far away from Hay Creek, the North Unit Irrigation District was established. Its first meeting was held in Jefferson County's original seat of Culver in 1916, in Judge Boegli's office. The district had 133,000 acres of land, but no money to dig ditches. Its very legality was challenged in court by a group of

Bridges over the Crooked River near Redmond, 1938. *Oregon Historical Society 94335*

landowners. For two decades, until the New Deal came to the rescue, the promise of water offered by the North Unit Irrigation District went unfulfilled.

Farming remained a hard and unprofitable business and a poor man's life. Ranching, as before, fared better in North Central Oregon. In Jefferson County, a few ranches flourished and bought up old abandoned homesteads. Priday and Morrow & Keenan have already been mentioned. Along the Metolius, the Fly Creek and Three Rivers ranches expanded in this manner. Carl Smith owned the former, consisting of 17,000 acres on the Lower Desert, formed largely by paying back taxes on abandoned homesteads. He sold his land and 17,000 head of sheep to his brother Marion and moved to the Willamette Valley. Marion Smith later sold the Fly Creek Ranch to H.M. "Black Hans" Hanson of Long Creek. That same year, Harry Heising, Dan Heising's son, sold the 11,000-acre Three Rivers Ranch to E.L. "Red" Braly of Prineville.

One ranching enterprise that flourished briefly was the Black Butte Land & Livestock Company. It was incorporated in March 1902, had its headquarters on the Swamp Ranch, and grazed enormous herds of cattle and many bands of sheep between the banks of the Deschutes and the lower parts of the Cascades. The company was dissolved in 1918. However, one of its owners, William Wurzweiler, built a house on the Black Butte Ranch outside Sisters. Wurzweiler's son, Max, inherited the ranch, which he sold during the Great Depression to Steward S. Lowery of San Francisco.

In Crook County, too, ranches expanded by buying out depressed home-steaders or paying taxes on their land. The great success story among the home-steaders there was Charles and Effie Sherman. They had arrived in the Gilchrist Valley north of Fife in 1909 to homestead a 160-acre claim. The Shermans did not give up during the tough times and bought the claims of neighbors who did. Eventually the Sherman Land & Livestock Company had 53,000 acres and 3,300 head of cattle. The Hudspeths bought them out in 1958.

The most prominent ranching outfit in Crook County in the period between the wars was the S.S. Stearns Cattle Company. It was formed after Sidney S. Stearns bought out his partners Thomas Baldwin and Joe Howard. The local newspaper reported on many of the company's activities, such as movements of their cattle from place to place. Known popularly as the "Triangle Outfit" from its brand, the Stearns Cattle Company controlled most of the land between Prineville and the future side of the Bowman dam.

Prineville itself remained a cattle town. The Oregon Cattlemen's Association, founded in 1913, held its state convention in Prineville in 1915. Four towns became headquarters of the association over the years, starting with Baker City, then Burns, and then Canyon City before Prineville had that distinction for about 20 years when the state office was located in the Ochoco Inn.

But something else was happening economically in the remote areas of North Central Oregon. Something other than moving livestock or raising crops or dig-ging ore. Something, in fact, that had nothing to do with agriculture. It began shortly before the Great War.

Most pre-20th century American resorts were situated on oceanfront or lake shores, which did not recommend North Central Oregon as a site for such busi-nesses. However, the region did have lakes, and also three rivers, located amid a natural beauty rivaled by few other regions in America. It also had marvelous fishing and hunting deemed critical to the success of resorts in the interior West. Thus, the best early resorts in Central Oregon would be along the banks of the scenic Metolius and Deschutes rivers, and lakes in the Deschutes forest. Soon, summer houses would replace homesteaders' cabins in these areas.

The idea of an actual resort in Central Oregon was a novel one when Dan Heising paid $3,000 to Lee Cover for the old Bamford place on the Metolius. On June 8, 1908, he opened the Heising Resort for hunters, fishermen, campers, and anybody else interested in paying to spend some time along one of America's most beautiful wild rivers. Mostly, though, it was for fishermen, and they came from far away to angle in the Metolius, which even a half-century later would be crowded with salmon, trout, and other fish. The *Bend Bulletin* closely followed activities at this as-yet-unique business, reporting on the various activities there from season to season and listing the distinguished visitors. The newspaper's owners, the Putnams, were among its guests in September 1913, along with Copper Trust founder Thomas Lawson and his son-in-law Henry McCall. The Heisings were successful enough to expand their holdings along the south bank of the Metolius. They sold the 137-acre resort in 1930 to San Francisco capitalist Harold Mack. He made it a summer house.

A dozen years later, in 1943, the old resort was leased to Cliff and Marjorie "Susie" Ralston. With five guest cabins in addition to the main house, the Ralstons renamed it the Circle M Dude Ranch and reopened it to guests. They operated it for a decade. After going through various owners, this first Central Oregon resort was torn down as a fire hazard in 1960.

Another San Francisco capitalist, John Gallois, stayed at the Heising ranch while waiting to have his car repaired during a trip through the region. The Metolius impressed him so deeply that he bought three acres of land from the Heisings along the river, where he built a summer house. He sold it in 1947, and a year later it was acquired for $20,000 by Eleanor Bechen of Bend. She established the ten-unit resort "House on the Metolius"; guests have included movie stars and an ex-president.

Shortly before the Great War, wheat farmers from Sherman County discovered the splendid fishing, huckleberry-picking, and natural beauty of the Metolius. They began to go there after harvests were in, relaxing on the Updike place under tall ponderosas while their fishing lines bobbed in the tumbling white waters. In the summer of 1915, three Sherman County families—the Belshes, Hansens, and Henrichs—went by automobile to the World's Fair in San Francisco, and on their return trip the men drove off the main road to the Updike place to show their wives the wonderful retreat they had found. It delighted the women as much as it had the men. The families decided that they wanted to have summer houses there, so they got in touch with the U.S. Forest Service.

The USFS agreed to lease out three lots for a period of 99 years. The families then told their friends and relatives in Sherman County about their new vacation spot, and invited them to share it. However, to reach the place it was necessary for visitors to leave the main highway and travel over often ungraded, always unmarked, roads through the Crooked River and Deschutes canyons, across the Lower Desert, and over Green Ridge to the Metolius. The Sherman County men solved the problem of unmarked roads by marking them, and in a most unusual way: they gathered up all the discarded license plates they could find and nailed them two-crossways to trees and fence posts along the whole route as cynosures.

Of course, when new visitors saw the area, they too wanted summer houses there and made their own arrangements with the Forest Service. Because these people were from Sherman County, the place became known unofficially and then officially as Camp Sherman. They began building cabins in 1918 and by the next year there were a half dozen. Dick Fuller started a summer store in a tent, and later Frank Leithauser assumed ownership for a couple of seasons. Leithauser also became the first Camp Sherman postmaster. Ross C. Ornduff bought the store and built a new building for it, then sold it a few years late to R.C. Foster.

By the end of World War II, there would be 60 houses at Camp Sherman and it would be the biggest resort on the Metolius, a vacation place for Wall Street and Hollywood celebrities. For years, though, it was only a summer getaway for prosperous Sherman County residents, who passed a few weeks there picking huckleberries, hunting deer, and fishing. Independence Day found many of them at a big communal picnic, followed by a trip to Henry L. Corbett's summer house for ice cream, and finally an afternoon swim in Suttle Lake.

The Lake Creek Lodge was started by Martin Hansen after he bought a homestead from Ed Carney of Prineville in 1919. Hansen's resort gained no small part of its popularity from the meals prepared by Mrs. Hansen, said to have been a superior cook. They sold the resort in 1935.

Meanwhile, the banks of the Metolius opposite the Warm Springs Reservation became dotted with summer houses, some of which were rustic and some quite fancy. A famous temperance advocate, Dr. Clarence True Wilson, had a summer home below the Allingham place. Among the people who visited was writer Harold Bell Wright, whose novels, *The Shepherd of the Hills* and *The Winning of Barbara Worth*, each sold more than two million copies. He stayed there during part of one summer.

The biggest summer house on the river was built in 1929 by John Zehntbauer, president of the Jantzen Knitting Mills. It stood on three acres of land he had bought a few months earlier from the Heisings. The 12-room house cost a then magnificent sum of $40,000, its most impressive feature being an enormous picture window in the 40-foot-long living room, enabling people sitting at the big fireplace to look out at the snow-covered Cascades. Included on the property was a greenhouse, saddle house, garage with maid's quarters, and an orchard. A big fountain stood in front of the house. The house was destroyed by a fatal Christmas morning fire in 1957.

Long before Sisters developed into a resort locality, the state's first dude ranch was developed five miles north of the town. Henry L. Corbett of Portland sold the Sundown Ranch to its former manager, Ben Tone, and Gilpin Lovering of Philadelphia. They put in a club house and log cabins that were isolated from one another but all equipped with running water. They opened it as a dude ranch in 1923. It lasted about two years.

A woman who developed a resort during the economic turmoil of the 1930s was responsible for one of Central Oregon's best known camps. Donna Gill established Camp Tamarack at Dark Lake, near Suttle Lake, in 1935, and for 20 years operated it as a private resort for girls. In 1955, she would buy the 600-acre Indian Ford Ranch at Sisters and remodel it into a guest ranch.

No resorts developed along the Deschutes, but many regarded the river itself as a vacation spot because of the spectacular fishing. When John Y. Todd owned the Farewell Bend Ranch, he employed a caretaker, who allegedly could light his morning fire, walk to the river, catch trout for breakfast, and return to the house before the frying pan got hot. When the Rod and Gun Club of Madras started its annual fish-fry at Cowles Orchard in 1910, a single fisherman could catch up to 100 trout; most would be more than a foot long. Later in the 20th century, fishing season opened with the banks of the Deschutes crammed tight with anglers.

Deschutes County had its first lake resort about 1913. The Forest Service issued a permit to Fred Shintaffer to establish the East Lake Resort. Other resorts were established in the years prior to the Great Depression: Odell Lake, Elk Lake, Suttle Lake, Crescent Lake, and the Paulina Lake Resorts by 1926, with South Twin and Summit Lodge resorts opening in 1928.

Another form of recreation began in earnest in Central Oregon when two boys were reported missing in the Cascades. A group of experienced skiers went up into the mountains to search for them. They were unable to locate the boys, but during the search they had an opportunity to exchange ideas and opinions. What they all had in common was skiing. And the group, consisting of Chris Kostol, Emil Nordeen, Nels Skjersaa, and Nils Wulfberg, decided to form a skiing club. In 1927, they formed the Skyliners, with Carl A. Johnson as president, and with membership open to anyone interested in skiing. Louis Hill, the president of the Great Northern Railroad, donated land at Windy Ridge on the McKenzie Highway where the group built their first lodge and ski jump.

But most Central Oregonians had little time in the coming years to enjoy resorts or skiing. Tough times were coming for the whole world, and Central Oregon was not so isolated that it could escape them.

33

THE GREAT DEPRESSION
1929–1935

N EWSPAPER COLUMNIST Will Rogers warned in the early 1920s that America was headed for economic disaster. Throughout the decade he sounded the alarm. People smiled. Will could tell a joke, they thought, but he could not predict economic trends worth a hoot.

People in cities believed the economy was great, and that it would get even better. In the "Roaring Twenties," everything appeared to be booming, to people in the cities. Rural America was not booming. Parts of it were in serious economic trouble. But that was normal for rural America; nobody worried too much about it. The rural localities of Central Oregon—that is to say, the areas outside Deschutes County—muddled along. But rural Central Oregon was hit hard by the Coolidge recession, which fell especially hard on agriculture.

Before the recession, Madras had two banks: the rebuilt Madras First National and the Madras State Bank that had been organized in 1909. The latter closed its doors on December 8, 1926. At fault was the recession, during which the Madras State Bank had overextended itself trying to help Jefferson County farmers. The Madras First National Bank feared that the closure might set off a rush on it as well. Directors sent to Portland for a large amount of cash, then piled it behind the cages to reassure depositors. The cash also served to tide over customers who had lost their money in the other bank and needed immediate cash. The Madras First National survived, but 15 days later the Crook County Bank in Prineville also shut its doors. G.M. Cornett and Charles M. Elkins had been among the local business luminaries associated with the latter institution, a prominent presence in Prineville for more than two decades. Like the Madras State Bank, the Crook County Bank would never reopen.

The strong economy for towns and cities, and weak economy for rural areas, was reflected by the population shifts within North Central Oregon from 1920 to 1930. The population of industrialized Deschutes rose from 9,622 to 14,749, while Wheeler with its new Kinzua complex inched up by 8 residents, from 2,791 to 2,799. But the predominantly rural counties joined aging Wasco in a population slide. Wasco dipped from 13,648 to 12,646, Crook from 3,424 to 3,336, Sherman from 3,826 to 2,978, and Jefferson from 3,211 to 2,291.

Will Rogers was not alone in warning that the United States could not long prosper while the federal government continued to borrow money instead of raising taxes. But President Calvin Coolidge disliked taxes. He borrowed. Of every dollar the federal government spent during his administration, warned

Rogers, 25 cents went for interest on the national debt. Everyone, not just Uncle Sam, was borrowing. States and municipalities did it for funding public projects. Prineville had borrowed $300,000 to build its railroad; the O.I.D. borrowed $1.1 million to construct its dam. Corporations borrowed, often without collateral. Corporations also issued—as they always had—stock certificates that had more water in them than the Ochoco reservoir.

In October 1929, the stock market collapsed and the Great Depression began. In Oregon, the income per capita tumbled from $640 in 1929 to $337 in 1933. The Hoover administration reluctantly ditched free enterprise by establishing the Reconstruction Finance Corporation, but it was not enough. Not until Franklin Roosevelt took office in 1933 did the government really begin to dig the country out. The depression bottomed out in 1933–1934. A recession hit in late 1937, but the economy remained sound from 1935 onward. Prosperity, however, remained elusive until 1941.

At first the depression little bothered Central Oregon residents. It found local ranchers shipping out record numbers of sheep, and farmers producing bumper crops of alfalfa and other grains. Business in the stores slowed, but people still had money in their pockets. They knew about the depression from the radio and Portland newspapers. Times were tough, but there had been tougher times. Depressions seldom lasted longer than a few years. If President Herbert Hoover took the sort of aggressive action that President Theodore Roosevelt had taken against the 1907 depression, it might end before it caused real trouble. North Central Oregon might escape altogether.

What Central Oregon could not escape even briefly was an accompanying disaster: the drought that afflicted the West and brought the Dust Bowl. The drought hit some areas sooner than others, beginning in the late 1920s and striking hard everywhere during the early 1930s.

The first areas of Central Oregon to be impacted were those that already had little water. Some of the few farmers still trying to eke out a living on the Great Sandy Desert were forced out. The population of the Fort Rock Valley had been about 1,000 during World War I but would fall to about 100 before World War II. A third of the homes in town stood empty, and every one of the two dozen houses between Silver Lake and Fort Rock was empty, the windows broken. All the hamlets and little towns of Central Oregon developed a rundown, dusty, abandoned look. No money was available for upkeep or repairs.

Some of Bill Brown's horses died of thirst because they had been prevented from reaching a spring on Wagontire Mountain when rancher Frank Dobkins put up a barbed wire fence along it. Their deaths created a national furor. In May 1930, President Hoover signed an executive order to reopen a road to the spring. However, the drought prompted others near Wagontire Mountain to abandon Brown's policy of open water holes. The Hutton family, who had settled on Wagontire Mountain at the behest of Bill Hanley in 1884 and some of whom had worked for Brown, controlled more than 9,000 acres on the mountain. This was the largest amount of land anyone there had, and theirs was also some of the best acreage, grazing 3,100 head of cattle. In the early 1930s, the Huttons fenced off all of their water holes. Other ranchers sued for access in 1934. Some ranchers apparently resorted to fence-cutting. The acrimony became bitter.

Central Oregonians even got a brief taste of the Dust Bowl. The over-farmed soil in the Midwest had begun to blow away, leading to the misery that John Steinbeck described in the opening pages of *The Grapes of Wrath*. In mid-April 1931, a storm of yellow dust blew out of Montana, over north Idaho, and down into Oregon. It swept across Central Oregon, continued over the Cascades and also up the gorge, smothered Portland, flew over the Coast Range, and out into the Pacific, where ships miles from land had to sail through red-dust smog.

In Central Oregon, the strong storm riding on a northeast wind rolled a sea of yellow dust through *everything*. It blew for a day, and then suddenly stopped. Several hours passed in calm. Then the wind blew strong again, but this time in the exact opposite direction. The sun had turned very pale, and the dust was so fine that no door or window could shut it out. It came inside houses so thickly that people could not see each other across a room. The choking dust drove people to whatever shelter they could find, and no shelter was adequate. It took the paint off cars and houses, it jammed machinery. Cars and trucks stalled. Comprised of topsoil, it lifted up and took away additional topsoil in some North Central Oregon areas.

The worst hit locality was along the Metolius, which may have been raked over by the center of the strange storm. No funnel clouds were reported, yet the winds apparently equaled the force of a tornado. First, a tidal wave of dust rolled over, the same as everywhere else in the region, and then silence followed. After awhile, the wind suddenly picked up again, with a ferocity never since seen in Central Oregon. It ripped huge pines out by the roots and threw them around like straw in a whirlwind. Thousands of trees crashed to the ground. People, whipped by the dust-laden wind, fled to open places to escape the falling pines. Huge trees that had lined the banks of the Metolius at the time of the Fremont Expedition were ripped from the ground like saplings, and slammed into others that were meeting the same fate.

The Forest Service later estimated that the winds blew down more than ten million board feet of timber along the river. Had the summer crowd been at Camp Sherman and the other Metolius resorts and summer houses, authorities believed there would have been deaths. As it was, the storm damaged many houses and destroyed 12 entirely. Among the latter was Henry L. Corbett's big summer house, hit by a falling tree that caused embers in the fireplace to fly out onto the floor and start a fire. The storm terrified the few people at Camp Sherman, and injured some of them. A tree crashed onto the roof of the Camp Sherman store, trapping Mrs. R.C. Foster in the debris until she could be dug out.

Martin Hansen drove her to a doctor in Redmond, who treated her for a broken leg. Even after the storm passed, weakened trees continued to fall to the ground. Walking through the woods, or close to them, suddenly became a precarious thing to do.

Other districts were not hit as hard, but did not escape. The government estimated that between three and five million board feet of timber was blown over in the Ochoco National Forest. Power and telephone lines were knocked down, leaving town residents without electricity or communication. For awhile, Prineville was completely isolated from the rest of the world, and Bend had no communication to the north. Weirdly, only days after the storm passed, eight inches of snow fell at Hampton Butte in less than three hours.

Three months later, a fire broke out along the Metolius near the ruined forest and began to burn along both banks of the river. Firefighters went in to contain it before the flames could reach the downed timber, more than 10,000 trees. However, airborne embers preceded the main blaze, setting spot fires miles away. Embers landed on and ignited the fallen timber. Alarmed officials summoned hundreds of men to fight the inferno that rolled a blanket of smoke over North Central Oregon. The blaze burned down two sets of cabins before firefighters finally stopped it. Altogether, the Metolius fire of 1931 burned 4,000 acres on the south side of the river and 2,000 acres on the Warm Springs Indian Reservation.

By that time, the Great Depression had begun to impact Central Oregon. Money became tighter. People withdrew money from banks to meet expenses, and had less money to deposit. In February 1931, a bank failed in Redmond. But there was no run on other banks, no panic. People continued to go about their lives, more nervous but still claiming confidence.

In late August 1931, oil explorations excited people in Wheeler and Crook counties. A Northwest Petroleum Corporation geologist spoke at the Prineville courthouse about his firm's scheme to drill a well at Mitchell. He expected to hit oil or gas at less than 2,500 feet. Other big oil companies and independent producers had rushed in and leased land. Much of the Upper Country had gone under lease, and a well would soon be drilled at Suplee.

But on Tuesday, September 1, 1931, the Prineville National Bank failed to open its doors. Started ten years earlier as the Bank of Prineville, it had capitalization of $50,000. J.L. Karnopp of Portland was president, but several local residents owned stock. Harder times had led to withdrawals of more than $67,000 during a three month period while deposits came to only $40,000. Recognizing that the little bank could not survive this gradual drain, its officers called in federal bank examiners. It still had about $80,000 in deposits. The local First National helped out people whose money was trapped in the failed bank. When the Prineville National's books were finally closed in 1935, it had paid depositors almost 75 cents on the dollar. Lake M. Bechtell, a former director, bought its remaining assets.

Only one bank remained in Prineville. The First National, where Harold Baldwin had succeeded his father as president, reported deposits of $316,913.36 on March 31, 1932. More than three decades would pass before Prineville again had two banks. After the depression reached Crook County, it settled in hard. Money became scarce. By April 1932, the Lyric Theater had suspended operations for lack of business. Crook County retail sales fell by half from 1930 to 1935, from $1,040,000 to $523,000

Other bank failures in Central Oregon followed. Down in Harney County, the First National Bank of Burns closed its doors on July 5, 1932. It never reopened, and lost its building early in 1934. Also, the 13-year-old Mitchell State Bank closed its doors forever on September 1, 1932, the anniversary of the failure of the Prineville National. Of course, the Bank of Fossil, run by highly competent Annie Steiwar, survived this wrenching period of drought and depression, one of the few small lending institutions to do so.

In Bend, both Brooks-Scanlon and Shevlin-Hixon shut down their sawmills in January 1932. They did not go out of business, but would cease to operate until economic conditions improved. The closing of these two giant sawmills, and the auxiliary enterprises that depended on them, threw thousands of men out of work. The Bend boom gave way to a horrible bust. Public assistance projects were launched but were inadequate while Hoover remained in the White House.

As often happens when tragedy strikes, heroes and heroines came forth. In Central Oregon, the Erickson family appeared in that role. Peter Anderson Erickson had come to America from Sweden when six years old, grew up in the "Old Northwest" in the east, and married a Norwegian immigrant before moving to Potlatch, Washington, to work in sawmills. He arrived in Central Oregon in 1916 after he filed on a homestead near Paisley. But instead of becoming a farmer, he bought a candy store in Bend. Aided by his wife, and sons Art and Carl, after he added groceries to his inventory Erickson succeeded as a businessman in Bend's prosperous boom era of the 1920s.

When the depression arrived, and other businessmen failed, Erickson survived. More than that, he expanded. In the very depths of the Great Depression, while many believed America would soon sink into revolution, he built a new establishment on Wall Street that became two stores: Erickson's, where customers could buy on credit, and Kwality Kash, where prices were lower but only cash was accepted. Another Erickson grocery, the Economy, opened on Bond Street. Eventually the Ericksons would have 20 stores throughout Oregon, with 7 in Central Oregon, and Carl Erickson would also be involved with The Smart Shop, Bend Hardware, Lumberman's Insurance, and Deschutes Federal Savings. In Prineville alone, Erickson would have a large grocery store and a large department store. And he did not do it by pinching pennies. Throughout the depression, the Ericksons allowed people to have food when they could not pay cash, and accepted their credit when most merchants would not dare. The Ericksons trusted that people would pay their tab when able, although in some cases the debts became substantial. Also, Betty Erickson bought new clothes for some girls from poor families at The Smart Shop.

Farmers and ranchers suddenly found themselves in the same situation as most everyone else. A bushel of wheat that sold for $1.03 in 1929, went for 38¢ in 1932, and a pound of wool dropped from 98¢ in 1929 to 46¢ in 1932. The drought got worse. Farmers and ranchers who had no water in 1933 waited for the weather to improve in 1934, but the drought hung on, as tough as the depression itself.

Many farmers and ranchers lost everything. Even Bill Brown. Demand for horses had already declined after farmers switched to tractors and the military to trucks and armored vehicles. The depression caught Brown overextended. In 1930, foreman Fred Houston rounded up 1,013 horses and drove them to Bend. Freight cars then took them to the Schlosser Brothers' Packing House in Portland, where they became dog food and chicken feed. To save what remained until the economy rebounded, as Hoover had promised it soon would, Brown began borrowing money from the Pacific Wool Growers Credit Corporation: $41,000 in July 1932, $44,200 in February 1933, $47,150 in December 1933, and $47,114 in June 1934.

He repaid each loan except the last. In March 1935, he received a $31,900 loan that he covered with a chattel mortgage on his sheep. This, too, he could not repay. On June 1, 1935, Brown lost his land, buildings, and livestock to Pacific Wool Growers when it foreclosed. By that time all of Brown's horses had been rounded up and sold. He retired to the Methodist Old Folks Home in Salem. Although he had donated money to help build it, he had not reserved a place for himself and had no money. His brothers paid the $1,000 to get him in, and he died there in 1941.

Some people looked to mining for escape from the poverty produced by the depression. The Alaska Juneau Mining Company reopened the Oregon King in 1933. New buildings were put up, people employed. But not for long. It closed, again apparently because of lawsuits.

In the summer of 1934, two schoolboys eating lunch while prospecting in the Horse Heaven locality near Ashwood discovered cinnabar. One boy's father, Ray Whiting, together with C.C. Hayes, bought an existing claim there, and in association with Robert Betts and Capt. E.W. Kelley organized Horse Heaven Mines, Inc. Sun Oil Company bought the mine in 1936 and by 1944 extracted 100,000 tons of cinnabar to produce 15,000 flasks of quicksilver.

Not far away, other cinnabar mines were developed in Crook that made the county one of America's largest producers. This boom continued until World War II, when manpower shortages and falling mercury prices closed the mines. Even during the depression, though, the mines in Jefferson and Crook counties employed relatively few people, while many needed work. Crook County continued to hope for sawmills, but, noting the fate of Brooks-Scanlon and Shevlin-Hixon in Bend, hoped more for oil wells. Neither mills nor wells came.

Crook County's single unit school district provides a good example of what happened in the county and throughout the region. The district's total budget for 1929–1930 was $66,553. The superintendent earned $2,400 a year, the clerk $1,200, and the two principals $3,350. The 1930–1931 budget was $65,350.41. La Selle Coles, a high school teacher and football coach hired in 1929, recalled that he received a $40 raise in 1930. The budget for 1931–1932 was $62,404.61.

The big cuts began with the 1932–1933 budget. The superintendent's salary fell $300, the clerk's $30. The total budget was $56,584, but this amount now included the high school. The county unit budget for the schools included in the previous years was only $48,144.14, or a cut of 27 percent from 1929–1930.

In March 1933, the school board decided to cut all teachers' salaries by 15 percent for 1933–1934. This included 20 elementary and 6 high school teachers. Teachers in one-room schools would receive $675. The clerk's salary would be cut 10 percent immediately, 15 percent in September. The district paid the salaries in warrants, discounted 10 percent. The board decided that it would run the high school unless indebtedness reached the previous year's level, then close it. CCHS managed to get through the year, but just barely.

In April 1934, the board gave CCHS teachers contracts for 4½ months, with the understanding that they would be extended another 4½ months if the money became available. It did. The county unit budget for 1934–1935 was only $45,000. It hit bottom in 1935–1936, when the elementary schools budget (the old county unit) was only $41,580, and the high school $9,975. The superintendent's salary sank to $2,000, and the two principals together received only $2,175. In 1936–1937, with national recovery well underway, the board approved a $45,000 budget for the elementary schools and $12,500 for CCHS.

The board understood that people were having a tough time and sought only the money essential to keep the schools going. For their part, voters did not reject levies during the depression. Indeed, on September 11, 1935, the board authorized $29,000 in bonds to supply 55 percent of the cost of a new high school. It razed the old one and, in 1936, 5 teachers and 95 students moved into a new building at Third and Fairview.

The City of Prineville Railway, already in trouble, sank deep into the red. The progressive ideas that had led to the building of the railroad and the Ochoco dam now looked like folly. In 1930, the city defaulted on interest payments of $23,100 on the railway bonds. Rail shipments fell, and income with it. The railroad cut salaries and stopped maintenance. Soon the railway itself began to come apart. Weeds grew over the tracks. Trains derailed. Its manager begged the common council for money, but the town itself had cash problems. Finally, to keep the railway alive, the council included it in the city's annual budget.

On January 2, 1934, the Prineville Common Council passed Ordinance 300. Its arrogance was exceeded only three decades later when another council tried to force residents to get building permits before they could paint the interiors of their houses. Ordinance 300 required that every professional person or businessman in town obtain a business license, and also file monthly statements with the city recorder showing how many pounds of merchandise they had received or dispatched by any means other than the railway. They would be required to pay a fee of 10¢ per 100 pounds for all such shipments. (Historians Frances Juris and John F. Due later wrote that it was an attack on the truckers, whose competition had reduced the railway's profits for years.) Whatever its intent, businessmen already pinched by the depression petitioned for its repeal. In April, the council reluctantly complied.

With interest payments on the railway bonds halted, the city began repurchasing the outstanding bonds. It bought about $188,000 worth for 10 to 15 cents on the dollar. In 1937, it issued $197,000 in new general obligation bonds to replace the bonds still outstanding, but at interest rates of only 1 to 4 percent. Most town leaders in Prineville still believed in the railroad. The depression now was beginning to yield to FDR's New Deal, and Crook County still had all that timber standing in the Ochoco National Forest, waiting for sawmills.

34
THE NEW DEAL
1933–1942

THE LAST BELLWETHER COUNTY in America was Crook. From its founding until 1992, it voted for the national winner in every presidential election. In 1932, Crook residents gave Franklin D. Roosevelt 824 votes, Herbert Hoover 638.

After taking office in March 1933, Roosevelt inaugurated the programs known as the New Deal. Contrary to political myth, this did not involve great expenditures of money (FDR started his administration trying to balance the budget), but rather a change in spending priorities, a "new deal" of the cards. Emphasis went to public works and other projects designed to get people back to work and the economy back into gear. Once people had jobs again, the New Dealers believed, the economy would gain forward momentum, and recovery would follow.

Help came fast to Central Oregon. Farmers received loans, and also information about how to sell livestock to the government. The federal government drilled wells for drought relief. The federal highway aid program funded improvements of Highway 28. Prineville Mayor W.B. Morse and the common council asked town residents for suggestions about how to spend Reconstruction Finance Corporation money coming there through the state. Possibilities included new lighting, sewer, or water systems.

Only 27 days after his inauguration, Roosevelt established the Civilian Conservation Corps to employ young jobless men in rehabilitating forests and other natural resources under direction of the U.S. Army (in the camps) and government agencies (in the field projects). Within a month, the CCC established a camp near the Maury ranger station in the Ochoco National Forest. By early June, 67 CCC men under army control were at the site and at a second camp. The CCC opened another camp at the Rager ranger station, and the June arrival of 174 men from New York raised the total number of CCC workers there to more than 300. These men became friends of local residents. The populations of the camps exceeded those of any community in Crook except Prineville.

When Prineville residents rode out to the CCC camp at Maury to play baseball and eat hotdogs on Independence Day, a reporter tagged along. He described the Maury CCC camp in the next issue of the *Central Oregonian*:

"The camp is beautifully laid out in a small valley with spring water piped to all parts of the camp. The living quarters are army tents arranged along both sides of a 'street' and each tent is equipped with a stove, table, bunks and other conveniences. The mess hall is a large and convenient building, built in sections so it can be taken down and moved to a new camp when cold weather drives the C.C.C. workers from Maury. Each section has an opening for a window which will be screened for summer use and will accommodate a window whenever weather conditions call for protection from cold or storm. Army tarpaulins provide a roof over the table and a tarpaper roof has been built over the supply room. Cooking is done in the open. A tarpaulin roof covers the work kitchen. Boys are assigned to kitchen duty under the chef and gather in groups to peel and slice potatoes, prepare meat for cooking and mix and mould bread for baking. A huge dutch oven has been built beside the ranges, a cooler with large capacity has been built and many modern conveniences unknown to the old army camps and frontier construction camps make life more pleasant for Uncle Sam's workers."

The reporter said visitors marveled at the camp's beauty and the comforts of the workers, who were "protecting the forests from fire, developing water projects, building roads and fences, and otherwise making the Ochoco national forest into a more accessible and more pleasant playground while enhancing its value as a stock range and potential timber supply."

Prineville residents became so enthusiastic about FDR's programs by October that they marched in their support:

PROCLAMATION

Whereas, the entire United States is engaged in a gigantic experiment designed to restore prosperity and destroy the present depression; and

Whereas, Each and All of us without exception must get in line in the business army of the United States and by our undivided and whole-hearted cooperation aid the Government in its endeavor to relieve the present situation; and

Whereas, the effectiveness of the legislation enacted to assist in lifting the clouds of depression depends on universal support, and

Whereas, it is fitting and proper that a public expression of approval and support of the National Recovery Act be given by the City of Prineville and the citizens thereof,

Therefore, by virtue of the authority vested in me as Mayor of the City of Prineville, Oregon, I hereby declare and proclaim that from the hours of 2:30 p.m. to 5:00 p.m. on Friday, the 27th day of October, 1933, to be a holiday and further declare and proclaim that on said day at the hours set that the City of Prineville, Oregon, and the citizens therefore assemble for the purpose of displaying and declaring to the United States its undivided support of the National Recovery Act and the principles therein set forth.

Given this 25th day of October, 1933.

W.B. MORSE,
Mayor of the City of
Prineville, Oregon

Organized by the American Legion Americanization Committee, Morse led a parade consisting of floats, fire trucks, government employees, businessmen, and various other groups, all carrying N.R.A. banners. Prineville became the first town in Central Oregon to hold an N.R.A. parade. Federal law exempted towns of less than 2,500 from compliance with N.R.A. regulations, but grateful residents did not care.

They soon had other Roosevelt programs to cheer about. In March 1934, the federal Civil Works Administration employed 67 men to build a municipal airport on the sage and juniper flat on the mesa south of Prineville. They dedicated it in August. A new mayor, W.R. McCormick, officiated for the city, and Judge Marion "Dick" Biggs for the county. Lieut. Wistar Rosenberg landed the first airplane.

On January 30, 1935, Prineville joined 5,600 other communities in holding a President's Birthday Ball. The local ball committee consisted of W.B. Morse, Marion Biggs, R.W. Zevely, and Harold Baldwin. The American Legion formed a committee of Asa Battles, Sylvain Michel, and Joe Mason to assist with preparations. They kept expenses down hoping to make a profit on the dance, 30 percent of which would go to the Birthday Ball Commission for Infantile Paralysis Research, with the remaining 70 percent equally divided between the Shrine and Doernbecker hospitals in Portland.

Other areas of Central Oregon were benefiting as much as Crook from the New Deal, and from some of the same agencies and projects. Among the many other CCC camps that the administration opened in 1933 was one at the John Riggs Race Track, on the old Potter homestead at the head of the Metolius. Known as Camp Sisters, its 215 corpsmen built most of the roads found today near Camp Sherman. They improved the main roads, built new fire roads, established trails and picnic grounds, put up historical and boundary markers, and improved the existing campgrounds. The camp survived until 1942, when the CCC program ended during World War II.

It was not the CCC or the Civil Works Administration, however that upgraded another airport in the area—indeed the closest one to Prineville's new facility—but the Works Projects Administration. In 1924, the Redmond Commercial Club had joined forces with the local American Legion post to promote the building of a Redmond airport. The chief promoter was John Ray "J.R." Roberts. The group bought a 160-acre tract of land east of town and began laying out the facility. No big push happened, only steady effort over the years. They graded two runways. During the New Deal, the federal government contributed money to the project and sent WPA workers to labor on the desert alongside the Redmond volunteers. Eventually, just in time for its heavy use in World War II, 7,000 feet of runways were paved. Commercial flights began in 1940, and in June 1941, the airfield was named Roberts Field.

Two projects were completed in 1937 that were outside Central Oregon but nevertheless had a huge impact on the region. Immediately after he took office in 1933, Roosevelt had pushed for dam construction on the Columbia. Michael Baughman and Charlotte Hadella (2000) have noted that in the 700 miles from St. Louis to the Gulf of Mexico the Mississippi falls only 100 feet, but in the 400 miles across Washington state the Columbia drops more than 1,000 feet. This is ideal for dams, and the Roosevelt Administration proposed building ten on the Columbia. The largest, of course, was the Grand Coulee, the biggest concrete structure on earth, which produced two million kilowatt hours of electricity. An Eastern congressman moaned that there was no one in the deserts of the interior Northwest to buy such power, only "rattlesnakes, coyotes, and rabbits." However, another dam, Bonneville, was completed in 1937. In years to come, the Bonneville Power Administration would become a principal supplier of electrical energy to Central Oregon, and would string lines across the region and build substations.

The other out-of-region event of 1937 was the dedication of Timberline Lodge, built under the auspices of the New Deal on an old landslide on Mount Hood. Many Central Oregonians would stop and dine there over the years, and some would ski the nearby runs. Timberline set the precedent for other ski resorts (including the big Central Oregon resort built decades later on Mount Bachelor). Some Central Oregonians were present when President Roosevelt dedicated Timberline Lodge, including Judge Biggs and four members of the Stearns family.

Not everything about the New Deal involved economic recovery and this was demonstrated in northwestern Deschutes County. Part of the Roosevelt Administration's focus was the conservation of national resources. Roosevelt established the Three Sisters Primitive Area in 1937 with a total area of 191,000 acres, and the following year added another 56,000 acres. About the same time, the government established the Mount Jefferson Primitive Area with 85,033 acres.

On the Warm Springs Indian Reservation, a new hospital was built during these years, as well as a new boarding school with dormitories. Members of the tribes voted in 1938 to accept the Indian Reorganization Act. They adopted a constitution by which an eleven-member tribal council would govern the reservation. The eleven members would consist of eight who would be elected by a vote of the whole tribal citizenry every three years, and three chiefs, one from each of the three tribes living on the reservation.

Roosevelt put together several New Deal programs to aid farmers and ranchers. With most of Central Oregon still dependent upon agriculture, these programs proved important for both immediate relief and long-term benefits. The administration believed that in order to stabilize prices it was critical to reduce the over-supply of farm products, with the goal of eventually allowing farmers to increase prices and live on the income from their labors and assets. To this end, Roosevelt put forward and Congress approved the Agricultural Adjustment

Act of May 12, 1933. American historian Samuel Morison has noted that when Hoover left office, wheat and corn were fetching less per bushel "than…in the colonies 300 years earlier."

The AAA authorized payments for not planting crops. But it also called for the slaughter of livestock. This was because the 1933 farming year had started before the AAA was activated, so the surplus had to be stopped from increasing before it could be decreased. Millions of animals were slaughtered, and Roosevelt had the 100 million pounds of edible meat frozen by the Federal Surplus Relief Corporation and distributed to starving Americans. Most of the animals slaughtered were pigs (more than six million of them) and cattle. But the administration also believed that too many sheep grazed the land. Deschutes County's agricultural office received a federal order to buy and slaughter 5,000 of them. Their meat was to be sent to St. Louis to be canned and distributed to the hungry, and 1,000 of their pelts were to be dried and sent to Portland. But the only way to dry the pelts was to hang them over fences. As a result, an early symbol of the New Deal in Central Oregon became the fences of Deschutes County's farms and ranchers laden with the white wool of drying sheep pelts, a scene reminiscent of the 1880s' "double winters."

Crook County farmers received great news in January 1935: the Reconstruction Finance Corporation would rescue the Ochoco Irrigation District. The O.I.D. had been rebuffed years earlier when it offered bondholders several settlements after defaulting on its bonds. The depression would have made even those offers impossible to fulfill. The district and Oregon's congressional delegation tried to interest the RFC. Meanwhile, the O.I.D. reduced its projection of the amount of irrigated land from 23,000 acres to 8,500, about 1,820 belonging to the Oregon & Western Colonization Company. Finally, the RFC announced through the congressional delegation that it would pay slightly more than 20¢ on the dollar for the bonds and the construction warrants. The farmers whose 8,500 acres would carry the $285,000 debt would have 30 years to pay it off.

Like the O.I.D., the North Unit Irrigation District in Deschutes County became a big beneficiary of the New Deal. The CCC established Camp Redmond outside the town of Redmond, east of the railroad tracks, on property leased from the Deschutes County Fair Association. By September 1938, the camp had 43 buildings, including 12 barracks, officers' quarters, a main office, assembly hall, recreation hall, heating plant, infirmary, schoolhouse, laundry, supply depot, commissary, and three mess halls, connected by two miles of wooden sidewalks.

On October 23, 1937, the North Unit Irrigation District voted 179 to 10 to contract with the Bureau of Reclamation to build the irrigation system. The district agreed to repay the Bureau $8 million over 40 years. The work would be undertaken by CCC men from Camp Redmond. Three of its four companies went up the Deschutes River and established a new CCC camp of 34 buildings, called Camp Wickiup. They then began constructing a storage dam for irrigation water, later named Wickiup Reservoir. The other Camp Redmond company began digging a ditch early in 1939 that eventually was 12 miles long, 40 feet wide, and 6 feet deep. This was done by pick, shovel, and blasting powder. The work of digging and then riprapping the canal with stone lasted from 5 a.m. to midnight in three shifts. Although the outbreak of World War II ended the CCC's involvement, the project continued for almost a decade, with the U.S. Reclamation Service overseeing the wartime labor being done by a unit of conscientious objectors, and the post-war work accomplished by other laborers. Water went through the farthermost lateral in North Agency Plains on July 3, 1948.

Throughout the depression and in the years that followed, however, the state government refused to declare a moratorium on collecting overdue property taxes, often years in arrear because of the long period of drought and depression. Foreclosures became commonplace in Central Oregon. This created hardship not only for the unfortunate tax delinquents, but the foreclosures also took private land off the tax rolls, forcing government to raise taxes on everyone else to cover the balance.

As important as the New Deal programs were for farmers and ranchers, the end of the drought in 1935 helped them more. However, it also led to the worst winter of the decade. It began on or about January 9, 1937. In North Central Oregon it snowed for six days and six nights without interruption. The snow depth measured as little as three feet in some areas, more than five feet in others. In Bend, snow fell for 29 out of 31 days. The temperature there dropped to 20 degrees below zero, but that was not the worst of it. One rancher near Cold Camp, who had five feet of snow on the ground, reported that the temperature there was as low as 35 degrees below zero for many weeks. The conditions became so bitter that students of the Donnybrook School boarded with their teacher to avoid traveling between their houses and school.

Americans have always loved to start new enterprises, and even the Great Depression could not stop them. The rich ran the danger of increasing their tax vulnerability if they succeeded, and the poor might not have enough "jack" to swing a deal, but people rich and poor would try anyway. Most, of course, went broke. Location is not all that matters in business; timing is also critical. It just was not the best time. But some businesses did survive and even actually flourished. A couple that did survive—and flourish—became important features of life in Central Oregon during the decades that followed.

Myrl Hoover was a young fellow whose father George had a garage in a stone building on Greenwood Avenue in Bend. Myrl became well-known because he often was at the garage dispensing gas at the curb pump. He was accustomed to cars and had no problems driving the unpaved, very narrow, Deschutes mountain roads that intimidated many motorists. One day, in 1929, Myrl had stopped for gas at a Redmond station on his way to Portland and encountered four people who were stranded because they had missed the bus to the same city. He offered to drive them there over the old Barlow Trail in his Model A Ford, and they accepted. During the journey he began to realize that he had stumbled onto something that could be turned into a business: busing passengers between Bend and Portland over the Barlow Trail.

No sooner the thought than action. Arriving in Portland, he traded his car for a 1926 Cadillac that could seat seven people. Hoover then applied for a Public Utilities Commission license to carry passengers for pay on alternate days between Bend and Portland. In June 1929, brothers Myrl and Maurice Hoover officially went into the bus business as Mount Hood Stages, Inc. Myrl drove one day, and a partner he took in who also had a large car, R.D. Davis, drove the next. They advertised that seven dollars would get a passenger to his destination in seven hours. When the depression hit and business declined, Davis dropped out, and Myrl's father replaced him by using his own Hupmobile.

The slack in business proved temporary because people turned to buses in preference to private automobiles as money tightened. In the spring of 1930, the little company acquired two more Cadillacs. Maurice Hoover now became one of the drivers, Prince Staats another. The following year, Hoover's firm absorbed the Columbia Gorge Stage Line, opening a Bend-The Dalles route, with the former owner, Dell Mattson, becoming a driver. William "Bill" Niskanen, a Brooks-Scanlon accountant who kept the books for Mount Hood Stages, bought stock in 1933 and later became the general manager. Over the years the bus line opened routes to Klamath Falls, Eugene, and points east, and changed its name to Pacific Trailways. And for decades to follow, bus travel in Central Oregon meant Pacific Trailways.

In 1938, the *Bend Bulletin* received a license from the Federal Communications Commission to operate a 100-watt radio station. At the time it was legal for a newspaper to own a radio station, usually incorporating the paper's initials in the station's call letters, such as the *Oregonian's* KOIN (Oregon's Independent Newspaper) and the *Oregon-Journal's* KPOJ (Portland Oregon Journal). The *Bend Bulletin* identified its station with the town, KBND. It began broadcasting in December 1938 from the basement of the Pilot Butte Inn with its tower on the Deschutes. The *Bulletin's* advertising director and part owner, Frank Loggan, became the station manager. In 1945, he sold his interest in the newspaper and bought control of the radio station. Other stockholders included Mary Brown of the *Redmond Spokesman*, Bob Dickenson, and ex-broadcaster Kessler Cannon.

A Baptist minister, the Rev. Ted Goodwin, father of a later 9th U.S. court of appeals judge, believed that Prineville's news should be on the station. In 1939, he bought an hour three times a week for his "News of Prineville" show, sponsored by local businesses. Goodwin eventually tired of all the trips back and forth over the rough road between the two towns, so he installed broadcasting equipment in his Prineville house, giving KBND its first substation. The program lasted for many years and was popular throughout KBND's broadcast area.

The decade ended on an upbeat, again thanks to the New Deal. In 1939, using WPA money, Deschutes County built a new courthouse in Bend. By then the town's population was over 10,000, and the timber industry was back on its feet, with both Brooks-Scanlon and Shevlin-Hixon employing workers to turn out lumber for construction and housing projects sparked by the national recovery.

In 1938, the recovery led to a reversal of the usual flow of money. Instead of government sending money to prop up economic activity, in that year the Union Pacific and the Spokane, Portland & Seattle loaned the Prineville Railway $28,000 so that it could patch its tracks. The tracks and equipment had deteriorated so badly that the money came almost too late. And why would the big railroads care? Because the City of Prineville Railway now was shipping something over its 19 miles of track that it dearly wanted to continue hauling: lumber, and lots of it.

35

SAWMILLS FOR PRINEVILLE
1937–1941

T HE NEAREST TIMBER to Prineville stood many miles from town and any potential sawmill. Prineville itself was not situated adjacent to forests like Bend and Sisters. Reaching the woods before the advent of logging trucks in the 1930s would have required the laying of many miles of very expensive railroad track. The cost was prohibitive. This delayed the development of the Prineville lumber industry until trucks became available.

However, after the sawmills arrived, the City of Prineville Railway provided the shipping means that the progressives had predicted. In a superb combination of private enterprise and public ownership, the mills and the city railway would work together to form a seamless economic machine, the likes of which would not be found in any other community in the world, and a town far from the woods rose to a preeminent position in the American lumber industry.

But first it had to attract sawmills. Soon after Prineville built its railroad, reports circulated that A.R. Rogers of Minneapolis and W.A. Pickering of Kansas City would build a mill to cut about two billion board feet of timber that they owned in the Ochoco forest. Instead, in 1923, R.A. Booth, O.M. Clark, E.S. Collins, and other lumbermen bought 55,000 acres of timberland from the Rogers' firm, and cutting rights on land belonging to the Oregon & Western Colonization Company.

They organized the Ochoco Timber Company and looked for someone to build a mill. Booth, a Springfield lumberman, became the firm's first president and the principal promoter of the Ochoco forest's prospects. In 1925, he and his son showed Shevlin-Hixon executives around the area. Rumor spread that Shevlin-Hixon would build a Prineville sawmill. They had recently sawed out their timber holdings at Bimidji, Wisconsin. But Shevlin-Hixon stayed away. Booth labored on.

Also in 1925, local residents built a sawmill northwest of Prineville. F.S. Davidson and 18 employees cut roughly 25,000 board feet a day. Davidson Brothers used nine trucks and three heavy horse teams. Ochoco Box & Lumber Company leased the mill in 1929 and employed more than 50 men. The depression shut it down in 1932.

W.L. "Pop" Forsythe had left home when only eleven to work in sawmills. By age 17, he was managing one. He worked for Davidson Brothers and for Dant & Russell's Redmond sawmill. Forsythe drew Howard Crawford's attention to the idle Davidson mill. Crawford, president of the Tum-A-Lum Lumber retail chain, bought it. Forsythe and Crawford organized the Pine Products Company with Forsythe as president, Crawford as secretary, and Spokane lumber wholesaler Howard Soderberg as another incorporator. The mill reopened in March 1935 under Forsythe's management. It burned down the following year. The Endicott logging camp, which supplied it, continued to operate while the mill was being rebuilt. In Spring 1937, with 35 men producing 50,000 board feet of lumber daily, the mill went to two shifts.

The Alexander Yawkey Timber Company of Wausau, Wisconsin, owned the second largest stand of private timber in Crook County. Ben Alexander, president of the Masonite Company, and C.C. Yawkey, owned most of the stock. In 1937, they incorporated an Oregon firm, the Alexander-Yawkey Lumber Company. J.F. Daggett of Klamath Falls became vice president and general manager. Daggett announced that it would build a sawmill near the junction of Little McKay and Big McKay creeks, about 14 miles northeast of Prineville. The planer and drying yards would be in Prineville, the offices in the Robinson & Clifton Building. The initial investment was $200,000.

When the mill burned in 1940, the owners had it rebuilt. A year later, after 60 percent of their employees were discovered to be members of the American Federation of Labor, the A.F.L. became the bargaining union. The "A-Y" moved its mill to Prineville in 1943. An arsonist destroyed it less than two years later. The company rebuilt it just in time for an A.F.L. strike that closed 494 sawmills nationwide, including the "A-Y."

Meanwhile, R.A. Booth had little success finding someone to build a sawmill for the Ochoco Timber Company. After it defaulted on a mortgage payment to the Northwest National Bank of Minneapolis, it went bankrupt. Booth and his partners watched in frustration while Crawford, Alexander, and Yawkey entered the area to profit from the lumber boom that New Deal construction programs had sparked. Booth finally proposed to the Roosevelt Administration that the federal government purchase 28,000 acres of the company's timber land for inclusion in the Ochoco National Forest. In return, the company would use the money to build a sawmill at Prineville that would provide jobs. Shortly before the 1936 general election, President Roosevelt personally endorsed Booth's proposal in a letter to B.F. Irvine, editor of the Portland *Oregon Journal*. On December 16, 1937, the administration approved federal buying of 20,989 acres of forest land from the Ochoco Timber Company for $288,000. The Ochoco firm still retained 52,577 acres, and bought an additional 15,000 acres from the Oregon & Western Colonization Company and laid plans for a sawmill.

The stockholders decided to establish a separate operating company for the sawmill, capitalized at $100,000. In January 1938, they held the first board meeting of the new Ochoco Lumber Company in Portland's Imperial Hotel. They hired as office manager and accountant Stuart J. Shelk of Linnton, a nephew of W.W. Clark, president of western Oregon's Clark-Wilson Lumber Company and secretary-treasurer of Ochoco Lumber. Many prominent families would hold stock in the two Ochoco companies over the years, including the Hill railroad family, and Truman Collins would briefly be president of the sawmill company. Shelk himself was a grandson of O.M. Clark.

At the turn of the century, O.M. Clark had owned sawmills and flour mills in Michigan in partnership with O.P. Pillsbury. When they split, Clark took the sawmills and Pillsbury the flour mills. Pillsbury made it bigger in flour than Clark ever did in lumber, but Clark did just fine. Arriving in Oregon in 1902, he built the Clark-Wilson mill on the Willamette. When a 1920 fire destroyed a nearby mill, Clark took stock in the company in return for putting up enough money to get them back into business. It became Willamette Industries. Around 1923, Clark had bought Ochoco Timber stock when Booth organized the company.

The eldest of Clark's three children married Linnton jeweler Lewis Shelk. Their son Stuart was born in Portland in 1905. From the age of 12 he worked in his grandfather's Willamette sawmill when not in school. He studied accounting at Oregon State College, earning his degree in 1929, a bad year to start any new career. His grandfather died the same year, and his uncle took over the mill. The uncle hired him to be a timekeeper. Shelk later became the purchasing agent. He remained until 1938, when he jumped at the chance to escape to Prineville.

In April 1938, the firm announced that it would employ 25 men to build the mill. It selected a site just south of Ochoco Creek on the east side of Combs Flat Road. The first carload of lumber went out over their new spur in October. A strike closed the mill in 1941 when the owners rejected wage demands, and four employees refused to join the IWA-CIO union. After four weeks, the company capitulated, agreeing to a wage hike and an eight-hour work day. Remembering their experiences during the depression, the tight-fisted board members admired Shelk's natural conservatism as well as his business ability. They promoted him to general manager in 1944. Shelk, in turn, invested in the firm over the years and eventually became a major partner.

Paul B. Kelly contracted with Ochoco Lumber in 1938 to do all of its logging. The firm's nearest timber was 30 miles distant, and Kelly cut, hauled, and delivered it to the mill pond. He remained Ochoco's only contractor until 1941, when he bought a big tract of timber from the Connollys of Mitchell and announced that he would build a mill of his own. It would employ 75 men. He built the Paul B. Kelly Lumber Company mill about a mile from the Ochoco Highway, two miles east of the Wildwood forest camp, and installed a planer at Prineville. He planned to cut about 20 million board feet a year. Although Kelly remained a big player in the Prineville timber game until 1952, he shut down the mill in 1943 and later sold it to the Valley Tie & Lumber Company of Orofino, Idaho.

In 1939, Johnnie Hudspeth moved to Prineville from Bend. A few years earlier no one in Prineville had ever heard of him. The time would come when many people outside Prineville believed he owned the town.

Joseph D. and Minerva Jane Robinson Hudspeth lived in Marble, Arkansas, when their son Johnnie was born on April 8, 1908. The timber family later moved to Kiowa, Oklahoma. They had other children: Fred, Claude, Clarence, Lloyd "Speck," Goldie, Mabel, and Jewell. The energetic and brilliant Johnnie became the family's real leader at an early age. After the Hudspeths sawed out their timber in the Southwest, they looked to Central Oregon. Having cut scrubby stands of small pine for decades, they were impressed by the great tracts of old growth ponderosa growing in the Ochocos.

In the autumn of 1936, Johnnie Hudspeth, his extended family, and a crew of workers, arrived in Central Oregon aboard five trucks loaded with people, furniture, and portable sawmill equipment. He also brought along five mules to do the logging. The family bought timber near old Camp Watson in Wheeler County. Joseph and two of his sons ran the mill, while the other sons worked in the lumber business elsewhere. According to one story, during their first winter Johnnie Hudspeth declared, "I'll walk out of here with a million dollars or a pack on my back," to which an employee replied, "Well, sonny, you'd better start walking." So little confidence did the workers have in the operation—its portable sawmill sitting in timber miles from the railhead, run by newcomers from Oklahoma—that the Hudspeths had to pay their employees every week in cash.

These workers were not the only skeptics. Conventional wisdom declared it impossible to profit on lumber hauled to the railhead from the east side of the Ochocos. The Hudspeths had arrived with equipment and money, but many prejudiced Oregonians contemptuously dismissed them as "Okies." The Hudspeths reinforced the "Okie" stereotype by logging in the backwoods with mules. When the Hudspeth mules first appeared in Bend, young Brooks-Scanlon executives went out for a look and burst into laughter.

But these particular "Okies" had cash, experience, an appreciation for Central Oregon's tall timber, and the peculiar business skills of Johnnie Hudspeth. A man of enormous drive and ambition, he was also a superb promoter and skilled gambler.

The Hudspeths trucked their lumber from Camp Watson to Prineville. There they loaded it onto flatcars and shipped to the main line, then up to a box factory at Bridal Veil. The mill cut up to 40,000 board feet of fine grade lumber daily, and had its output contracted for a year in advance. Johnnie Hudspeth logged all day and piled lumber at the mill at night. One brother moved to Prineville in July 1937 to supervise the shipments. About a year later, the family leased Lyle Gillmor's garage at Second and Main to service their trucks. As mentioned earlier, Johnnie Hudspeth would move to Prineville in 1939.

In May 1940, the Prineville Common Council granted Johnnie Hudspeth a 20-year lease (at $1 a year) on a six-acre tract in the town's industrial park. He installed a planer there to finish the rough lumber hauled from the sawmill, now moved from Camp Watson to a site near Mitchell. By 1943, when the

Johnnie Hudspeth (center), with brothers Fred (left) and Claude, at the 1947 champagne launching of the Prineville sawmill that would make Johnnie the most famous tycoon in Oregon. *Bowman Museum, Crook County Historical Society*

firm opened an office in the Robinson & Clifton Building, it had a sawmill on Bridge Creek, the former Central Oregon Lumber Company mill near Mitchell, the former Erickson Pine mill also near Mitchell, and two portable sawmills. Soon the company was producing 150,000 board feet a day. Hudspeth used the income to buy more timber, or forested land for $1.25 an acre. Lumbermen who earlier had laughed at the Hudspeths now resented the "outsiders" turning a profit on their turf. Every year, more of the Hudspeth company's operations moved toward Prineville.

The industrial revolution had arrived in Crook County. It brought immediate and permanent change. Prineville went from a rural backwater to the most industrialized community in Central Oregon, a distinction that lasted into the 1990s. It came at a price. The town's quiet, easy pace surrendered to a faster, noisier one. The sawmills and planers made noise day and night. Trains chugged over the tracks, their plangent whistles echoing through the valley, hauling lumber to the main line. Weekday mill whistles became as familiar as the Sunday church bells. Not until the Reagan era, when Ochoco Lumber closed for retooling while the other sawmills shut down for lack of orders, would Prineville again know a sustained period of silence. Weekday mornings, people found half-burned sawdust from the wigwam burners deposited on their car windshields. Stagnant air caused thick smoke from the mills to inundate the entire valley. Overloaded log trucks rocketed down Third Street, and churned up great clouds of dust over the region's dirt roadways.

From 1920 to 1930, Prineville's population had fallen from 1,144 to 1,027, Crook County from 3,424 to 3,336. But from 1930 to 1940, Prineville's population rocketed from 1,027 to 2,358, Crook County from 3,336 to 5,533. It is unlikely that any part of this increase preceded the building of the first sawmill.

36
HOME FRONT
1941–1945

MOST PRINEVILLE RESIDENTS learned about the Japanese attack on Pearl Harbor from radio. Although shocked, nobody panicked. A few small groups gathered on street corners to discuss the news. The following day, when President Roosevelt asked Congress to declare war on Japan, all business activity ceased while people listened to the radio broadcast in stores and downtown offices. Everyone wanted to know more than what they were getting from news reports. Rumors were rife.

On December 9, the Lions Club held a regular meeting in the dining room of the Ochoco Inn. When Roosevelt began addressing the nation again, they turned up the radio and suspended the meeting. Downtown and in homes, groups gathered around radios. The Crook County Defense Committee met. Organized long ago in response to a war that appeared imminent, it had been lulled, by a relative calm, into weeks of inactivity. Now committee members agreed that their organization should be expanded. They chose Cecil Youngstrom as coordinator for defense activities.

People had been preparing for Christmas. They tried, nervously, to continue. The Lions Club decided to go ahead with plans for a free show for children on December 20, and a Christmas tree program in Pioneer Park on Christmas Eve. Mrs. May Barney, the Garden Club president, announced that their club-sponsored Christmas lighting contest would proceed as scheduled unless the government banned outdoor Christmas lights. Anyone wishing to enter, said Barney, could fill out an entry blank and drop it into boxes at the Ochoco Pharmacy, Sprouse-Reitz, Erickson's Food Market, or the Michel Grocery.

Later, the club would offer Defense Savings Stamps as prizes. The war dominated every mind. Crook County had 998 men registered with the Selective Service; 55 already had gone into the army. Many residents knew someone who had been at Pearl Harbor, and the scanty news coming from there was already gagged by wartime restrictions.

Within days, school officials had compiled information from newspapers, radio, and pamphlets informing residents about what to do in case of an enemy attack. The information was printed and distributed to CCHS students to take home. The *Central Oregonian* summarized war news from United Press dispatches and reported international as well as community developments. It asked young men planning to enlist in the navy at Bend to see the "*Central Oregonian* navy editor" for information and a pamphlet titled "Life in the U.S. Navy."

Gordon Bath, a geophysicist conducting a mining survey in the county's mercury-producing area as part of a state and federal program, held the rank of Second Lieutenant. The army called him up within hours of the Japanese attack on December 7, stopping the important survey.

Youths rushed over to Bend to enlist. The Prineville draft board, consisting of Asa Battles, Percy Smith, and Carey Foster, waited for government instructions. The county's Red Cross committee began trying to raise $1,000 as its share of a $50 million national fund. Local farmers promised to do their bit to increase the food supply.

County defense coordinator Youngstrom soon announced that, subject to army approval, Prineville would hold a practice blackout on the night of Sunday, January 18. Every light and fire in town would have to be extinguished, and all traffic stopped except emergency vehicles. Anyone violating the blackout, or otherwise breaking any law, would be fined up to $250 and jailed for 50 days. Mayor J.H. Rosenberg said that the blackout and all-clear signals would be a two-minute blast of the fire siren. Sylvain Michel would become head of the air raid warden service.

Residents gradually became accustomed to young men leaving for duty, tire collections, bandage rolling, gasoline and food rationing, extra hours on the job, no vacations, and other aspects of home front life. For March 1943, Crook County took first place in the United States in *per capita* war bond purchases by local residents.

The war had a greater impact on Deschutes and Jefferson counties. Though far from the battlefields, these localities included key installations in the American war effort. Of course, Brooks-Scanlon, Shevlin-Hixon, and other mills worked overtime, as did heavy industries throughout the country, but three big military facilities were built in the western districts of the region that were directly important to war planning.

The installation that had the greatest impact at the time was the Henry L. Abbot Engineer Replacement Center, 15 miles south of Bend, on the site of modern-day Sunriver. Although the Center cost more than 4 million dollars to build (well over 20 million in today's dollars), it was not the facility itself that had the most impact, but rather the activities staged there by Gen. Alexander M. Patch's IV Army Corps. Designated the "Oregon Maneuver," it brought more than 100,000 soldiers into Central Oregon in 1943 to practice war operations across four counties in preparation for the real thing.

The influx of such a large body of men into a mostly rural region, where the total population of the counties did not approach even half their number, produced a number of temporary changes. Soldiers trained and maneuvered across private as well as public lands, cutting and then mending fences, scaring cattle, upsetting dogs, and generally impressing many residents and amusing a few. In their free time, they visited relatives living in the region, toured such scenic draws as the Crooked River Bridge and Petersen's Rock Garden, and dined at the Pine Tavern or caught a film at the Tower Theater. Not only Bend and Redmond, but Madras, Sisters, and Prineville were host to large numbers of visitors in uniform. Aircraft participating in maneuvers flew over towns, ranches, and farms so constantly that silence was unusual. A few soldiers died during the training, drowning in the region's rapid rivers or succumbing to other accidents.

Army engineers built several bridges over the Deschutes for the mock battles, which were left for the use of local civilians at the conclusion of the exercises. Residents used these soundly constructed bridges for decades.

The army occupied the Engineer Replacement Center for less than two years before closing it, and shipping out the soldiers to fight in the Pacific and Europe. Some veterans of the war remembered their favorable impressions of the people and region, and returned to settle. Among these was young Dwight Newton, a future writer who, when he had spare time in the army, devised plots for western stories.

Huge aerodromes at Madras and Redmond were the other two large military facilities established during the war. If the Japanese invaded the West Coast, the government planned to bomb enemy positions from these bases east of the Cascades, which in the meantime would be used for pilot training. The big base at Madras, abandoned after the war, has largely been forgotten, but the smaller aerodrome at Redmond had a different fate.

The army took over Roberts Field with its 7,000-foot-long runways to establish a training base for airmen flying P-38 "Lightning" fighters and B-17 "Flying Fortress" bombers. Huge hangars were constructed for these planes and others. Civilian aircraft could no longer land at Roberts, but instead had to use an airstrip at Cline Falls. The Roberts facility became well-known to airmen throughout the country. The base published its own newspaper for the men and women stationed there, the *Redmond Fortress*. Army Air Force planes flew throughout Central Oregon and the noise of the large B-17s rattled windows, stopped hens from laying eggs, and caused cows to cease giving milk. A number crashed, and years passed before some of them were found. Even decades later, one missing bomber was discovered rusting away in the Ochoco National Forest. Bombers also flew back and forth between Central Oregon and a base in Texas.

After the war, the town of Redmond bought the airfield and all its facilities from the Air Force for $1. The long bomber runway was shortened and again the facility became a municipal airport. B-17s again would be based there, when the Forest Service acquired surplus planes for smokejumpers and its fire fighting program. The Redmond Airport became the largest airfield in Central Oregon and one of the biggest in the Pacific Northwest. Its powerful searchlight flashed through the nights long after the war, visible over the desert for many miles, even east of Powell Butte.

The need for minerals during the war led to yet another reopening of the Oregon King near Ashwood in 1942. Jack Edwards leased the mine to Fenton and Custer Young, and they operated it for several years before the shaft reached other claims. Then it was shut down, again.

No spectacular government facilities or war-related industries came to the Warm Springs Indian Reservation. However, the Warm Springs Indians did not sit out the war, any more than they had sat out the earlier, considerably smaller conflicts against the Paiutes, Modocs, and Bannocks. Seventy Indians from the reservation served in the armed forces.

While the war benefited the economy of most of Central Oregon, it did not benefit every community and actually hurt some areas. Especially Shaniko. In the summer of 1942, the Union Pacific applied to the Interstate Commerce Commission to abandon its line to Shaniko, claiming that it had lost money for two years. Stunned residents of Wasco, Jefferson, and Sherman counties, led by Giles French, appealed the decision, and the ICC scheduled a hearing. Before it could be held, the Reserve Metals Corporation, a federally-owned military supply operation, seized the line to confiscate the rails for use in the war effort. French and other representatives rushed to Washington, D.C., before the government could rip up the tracks, appealing to the War Production Board and Sen. Charles L. McNary of Oregon.

The War Production Board became convinced that the line really was essential for transporting grain from the area and ordered the Reserve Metals Corporation to desist. The line was returned to the Union Pacific, much to the latter's distress. The Union Pacific pressed its application to vacate, and in July 1943 the ICC finally gave the railroad permission to abandon the Shaniko tracks. Local residents could do nothing to stop it. On November 30, 1943, the last train left Shaniko, and soon the rails were pulled up from what had once been the terminal that served all of Central Oregon.

The war years also adversely affected Wheeler County. Until then, the county had grown in population, even while other rural areas declined. With the Ochoco highway running through the county, Kinzua shipping out trainloads of lumber, and repeated efforts to develop oil wells, Wheeler had been proportionally more stable than surrounding counties. Descendants of those men and women who had first penetrated the mountains to settle in this isolated area had, for the most part, remained. But the war changed that. Young men went into the military, while older men left to work in the Prineville and Bend mills, or the shipbuilding and other war industries at Portland and elsewhere. Except for brief visits, few of them ever returned.

Due to the war, Prineville changed its railroad in ways that would have important repercussions for the post-war timber industry. After Prineville's mayor, Dr. J.H. Rosenberg, died in 1942, the Common Council had to select a new mayor. The focus turned to a woman. Three of the six council members voted for May Barney, who had moved to town only 3 years earlier and had served on the council just 14 months. However, two ballots had ended in a deadlock, with two members declining to vote for her and Barney refusing to vote for herself. They called a recess and the three members convinced Barney to vote for herself. She became the only woman mayor in wartime Oregon.

A difficulty Barney and the council needed to tackle was the state of the Prineville Railway's equipment and tracks. Manager C.W. Woodruff had nursed the railroad through the depression and in 1938 started rebuilding it almost from scratch. He replaced most of the 19 miles of track, and added new spurs and extensions. But the war led to increases in freight traffic and other problems. Bitter complaints about the railroad's condition came from the Office of Defense Transportation and local sawmills. Trains crawled at a snail's pace to avoid derailment or damaging the tracks. Regardless, derailments sometimes occurred several times in a single week.

In January 1945, Paul B. Kelly took a seat on the Common Council; Mayor Barney appointed him as chairman of the railway commission, with Richard P. McRae and H.L. Munkres. The railway commission then signed a contract with Morrison-Knutson to do extensive maintenance work on a unit bid basis. At the commission's urging, the council replaced C.W. Woodruff after 21 years as railway manager with C.C. McGlenn. The town loaned the railway another $19,000. Probably at Kelly's urging, Alexander-Yawkey, Ochoco Lumber, and Pine Products each loaned the railway $8,000. Also, again at Kelly's request, the town transferred $10,000 from the sewer extension fund into the railway fund. McGlenn began rehabilitating the tracks and replacing old equipment, in essence yet again rebuilding the railway. He also built a new 1,250-foot spur to the Brown and Bozarth potato plants.

In the latter part of the war, a danger lurked over Central Oregon that almost nobody knew about at the time. Just outside the Klamath Indian Reservation, it led to the only civilian casualties resulting from direct enemy activity within any of the 48 states during the war. Two adults took five children for a picnic in May 1945 to a spot near the hamlet of Bly. When one of the picnickers found a very large balloon stuck in a tree, all but one in the group rushed over to discover what it was. It exploded, killing one of the adults and all of the children. It turned out that the huge balloon was one of thousands that the Japanese had booby-trapped and then released, to be carried by prevailing winds across the Pacific to the United States in hopes of starting large forest fires. Many had landed in Oregon, though the Japanese effort proved ineffective. The government had issued no warning about the balloons lest it cause a lowering of morale! A monument was placed on the picnic spot five years later.

By 1945, Central Oregonians had become all too familiar with the notices of battlefield deaths and new rationing restrictions. They cheered as Allied forces advanced across Europe and the Pacific. When word arrived of President Roosevelt's sudden death on April 12, schools closed immediately. Spirits rose again when Germany surrendered shortly afterward in early May. When it became obvious in the summer of 1945 that Japan also would soon surrender, the Prineville-Crook County Chamber of Commerce worked out a celebration closure schedule for local businesses. Storeowners placed signs in their windows announcing that they would shut down when word came of the surrender and remain closed the following day.

Shortly after 4 p.m. on a Tuesday in August, word did come. The fire siren blew and people rushed out of stores and offices asking one another, "Is it true?" People downtown cheered and honked their horns, sawmill whistles blew, and workers headed home early. Minutes after the siren started, restaurants, saloons, stores, and the state liquor agency all closed their doors. The following day, one restaurant opened part time and the *Central Oregonian* prepared its next issue, but everything else remained closed down. The business district was deserted, as well as the post office, courthouse, and schools. The sawmills were quiet.

Businesses, excepting the mills, reopened on Thursday, even though President Harry Truman had designated Wednesday and Thursday as holidays for federal employees. Churches held special services.

Prineville was about to enter the post-war period—an era of high hopes, a flourishing economy, and contentious labor problems. Prineville, which had missed out during the Roaring '20s, would have a central seat in a thriving post-war future. The former cow town was about to become a prosperous, corrupt, free-wheeling boom town. Cash would flow. Lumber executives would buy or build houses on the Ochoco and Loma Vista heights. Returning veterans would find jobs in new sawmills and in auxiliary industries. Before the decade ended, more pine lumber would be shipped out of Prineville than any other railhead in the United States.

37

THE SMOKESTACK AGE
1946–1952

ETWEEN V-J DAY and September 26, 1946, 5,599 new lumber firms began business in Oregon. Some started up in Central Oregon, though the pre-war companies still held the ascendancy. In the region, timber remained the new, big, and profitable industry, while agriculture's importance continued a long decline. Many could reap profits in timber, few in agriculture. It did not matter if a person owned a sawmill or ranch, or worked in a sawmill or on a ranch, it was the same. But the days of the timber boom, too, would be limited, and everybody knew that from the start. People in the Pacific Northwest remembered why many of the big mills that had begun in the "Old Northwest" in the upper central part of the United States were no longer there.

It would be difficult to record the names of all the area's post-war sawmills. A list of the companies using Highway 28 included the C.L. Pine Company (35 employees), Blue Mountain Lumber (225), Lawford Lumber Company (40), H.G. Foran Lumber Company (75), Pine Products Company (175), Hudspeth Sawmill Company (40), Evans Lumber Company (75), Midstate Lumber Company (30), Ochoco Lumber Company (150), Kimberly Lumber Company (n.a.), Valley Pine Company (15), Central Oregon Lumber (12), Wells & Nash Lumber Company (32), Mitchell Pine Lumber Company (85), Hudspeth Pine, Inc. (185), Hudspeth Sawmill Company No. 2 (75), Alexander-Yawkey Lumber Company (250), Forest Products Company (20), and Willis Spoo-Roach (40). In 1948, Alexander-Yawkey and Hudspeth Pine each had an annual payroll of $1 million, Ochoco Lumber Company $650,000, Pine Products $495,000, Evans Lumber Company $480,000, Hudspeth Sawmill Company No. 2 $275,000, and Hudspeth Sawmill Company $125,000.

Late in 1942, the Spoos had shut down the Mitchell Pine Lumber Company to retool. It replaced all its motors, equipment, and machine parts with new equipment bought from the Prineville Machine & Supply Company. Willis Spoo oversaw the family's remaining interests at Sisters until they closed them out during the war. He removed the mill to Post in 1946, where he ran it for four years. About the same time that Spoo put in the Post mill, he built a small mill about ten miles west of Mitchell. He oversaw operations from Prineville.

The Post mill was sold in 1950 to John White. Three years later, Spoo bought a large mill at Elgin, but it burned down a couple of years later. Spoo, who had become one of the legendary Central Oregon timber figures along with such men as Paul Kelly and Phil Dahl, sold all his holdings and moved to Colorado.

The Heppner Lumber Company put in a stud mill at Spray in 1940. Frank Crawford ran the mill, then the Hudspeths, and later Walt Lindstrom, then Barney Malcolm, and finally in 1971 it was acquired by the Kinzua Corporation. The latter, in 1953, became the successor to Kinzua Pine Mills after Eastern interests acquired it. By that time it used its own chain-driven Mack logging trucks as well as trains. Kinzua named its logging subsidiary Eastern Oregon Logging Company. Kinzua also bought Heppner Pine Mills and its timber holdings in 1959, and then, in 1971, the aforementioned Heppner Lumber Company. However, two years later it dismantled the Spray mill.

Jefferson County missed out on the post-war timber boom. Most of the timber cut there was trucked to out-of-county mills such as the Tite Knot and Brooks-Scanlon. The only Madras-area mill, located on La Monta Road three miles south of town, operated for only three years. This was the D & L Lumber Company, a partnership of lumberman George "Bud" Dimick and trucker Winton Livingston, established in 1946. Livingston logged a million board feet of timber off Grizzly Mountain and hauled it to the sawmill, where Dimick cut it into rough lumber.

The Warm Springs Indian Reservation fared better. Large amounts of timber stood in the mountainous western regions of the reservation, and the tribes contracted with local lumbermen in a way that produced immediate income and long-term employment. It began in 1942 with the Schoolie Timber Contract, sold to a firm called the Warm Springs Lumber Company. Five years later, the Tite Knot Pine Mill of Redmond purchased the Whitewater Timber Sale, and two years later the same firm acquired the Simnasho sale.

Three partners logged Warm Springs timber under contract with the tribes. In 1948, Phil Dahl bought his stepfather's heirs interest in the Tite Knot Pine Mill, while Sam Johnson bought out his father Orie Johnson's interest in the same business. Dahl built a sawmill on the reservation, named Dahl Pine, Inc., in partnership with Sam Johnson and Harold Barclay. Dahl Pine also established a planer in Madras in 1955 directly south of the Warm Springs Lumber Company loading dock. Another firm in the combine was the Harold Barclay Logging Company. In 1955, they opened a plywood mill at Madras, with $500,000 of capital stock, named Jefferson Plywood.

Dahl owned about half the complete operation, while Johnson and Barclay each had about a quarter. Tite Knot and Dahl Pine each produced 20 million board feet of lumber annually. Dahl's experience in dealing with the tribes would serve him well in the mid-1960s when he won the contract to buy 170 million board feet of timber on the Spokane Indian Reservation.

Later the tribes expanded their own involvement in the business. In 1961, Johnson sold his interest in Tite Knot to Dahl and bought out Dahl's interest in Jefferson Plywood. He and his new partner, Pershing Andrews of Madras, continued to use timber bought from the Confederated Tribes. In 1967, the

Warm Springs Indian Reservation purchased the mill from the Jefferson Plywood Company for $3.2 million.

The biggest change outside Prineville came in Bend. With a population of 11,000, and half its workforce employed in the timber industry, Bend remained very much a mill town after the war. However, unlike Prineville with its five medium-sized mills, Bend was dependent on only two big mills. If one mill went under, it would extensively hurt the town. And one mill was about to go under.

Before the war, Shevlin-Hixon had employed 1,400 workers, Brooks-Scanlon 1,100. The war had meant profit for most large industries despite heavy wartime taxes. But the big bonanza for the timber industry would come with the postwar housing boom. Lumber was needed desperately and almost any size or grade would find a ready buyer. The giant Bend sawmills ran full bore. Most of the logs being sawed by Central Oregon mills came from private land. The federal and state governments sold timber, but it remained less desirable than private timber. Government timber not only cost more, it also came with pages and pages of rules and regulations. Some lumbermen could not imagine remaining in business without access to private timber. As a consequence, many operators quit business in the early 1950s when private timber began to disappear.

Entering the 1950s decade, both Shevlin-Hixon and Brooks-Scanlon realized that they could not survive together as they had in the past. Always before they had cooperated. Now they could either continue to do so by agreeing that one would go out of business and the other survive, or they could turn upon each other in a savage competition for a diminishing supply of private timber. In a movie it would have been the latter, but this was reality. Executives of the two companies met and discussed how to efficiently resolve the matter. The obvious solution was for one company to buy all the assets of the other.

A story believed in Bend for decades claimed that the decision of who would buy and who would sell was reached by simply flipping a coin. Actually, the decision seems to have been concluded in a more complicated, if less colorful, manner. Shevlin-Hixon's board asked Brooks-Scanlon for a figure at which they would sell their assets. Negotiations for the sale of Brooks-Scanlon were already underway when the last surviving member of the Shevlin family died. The man's widow, however, wanted out of the company. This suddenly reversed everything, and Brooks-Scanlon began negotiating to buy Shevlin-Hixon. They struck a bargain: Brooks-Scanlon would take possession of Shevlin-Hixon's mill and timber on January 1, 1951.

The last tree cut by the Shevlin-Hixon Lumber Company fell on December 9, 1950, in Klamath County. The company selected a 73-year-old man who had been employed by Shevlin-Hixon since 1914, and who had seen the mill start up, to send through the last log. Crying, J.N. Mahoney did so on December 23. The mill whistle blew for the last time, and the workers slowly streamed out of what had once been the largest pine mill on earth.

Brooks-Scanlon absorbed the timber into its own inventory and began dismantling the Shevlin-Hixon facilities. This included the 100-foot-high burner, which had four-foot-thick fire brick walls covered with steel plates. The burner had to be dynamited. Sheep ranchers bought salvaged steel for use as water tanks. Soon, only the Brooks-Scanlon mill remained, but even as late as 1960 it would hold 200,000 acres in Oregon containing 960 million board feet of timber, 80 percent of it Ponderosa pine. In fact, all of the other Central Oregon sawmills, excluding only the huge Edward Hines Lumber Company in Burns, had less capacity altogether than Brooks-Scanlon had.

Meantime, Leonard Lundgren announced that he would build a new sawmill in Bend. This provided work for some former Shevlin-Hixon employees. Lundgren hired 100 men when opening the new mill in mid-1951. The firm, initially called Lundgren Lumber Company, later became Lelco Inc. Its office was located on Woodland Boulevard and the shops and veneer plant on D Avenue.

Lundgren also bought the old Hitchcock sawmill in Sisters from Dant & Russell in 1953. Dant & Russell had shut down the mill, which had a $300,000 payroll, blaming the closure on the Forest Service for not making more timber available for logging. Ralph Crawford, Deschutes National Forest supervisor, admitted that more timber could be sold but said that the Forest Service lacked enough qualified employees to prepare the sales. It was exactly the sort of problem that made private timber more desirable than government trees. Lundgren reopened the mill and operated it for a decade. Lelco lasted until the late 1960s, when the lack of timber and the ever higher prices commanded for what remained available drove Lundgren to sell all of his holdings to Brooks-Scanlon. The latter dismantled the mill.

The Shevlin-Hixon closure began a long decline for the timber industry in Bend. Lelco absorbed only part of the huge mill's former workforce. While Brooks-Scanlon remained the really big employer, in a few years it, too, would begin to skive back its labor force by increased reliance upon modern technology in sawmills and logging. The private logging trains, rails, and moveable camps would soon be a thing of the past.

Where Bend's future lay was not obvious in 1951. But whatever happened, barring the discovery of oil at Madras, Prineville, or Mitchell, or perhaps at Paulina or Suplee or Antelope, Bend would probably remain the region's big town.

More than a year before Shevlin-Hixon shut down, the circulation manager of the *Bend Bulletin*, Leslie Schwab, had driven to Bend High School during the late afternoon of September 20, 1949, to attend the first class of night courses he had signed up for in English composition and constructive accounting. One hundred and six other new students had enrolled for night classes. Only eight courses were offered. The sponsor was not actually the high school itself, but a brand new educational entity that used the school's building because it had none of its own. It was allowed by a new act passed in the legislature at the urging of Dr.

John "Jack" Cramer and sponsored by senators Richard Neuberger and Austin Dunn. It was being promoted locally by Bend school superintendent James W. Bushong and the school board of Glenn Gregg, Dr. Joseph Grahlman, Leonard Standifer, Vance Coyner, and Grace Elder. The new institution opening that Indian summer day in 1949 with an $8,000 budget was called Central Oregon College. It was the first college ever in Central Oregon, and, today as Central Oregon Community College, remains the only public college in the region. The day would come when it offered an extensive curriculum in forestry, but also the day would come when that course would have fewer applicants than the number of students signing up for downhill skiing.

Two years after the big mill shut down, and at the same time circulation manager Schwab moved to Prineville, a new owner would take charge at Judge Robert Sawyer's *Bend Bulletin*. Back in 1913, Sawyer himself had been hired by George Putnam, the paper's publisher. Putnam had noticed that Sawyer's letters to the little weekly had both good style and good things to say. This aroused his curiosity because the letters came from a lumber worker. When he investigated, Putnam discovered that young Sawyer was no ordinary laborer. For one thing, he had a law degree earned at Harvard College.

A native of Bangor, Maine, Sawyer had practiced law for awhile in Boston before he moved out West and wound up in the booming mill town of Bend. Putnam hired him as a reporter for $75 a month. In 1915, he promoted Sawyer to editor. Sawyer oversaw the conversion of the weekly into a daily the following year. In 1919, when Putnam returned east to participate in his family's book publishing business, he appointed Sawyer manager of the *Bulletin* and left him in charge. Later, he sold the newspaper to Sawyer.

During the next 30 years, Robert W. Sawyer became one of the state's most prominent and powerful citizens. For seven years, Sawyer was Deschutes County judge, and thereafter he was known to most people as Judge Sawyer. His work on behalf of Deschutes County included leading the effort to raise money to construct a new building on Hospital Hill for St. Charles Memorial Hospital, and to secure more reclamation and irrigation projects in the county.

Sawyer's replacement entered the region in 1953. Judge Sawyer and co-owner Henry N. Fowler sold the *Bend Bulletin* to a young editor of the *Stanford Review* magazine, Robert W. Chandler. Anyone who believed that the change in ownership would lead to a change in the prominent part that *Bulletin* editors had played in Deschutes County affairs quickly learned otherwise. He would become one of the most powerful political voices in Central Oregon without holding political office.

Born in 1921 in Marysville, California, Chandler was raised on a farm and educated in Yuba City public schools. He earned a degree in journalism at Stanford University, and worked briefly on a couple of California weeklies before he secured a job as a *San Francisco Chronicle* reporter. After a short period, he was hired by the United Press, and traveled extensively throughout the West as a reporter and temporary bureau manager before the outbreak of World War II. Chandler served in the army in the Pacific Theater, from Australia to New Guinea to the Philippines to Korea to Japan. Along the way he made an impressive number of friends and established a wide network of contacts, among them men who in the future would be important political leaders in their countries. After the war, he joined the news staff of the *Denver Post* until he became the editor of the *Stanford Review*.

Chandler proved to be an even more powerful influence in Bend affairs than Sawyer had been, and also a much more controversial one. Many people liked and respected him, but others hated him with a passion. To supporters he was a dedicated professional journalist intent on turning the *Bulletin* into a first-class newspaper, while also using it to influence the politics and growth of Central Oregon and the whole state in a positive manner. Enemies viewed him as a yellow journalist intent on building a newspaper empire while putting roadblocks in the path of progress. One thing everybody could agree upon, friend or foe, was that he wielded an immense amount of influence in the region and the state. Chandler was fond of the adage: "Never pick a fight with someone who buys ink by the gallon." In a fight he could be either enlightened and far-seeing, or obstinate and stubborn. Either way, his control over the *Bulletin*, and eventually seven other newspapers (including the *Redmond Spokesman*), made him formidable.

Another arrival in post-war Bend also wielded a pen, and did it better than Chandler, though without changing much about the town or the region. This was Dwight Bennett Newton, soon to become Central Oregon's leading author and one of the most famous Western writers in the world. Newton was born about 1916 and raised in Kansas City. He attended a local university, planning to become a teacher, and earned a master's in history. A fellowship was awarded to him, with which he intended to earn a Ph.D., but World War II intervened. He was drafted into the army and sent off to Camp Abbot in Central Oregon. Newton arrived there already a professional writer.

Although he had planned to become a teacher, his real interest since age seven had been writing. He did not know what he would write, only that this was what he wanted to do. Then, when he was 12, he had been hanging around the house one rainy April day and discovered a pulp magazine of his brother's. Reading a story written by Max Brand, he so liked its language, scenery, and action that he decided he wanted to write Western stories. Newton began writing and mailing them to publishers, but nine years passed before his first sale, for $60, of a 12,000-word novelette called "Brand of the Hunted."

He wrote while serving in the army and recorded numerous plots for future work. When he returned to civilian life in 1946, he had sold a novel and 50 short stories. Newton moved to Bend to live and work as a professional writer, all thoughts of supporting himself as a teacher gone. In the years that followed, he became one of the most prolific Western writers in the country, and his books were translated into many foreign languages. His 1948 novel *Range Boss*, which sold 450,000 copies, became America's first original paperback. Five years later he was one of the founders of the Western Writers of America, and served as its secretary-treasurer for a decade. Before he quit writing shorter pieces in 1951 following the end of the pulp magazine era, he had seen 175 of his short stories and novelettes published.

In later years, he would write a Hollywood novel, 40 to 50 television scripts (he was the original writer for the popular television western "Wagon Train"), and 50 western novels, among them three classics of the genre: *The Big Land, Hangman's Knot,* and *Crooked River Canyon.* The latter, as well as several other novels by Newton, drew on the early history of Central Oregon for inspiration. *Crooked River Canyon,* for example, focused on the Vigilante era of early Crook County.

After Shevlin-Hixon had closed, after Central Oregon College had opened, and while Dwight Newton was typing his fictional stories about the Old West, a man who had fought the Vigilantes in real life was still in the saddle, and would soon, one last time, ride down a Prineville street.

The Pine Theater, opening in September 1938 with a showing of *Give Me a Sailor*, became the flagship of the K & D chain. *Bowman Museum, Crook County Historical Society*

38
CAPITAL OF THE WORLD
1953

EE EVANS arrived in Prineville in 1944. Born at Wewoka, Oklahoma, in 1908, Evans had attended Tulsa University and received a bachelor's degree from Central State Teacher's College. Employed as the Ward School principal in Seminole, 1933–1934, the following year he became Seminole County's chief deputy clerk. In March 1934, Evans married Goldie Hudspeth, sister of Johnnie Hudspeth, and two years later entered the retail lumber business in Wewoka. In 1942, he followed the Hudspeths to Central Oregon. He had business ties there even earlier as a partner in the Bridge Creek Lumber Company. Evans acquired timber holdings in Grant County and in 1944 had an interest in the Valley Lumber Company of John Day. That same year he moved to Prineville, living in a renovated barn on Loma Vista Heights. He built the Evans Lumber Company sawmill (later renamed Evans Pine) west of Prineville on La Monta Road. For decades the mill would be one of Prineville's largest.

Other Crook County sawmills and moulding mills operating during the post-war housing boom included Endicott and Ammons, with a mill on Dairy Creek; Midstate Lumber Company; Grizzly Lumber, near Prineville; and Midstate Manufacturing Company, whose president was J.F. Daggett. Lumber Re-Milling Corporation, a secondary wood products firm, had an annual payroll of about $100,000 for its 22 men in 1950, before it built a new $200,000 plant on La Monta Road. Its president was F.D. Stapp Sr. Ochoco Cedar Corporation, with an office in the Bowman Building, had Lake M. Bechtell Jr. as president. Ochoco was taken over by E.L. "Red" Braly in 1951 for the benefit of its creditors, and he moved the mill to California. For years, Walt Demaris had a sawmill on McKay Creek.

Two sawmills started up near Paulina after the war. The Still-Van Mill on Roba Creek was owned by Marion Stillwell and Jack Vandevert. Its competitor drove the mill out of business, but Stillwell remained active in the Central Oregon timber industry until the mid-1950s. He later became one-third partner in a big Boise hotel. The Paulina Lumber Company built its mill on Beaver Creek. Organized May 1, 1946, as a partnership including Red Braly, Pat Moore, and Louis Davin, it had an office in the Robinson & Clifton Building. Ferguson & Miller Logging Company, owned by Harold Foran, later bought it.

In addition to the sawmills, several big logging companies overshadowed the many small ones. The first big contractor was Paul Kelly. Endicott Logging Company later replaced Kelly as Ochoco Lumber's contractor. Jack Patterson, a big independent in the early 1950s, operated in Oregon and Washington, helping to build dams as well as log timber. One bad season could wipe out a logging company. The business resembled construction firms, requiring a heavy investment in equipment, often with borrowed money. Ochoco Lumber made contracts with select firms, helping to assure their stability, which also increased Ochoco's ability to control its own future. Some millowners contracted for logging, while others built their own fleet. Hudspeth eventually owned 90 log trucks.

Johnnie Hudspeth had continued to expand his organization. Although Hudspeth himself lived in Prineville and had an office in the Robinson & Clifton Building, most of his company facilities remained in Mitchell. The Hudspeths had built houses there for their workers. But remote Wheeler County was a poor location for a growing business like Hudspeth's. Mitchell and Spray received electrical power, when they received it at all, from a diesel plant, and juice from the Rural Electrification Administration would not reach southern Wheeler and northern Grant counties until Easter Sunday 1953. It remained one of the most isolated areas in the Pacific Northwest.

Hudspeth's move to Prineville came in 1947. He decided to build a big sawmill on the tract (now expanded to 40 acres) where he had installed the planer. Workmen were still building the Hudspeth Pine Inc. mill Saturday morning, November 19, when Johnny's wife, Floreine, smashed a bottle of champagne on the first log to roll toward the saw, launching the facility. The mill could cut 70,000 board feet a shift. And Johnnie Hudspeth announced during the ceremony that the family would move their headquarters from Mitchell to Prineville.

In a few years, the Hudspeth companies became the largest manufacturer of yellow pine lumber in America. Johnnie Hudspeth, expanding into ranching in a big way, also would become the largest landowner in Oregon and own the biggest herd of Purebred Herefords in the United States. His companies would pave roads, build the Bowman dam, retail automobiles, distribute oil, fabricate machinery and tools, and own everything from feed lots to Ashland's famous Marc Anthony Hotel. Nobody who ever lived in Central Oregon became a bigger legend in his own time. During the 1950s and 1960s, when he was widely viewed as the richest man in the state, the names "Prineville" and "Hudspeth" were paired in the minds of most Oregonians.

In 1947, the new Hudspeth mill meant jobs. Especially for people from Arkansas and Oklahoma who had blood or friendship ties to the Hudspeths. Especially for soldiers back from the war. Especially for young men with young families.

The biggest shipping center in America producing lumber to satisfy the country's housing needs had its own housing shortage. Families arrived crammed in cars and pickups, with nothing waiting except a job. Dirt floor shanties rose in "Little Arkansas" and its less impoverished neighbor, "Little Oklahoma." Everywhere carpenters labored, building new houses of all sizes. Johnnie

Hudspeth would soon have the biggest house of all, with ten bedrooms and even more bathrooms.

Prineville's population, which already had doubled from 1935 to 1940, rose from 2,358 in 1940 to 3,233 in 1950, while Crook County's population shot from 5,533 to 8,991. Gambling, prostitution, alcoholism, and crime also increased. Slot machines decorated the fraternal clubs. Police collected payoffs from gambling dens and brothels, and at least one police chief blackmailed town council members. Radio commentator Walter Winchell claimed that Prineville had more suicides *per capita* than any other community in the United States. The population boom created challenges that had to be met fast, with little preparation.

First, a hospital. Dr. Raymond Adkisson had converted Mack Cornett's mansion into a hospital in 1940, but the town needed a modern facility. In 1948, civic leaders agreed to build one. Because no private company would do it, the community itself would.

Organizers chose J.F. Daggett and rancher Claude Williams as general chairmen of a money drive, and Carey Foster as the campaign organization chairman. They hired professional money-raiser Louis Barr to spearhead it. Virtually everyone joined the effort. Within three weeks pledges reached $382,682. The money came from local residents, not one dime from the federal government. It took a year to build Pioneer Memorial Hospital on the Ochoco Heights between Elm Street and the town's tall, slender, wooden water towers. Dedicated on Sunday, May 28, 1950, a few days later PMH received patients from the old Prineville General Hospital.

Trouble meanwhile beset the schools. In June 1945, the school district had hired Cecil Sly as superintendent. Born in Michigan in 1897 and raised in Washington, Sly had been a school teacher, coach, and superintendent. Eighteen inches of snow on the ground could not convince this tight-fisted conservative to cancel school for a day. Parents approved. Children often hated him as they trudged to school while pupils in Madras or Bend got the day off with less snow than Prineville. Sly had arrived when changing economic and demographic conditions accompanying the war's end put great strains on the district. For example, rising living expenses had caused teachers and other district employees to seek raises. But the big problems came from the increase in the student population.

The district had built a new elementary school in 1939, the Crooked River Grade School. Hardly had its doors opened before a pre-dawn fire gutted it. Insurance covered most of the damage, and the school reopened in time to catch the first wave of timber-boom children. Soon, Crooked River had to double-shift its children because the classrooms were inadequate. The school crammed pupils into an annex, the cafeteria, and a Quonset hut. The double-shifting ended on February 4, 1946, when the district opened the new Ochoco Grade School at the west entrance into town. But more and more young families kept arriving, especially after Hudspeth Pine opened.

Total school district enrollment reached 887 students in 1944, 968 in 1945, 1,077 in 1946, 1,182 in 1947, 1,494 in 1948, 1,659 in 1949, 1,757 in 1950, 1,804 in 1951, 1,841 in 1952, and 1,935 in 1953. The baby boomers began to reach the first grade just as the timber boom passed, and the pressure of ever more pupils entering the schools continued until the early 1960s. Elementary schools experienced the worst pressure. Statistics show the impact of Hudspeth's new mill: 921 elementary students in 1947, 1,172 in 1948. The district sought money to build yet more schools while trying to make more room in existing facilities. In a single year, Crooked River Grade School leaped from 140 first graders to 218. Most classrooms there had 35 to 40 pupils, one had 44. Crooked River returned in the 1950s to double-shifting for the first, second, and third grades. The school had a capacity of 375 pupils but a student population of 931.

In February 1949, the school board put before voters a $500,000 bond issue to build a new high school. Crook County, which had approved the construction of a high school in the depths of the Great Depression, now hesitated. The district's budget had shot from $59,879.88 in 1940–1941, to $153,937.47 in 1944–1945, and had more than doubled that by 1949. In 1945 alone, property taxes in Prineville rose a whopping 51 percent. Increased prosperity brought increased costs. People felt the bite. The bond issue went down to defeat.

More stunning, on June 20, 1949, the district suffered its first-ever levy defeat. The board trimmed the budget to $368,699.99 and called a special election. This time voters approved it three-to-two.

On January 5, 1950, the board put the $500,000 high school bond issue up for vote again and canvassed energetically. It passed, with over 1,000 people casting ballots in the largest turnout for a school election up to that time. The new CCHS opened on the banks of Ochoco Creek in 1951. That same year the district built a new school at Lone Pine.

The district, in common with others throughout Oregon, wanted to eliminate rural schools such as Lone Pine. School officials believed it would be easier to bus students to central schools where a better education could be provided. By 1931, only 15 rural schools remained; 10 remained in 1945. During the following decades, the district closed the Mill Creek, Fife, Shotgun, Suplee, and Howard schools. Lone Pine would survive until 1986, leaving only Paulina and Powell Butte. Every rural school closure brought people in from the affected localities to protest at board meetings. Post area residents even stirred up a state investigation of the board's decision.

For all the problems, life in Crook County was good after the war. Times were getting better. If the mills were loud and spewed smoke and ash into the air, they provided jobs and stability. If some city officials and police were corrupt, it was nothing new, not untypical of small towns of the era, and not oppressive. If the town was growing too fast, it was better than not growing at all.

Soon after the New Deal's turning around of the economy, several successful businesses had been founded that were not part of the forest products industry. Stephen Yancey's son Orville had been born in Prineville in 1896. He became a statewide debating champion while at CCHS and later attended Willamette University. After living in Canada, Yancey returned to Crook County, where he bought a ranch and the City Transfer & Storage Company. He began building a packing plant on his ranch in October 1939 and two months later opened the Prineville Packing Company. Each year he processed about 2,000 hogs and 1,000 head of cattle. Yancey retailed much of it through Erickson's Food Market.

Zbindon Brothers built Prineville's first potato warehouse in 1943 on land belonging to the railway. Two years later, Roy Brown established another north of town, and Mel Bozarth & Company built one about a mile west of Prineville. Potatoes became the big Crook County farm crop for decades.

Ken Piercy arrived in Prineville in 1937. He was born in Deer Park, Washington, in 1912, and his family had moved often before they settled at Coos Bay. His brother Denzel bought a theater at Junction City in the Willamette Valley in 1934, and 23-year-old Ken invested in the business. The brothers borrowed $350 to start their firm, which they grandiosely called K & D Theatres Corporation. In September 1934, they bought Prineville's old Lyric Theater. Piercy moved to Prineville three years later to manage it. He opened the Pine Theater in 1938. It became Prineville's main theater, while the Lyric, located in one of the Ochoco Inn "stores," was relegated to showing second rate movies until it closed in 1954. After army service during World War II, Piercy continued to expand the company. Among the K & D drive-in theaters was the Patio Drive-In on the east side of Prineville. Although K & D developed a chain, even decades later Ken Piercy could often be found at the Pine Theater on Friday nights, a well-dressed, tall, slender man with a small mustache watching the show while he also eyed the business.

But the biggest non-timber business that would appear in Prineville actually did start with a tie to timber. In 1938, Fred Hudspeth had married Margaret Harlan in Bend. Her sister had earlier married the Portland *Oregon Journal* regional distributor, Leslie Schwab.

Born in 1917 in Bend, and raised in Minnesota as well as a Brooks-Scanlon logging camp in Deschutes County, Schwab was orphaned in his mid-teens. He remained in school, worked hard, and with newspaper routes in Bend earned a larger income than the school superintendent. After graduating from high school, he married Dorothy Harlan and continued in newspaper distribution. He joined the Air Cadets during World War II but saw no action. After the war, he returned to Bend as the circulation manager for the *Bend Bulletin*. Schwab always had been fascinated by business and anxiously wanted to go into a business of his own. He had ambition and hustle but no money.

Schwab's kinship by marriage to the Hudspeths provided the key. Fred Hudspeth offered to help him buy a business if Schwab found one he wanted. Schwab investigated many, and decided that he liked best a small O.K. Rubber Welders shop across the creek from the new high school in Prineville. Little more than a shack with an outhouse in back, owner Marshall Winn and one employee retreaded tires, fixed flats, and sold new tires. Schwab had never fixed a flat in his life, but he believed that the business had potential. The Hudspeths liked the idea, too, because they regularly needed tire work done on their dozens of logging and ranch trucks. It was finally agreed that Johnnie Hudspeth, Fred Hudspeth, and Les Schwab would buy the business and that Schwab would manage it. But then Johnnie changed his mind. This seemingly bad news may have been one of the best breaks Schwab ever had. In the end, Fred loaned Schwab $11,000 to buy the business, and Schwab also sold his house and borrowed on his life insurance. He moved to Prineville, and, without partners, took over the shop on January 1, 1952. Winn had made sales of about $32,000 his last year, but in his first year Schwab's were $150,000.

Schwab had two big advantages. One was the Hudspeth trade, which gave him far more truck work than any other tire dealer in the region. The other was a genius for business. Schwab proved astute at developing new programs, some for employees and some for customers. He wrote his own radio advertisements so they would not sound like everyone else's, initiated profit sharing years before it became popular, and cleaned up his stores while other tire stores were greasy and dirty. He soon bought a second store in Redmond. Later, a third at Bend. Next, Madras. He continued to buy and build stores. He eventually broke his contract with O.K. Rubber Welders, saying that they had not played fair with their dealers, and went straight independent. He called his firm Les Schwab Tire Centers. In time, it would make Prineville the headquarters of the largest retail tire company in America, with huge mixing warehouses and the country's biggest retreading plant. That came later, but the roots of it were laid at the peak of the timber boom, when logging trucks clogged Prineville's streets and mill smoke hung over the Ochoco Valley.

Unlike Hudspeth and Schwab, many who became successful in Crook County later moved elsewhere to pursue their success. For example, Lee Evans. He left in August 1950 for Santa Rosa, where he and Paul Kelly had acquired a huge stand of timber. Evans later expanded his interests into the oil business in Oklahoma and various other investments. But he was not through with Central Oregon.

After World War II, the federal government decided to sell Camp Abbot. The land wound up in the hands of the Hudspeth Land & Livestock Company. When the Hudspeths decided to sell, their brother-in-law Lee Evans bought it up. He formed a partnership with two men from western Oregon, John Gray and Donald McCallum, to develop a resort community. Fifteen miles south of Bend, with five miles of property along the Deschutes, it was an ideal place, although many people laughed at the idea. In 1968, Sun River Properties, Inc., sold its first parcel, and in 1969 the lodge, condos, and recreation facilities opened. Thus Sunriver, too, could be traced to the Prineville timber boom.

While companies came and went, some other aspects of life in the region continued much as before, but with new features. People in Powell Butte had wanted to build a community church following the war. In 1946, they started the Lord's Acre Sale and Auction to raise money for the project. It worked so well that even after they put up the nice big brick church, they continued holding the annual sale and auction. The money it raised was used to maintain the church, support missions and religious colleges, and provide scholarships to young people training for church service. The event attracted national attention. Several thousand people began showing up every year. People in Powell Butte prepared all year long for the sale.

Four KYJC employees in Medford wanted to start a radio station of their own and picked Prineville. Colin R. Matheny, Jed Stuart, Mike Miksche, and Bob Bruce applied for a license in 1948, but red tape at the Federal Communication Commission held it up for more than a year. Some local residents invested in Radio Central Oregon, including Robert Lister, Paul Kelly, Claude Williams, and W.B. Morse. The Medford group erected a 34 x 34 foot building on the Madras Highway, installed equipment, and put up the 305-foot-high tower that became the tallest man-made structure in Central Oregon. The total investment was about $30,000.

When the station went on the air, January 31, 1950, the temperature in Prineville was -40. A propane tank used to heat the little building froze up at night. As a result, there was no heat and the temperature inside the station was below zero. Broadcasters wore heavy coats and blankets while they worked. The 1,000-watt station sent its signal up the Crooked River Valley, and was heard in 14 counties from Goldendale to Klamath Falls. Even decades later, people driving to The Dalles who could not pick up the more powerful Bend stations could easily hear KRCO.

But some things had not changed. Flooding remained a serious problem for Prineville during the 1950s. The decade's first big flood came in March 1952. The Crooked River overflowed its banks when the winter snows melted. High school students joined volunteer firemen, city and state police officers, city and county employees, and dozens of volunteers in building a dike to return the river to its channel. The Riverside Addition was inundated and 125 people evacuated. The Red Cross was called in, and, together with the Eagles Auxiliary, helped the people displaced by the flood. The Baptist church and the Ochoco Inn provided shelter for many. From the Viewpoint, on the rimrock mesa west of town, people looked down to see houses below completely surrounded by water, as though they were sitting in a lake. The flood caused more property damage than any since 1902.

The Ochoco dam, which always leaked badly, had been ruled unsafe in 1947, and the Bureau of Reclamation repaired it.. The Bureau packed it with boulders and gravel to weight it and stop the leaks. The work started in 1949 and was finished the following year. Soon boat races were held on Ochoco Lake. But the Ochoco dam had no influence on Crooked River, and the stream flooded often. Arthur Bowman and LaSelle Coles continued to lobby the federal government to build a dam on Crooked River. When the government finally agreed, in a few years a Hudspeth firm would build it.

Agriculture, too, remained a prominent feature of Central Oregon life. It paid little, if anything, but many people continued to eke out a living from it. Almost only the big ranches could turn a profit. The Hay Creek Ranch continued to go through successive owners. Fred Wickman sold it to A.J. Smith & Sons of Big Fork and Kalispel, Montana, in 1952, but took it back a couple of years later. The Curtis Martin family of Portland later acquired it. When the Martins sold it to J.W. Chase & Son of California, they received more than $2 million.

A sampling of the many ranch sales during the post-war period gleaned from newspapers, with private and public acreage combined, would include these well-known spreads:

- The 1946 sale of the 45,000-acre Wayne Houston ranch to Jack and Walter Kittredge of Silver Lake for over $60,000. The Bear Creek spread had been started as a homestead by Wayne's father, J. Floyd Houston, in the late 19th century. Included in the sale were 500 head of cattle.
- The 1946 sale of the 46,000-acre Keystone Ranch by Howard Mayfield to J.J. Jacob & Sons of Malin.
- The 1951 sale of the old Bryson place, with 11,040 acres of land and 500 head of cattle, by Walter Bolton to William R. McCormack, for over $100,000.
- The 1951 sale of the lease on the 52,000-acre Robert Lister Stock Ranch near Paulina to the Gill Cattle Company of California.
- The 1951 sale of the William C. James ranch in the Mauries to Aloysius A. Ryan of The Dalles for over $60,000, involving 10,070 acres.
- The 1951 sale of the 10,000-acre Joe Keerins ranch at Suplee to Frank Humphrey of Reno.
- The 1951 sale of the 75,000-acre Mills Land and Livestock spread on the Silver Creek range in the Snow Mountain district, which had been in the Mills family since the 1880s, to Robert Sartain of Sacramento and Elko County, Nevada, along with several hundred head of cattle.
- The 1951 sale by Parr Norton of his upper Trout Creek ranch, consisting of more than 10,000 acres cut from the old H.L. Priday ranch, to his nephew Andrew A. Norton.

- The 1951 sale by Harry Heising of the 11,000-acre Three Rivers Ranch at the confluence of the Metolius, Deschutes, and Crooked rivers, to Red Braly.
- The 1951 sale by Earl Bush of the 10,000-acre Izee Ranch, 90 miles southeast of Prineville, to Charles Jackson. It grazed about 700 head of cattle.

The Gill firm was especially active. Operated by Fred Gill, with headquarters in Exeter, California, the Gill Cattle Company had interests in California, Oregon, Wyoming, Montana, and Arizona. For years it was a major player in Central Oregon's cattle business. It leased the Corbett and Roy McCallister ranches on Crooked River, paid $410,000 for the 40,000-acre Kueny ranch in the Steens Mountain country in 1952, and, the following year in a multimillion-dollar deal, bought the 420,000-acre Roaring Springs Ranch at Frenchglen.

From 1949 to 1969, the number of farms and ranches in Deschutes County fell from 937 to 503, in Crook from 472 to 293, in Jefferson from 567 to 356, and in Wheeler from 189 to 110. The sheep population in Central Oregon also fell, in 1949 there being 3,000 in Deschutes County, and the same number in 1969, but in Crook County the number dropped from 14,000 to 2,000, in Jefferson County from 14,000 to 2,000, and in Wheeler County from 18,000 to 6,000. Cattle population rose from 88,000 in 1949 to 139,000 in 1969.

As the importance of agriculture in the region diminished, people wished more than ever to preserve its homespun culture. What was earlier simply the way people lived became an ideal to be praised in fairs and rodeos and political speeches. The old West was dying, and people did not want it to go…at least not entirely.

While the world war still raged, the Sisters Rodeo, "The Biggest Little Show in the World," began at the Creighton place near the Sisters airport in 1943. There was no parade that first time. The McCoin Ranch of Terrebonne supplied the stock. Top riders appeared because the rodeo sponsors offered $500 prize money for each event, which was very high for the time.

As the Pacific war wound down, ranchers and other Crook County residents planned the first ever Crooked River Roundup, holding it on Labor Day weekend 1945. It began Saturday night with a combination queen's ball (featuring the crowning of the roundup queen) and a buckaroo dance in the school gymnasium. Sunday, at 10 a.m., a parade wound through town, then at 1:30 p.m. a rodeo began at the fairgrounds. At 5 p.m., a baseball game began at Davidson Field between the Prineville Townies and the Portland All-Stars. Monday, Labor Day, started with another 10 a.m. parade and concluded with the 1:30 p.m. rodeo. Five main events were held on Sunday and Monday, with $2,500 in prizes.

It became one of the Pacific Northwest's most important rodeos. The Warm Springs Indians participated each year and contributed greatly to its success. While they might live in houses on the reservation, at the Crook County Fairgrounds they pitched tepees. A man closely associated with the bigger Pendleton rodeo arrived in 1951 to lead the parade for that year's Crooked River Roundup: James Blakely. Yes, the same James M. Blakely who in 1884 had led the Moonshiners showdown with the Vigilantes in the dusty street outside Til Glaze's saloon.

Blakely often led rodeo parades on his favorite palomino and participated in other events celebrating Oregon's frontier days. In spring 1939, the Portland *Oregonian* had published Blakely's account of the Vigilantes and Moonshiners, as told to reporter Herbert Lundy. It had ignited a history binge in Crook County, with oldtimers recounting past events and the *Central Oregonian* running special articles. It became absurd, the newspaper reporting the year's first council meeting under a headline announcing that the council had begun its fifty-eighth year.

In 1951, Blakely also appeared as the special guest at a big buckaroo breakfast on the Breese ranch. Orville Yancey prepared the breakfast over a ditch near the house. Doris Breese remembered 40 years later that Blakely was gracious, quiet, mild-spoken, proud, and—the feature everyone who met him always commented upon—stood straight as an arrow. John Combs had died four years earlier, leaving Blakely probably as the last Moonshiner.

He was certainly one of the few Oregonians still walking and riding who had been an infant when Superintendent of Indian Affairs Joel Palmer negotiated with the Indians of Central Oregon for their cessation of claims to the region in return for the Warm Springs Reservation. And the last alive who rode into the Grizzly Mountain area when no other white settlers lived there. Everything else—the range wars, the land frauds, the homesteader boom and dust, the world wars, the depressions and recessions, prohibition and repeal, the building of the sawmills, the closing of the world's biggest pine mill, the coming of trains and automobiles and airplanes, and the many openings and closings of the Oregon King Mine—had happened since young Blakely cupped cold fresh water from Willow Creek up to his desert-parched mouth.

Blakely died at College Place, Washington, on January 23, 1953, at 100 years of age. People throughout Oregon sent floral arrangements to his funeral in Enterprise, Oregon. In August, a splendid bay led the parade that started the Crooked River Roundup. Although saddled and bridled, James Blakely's favorite horse this time carried no rider. Crook County residents in this manner honored and said goodbye to the special friend who had led their revolution against terrorism.

They also understood that the last of the great original pioneers had gone to his reward, and the pioneer era of the Crooked River country had passed into history.

SELECT BIBLIOGRAPHY

Newspapers

Bend Bulletin
Central Oregon Recreation
Central Oregonian
Crook County Journal
Deschutes Echo
Madras Pioneer
Ochoco Review
Oregonian
Prineville News
Prineville Review
Redmond Spokesman
Statesman-Journal
Times-Mountaineer

Government Records

Crook County Commissioners' Journal.
Crook County Deed Books.
Crook County Unit School District, Minutes 1921–1991.
Oregon Blue Book, 1949, 1973–1974.
Prineville, City of, Minutes of Common Council.
State Highway Commission, Maps, 1918, 1920, 1922.
State Highway Commission, Engineer Reports, 1895–1940.
State of Oregon v. James M. Barnes, Case File.
State of Oregon v. William Thompson, Case File.
Statewide Hazard Analysis, Draft for Crook County, 1984.
Wasco County Census, 1880.

Articles and Essays

"(The) Blakelys," *Statesman-Journal* (August 3, 1975).
"Blakelys Made History when Six-Guns Ruled," *Central Oregonian* (January 29, 1953).
Brogan, Phil F. "Billy Chinook...His Lake," *Oregon Motorist* (April 1969).
_____. "Billy Chinook: Indian Warrior 'True Friend,'" *Oregonian* (October 15, 1978).
Church, Foster. "The Campaign for Crook County," *Sunday Oregonian* (July 12, 1992).
"(The) George Langdon Story," *Central Oregonian* (October 28, 1982).
Goodwin, Ted. "Around and About," *Central Oregonian* (January 29, 1953).
"Jim Blakely Dies at Daughter's House," *Record-Courier* (January 29, 1953).

"Jim Blakely, Pioneer Sheriff of Crook County Dies at 100 Years of Age," *Tribune* (January 29, 1953).

Lundy, Herbert. "When Juniper Trees Bore Fruit," *Oregonian* (March 12–28, 1939).

Nichols, M. Leona. "The Saga of William Walter Brown," *Sunday Oregonian* (October 23, 30, 1932).

Veazie, A.L. "Address at the Dedication of a Monument to the Pioneers of Crook County at Prineville, August 7, 1938," *Oregon Historical Society* (December 1938).

Washburn, Sherman A., ed. "Historical Perspectives," *Oregon Health Bulletin* (August 1972).

West, Oswald. "Bill Brown Entertains the Governor," *Oregonian* (November 20, 1949).

Wright, Tom. "Rain Helps 'Baptize' Round Butte Project," *Statesman* (June 18, 1965).

Young, F.G. "Financial History of the State of Oregon—III," *Oregon Historical Quarterly* (June 1910).

Books and Reports

Applegate, Shannon, and Terrance O'Donnell, eds. *Talking on Paper: An Anthology of Oregon Letters and Diaries,* vol. 6 (1994).

Baehr, Russell. *Oregon's Outback: Tales and Legends from Beyond the High Cascades* (1988).

Ballou, Robert. *Early Klickitat Valley Days* (1938).

Bancroft, Hubert Howe. *History of Oregon, 1848–1888,* 2 vols. (1886, 1888).

Baughman, Michael, and Charlotte Hadella. *Warm Springs Millennium: Voices from the Reservation* (2000).

Beckham, Stephen Dow, Rick Minor, Kathryn Anne Toepel, and Ruth L. Greenspan. *Prehistory and History of the Ochoco National Forest, Central Oregon* (1987).

Biographical Directory of the United States Congress, 1774–1989 (1989).

Brimlow, George Francis. *Harney County Oregon and Its Range Land* (1951).

Brogan, Phil F. *East of the Cascades* (1964).

Campbell, Arthur H. *Antelope: The Saga of a Western Town* (1990).

Carey, Charles Henry. *A General History of Oregon Prior to 1861,* vol. 2 (1935).

Caterpillar Tractor Company. *Men of Timber: The Presidents of the Pacific Logging Congress* (1954).

Clark, Keith. *Redmond: Where the Desert Blooms* (1985).

————, and Donna Clark, eds. *Daring Donald McKay; or, the Last War Trail of the Modocs* (1971).

————, and Lowell Tiller. *Terrible Trail: The Meek Cutoff, 1845* (1966).

Cline, Gloria Griffen. *Exploring the Great Basin* (1963).

————. *Peter Skene Ogden and the Hudson's Bay Company* (1974).

Collier and Son Corporation, P.F. *World Atlas and Gazetteer* (1942).

Corning, Howard McKinley, *Dictionary of Oregon History* (1989).

Crook County High School Economics Class, ed. *Landmarks in Fifty Years of Education in Crook County High Schools* (1952).

Crook County Historical Society. *Crook County Timber History: A Narrative* (1997).

————. *The History of Crook County, Oregon* (1981).

————. *The History of Crook County, Oregon* (1994).

Deschutes County Historical Society. *A History of the Deschutes Country in Oregon* (1985).

Due, John F., and Frances Juris. *Rails to the Ochoco Country* (1968).

_____, and Frances Juris Rush. *Roads and Rails South from the Columbia: Transportation and Economic Development in MidColumbia and Central Oregon* (1991).

Farrell, Alice M., ed. *Jefferson County Reminiscences* (1957).

Fiedler, Frank X. *Blazing a Trail: The 50-Year History of Central Oregon Community College* (2000).

Fremont, John Charles. *Memoirs of My Life* (1886).

_____. *The Explorations of John Charles Fremont,* 2 vols. (1970).

French, Giles. *Cattle Country of Peter French* (1964).

Fussner, F. Smith, ed. *Glimpses of Wheeler County's Past: An Early History of North Central Oregon* (1975).

Glassley, Ray H. *Indian Wars of the Pacific Northwest* (1953).

Gray, Edward. *William "Bill" Brown, 1855–1941: Legend of Oregon's High Desert, Including a History of the Wagontire Mountain Range Feud* (1993).

Gribskov, Joyce. *Pioneer Spirits of Bend* (1980).

Griffin, Dorsey. *Who Really Killed Chief Paulina?* (1991).

Haas, Ben. *KKK* (1963).

Hansen, Laura Bishop Varco. *The High and the Low Deserts and the Plainview Years* (1980).

Hatton, Raymond R. *Bend in Central Oregon* (1978).

_____. *High Desert of Central Oregon* (1977).

_____. *Pioneer Homesteaders of the Fort Rock Valley* (1982).

_____, with Lawrence A. Chitwood and Stuart G. Garrett. *Oregon's Sisters Country: A Portrait of Its Lands, Waters, and People* (1996).

Helms, Irene H. *Remembering—School Days of Old Crook County* (1980).

Heritage '75 (April 7, 1975).

Heritage '76, Judi Schley, ed. (July 22, 1976).

Heritage '77, Gary Newman, ed. (October 26, 1977).

Hill, Geoff, ed. *Little Known Tales from Oregon History,* vol. 1 (1988).

_____. *Little Known Tales from Oregon History,* vol. 2 (1991).

Holbrook, Stewart H. *The Age of the Moguls* (1954).

Jackson, Royal G., and Jennifer A. Lee. *Harney County: An Historical Inventory* (1978).

Jefferson County Historical Society. *History of Jefferson County Oregon, 1914–1983* (1984).

Johansen, Dorothy O., and Charles M. Gates. *Empire of the Columbia* (1967).

Juris, Frances. *B.F. Nichols, "Father of Crook County"* (1999).

Lord, Elizabeth. *Reminiscences of Eastern Oregon* (1903).

Lowry, Nita. *The Triangle Outfit: The True Story of One Man's Dream and the Many People Who Helped Make It a Reality in Central Oregon Country* (1995).

McArthur, Lewis A. *Oregon Geographic Names* (1974).

McCall, Dorothy Lawson. *The Copper King's Daughter* (1986).

_____. *Ranch under the Rimrock* (1972).

McCart, George, Lawrence Nielsen, and Doug Newman. *Pioneer Roads in Central Oregon* (1985).

McCarthy, Linda. *A History of the Oregon Sheriffs, 1841–1991* (1992).

McNeal, William H. *History of Wasco County* (1953).

Meier, Gary and Gloria. *Oregon Outlaws: Tales of Old-Time Desperadoes* (1996).

Miller, May. *Golden Memories of the Paulina Area* (1974).

Morison, Samuel Eliot. *The Oxford History of the American People* (1965).

Myers, Gustavus. *History of the Great American Fortunes* (1937).
Oliphant, J. Orin. *On the Cattle Ranges of the Oregon Country* (1968).
Oliver, Herman. *Gold and Cattle Country* (1962).
Puter, S.A.D., and Horace Stevens. *Looters of the Public Domain* (1907).
Rees, Helen Guyton. *Shaniko People* (1983).
Scott, Harvey W. *History of the Oregon Country*, vol. 2 (1924).
Scott, Walter L. *Pan Bread 'n Jerky* (1968).
Shaver, F.A., with Arthur P. Rose, R.F. Steele, and A.E. Adams. *An Illustrated History of Central Oregon, Embracing Wasco, Sherman, Gilliam, Wheeler, Crook, Lake and Klamath Counties, State of Oregon* (1905).
Sifakis, Carl. *The Encyclopedia of American Crime* (1982).
Snyder, Keith. *Prineville Business History, 1868–1922* (2004).
Stinchfield, Janet L., and E. McLaren, eds. *The History of Wheeler County, Oregon* (1983).
Thompson, William. *Reminiscences of a Pioneer* (1912).
Turnbull, George S. *History of Oregon Newspapers* (1939).
Unruh, John D., Jr. *The Plains Across: The Overland Emigrants and the Trans-Mississippi West, 1840–60* (1979).
Vaughan, Thomas, ed. *High and Mighty: Select Sketches about the Deschutes Country* (1981).
Voegtly, C.H. *An Illustrated History of Baker, Grant, Malheur and Harney Counties* (1902).
Williams, Elsie Horn. *A Pictorial History of the Bend Country* (1983).

Other Sources

Bentley, Fay Van Scholack. "William Walter Brown; Homesteader, Sheepman, Pauper," undated *Central Oregonian* newspaper clipping.
Clark, Cleon and Wanda. Unpublished interview with Fred Houston, 1975.
"Grizzly Settlers of Pioneer Stock." Undated, unidentified newspaper clipping.
Hodgson, Allen. "History of the Ochoco National Forest," 1913, unpublished.
"Jim Blakely–Sheriff Extraordinary." Unpublished, undated manuscript, Bowman Museum, Prineville.
Lockley, Fred. "Impressions and Observations of the *Journal* Man," *Oregon Journal*, undated reprint.

CHAPTER INDEX OF PERSONAGES

Capt. Charles La Follette—commander, Oregon militia's Camp Polk.

Samuel Hindman—homesteaded near Camp Polk, ca. 1870; later Sisters townsite.

Chapter 5: Empty Except for Indians and Gold, 1853–1864; pp. 26–30

Billy Chinook—relocated to Warm Springs Reservation, 1857.

Joel Palmer—negotiated Warm Springs treaty, June 22, 1855.

Chief Que-pe-ma—independent minded Tygh headman.

Dr. Thomas Fitch—Warm Springs physician; organized defense against Paiutes.

J.L. Adams—claimed to know Blue Bucket mine location.

Henry Griffin—discovered gold, Powder River valley, 1861.

William Aldred—found gold at Canyon Cr.

Chapter 6: Paulina War, 1859–1867; pp. 31–39

Paulina—Paiute war leader.

Chief Ochoco—frequently camped in Ochoco Valley.

Dr. Thomas Fitch—led Warm Springs war party, 1859.

Wahveveh—Paulina's brother; killed, Lake Harney battle.

Capt. John Drake—Oregon cavalry company leader, 1864.

Lt. McCall—led attack ordered by Capt. Drake.

Chief Stockietly; Stock Whitley—Indian scouts leader; fatally wounded by Paiutes.

Lt. Stephen Watson—killed in battle with Paiutes.

J.W.P. Huntington—Oregon Indian superintendent (1864); opposed extermination.

Chief Winnemucca—major Paiute leader.

Chief Howluck—warring Paiute leader, Southern Oregon/Northern California.

Dr. William Cameron McKay—Indian/Scot ancestry; agency physician, scout, interpreter.

Billy Chinook—with scouts, killed Tamowins.

Tamowins—Paiute shaman.

Capt. L.L. Williams—defeated by Paiutes between Burns and Harney Lake.

Lt. Reuben Bernard—First U.S. Cavalry.

George L. Woods—Oregon governor; demanded Paiute extermination.

Edwin M. Stanton—U.S. Secretary of War.

Gen. George Crook—implemented harsh war policy.

John Darragh—army scouts leader.

Lt. William Borrowe—instructed scouts to take no prisoners.

Queapama—Wasco leader, murdered in parley with Paulina.

Chief Poustaminie—Tygh headman, murdered by Wahveveh's Paiutes.

James Clark—Burnt Ranch, John Day River; Clark and Maupin killed Paulina, 1867.

George Masterson—James Clark's brother-in-law.

C.W. Myers—Bridge Cr. stage station.

Bud Thompson—leader of packers.

Howard Maupin—stage station operator; helped kill Paulina.

Perry Maupin—son of Howard Maupin.

John Atterbury—joined party pursuing Paulina.

Henry Wheeler—stage line operator.

H.C. Paige—Wells Fargo messenger.

C.W. Meyer—Bridge Cr. stage station operator.

William Ragan—joined Clark and Maupin, pursuing Paulina.

Andrew Clarno—stage station operator.

Chief Natchez—occupied Malheur Reservation.

Chief Egan—"   "

Chief Owitze—"   "

Chapter 7: Roads Enter the Wilderness, 1846–1880; pp. 40–48

Samuel Barlow—pioneered Barlow Road near Mount Hood, 1846.

Andrew Wiley—explored Hogg Pass/Wiley Pass.

John Templeton Craig—McKenzie Pass road builder.

Andrew Jackson Tetherow—Deschutes canyon ferryman.

John Y. Todd—(Tygh Valley rancher/blacksmith) Deschutes toll bridge.

Robert Mays—"   "

Ezra L. Hemingway—toll collector; Todd/Mays partner.

Joseph H. Sherar—long-time Deschutes bridge owner.

Howard and Perry Maupin—established Deschutes ferry.

W.E. Hunt—purchased Maupins' ferry.

Felix Scott Jr.—McKenzie Pass wagon road builder.

Marion Scott—brother, Felix Scott Jr.

John McNutt—partner, Felix Scott Jr.

Henry Spalding—famous Idaho missionary; pioneered Cascades route.

Ritchie—driver on Scott Trail.

Cunsil—" "

Marion Scott—Hay Cr. cabin occupant, Indian raid, 1866.

Presley Scott—" "

Charles S. Hardison—" "

John B. Evans—" "

Thomas J. Evans—" "

Lem Jones—" "

Mr. Mills—" "

B.J. Pengra—promoter, Oregon Central Military Road.

Luther Elkins—developer, Willamette Valley & Cascade Mountain Wagon Road Co.

Elisha Barnes—sued (lost) regarding fraudulent road land grants.

Grover Cleveland—U.S. President (1885–1889, 1893–1897).

Lazard Freres—Paris banking house; purchased controversial land grants.

David Cahn—later purchaser, disputed land grants.

Alexander Weill—" "

Col. T. Egenton Hogg—unsuccessful transcontinental railroad tycoon.

Francis Kerr—investor, Col. Hogg's scheme.

Capt. Henry Mosely—" "

Chapter 8: The Monopoly, 1860–1880; pp. 49–50

Capt. John C. Ainsworth—co-owner, Oregon Steam Navigation Co.

Robert R. Thompson—" "

Simeon G. Reed—" "

Chapter 9: Early Settlements, 1867–1900; pp. 51–61

David Wayne Claypool—Mill Cr. settler, 1867.

Raymond Burkhardt—" "

Calvin (or George) Burkhardt—" "

Capt. White—" "

William Smith—" "

Elisha Barnes—" "

Louisa Elkins—David Claypool's wife.

Susanna Glenn—Elisha Barnes' wife.

Peter "Pete" French—Eastern Oregon cattle baron; Elisha Barnes' brother-in-law.

George W. Barnes—Elisha Barnes' son; Mill Cr. settler.

William Elkins—early settler, Ochoco/Mill creeks.

Ewen Johnson—" "

James Blakely—(father) Western Oregon; captain, Rogue River War; legislature member.

James M. Blakely—(son) homesteaded 14 miles north of Prineville, Willow Cr., 1869.

Kennedy and Ellen Montgomery—early Willow Cr. settler(s).

S.W. Wood—" "

Perry Read—" "

William Pickett—first schoolmaster.

William S. Clark—Ochoco School District chairman: trailblazer with Lew Daugherty.

George H. Judy—school district secretary.

Ewen Johnson—school district director.

William Marks—" "

Edmund F. Veazie—" "

James A. Crawford—second schoolmaster.

Ike Schwartz—builder, steam-powered sawmill.

Francis B. "Barney" Prine—founded Prine community, 1868; blacksmith/storekeeper.

David Prine—Barney Prine's brother; early settler.

Elizabeth Prine—David Prine's wife.

William Heisler—competing storekeeper.

Lew Daugherty—blazed trail with William S. Clark from The Dalles.

Alexander Hodges—moved to Prine community, 1870.

Monroe Hodges—Alexander's brother; purchased Prine cabin, 1871; platted Prineville.

Mack Cornett—took over The Dalles-Prineville stage route.

Lige Haight—built toll gate, Cow Canyon.

Til Glaze—hard character.

Hank Vaughan—famous gunfighter.

Benjamin Franklin "Ben" Allen—Allen Cr. settler; sheep ranching tycoon.

Matilda Tate—Ben Allen's wife.

William "Bud" Thompson—Hay Cr.; former newspaperman.

S.G. "George" Thompson—Hay Cr. settler; Bud
Thompson's brother.
Joachim Miller—mining country express man;
became national literary figure.
Henry and Thomas Gale—Roseburg news-
papermen; wounded Bud Thompson in
gunfight.
Thomas Ward—Nevada miner, started Shaniko.
August Scherneckau—Indians called him
"Shaniko."
Henry Heppner—storekeeper; Heppner, Or-
egon, namesake.
Robert Warren—Willoughby (Grizzly) post-
master.
Margaret Morrow—described Grizzly School.
Charles C. Maling—Englishman; founded Wil-
low Cr. sawmill.
Charles Durham—Englishman; Trout Cr.
tributary sawmill.
Clark Rogers—first homesteader, The Cove.
T.F. McCallister—traded Prineville house/lot
for Rogers' homestead.
Ben Beeman—early Culver settler.
Joel Allen—settler, Deschutes' east bank.
Steve Staats—" "
Sidney "Sid" Stearns—" "
Marshall Clay Awbrey—settler, Deschutes' west
bank (now in Bend).
Samuel Hindman—Squaw Cr. settler; estab-
lished post office/trading post.
John Templeton Craig—mail carrier; froze to
death, 1877.
J.B. Claypool—Squaw Flats settler.
David W. Claypool—settler near Indian Ford
Cr.
Christian W. Meyer—Alkali Flat stage station/
inn, 5 miles east of Mitchell, 1863.
"Alkali Frank" Huat—" "
Andrew Clarno—cattle rancher, William
Snodgrass's partner.
William Snodgrass—cattle rancher, Clarno's
partner.
Dan Leonard—inn on Condon-Fossil road.
Howard Maupin—stage station operator,
Antelope Valley.
Nathan Wallace—purchased Maupin's prop-
erty; relocated to new Antelope townsite.
Ezekiel Waterman—established Waterman Flats
stagestop/inn.
Caleb Thornburg—town of Caleb namesake.
E.B. Allen—rancher/founder, Caleb.

S.G. Coleman—" "
R.N. "Mose" Donnelly—early Richmond settler.
"Pike" Helms—arguments caused town name,
Contention.
Jerome H. Parsons—" "
Frankie Parsons—Parsons' daughter; persuaded
renaming Contention as Twickenham.
Mary E. Spray—platted Spray.
George Jones—Antone stockman, farmer,
prospector.
Antone Francisco—Portuguese native; town of
Antone namesake.
John Hipple Mitchell—bigamist, swindler, U.S.
senator.
William "Bawdie" Johnson—founder of Mitch-
ell.
Thomas Benton Hoover—rancher; established
Fossil post office.
Thomas Watson—with Hoover, moved Fossil to
Butte/Cottonwood Cr. junction, opened
store.
George Millican—early settler/rancher; Mil-
lican namesake.
P.B. Johnson—first Millican postmaster/stor-
eowner.
Francis Forest—cattle rancher/storekeeper;
town of Forest namesake.
Dr. James R. Sites—Deschutes homesteader;
farm later became Lone Pine.
Philip G. Carmical—stage station owner,
Carmical's Crossing.
Charles, George, and Walter O'Neil—store own-
er; Carmical's Station renamed "O'Neil."
Logue Cecil—upper Silver Cr. settler.
Robert Baker—early Silver Cr. settler.
James Elkins—horse rancher, Grindstone/Bea-
ver creeks.
Billie Adams—Beaver Cr. settler; later became
Paulina townsite.
William Noble—" "

Chapter 10: Bannock War, 1878; pp. 62–70

Monroe Hodges—extensive holdings, Prineville
Valley.
Alexander Hodges—" "
John Y. Todd—Farewell Bend cattle baron;
wintered in Prineville.
Bud Thompson—Prineville resident; arranged
Hay Cr. defenses.
James Blakely—" "

Marion Powell—first Prineville Sunday school superintendent.

Dr. Lark Vanderpool—Prineville's first permanent professional man.

Dr. James Roland Sites—Polk County physician; periodic resident, Prineville.

Dr. James Richardson—doctor, 1880.

Dr. H.P. Belknap—doctor, arrived 1881.

John E. Jeffery—published Prineville's first newspaper, *Ochoco Pioneer*, 1880.

George W. Barnes—Elisha Barnes' son; Prineville's first lawyer, 1880.

Benjamin Franklin Nichols—pharmacist; later, Barnes' law partner, legislator.

Joseph Hunsaker—took over Nichols' drug store, 1879.

Dan Richards—owned Occidental Hotel (formerly Hodges Hotel) by 1880.

William Circles—later Occidental Hotel owner.

Oliver Jackson—Jackson House operator.

A.B. Culver—took over Jackson House (aka Culver House), 1880.

Charles C. Maling—built planer, Prineville.

James A. Allen—established grist mill, Prineville.

David F. Stewart—grist mill manager after Allen sold out.

Barney Prine—recalled early Prineville's roughness.

Van Allen—tried to take over Prineville; gunned down, 1878.

Jeff Drips—Van Allen's partner; captured and acquitted.

James Chamberlain—Wasco County deputy, 1878.

Jerry Luckey—" "

Chief Egan—Paiute headman aligned with Idaho's Bannocks, 1878.

Chief George—Wasco leader, offered protection against Paiute/Bannock attack.

George Thompson—warned by Chief George about possible assault.

Perry Maupin—" "

Dr. David Baldwin—Hay Cr. sheep ranch owner.

Clanic—herder from Warm Springs agency.

Capt. Reuben Bernard—led attack against Paiutes/Bannocks, Silver Cr., 1878.

Pete French—volunteer, Bannock War.

Orlando Robbins—famous Idaho scout/volunteer.

Gen. Oliver Otis Howard—led pursuit of Egan after Silver Cr. battle.

James Clark—led Canyon City volunteers in Murderers Cr. fight.

Billy Stewart—Murderers Cr. rancher killed in Bannock War.

Gen. M.V. Brown—Linn County militia leader.

Charley Long—young cowboy volunteer with Bud Thompson.

Chief Winnemucca II—often remained free roaming in Central Oregon.

Chief Ochoco—" "

Chief Que-pe-ma—" "

Lt. Thomas W. Symons—U.S. Army surveyor.

Jim Kelsay—sheepherder, discovered grisly horse bones.

Dean Huston—witnessed horse skeletons.

H.D. Still—in 1934, found possible prospectors' cabin; buried gold rumors.

I.D. Basy—" "

John Hyde—Izee area homesteader, shot at by Columbia Indian, 1898.

George Cutting—posse member, killed in last Indian clash, 1898.

Ben Selling—former Oregon Senate president; owned interest, Prineville store.

Henry Hahn and Leo Fried—Prineville storekeepers.

Julius Durkheimer—Leo Fried's brother-in-law.

Mose Sichel—purchased Hahn & Fried store by 1889.

Til Glaze—(fiddle player) Prineville saloon proprietor.

Dick Graham—(coroner) " "

Henry Burmeister—" "

R.R. Kelly—" "

John Gagen—established soda bottling plant, Prineville.

Elisha Barnes—first Prineville mayor, 1880.

Joe Howard—Prineville drugstore co-owner; eventual Sid Stearns partner.

Tom Baldwin—" "

Sid Stearns—Farewell Bend rancher.

Chapter 11: Blood on the Snow, 1882; pp. 71–77

Bud Thompson—cattlemen's Vigilante leader.

Lucius Lambert Langdon—Newbill Cr.; executed by Vigilantes for Crooks/Jory murders.

Emma LaFrancis Langdon—Langdon's wife.

A.H. Crooks—murdered by Langdon in land claim dispute.

Stephen J. Jory—A.H. Crooks' son-in-law, murdered by Langdon.

Garrett Maupin—Howard Maupin's son; in earshot of Crooks/Jory shootings.

Howard Maupin—shot sheep herder two years earlier.

George Langdon—Lucius Langdon's brother on Mill Cr.

Powers—Prineville Justice of the Peace.

Til Glaze—(saloonkeeper) member of Bud Thompson's posse.

George Barnes—(Prineville lawyer) " "

Sam Richardson—" "

Charley Long—(cowboy) " "

John Luckey—(blacksmith) deputy sheriff.

James Blakely—member of second posse arresting Langdon.

Joe Schoolin—" "

Lucian Nichols—" "

Robert Smith—" "

W.H. Harrison—Langdon's young hired hand, lynched by Vigilantes.

W.C. Foren—with deputy Luckey, prepared Langdon's shackles.

Herbert Lundy—reporter quoting Blakely in Langdon affair.

Eugene Luckey—(blacksmith) reportedly at Jackson House during Langdon/Harrison affair.

John Summerville—(merchant) " "

Gus Winckler—(store manager) " "

Leo Fried—(storekeeper) eyewitness to Harrison's lynching.

Elisha Barnes—(president) Ochoco Livestock Association, the "Vigilantes."

Joe Hinkle—(vice president) " "

S.J. Newsome—(treasurer) " "

Al Schwartz—(rancher) with Blakely, condemned Langdon/Harrison murders.

Steve Staats—" "

Chapter 12: Reign of the Vigilantes, 1882–1883; pp. 78–88

Michael W. Mogan—Trout Cr. rancher; murdered by Morsey Barnes, Prineville, 1882.

Frank Mogan—Michael Mogan's brother; murdered by Bud Thompson, 1883.

Martha McCloud Mogan—Michael Mogan's widow; remarried his brother Frank.

Mattie Mogan—Martha Mogan's daughter by previous marriage.

Maggie Mogan—" "

Edward Michael Mogan—Michael and Martha Mogan's son.

Stella Elizabeth Mogan—Michael and Martha Mogan's daughter; died in infancy.

May Mogan—Mogan brothers' sister.

James Morris ("Morsey" or "Mossy") Barnes—shot Michael Mogan; found not guilty; allegedly committed suicide, 1895.

Dick Graham—saloon owner where Michael Mogan was shot.

George Barnes—Morsey Barnes' brother and attorney.

H.Y. Thompson—with Morsey's brother George, legally represented Morsey.

John Combs—witness to Michael Mogan's murder.

Perry Read—" "

William Gird—" "

E.L. Harpool—(Linn County resident) " "

Samuel Norman—(Linn County resident) " "

A.S. Bennett—circuit court judge.

M.A. McBride—district attorney.

Mays Shoater—represented Morsey Barnes at murder trial.

J.H. Gray—jury member.

Columbus Friend—" "

W.T. Vanderpool—" "

Ed Kutcher—" "

Frank Forrest—" "

Z.B. Offrell—" "

J.J. Brown—" "

Harry Thompson—" "

J.B. LaFollette—" "

T.J. Powell—" "

W.W. Dodson—" "

W.J. Saltzman—" "

Dick LeMert—decades later, claimed Morsey's ghost made noises upstairs where he allegedly hanged himself.

Benjamin Franklin Nichols—druggist, lawyer, legislative representative; introduced Wasco County bill.

Gen. George Crook—Crook County namesake.

Z.F. Moody—Oregon governor.

Sam Richardson—first Crook County clerk.

S.J. Newsome—first Crook County surveyor.

Horace Dillard—first Crook County treasurer; *Prineville News* publisher.

Gus Winckler—Vigilante; second Crook County treasurer.
George Churchill—first Crook County sheriff.
Ben Allen—Crook County commissioner.
Charles M. Cartwright—"   "
George Thompson—first Crook County judge; Bud Thompson's brother.
Elisha Barnes—Prineville's first justice of the peace.
John H. Mitchell—corrupt candidate for U.S. Senator.
Henry Cleek—rancher northwest of Prineville.
John and Price Thorp—wanted for possibly shooting at a Vigilante; accused of horse thieving along with James Townsend.
James Townsend—accused by Vigilantes of horse stealing.
David Stewart—individually critical of Vigilantes.
Steve Staats—"   "
James Blakely—"   "
John Combs—"   "
C. Sam Smith—"   "
Kate Robbins—neighbor of Al Schwartz.
Al Schwartz—spoke out against Vigilantes, shot in saloon.
Henry Burmeister—saloon owner where Schwartz was murdered.
W.C. Barnes—Elisha Barnes' second son.
Sid Huston—young man associated with Al Schwartz; lynched by Vigilantes.
Charles Luster—"   "
W.C. Foren—Vigilante; likely shot during lynching.
Hank Vaughan—celebrity gunfighter; professional gambler.
Charley Long—got in shootout with Hank Vaughan over card game.
Shorty Davis—First of two ranchers of that name to disappear without trace, 1883.

Chapter 13: Rising of the Moonshiners, 1883–1884; pp. 89–95

Frank Mogan—Michael Mogan's older brother; murdered by Bud Thompson.
Bud Thompson—Vigilante leader; murdered Frank Mogan.
George Langdon—left town after brother Lucius Langdon's murder.
M.A. McBride—district attorney.

Benjamin Franklin Nichols—charged Bud Thompson for Frank Mogan murder.
Johnny Douthit—town recorder; *ex-officio* justice of the peace.
Judge Thompson—put up Bud Thompson's surety money.
E.F. Foley—"   "
Elisha Barnes—"   "
James Cantrell—subpoenaed for Bud Thompson's grand jury hearing.
R.R. Kelly—(saloon owner) "   "
Thomas Cross—"   "
John Combs—"   "
Lucien Lytle—"   "
Joe Mills—"   "
Frank Barnes—(another son of Elisha Barnes) "   "
Martha Mogan—(later won $3,600 civil suit against Thompson; never paid) grand jury witness.
E.F. Foren—"   "
Garrett Maupin—"   "
May Mogan—"   "
George Churchill—(sheriff) "   "
George Barnes—"   "
Elisha Barnes—"   "
William Prine—"   "
C.E. Jenkins—"   "
David Prine—"   "
John Culver—"   "
Mr. Shelby—"   "
William Brown—"   "
Mr. Stuart—"   "
James Turner—"   "
A.B. Webdell—"   "
A.S. Bennett—circuit court judge presiding, Barnes and Thompson murder trials.
Steve Staats—Vigilante critic; murdered at Powell Butte.
Caroline Coffee—Steve Staats' wife.
William Staats—Steve Staats' son, rival to rancher John Sisemore.
Emma Turpin—William Staats' wife.
John Sisemore—William Staats rival; ranch developed into village of Bend.
Sid Stearns—Deschutes rancher.
John Newton "Newt" Williamson—stayed with Staats' body.
Mose Sichel—Prineville area resident.
Gus Winckler—threatened James Blakely; left town after confrontation.

Wagner brothers—opposed Vigilantes.
James Blakely—leader of Citizen's Protective Union, the "Moonshiners."
John Combs—co-founder, Citizen's Protective Union.
C. Sam Smith—" "
David Stewart—" "
Charles Pett—(partner with David Stewart) " "
T. Clay Neese—("little preacher") " "
David Templeton—Moonshiner leader.
Al Lyle—" "
Isaac Ketchum—merchant; a Moonshiner.
Til Glaze—did not join Moonshiners.
F.A. McFarland—(county judge) elected in Moonshiner revolution.
G.L. Frizzell—(county commissioner) " "
J.H. Garrett—(county commissioner) " "
W.R. McFarland—(county surveyor) " "
A.C. Palmer—(county clerk) " "
J.T. Bushnell—(county treasurer) " "
M.D. Powell—(county assessor) " "
D.W. Aldridge—(school superintendent) " "
Ben Allen—(sheep inspector) " "
Al Lyle—(state representative) " "
William Lewis—(state representative) " "
S.G. Thompson—Bud Thompson's brother.
Elijah A. "Amos" Dunham—purchased S.G. Thompson's land when Thompsons left.
Dwight Newton—novelist; author of *Crooked River Canyon*.
Charley Long—shot in Washington.
Hank Vaughan—killed in horse accident, Pendleton.

Chapter 14: After the Revolution, 1884–1888; pp. 96–100

Horace Dillard—*Prineville News* building burned, 1883.
Alexander Hodges—store sustained damaged.
Mrs. M.A. Holbert—millinery owner, suffered loss.
Doc Vanderpool—drugstore destroyed.
William Circles—saved nails, Occidental Hotel ruins.
R.R. Kelly—(saloon) destroyed, 1884 fire.
Bushnell—(harness shop) " "
Wilson—(saloon) " "
Til Glaze—(livery stable) " "

Charles C. Maling—Prineville mill owner.
Alva Tupper—sheep thief, escaped Prineville jail.
George Churchill—sheriff; built new jail on S.J. Newsome property.
David Stewart—constructed new Crooked River bridge.
Charles Pett—(carpenter) " "
Harley Belknap—built new Prineville courthouse.
A.J. Tetherow—Deschutes River ferry operator/bridge builder.
Newt Williamson—sheepman; defeated Blakely for sheriff; later a newspaper editor, state/Congressional delegate.
Ben Allen—prominent sheepman.
F.A. McDonald—county judge.
C.A. Van Houten—replaced McDonald as county judge.
W.S.A. Johns—followed Van Houten as judge.
John Combs—deputy sheriff; succeeded Williamson as county sheriff.
W.A. Booth—first lost to, then defeated Combs, in county sheriff election.
James Blakely—lost sheriff's election; later moved to Wallowa country.
Kennedy Montgomery—purchased Blakely's homestead.
Charles Requa—bought Blakely's Prineville home.
Binger Herman—first congressman to visit Prineville.
A.H. Breyman—organized First National Bank of Prineville.
John Summerville—" "
Charles Cartwright—" "
Thomas McClelland "T.M." Baldwin—original board member, First National Bank of Prineville.
Henry Hahn—" "
Leo Fried—" "
V. E. Allen—" "
Mose Sichel—" "
A.H. Breyman—" "
Charles M. Cartwright—" "
John Summerville—" "
Sol Hirsch—" "
I. Fleichman—" "
Ben Allen—president, First National Bank of Prineville.

George Barnes—lamented scab on sheep.

Ben Allen—rich sheep rancher.

Elias "Shorty" Davis—Eagle Cr. sheep rancher.

Ben Selling—held minority interest, Prineville Land & Livestock Co.

Julius Durkheimer—" "

Henry Hahn—partner, Prineville Land & Livestock Co., 1890.

Dr. David W. Baldwin—established Baldwin Sheep & Land Co., 1873.

C.A. Van Houten—purchased Baldwin Sheep & Land Co., 1884.

J.P. Van Houten—" "

H. Loneoy—" "

John Summerville—" "

John Griffin "Jack" Edwards—Hay Cr. Ranch; half interest, Baldwin Sheep & Land Co., 1898.

Charles Cartwright—sold interest to Edwards.

Sam Hill—noted national railroad entrepreneur; visited Edwards' ranch.

Edward H. Harriman—" "

Orlando Parrish—Hay Cr. rancher.

Elizabeth Sager—Parrish's mother-in-law; survivor, 1847 Whitman Massacre.

William Albert Priday—Hay Cr./Trout Cr. sheep rancher.

William Morris—Priday's brother-in-law.

Leslie Priday—expanded Priday holdings to 120,000 acres.

S.G. Thompson—(first Crook County judge); briefly, Hay Cr. area.

Bud Thompson—(Vigilante) " "

Duovery Thompson—" "

Amos Dunham—purchased Thompson brothers property.

Tom Hamilton—Trout Cr. rancher.

Bidwell "Bud" Cram—" "

William Walter "Bill" Brown—most famous Central Oregon sheep rancher.

Joe Foster—Bill Brown's neighbor.

Johnny Overstreet—Foster's shepherd, shot by Brown.

Mrs. Martha Foster—testified, Overstreet shooting.

Thomas Jefferson Shields—later, Harney County's first judge; took Brown in custody.

Alfred O. Bedell—protected Brown from lynching.

George Nutting—Crook County stock inspector, disappeared 1889.

John C. Sumner—Crook County judge.

George Dodson—searched for Nutting.

Tom Jones—Trout Cr. district rancher.

Phil Brogan—" "

Knox Huston—Upper Trout Cr. resident.

Sheriff Combs—possibly organized search posse.

Kenneth McClellan; "McClean, McClellahan, McLennan"—Australian; ex-convict.

John Moran—shot by McClellan.

Newt Williamson—noted McClellan's quarrelsome nature.

Pat Kelly—found murdered in bed.

Chapter 17: Crook County War, 1898–1916; pp. 123–133

Mr. Snodgrass—Izee Sheepshooters Association representative.

Warren Glaze—regarding Crooked River bridge lynching.

W.H. Harrison—hung by Vigilantes, 1882.

Jack Edwards—spoke out for sheepmen.

Shorty Davis—second man of this name to disappear, summer 1900.

Monroe Miller—Bill Brown employee; escaped attack on flock, 1903.

Guy McKune—Lake County resident; masked riders attacked sheep, 1904.

Charles McKune—Thompson Valley rancher; sheep corrals burned.

Creed Conn—Silver Lake merchant; murdered but death ruled suicide.

Bert Strychnin—"accidentally" killed Billy Wilson.

Billy Wilson—shot near Deep Cr.

Allie Jones—sheep shot on Mill Cr., 1904.

James Keenan—principal in Morrow & Keenan Ranch, Willow Cr.

U.S. Cowles—Hay Cr. sheepman.

James Jones—gunned down in sheepmen's range dispute, 1903.

Jack Edwards—influential Crook County sheepman.

Newt Williamson—(prosecuted two men for burning shearing plant, 1915) " "

Listers—prominent Crook County family; sheep ranchers.

Dunhams—" "

Fred Smith—Paulina sheepman.

Owen Keerins—Izee sheepman; stock poisoned, 1905.

Effie Bell—suffragette nominated for school board, 1906.

M.E. Brink—withdrew nomination to school board.

Statira Biggs—Marion R. Biggs' niece and law partner; appointed Prineville city attorney, 1915.

T.E.J. Duffy—Prineville city attorney; became 18th Judicial District judge.

David Stewart—Prineville mayor, 1916.

Katherine "Kate" Helfrich—typographer; La Monta postmistress; first 1903 smallpox alert; died in Portland.

John B. "Jack" Shipp—English born; building contractor, Warm Springs and Prineville.

Charles Elkins—hardware store proprietor, rancher.

Stephen Yancey—freighted Prineville's first electric power plant.

Miss Rhonda Claypool—Prineville waitress afflicted by smallpox, 1903.

Miss Laney Boyd—Hotel Poindexter guest contracting smallpox.

Dr. Taggart—oculist denying smallpox diagnosis; later nursed patients.

Dr. Van Gesner—physician diagnosing smallpox.

Perry Poindexter—afflicted by smallpox; survived.

Ralph Poindexter—(Perry Poindexter's young son) " "

Robert Harrington—Prineville town marshal.

Dr. Gail Newsom—administered smallpox vaccine to children.

Dr. J.H. Rosenberg—recovered from smallpox.

Ed Harbin—immune to smallpox; delivered groceries.

Dr. Woods Hutchinson—state health officer.

Percy Davis—nursed smallpox patients.

Chapter 19: Prosecutions, 1902–1913; pp. 148–158

Stephen A.D. Puter—Eastern timber companies agent; indicted for fraud.

Well A. Bell—lawyer; local U.S. land commissioner; deputy district attorney.

Almond C. Palmer—Prineville lawyer; former land commissioner; founder, *Deschutes Echo* (Bend).

Kate Helfrich—*Deschutes Echo* typesetter.

Theodore Roosevelt—U.S. President (1901–1909).

Francis J. Heney—special federal land fraud prosecutor.

John H. Mitchell—U.S. Senator; indicted for conspiracy, 1905.

William J. Burns—Secret Service investigator.

Newt Williamson—U.S. Representative; indicted for land fraud.

John Combs—recommended as regional forest inspector.

Binger Hermann—U.S. Representative; indicted for land fraud.

Senator Fulton—only Oregon congressional delegation member not indicted.

Dr. Van Gesner—indicted for conspiracy.

Marion R. "Dick" Biggs—(county judge) " "

Gov. George F. Chamberlain—appointed Biggs, 1903.

A.H. Kennedy—*Prineville Review* editor.

Frank William Gilchrist—rich Wisconsin timberman; indicted for conspiracy.

Ralph E. Gilchrist—" "

Patrick Culligan—" "

James G. MacPherson—" "

Herman W. Stone—" "

Charles M. Elkins—Prineville resident, indicted for conspiracy.

John Combs—" "

Judge M.E. Brink—" "

Donald Steffa—" "

Thomas H. Watkins—" "

Ben Allen—Portland resident; indicted for conspiracy.

Amanda Elkins—John Combs sister; Elkins' wife.

Almond C. Palmer—U.S. land commissioner; accused of fraud.

C. Sam Smith—indicted for attempting to intimidate witnesses.

Wilford Crain—Horse Heaven land fraud witness.

Harvey Scott—*Oregonian* editor.

Ralph Porfily—claimed transients accidentally burned hay shed.

Shorty Davis—disappeared rancher, 1900; real name, Leonidas J. Douris.

Christian Feuerhelm—claimed knowledge of Davis's disappearance.

A.J. Derby—Hood River lawyer, investigated Davis's true identity.

Constantine Douris—acquired Shorty Davis's estate, 1907.

John Bain—jury foreman, Horse Heaven land fraud trial.

Will Wurzweiler—reported land fraud verdict, *Prineville Review.*

Mr. Bennett—defense attorney, Horse Heaven land fraud trial.

Judge Hunt—presided, Horse Heaven land fraud trial.

William Howard Taft—U.S. President (1909–1913).

Warren G. Harding—U.S. President (1921–1923).

Chapter 20: Bend Becomes a Town, 1902–1914; pp. 159–164

John Sisemore—Farewell Bend storekeeper.

Jackson Vandevert—Little River homesteader, 1870.

Scroggins—early Bend area homesteader.

William Vandevert—" ”

William Staats—platted Deschutes, 1902.

Alexander Drake—key developer; Pilot Butte Development Co.; platted Bend townsite.

Charlie Cottor—Drake's attendant.

Charles C. Hutchinson—founder, Oregon Development & Oregon Irrigation companies.

W. Eugene Guerin—Bend banker; Deschutes Irrigation & Power Co.; organized Central Oregon Banking & Trust Co.

A.C. Lucas—purchased Pilot Butte Inn, 1905.

A.L. Goodwillie—banker; Bend's first mayor, 1904.

Hugh O'Kane—Bend saloon owner.

Mack Cornett—stagecoach line operator.

William A. Gill—produced automobile serving between Shaniko/Bend, 1905.

J.M. Lawrence—*Bend Bulletin* editor; Bend banking partner.

John Steidl—purchased bank, 1907; renamed Central Oregon Bank.

J.E. Sawhill—" ”

Charles S. Hudson—president, Independent First National Bank, 1909.

Woodrow Wilson—U.S. President (1913–1921).

Mrs. J.E. Sawmill—member, Ladies' Library Club.

Miss Mary Coleman—first Bend librarian, 1908.

William A. Laidlaw—formed Three Sisters Irrigation & Ditch Co., 1903; platted Laidlaw (Tumalo), 1904.

Col. T. Egenton Hogg—failed transcontinental railroad scheme.

A.P. Donahue—founded Laidlaw's *Chronicle*, 1905.

Chapter 21: The East Leaves, the West Grows, 1880s–1910s; pp. 165–174

C.P. Bailey—early Baptist minister.

H.W. Hendricks—founded *Fossil Journal.*

Charles Clarno—son of cattleman Andrew Clarno; ran steamboats.

Henry Wheeler—pioneer stage line operator; Wheeler County namesake.

Thomas Benton Hoover—Fossil's first mayor.

James Simpson Stewart—*Fossil Journal* editor.

R.N. "Mose" Donnelly—introduced Wheeler County bill, 1899.

Gov. Geer—made Wheeler County appointments.

William W. Kennedy—Wheeler County judge.

Eugene Looney—Wheeler County commissioner.

George O. Butler—Wheeler County clerk.

George S. Carpenter—Wheeler County treasurer.

O.B. Mills—Wheeler County school superintendent.

Frank Peaslee—Wheeler County stock inspector.

A.F. Peterson—built Wheeler County courthouse.

Daniel M. French—The Dalles banker; formed ranching enterprise with Henry Wheeler.

Joshua W. French—" ”

D.E. Gilman—purchased Henry Wheeler's interest.

J. Wood Gilman—" ”

Frank and Josephine Redmond—acquired 80 irrigation acres; namesakes of Redmond.

Ezra Eby family—the Redmond's neighbor(s).

B.A. Kendall—" ”

William Buckley—" ”

Z.T. McClay—" ”

F.M. White—Redmond mayor, 1910.

Frank McCaffery—Redmond town council.

M.E. Lynch—" ”

H.E. Jones—" "

G.W. Wells—" "

Guy E. Dobson—" "

Dr. J.F. Hosch—" "

J.R. Roberts—business partner; Lynch & Roberts Department Store.

Rowlee and Whitted—Redmond Hotel owners.

Ehret brothers—Redmond mercantile, 1905.

J.S. Jackson—built furniture and hardware store.

Harry Gant—Redmond Livery Barn.

G.L. Ehlers—Redmond bank, 1908.

Guy Dobson—Redmond Bank of Commerce, 1909.

J.M. Crenshaw—Methodist preacher, 1912; drummed out of Redmond.

Gov. Oswald West—enforced "vice" laws.

H.E. Jones—Redmond council member; held illegal poker games.

Z.T. McClay—town marshal; arrested for illegal poker.

Miss Hobbs—Gov. West's secretary.

Samuel Hindman—original Sisters area settler.

John J. Smith—first postmaster, 1888.

Jacob N. Quiberg—suggested Three Sisters name.

Alex Smith—platted town of Sisters, 1901.

Robert Smith—" "

W.T.E. Wilson—owned sawmill near Sisters.

Rev. C.P. Bailey—Prineville Baptist Church.

John Dennis—Hotel Sisters owner; donated church lots.

Rev. Ralph Towne—Sisters Presbyterian church.

George Aitken—Sisters drug store proprietor.

John Wilt—rancher.

John Allen—purchased Wilt's ranch.

Meredith Bailey—purchased ranch from Allen.

Maida Bailey—Bailey's wife; former Stanford University/Reed College librarian.

O.G. Culver—postmaster of Perryville, later called Culver.

Dr. W.H. Snook—practiced in Culver; later of Madras.

Dan Swift—homesteader, final Culver location.

Orla Hale—settled in Madras area, ca. 1887.

John Palmehn—platted future Madras, 1904.

Max Wilson—first Madras postmaster.

Max Putz—Madras Milling & Mercantile Co. partner.

Henry Dietzel—" "

Simon Peter Conroy—" "

Dr. T.A. Long—physician, farmer, drugstore owner.

Dr. Homer D. Haile—excellent physician when sober.

Charles Crowfoot—first teacher.

Whitfield T. Wood—discovered ore; town of Ashwood namesake.

Jack Edwards—Oregon King Mining Co. principal; besieged by lawsuits.

Sen. Charles M. Cartwright—" "

Thomas J. Brown—sued over Oregon King claim.

James and Addie Wood—platted Ashwood, 1899.

Max Lueddemann—published *Ashwood Prospector.*

Rev. R.N. Free—appointed to Warm Springs, 1878.

Chapter 22: Homesteaders, 1890s–1920s; pp. 175–181

Isabel McKinney—Oregon desert homesteader.

Breuner—shepherd; shot Tom Reilly.

Tom Reilly—homesteader; killed by Breuner.

Thomas Hamilton—Jefferson County stock baron; kind to homesteaders.

Jack Edwards—" "

Pete French—Harney County rancher despised by homesteaders.

Ed Oliver—homesteader, murdered Pete French.

John Isham—Madras basin homesteader; drilled good well.

Frank Loveland—" "

Fred Waymire—" "

Ed Kutcher—operated community threshing machine.

A.P. Clark—" "

Chapter 23: Farming Towns, 1890s–1920s; pp. 182–190

O'Neil brothers—O'Neil siding namesake.

Dr. James R. Sites—initially homesteaded Lone Pine.

Frank Forest—Forest namesake; drilled La Monta oil well, 1910.

Bill Brown—Buck Cr. storekeeper.

Jack Edwards—Hay Cr. storekeeper.

Abe Merchant—first Opal City area claimant.
Wilson family—Opal City restaurateurs.
Jerry Achey—early homesteader, La Monta area.
Col. Smith—" "
Bill Rodgers—"Desert" postmaster.
Lizzie Pringle—"Desert" postmistress.
Kate Helfrich—La Monta postmistress, 1896.
Walt Rice—La Monta drugstore owner.
Joe and Josie Weigand—La Monta stagestop operators.
Frank Loveland—drilled La Monta oil well, 1910.
Ed Wills—store started Grizzly, 1900.
John Lewis—purchased Wills' store, 1913.
Henry Cleek—former Grizzly area rancher.
Morrow & Keenan—stage operators.
Nick Lambert—rancher; Grandview storekeeper.
Mr. Ransom—Grandview blacksmith.
J.T. Monical—started town of Geneva.
Clark Rogers—homesteaded The Cove, 1879.
T.F. McCallister—traded Prineville house for Rogers' homestead, 1888.
William Boegli—purchased McCallister's property, 1905; now Cove Palisades State Park.
U.S. Cowles—Agency Plains farmer; Mecca site.
Will See—Mecca storekeeper.
G.A. Paxton—Paxton depot namesake.
Ora Vantassel—Vanora namesake.
Dr. W.H. Snook—Madras physician.
Volney Williamson—laid out Metolius.
John Powell—Powell Butte namesake.
Vandeverts—local ranchers.
Moses Niswonger—first Powell Butte postmaster, 1909.
J.E. Beckman—later Powell Butte postmaster.
Elof Johnson—moved Powell Butte store.
John T. Faulkner—Paulina postmaster, 1880.
Bill Brown—claimed Paulina residency.
Lee Miller—co-operator, Paulina Cash Store.
George Ruba—" "
Elmer Clark—built Hotel Paulina, 1906.
Wallace and Walter Post—town of Post namesakes, 1886.
Alfred Aya—mapped out LaPine, 1910.
Frank Bogue—storekeeper; founded Rosland, 1880.
Grandma Beasley—Rosland/LaPine hotel.
E.N. Hurd—established *LaPine Intermountain*, 1911.

Glen Roper—LaPine saloon owner.
John Masten—LaPine sawmill owner.
George Millican—town of Millican namesake.
Billie Rahn—sole Millican resident, 1940.
C.H. Coffey—homesteaded at Brothers, 1913.
Ray and Elizabeth Markham—early Brothers settlers.
Brookings family—established Halfway House, 1910.
Bert Meeks—purchased Halfway House, 1918.
Sen. William Borah—Halfway House guest.
Madam Schuman Heink—(opera singer) " "
Christi Matchinson—(baseball player) " "
Andrew Larson—boxer; La Monta teacher.

Chapter 24: Land Bust, 1910s–1920s; pp. 191–193

Johnny Morgan—Paulina-Suplee telephone operator.
E.M. Shutt—started *Antelope Herald*.
Harold Lenoir Davis—noted author; Pulitzer Prize.

Chapter 25: Arrival of Jim Hill, 1908–1911; pp. 194–202

James J. Hill—Great Northern Railroad mogul.
Edward H. Harriman—Southern Pacific Railroad empire; Hill's antagonist.
John F. Swanson—alias for John F. Stevens.
John F. Stevens—James J. Hill's chief engineer.
J.P. Hahn—Madras hotel owner.
David Stewart—partner, Central Oregon Railroad scheme, 1908.
Mack Cornett—" "
T.M. Baldwin—" "
Charles M. Elkins—" "
W.A. Booth—" "
Louis Hill—James J. Hill's son.
John E. Burchard—St. Paul lumberman, formed Oregon & Western Colonization Co. with Louis Hill.
W.P. Davidson—" "
Bill Hanley—Harney County cattle baron.
C. Sam Smith—reported planned Prineville railroad branch.
Newt Williamson—" "
George W. Boschke—Harriman construction boss.
Howard Turner—U.S. land commissioner, Madras.

Johnson D. Porter—Porter Brothers executive.
Matt Clark—Oregon Trunk land agent.
S.J. "Beany" Sellers—head cook, Madras celebration, 1911.
Al G. Barnes—circus owner.
T.M. Baldwin—incorporated Prineville & Eastern Railroad Co., 1911.
C. Sam Smith—" "
H.A. Kelley—" "
David Stewart—stockholder, Prineville & Eastern Railroad Co. scheme.
Mack Cornett—" "
Charles M. Elkins—" "
W.A. Booth—" "
G.N. Clifton—" "
T.H. LaFollette—" "
John R. Stinson—appointee, Prineville Commercial Club railroad committee.
H.P. Scheel—incorporated Metolius, Prineville & Eastern Railroad Co. scheme.
Thomas W. Lawson—Copper Trust founder, promoted Prineville railroad.

Chapter 26: Bend's Giant Mills, 1915–1916; pp. 203–208

Charles C. Maling—Upper Willow Cr. sawmill.
Charles Durham—Trout Cr. tributary, 1890; other sawmills.
Jack Dee—son of Durham's partner, Mr. Dee.
U.S. Cowles—Foley Cr. sawmill.
Mr. Hawkins—Grizzly Mountain sawmill, 1903.
Guyon Springer—purchased Grizzly Mountain mill.
William Peck—" "
Henry Window—" "
Sam Compton—possible Grizzly Mountain sawmill.
Harry E. Blackwell—Grizzly Mountain sawmill, 1919.
Mr. Fronhoffer—Coon Cr. sawmill.
John Steidl—Awbrey Butte water-powered sawmill, 1902.
Louis Hill—promoted regional lumber production.
Anthony J. Dwyer—A.J. Dwyer Pine Land Co.
S.S. Johnson—Deschutes Lumber Co.
A.T. Bliss—early timberlands investor.
F.W. and Ralph E. Gilchrist—early timber barons.

Alexander Drake—Bend area developer.
A.O. and D.E. Hunter—acquired Drake properties, ca. 1910.
Clyde McKay—Mueller Land & Timber Co. promoter.
Joe Scanlon—Brooks-Scanlon Lumber Co.
Dr. Dwight Brooks—" "
H.E. Gipson—" "
Thomas L. Shevlin Jr.—Shevlin-Hixon Co.
John E. Ryan—represented S.S. Johnson Co.
Frank P. Hixon—president, Shevlin-Hixon Co.
T.A. McCann—Shevlin-Hixon western superintendent.

Chapter 27: The West Secedes, 1907–1916; pp. 209–217

Charles Benson—obtained injunction, new courthouse project.
Alexander Drake—proposed county divisions.
James J. and Louis Hill—encouraged Central Oregon timber development.
Gifford Pinchot—U.S. Chief Forester.
Judge Bell—limited courthouse construction costs.
W.D. Pugh—Salem architect, designed Prineville courthouse.
Wright & McNeely—Portland contracting firm.
Jack Shipp—completed Prineville courthouse.
Guyon Springer—Crook county judge, 1913.
R.H. Bayley—county commissioner.
Willis W. Brown—" " (refused to vacate seat).
A.M. McE. Ball—hired for illegal audit, 1914.
Frank Elkins—Crook County sheriff.
Newt Williamson—shearing plant burned down.
Van Allen—deputy.
Willard H. Wirtz—district attorney.
W.L. Bradshaw—circuit court judge.
Gov. Oswald West—declined to enter audit dispute.
Bert Haney—Portland lawyer consulted in audit case.
J.F. Blanchard—county court.
H.J. Overturf—appointed to replace commissioner Brown.
E.T. Luthy—won Brown's seat, 1916.
George M. Brown—state attorney general.
Nathan G. Wallace—lawyer representing Springer in libel suit.
A.M. Byrd—(newspaper publisher) sued for libel by Springer.

John Dennis—Hotel Sisters owner.
Mrs. George Aitken—saved Sisters post office records/mail, 1923 fire.
Joe Duckett—Sisters sawmill, 1910.
Everett Ashmore—" "
Dow Dobkins—Sisters mill, burned 1936.
Floyd Dobkins—" "
Edward Henry Spoo—started E.H. Spoo & Sons Lumber Co., 1923.
Willis Spoo—managed family's Squaw Cr. mill.
C.G. Hitchcock—mills near LaPine/Sundown ranch (1934).
Claude McCauley—sold LaPine mill to Hitchcock.
Welch brothers—purchased LaPine mill, relocated to John Day.
Samuel S. Johnson—managed McCloud River Lumber Co., purchased timber.
Col. S. Orie Johnson—timber buyer; S.S. Johnson's oldest son.
Samuel S. Johnson—Col. S.O. Johnson's son, helped establish sawmills near Sisters.
Elizabeth A. Hill—married to Johnson.
Bert Peterson—Tite Knot Pine Mill, Sisters area.
Philip Dahl—managed Tite Knot Pine Mill.
Frank William Gilchrist—eastern investor, purchased Central Oregon timberland.
Joe Haner—agent for F.W. Gilchrist.
Frank Duschau—Gilchrist timber buyer.
W.A. Gilchrist—F.W. Gilchrist nephew, inherited family's timberland.
Ralph G. Gilchrist—" "
Frank William Gilchrist—F.W. Gilchrist grandson; established Gilchrist company town.

Chapter 30: A Small, Rural County, 1920s; pp. 236–244

Monroe Hodges—Prineville founder, died 1905.
George Barnes—murdered, Canyon City, 1911.
Ben Allen—died 1917.
T.M. Baldwin—died 1919.
C. Sam Smith—died 1920.
George Russell—purchased Smith's ranch.
David Stewart—died 1923.
Sid Stearns—died 1923.
Robert Lister—Prineville community leader.
Harry Stearns—" "
Statira Biggs—city attorney.
Lake M. Bechtell—replaced Statira Biggs; later mayor/district attorney.

Marion "Dick" Biggs—lawyer, local Democratic leader.
Carey Foster—served county court; son and grandson of livestock barons.
Ben Groff—served at county court.
Nora Stearns—county clerk, 1928; first woman elected to county office.
Hugh Lakin—owner Lakin Hardware and other businesses.
Lorene Winnek—daughter of drug store owner, married Lakin, 1912.
Arthur Bowman—justice of the peace, 1915; Republican party leader.
LaSelle Coles—worked with Bowman for Crooked River dam.
Isadore Michel—Prineville grocery store owner.
Blanche Michel—Isadore's wife.
Arthur and Sylvain Michel—Isadore and Blanche's sons.
Kit Love—married Arthur Michel.
M.E. Brink—Prineville judge.
John Combs—Crook County sheriff (1918–1920).
Olie Olson—" " (1920–1924).
Stephen Yancey—" " (1924–1928).
W.S. Ayres—" " (1928–1931).
Ben Groff—" " (1931–1938).
William Jennings Bryan—three-time Democratic presidential candidate.
Mary McDowell—Hotel Prineville owner, 1922 fire; rebuilt Ochoco Inn, 1923.
Pete Seggling—(Pastime pool hall) 1922 fire.
Harvey Cyrus—(jewelry shop) " "
Mrs. Mona Shipp—(building) " "
J.A. Stein—(mercantile business) " "
Mrs. Maling-Walker—(buildings) " "
T.J. Minger—(plumbing business) " "
Joe Gerardo—(meat market) " "
Dr. Tackman—(dentistry office) " "
R.L. Schee—(real estate office) " "
J.A. Gillis—(tailor shop) " "
Jay Upton—(firefighter; future Oregon senate president) " "
Dr. C.S. Edwards—(raised alarm) " "
George Holmes—(fire chief; raised alarm) " "
Will Wurzweiler—(Prineville mayor) " "
Jack Benton—(building) " "
Klondike Kate—(Prineville restaurant operator) " "
Newt Williamson—(postmaster) " "
R.L. Schee—(later occupied A.R. Bowmans's abstract office) " "

Thomas Baldwin—bought out by S.S. Stearns.

Joe Howard—" "

Dan Heising—opened Heising Resort on Metolius River, 1908.

Lee Cover—sold Bamford place to Heising.

Putnams—(*Bend Bulletin* owners) Heising Resort guests.

Thomas Lawson—(Copper Trust founder) " "

Henry McCall—(Thomas Lawson's son-in-law) " "

Harold Mack—San Francisco capitalist, bought Heising Resort for summer home, 1930.

Cliff and Marjorie "Susie" Ralston—leased Heising Resort, renamed Circle M Dude Ranch, 1943.

John Gallois—San Francisco capitalist, built summer house near Ralstons.

Eleanor Bechen—purchased Gallois' summer house, established "House on the Metolius," 1947.

Belshes, Hansens, and Henrichs—started Camp Sherman, 1915–1918.

Dick Fuller—(founder) Camp Sherman summer store.

Frank Leithauser—(first postmaster) " "

Ross C. Ornduff—" "

R.C. Foster—" "

Henry L. Corbett—summer house.

Martin and Mrs. Hansen—Lake Cr. Lodge.

Ed Carney—Prineville resident, sold homestead to Hansen, 1919.

Dr. Clarence True Wilson—temperance advocate; owned Metolius summer home.

Harold Bell Wright—novelist visiting Wilson's summer house.

John Zehntbauer—Jantzen Knitting Mills president, built largest house on Metolius, 1929.

Henry L. Corbett—Portland resident, sold Sundown Ranch.

Ben Tone—manager, later owner, Sundown Ranch.

Gilpin Lovering—Philadelphia resident, co-owner Sundown Ranch, 1923.

Donna Gill—established Camp Tamarack for girls, 1935.

John Y. Todd—old-time Farewell Bend Ranch owner.

Fred Shintaffer—established East Lake Resort, ca. 1913.

Chris Kostol—formed Skyliners ski club, 1927.

Emil Nordeen—" "

Nels Skjersaa—" "

Nils Wulfberg—" "

Carl A. Johnson—first president, Skyliners ski club.

Louis Hill—Great Northern president, donated Windy Ridge land to Skyliners.

Chapter 33: The Great Depression, 1929–1935; pp. 259–266

Will Rogers—famous humorist, gave warning of economic disaster.

G.M. Cornett—Prineville businessman; failed Crook County Bank.

Charles M. Elkins—" "

Calvin Coolidge—U.S. President (1923–1929).

Herbert Hoover—U.S. President (1929–1933).

Franklin D. Roosevelt—U.S. President (1933–1945).

Frank Dobkins—(fenced spring, 1930s drought) Wagontire Mountain.

Hutton family—(settlers since 1884; enclosed springs) " "

Henry L. Corbett—(summer home destroyed) 1931 wind storm.

Mrs. R.C. Foster—(injured at Camp Sherman) " "

Martin Hansen—(drove Mrs. Foster to Redmond doctor) " "

J.L. Karnopp—Portland resident; Prineville National Bank president; institution failed, 1931.

Lake M. Bechtell—purchased Prineville National Bank surviving assets.

Harold Baldwin—(First National Bank, Prineville) survived Great Depression.

Annie Steiwar—(Bank of Fossil) " "

Peter Anderson Erickson—eventually owned 20 Oregon stores; granted credit in depression.

Betty Erickson—bought clothes for poor girls.

Bill Brown—lost everything, Great Depression.

Fred Houston—Brown's foreman.

Ray Whiting—organized Horse Heaven Mines, Inc., near Ashwood.

C.C. Hayes—" "

Robert Betts—" "

Capt. E.W. Kelley—" "

La Selle Coles—Crook County high school teacher/football coach.

Charles L. McNary—Oregon senator.
C. W. Woodruff—Prineville Railway manager.
Paul B. Kelly—(chairman) Prineville Railway
Commission, 1945.
Richard P. McRae—(member) "   "
H.L. Munkres—(member) "   "
C.C. McGlenn—new Prineville Railway man-
ager.
Harry Truman—U.S. President (1945–1953).

Chapter 37: The Smokestack Age, 1946–1952; pp. 287–293

Willis Spoo—central Oregon timber capitalist.
Paul Kelly—"   "
Phil Dahl—"   "
John White—purchased Post sawmill, 1950.
Frank Crawford—operated Spray stud mill.
Hudspeths—(successor) "   "
Walt Lindstrom—(successor) "   "
Barney Malcolm—(successor) "   "
George "Bud" Dimick—partner, D & L Lum-
ber Co.
Winton Livingston—"   "
Sam Johnson—cut Warm Springs lumber.
Harold Barclay—"   "
Pershing Andrews—partnered with Sam John-
son.
Leonard Lundgren—Lundgren Lumber Co.,
later Lelco Inc.
Ralph Crawford—Deschutes National Forest
supervisor.
Leslie Schwab—took night courses, community
college.
Dr. John "Jack" Cramer—urged new commu-
nity educational act.
Sen. Richard Neuberger—promoted education
bill.
Sen. Austin Dunn—"   "
James W. Bushong—Bend school superinten-
dent, 1949.
Glenn Gregg—Bend school board member.
Dr. Joseph Grahlman—"   "
Leonard Standifer—"   "
Vance Coyner—"   "
Grace Elder—"   "
George Putnam—Bend Bulletin owner.
Robert W. Sawyer—purchased Bend Bulletin
from Putnam.
Henry N. Fowler—along with Sawyer, sold
Bend Bulletin.

Robert W. Chandler—purchased Bend Bulletin,
1953.
Dwight Bennett Newton—Central Oregon
resident; noted Western author.
Max Brand—pulp Western writer, influenced
Newton.

Chapter 38: Capital of the World, 1953; pp. 294–304

Lee Evans—Evans Lumber Co. (later Evans
Pine), Prineville.
J.F. Daggett—president, Midstate Manufactur-
ing Co.
F.D. Stapp Sr.—president, Lumber Re-Milling
Corp.
Lake M. Bechtell Jr.—president, Ochoco Cedar
Corp.
E.L. "Red" Braly—took over Ochoco Cedar
Corp., 1951; relocated to California.
Walt Demaris—McKay Cr. sawmill.
Marion Stillwell—owner Still-Van Mill, Roba
Cr.
Jack Vandevert—"   "
Pat Moore—partner, Paulina Lumber Co.
Louis Davin—"   "
Harold Foran—Ferguson & Miller Logging
Co.; purchased Paulina Lumber Co.
Paul Kelly—Central Oregon's first large logging
contractor.
Jack Patterson—big independent logging
contractor.
Johnnie Hudspeth—largest yellow pine manu-
facturer in America.
Floreine Hudspeth—married to Hudspeth.
Walter Winchell—national radio commentator.
Dr. Raymond Adkisson—converted Cornett
mansion to hospital, 1940.
J.F. Daggett—co-leader, Prineville hospital
fundraising, 1948.
Claude Williams—(rancher) "   "
Carey Foster—hospital campaign organization
chairman.
Louis Barr—hired to spearhead fundraising.
Cecil Sly—Crook County school superinten-
dent, 1945.
Orville Yancey—Prineville Packing Co.
Zbindon Brothers—Prineville's first potato
warehouse, 1943.
Roy Brown—potato warehouse, 1945.
Ken Piercy—Pine Theater, 1938.